Voice of Nonconformity

A portrait of WRN

Voice of Nonconformity

*William Robertson Nicoll
and the British Weekly*

Keith A. Ives

Ⓛ

The Lutterworth Press

The Lutterworth Press
P.O. Box 60
Cambridge
CB1 2NT
UK

www.lutterworth.com
publishing@lutterworth.com

ISBN: 978 0 7188 9222 7

British Library Cataloguing in Publication Data
A catalogue record is available from the British Library

To Val

My truest critic
My most devoted friend
My most patient support
My consort soul-mate

Contents

List of Illustrations

Preface

People who have shaped the history of their times have often left their imprint clearly on the pages of history. Yet there are those who were most influential that have often been either ignored or relegated to lesser roles. Sir William Robertson Nicoll is an individual who usually worked behind headlines and this study has tried to look at the several planes of influence and interest that he had, although each one merits fuller treatment. The original plan was to let words of the subject of this biography come through its pages, but this proved a mammoth task. The original MS was almost twice as long and contained large amounts of material from the subject. Although this was a fair way of allowing the subject to speak for himself, it was also considered tedious and often only succeeded in getting bogged down in detail. Instead, there has been an emphasis on seeing the man himself, as well as giving a reasonable comprehensive over-view of his career. WRN accomplished so much and this biography seeks to acknowledge that – a life of undoubted brilliant achievement. He was caught up in social, theological, cultural, and political movements of his day and made his distinctive contribution to them all, enforcing or enhancing the lead of others.

Mainly the sources available to the writer have confirmed the mainlines of WRN's life, which have been written over the years since his death in 1923, and this is an attempt to bring together all that has been written about him and to harmonise those comments and insights made about him. There has been an attempt to examine personal letters where they exist. This has generally proved a disappointment in the case of WRN. There have been discovered snippets of information about WRN's relationships with individuals – which adds some colour, but there has been nothing discovered that challenges or changes the basic pattern and understanding of the subject's life. However, it is now possible to appreciate and see WRN in his life-context and to be able to distinguish between what he attempted and what he actually achieved.

WRN was an extraordinary individual who confined himself to certain fields of life, 'narrow' constraints, but through methodical study, observation and much toil, he made himself a master of journalism. This achievement was all the more remarkable and enhanced by his having a severe disability, which would have finished most others' careers – yet at times WRN's disability acted as a spur for him in how he arranged his life and simply got on with life's tasks and opportunities. He had to get on with life and do what he could, as thoroughly and as well as he could.

The author has tried to give a rounded study of the man in his times. Nicoll, or Robertson Nicoll, which he often used to distinguish himself from other 'Nicolls', or as he became known by his family, WRN, was an individual who is difficult to sum up completely. Commentators, even his authorised biography by T.H. Darlow, though they captured much, yet to others, who also knew the subject, felt there was much left out. T.H. Darlow published his official biography of WRN in 1925 and he did such a fine job that there has never been any subsequent attempt until now. WRN's biography was written two years after WRN's death, but in spite of being a long-time friend and of having access to letters, family and friends, there are areas that he missed and assessments that would have been impossible to make at that time. These are some of the missed emphases of WRN's life, which mean that Darlow skewed the final picture. Such significant areas I have sought to rectify in this study. Biographical studies can become as conditioned by the author's times as those of the subject, but my interest in WRN began with the patchiness I discovered in modern assessments of him. Historians, who appraised and assessed the period 1886 to 1920, seemed to have an extraordinary range of interest or lack of acknowledgement of Nicoll. There were appreciations which saw him as having considerable influence, such as Willis B. Glover's *Evangelical Nonconformists and Higher Criticism in the Nineteenth Century* (1954), and James Munson's *The Nonconformists – in search of a lost culture* (1991). However, there were those who ignored his role completely, such as John W. Grant's *Free Churchmanship in England 1870-1940* (N/D c1946), E.R. Norman's *Church and Society in England 1770-1970* (1976), David Bebbington's *Evangelicalism in Modern Britain: A History from the 1730s to the 1980s* (1989). Furthermore there were eulogies in the contemporary press, such as one quoted by Darlow, "For many years Sir William Robertson Nicoll has been the intellectual leader of Nonconformity – the chief exponent of its thought, and the most effective advocate of its causes in the press. Both as a speaker and writer he has been looked to for guidance by the Free Churches."[1] High appreciation was understandable in the days just after Nicoll's death, but then Dr. D. Martyn Lloyd Jones, who ministered at Westminster

Chapel, London, from 1938 to 1968, wrote as one who had lived through the latter period, when Nicoll's influence was at its height. "I have always regarded W. Robertson Nicoll as one of the worst, because of the most subtle, influences in the decline of Nonconformity at the end of the last century and the beginning of the present century."[2] So was WRN too liberal for conservative Evangelicals and yet too conservative theologically for Liberals to remember him?

Then there were other questions I wanted to investigate and here WRN's life was a rich basis in which to ask some more general questions:

What happened to the second generation of the Scottish Free Church to cause them to take the lead in accepting many of the conclusions of higher criticism?

What factors caused the considerable size and influence of the Nonconformist churches to decline, so that they failed to recover their prominent position?

What place was there for culture and sophistication as a cause of dampening spiritual zeal and evangelistic advance?

Can the Kingdom of God become mistaken for temporary political success?

These questions and others intrigued the author to investigate further. WRN was a dominant figure of the times and I felt that his life and work would help contribute to an understanding of his attitude and concerns during that stormy period from 1885 to 1920. Therefore, it was with the eventual hope of trying to write a biography that seeks to set him in his chronological context and so review the whole life and achievement of a remarkable man.

My study of William Robertson Nicoll has taken quite a few years. There have been different periods of intensity at times significant enough for my wife to speak of my 'obsession'. I have successfully submitted a study for a Master of Theology degree, but further research has deepened my appreciation of WRN and some of my original conclusions have been modified. This is a biographical study and mainly concerned with the public side of the man. Strangely, for one who released much personal information in his writings, WRN remained a little distant, remote to many, but never to his close friends, and family.

I am very conscious and grateful to the kindness, generosity and help that I have received in getting to this stage. The staff of the libraries at New College, Edinburgh, the University of Aberdeen, St Andrews University, Birmingham University as well as the British Library, The Guildhall of London Record Office and the Evangelical Library, I owe my appreciation for their dedication and support in dealing with my requests. Various friends and colleagues have encouraged me and I am grateful to them all. Dr. David Bebbington of Stirling University has been most attentive and encouraging, even finding valuable time to read and re-read some of my writing. My indebtedness has been to so many, especially those who let me respond to their question, 'Who is Nicoll?'

Additional material about WRN can be found at
http://www.keithshistories.com/extra-pages-to-wrn/

1

Growing Up in Aberdeenshire
1851-1870

William Robertson Nicoll was born on 10 October 1851 at Kildrummy, the next parish to Auchindoir, deep in the valley of the river Don, in rural Aberdeenshire. The eldest son of the Reverend Harry Nicoll of Auchindoir and Jane Robertson, a pure Celt from a branch of the Macleod clan and descended on his mother's side from the Robertsons of Struan – a heritage of which he was always intensely proud. Harry was born in 1812 on a farm near Lumsden, and not content with the simple life to which he seemed destined, instead undertook years of intense study towards qualification as a teacher at Aberdeen University. He was ultimately appointed the schoolmaster of his native parish of Auchindoir in 1834. Harry Nicoll did not, however, intend to long remain a schoolteacher: his true ambition was to become a minister in the Church. A further period of study saw him not only gain his licence to preach, but also a fascination with books and with theological scholarship that would last a lifetime, a fascination that he would ultimately bequeath to his son. Harry Nicoll found complete fulfilment and satisfaction as the minister of the Free Church in Lumsden, and he lived happily as pastor to his congregation until his death in 1891. Harry was, in his son's words, content with

> the honour he ever received...from his own people. He dwelt among them all his life, and was schoolmaster and minister in their midst for two generations. He loved them and the parish. During his ministry, he was not absent a week a year on an average from his own home. He knew every house, every tree, every flower, and every stone of the 'primitive, russet, remote country' in which he lived and died.[1]

WRN shared the same love of knowledge that had led his father from field to pulpit, but harboured a grand ambition that was very much his own.

Harry Nicoll identified with the Free Church of Scotland from its formation following the 'Disruption' of 1843, that is, the exodus of 479 protesters, ministers and elders from the Church of Scotland General Assembly in Edinburgh that formed its own Assembly in the wake of the 'Ten Years' Conflict'.[2] The 'rebellious' churchmen had attempted to end the power of patronage, whereby landowners could appoint ministers, sometimes in spite of the wishes of a particular congregation, but they were thwarted by the minority 'Moderate' party in the Assembly, who were supported by the distant and remote Parliament in London. Their gifted leader, Thomas Chalmers, organised the resulting Free Church of Scotland, which was both vigorous and spiritual. Many of the Evangelicals were Calvinistic in their view of the Church, much inspired by their historic past, particularly the achievements of John Knox and the Covenanters, but had been reawakened by the Evangelical Revival. Indeed, as Wright and Badcock put it, "For those who had gone out, the Disruption marked a new Reformation which would both restore the Scottish Church's spiritual independence and purity of doctrine, and liberate Scottish moral and intellectual life from aristocratic patronage and state-supported privilege".[3] Harry Nicoll was caught up in the excitement and his son, using his father's diary, quoted a comment from 1840 showing the strength of his father's feelings: "It appears to me doubtful whether Christianity authorises any man or any body of men to compel me to contribute to its support."[4]

Harry Nicoll's decision to stand with the Free Church of Scotland was made in spite of the weak support for its cause in the predominantly agricultural community of Aberdeenshire, where many favoured the Established Kirk.[5] However, the national events took time to percolate through to Lumsden. Harry discusses the period in his diary:

> This month has been passed in considerable anxiety re-
> garding the state of the church and my own future prospects.
> I have been delighted at the firm and disinterested spirit
> shown by the ministers of the Free Church, and the
> secession has been nearly twice as large as I supposed it
> would be at first. I daily expected after the Disruption to
> be appointed to preach in Lumsden village, but the month
> passed away and no appointment came. I feared I would
> be directed to continue teaching until the law regarding
> schools should be determined. I would be most unwilling
> to agree to this. Cannot think I have any legal right to
> hold a school after leaving the Establishment, and have

little pleasure in remaining here in such circumstances. Comforted by the words, 'Cast your care upon Him, for He careth for you'.[6]

Harry Nicoll's decision was a matter of conscience, but also an opportunity to realise a personal dream. By standing with the Free Church from its unpopular outset, he "became…the first Free Church minister of Auchindoir…[where] he preached to about a hundred people in a plain, barn-like building with whitewashed walls and bare deal pews".[7] His son later reflected on his father's attitude to the events surrounding the culmination of the Disruption, for he saw that, although his father truly identified with the Free Church cause, at the same time this did not stir him to any violent or controversial position towards the Established Church. He wrote,

> I have often heard the ministers who came out repudiating the word sacrifice in connection with their abandonment of State aid and privilege. In the Presbytery of Alford, to which my father belonged, no minister came out and no schoolmaster except himself. Feeling ran very high in those days, but my father continued on friendly terms with some ministers who remained in.[8]

The son, like his father, developed an inclusive and open approach to others from different backgrounds and viewpoints, though he knew where he stood and could defend that stance with knowledge and vigour, if required.

Harry Nicoll's family consisted of three sons and two daughters (in order of descending age): William, Maria, Eliza, George and Henry.[9] His wife died when WRN was a boy of eight. Recalling his mother later in life, WRN wrote that

> My mother was a bright, warm-hearted, eager girl, exceedingly well educated for her time. Though she was sixteen years younger than her husband was, the marriage was one of perfect union. It was clouded early by her falling into consumption. This seemed even to strengthen the tie between husband and wife. From the first, she was associated with my father in his studies. His wedding gift to her was an Italian edition of Ariosto, and they read together regularly till her health broke down.[10]

WRN also wrote of the terrible blow the death of their mother was for all the family. "In spite of all that could be done my mother grew steadily weaker, and died eight years after her marriage, leaving four children.... I remember that on the night of her death my father announced the heavy tidings to the frightened little children huddled together in the kitchen. He told them with a smile, and we wondered why he smiled".[11] The "four little children were left to the care of the devoted maid Mary and the scholarly father who, with his much reading, and with gardening and carpentering besides, must have found his days assiduously filled".[12] This early loss was to prove formative, opening up in WRN an extraordinary capacity to empathise with those who suffered bereavement. At the time, however, the sad little family found that in their rural setting the comfort of human company was not abundant; diversion and solace was instead sought in their father's library. The youngsters came to regard books in the way that other children might appreciate the costliest of toys, and the value of this youthful exposure to knowledge and the written word was far from lost on them. WRN later reflected, "The loneliness of those years I look back upon with gratitude".[13]

WRN was a child of a country manse, a Scottish term given to the home of a minister, a fact which never ceased to exert influence upon his life. The family home was in Lumsden, situated in a rather remote and bleak part of the Aberdeenshire Highlands. WRN referred to the town as having the 'strange, wasted beauty' of a little hamlet on the edge of Lumsden Moor.[14] The village was relatively young, having been built only in 1825 on the high road between Strathbogie and Strathdon, some thirty four miles from Aberdeen. Despite its youth, however, Lumsden's rural character was strong, the distinctive cottages which comprised the village surrounded by the smell and smoke of the peat fires. As he followed his father into the church, so he also inherited rights to the manse in Lumsden after his father's death, eventually he left it to his own family. His second wife wrote of his deep attachment to his native hills, and her husband loved George Macdonald's reflections about living in Lumsden: "Many a night I had watched the moon shining down on the hills and the valley without being able to put in words the look she wore then – a look I could not see in other places.... It is not the same anywhere else ... how true it is that we do not alter much! The externals change and the surroundings, but in our inmost souls we are what those early years and teachers made us."[15] It was to Lumsden that he returned for most of his summers, particularly after he had settled in London, a habit cultivated not least to keep him in touch with his roots.

Life in the manse was ordered around the seasons, and the summers seemed brief, the purple finery of fresh heather on the surrounding hills

Harry Nicoll, WRN's father

would fade all too soon. Lumsden was no place of grand beauty, but it managed to kindle a poet's appreciation in the youthful WRN. Despite those short summers and their ephemeral charm, however, it was the long dark winters which defined life in the village. WRN later reflected upon these dreary times:

> Looking back, it is the winter that strikes me as the dominant influence of the region. It was very long and very rigorous. The countryside was famous for its snowstorms,

the huge drifts they left behind them often impeding traffic for days. It was impossible to work out of doors during the dark, roaring nights and the scarcely brighter days. People were thus thrown upon their own resources, and were either made or marred by their use of the winter.[16]

WRN soon learnt to copy his father's example, however, and found these long winter evenings to be just the thing for serious reading.

WRN's childhood in the village of Lumsden was hard – even austere. He had many things in common with a typical hero of one of the popular Scottish novels he would do much to popularise: For there was the early death of his mother, his father's fanatical pursuit of his passion for collecting books, half-starving himself and his family so that precious volumes might be added to his library. Despite these difficult beginnings, however, WRN always maintained his loyalty to his home and had deep and highly personal reasons for his love of sentimental tales of rural Scotland. The roots of at least part of this attachment are found in the same year in which his mother died, when WRN entered the parish school of Auchindoir. In the village school, the schoolmaster had no assistant, only a pupil teacher, for as many as 130 pupils. "I was eight years old when I went to Mr Wilson's school … in order to commence Latin and prepare myself for the University … the school was largely attended, particularly in the winter."[17] In recalling his teacher John Wilson, WRN noted that "Mr Wilson did us a rare service in bringing to our minds at that early and susceptible age a sense of the beauty and the glory of literature. He taught me that Homer and Virgil were poets to be read and enjoyed. Moreover he set us to think for ourselves, and he criticised what we were reading."[18] Despite the quality of Wilson as instructor, however, the fact remained that the local school was terrifically overcrowded, and the incentive to ensure his son an eventual place at university meant that Harry Nicoll thought it a good idea for his son to attend the Grammar School at Aberdeen for the final part of his preparation. WRN proved a strong student, winning some school prizes for Latin composition,[19] and even began to contribute poetry to the local papers such as *Free Press* and the *People's Journal*. Not only was this the beginning of his lifelong interest in poetry, but he also began his practice of using pseudonyms, in this case 'Nicholas Maitland'.

For Harry Nicoll, books were the link to the idealised academic way of life of the scholar.[20] In this he was not alone, for in the second half of the nineteenth century there developed a sense of distance between the minds of many ministers and their congregations, which has been attributed to an inordinate love of books. Books were tools of the trade for ministers and brought knowledge and inspiration from the rich heritage of the past. Yet they could also sharpen a sense of sophistication and love of learning in its own right, leading some ministers to dwell in a world apart, a world more interesting and predictable than that inhabited by so many of their parishioners. Harry Nicoll was very much a part of this intellectual cadre, and through growing up in the shadow of such a man, WRN gained more than just a love of books – he also gained an appreciation of good style, which would prove invaluable to him in his career as a journalist. In discussing the breadth of his father's collection – and thus the range of texts he had at his disposal in his youth – WRN wrote that

> My father possessed a library, as distinct from a mere collection of books. That is he aimed at accumulating the standard works in English Literature in every branch of it. He had theologians, philosophers, the biographers, the historians, the novelists, the poets, and to a certain extent the scientific writers. There was, perhaps, no really standard author who was not represented among his books.[21]

Alongside this desire for knowledge, Harry Nicoll also bequeathed to his son a lively scepticism and interest in debate which could only truly be satisfied by the achievement of a high degree of scholarly credibility, which required, of course, an openness to texts of all types.

> We knew that he was profoundly religious – that religion was with him first and last. We learned our Psalms and chapters, and went to church and Sunday school, but my father never spoke directly to any of us about religion. On Sundays, we sat in a room where there were none but books concerning religion. Among them, however, were sceptical books side-by-side with the others…we were quite free to read any of these, and I read particularly some books of Francis Newman and was rather impressed by them. Walking one day with my father, I said tentatively, 'There are great difficulties about the Old Testament'. 'Oh yes, what have you been reading?' I told him. 'Yes', he answered, 'you know Francis Newman is always unfair, but there are great difficulties about the Old Testament.' This was all that passed.[22]

Harry's detached interest in all matters theological was undoubtedly a model for WRN, even if it was a model he didn't follow completely.

Indeed, the two men were quite different in this respect. Harry was consciously able to keep his individual ideas and influences out of his preaching. As his son observed, "Though he spent much time and pains on his sermons, he did not cut a channel between them and his reading... he never told anecdotes, very rarely used illustrations, made it a principle never to employ the first personal pronoun or to relate any experiences of his own. He had no poetical quotations, and he abhorred perorations. His sermons were clear, able, and deeply reverent expositions of evangelical theology."[23] WRN would cut a different path, learning to use, plunder and promote his latest reading to the full in his career as a journalist.

Within the realm of theology, however, the divide between father and son was far narrower. Harry's ability to maintain the divide between his private reading and public preaching was developed with time into a scholarly skill of sorts, dedicated to keeping conflicting viewpoints suspended in his mind and living with the tensions without seeing the need to reconcile them. He became interested in the new views emerging in Germany concerning the Old Testament, but grew alarmed when similar views were applied to the New Testament. As he developed as preacher and thinker, WRN came to hold a very similar stance, as indeed did others. There was a kind of 'intellectual schizophrenia', or 'believing criticism' in which father and son were able to follow the latest findings of biblical criticism, yet at the same time retain a warm piety for preaching, prayer and devotional living.[24] WRN was, like his father, able to hold ideas in suspended judgment, awaiting the 'full' truth to be revealed in due time. It was an attitude of detachment, often adopted by scholars to achieve objectivity, or for the more prosaic reason of survival within a conservative milieu under increasing pressure from developing theories. The inherent complexity of this stance, however, could lead many with non-academic minds to mistake this intentional detachment for substantial doubt.

In tracing the history of this development, some have reflected on the subtle move in Free Church seminaries in which the Reformation emphasis on the need for an 'educated ministry' became over-stressed to the degree of creating a 'scholarly ministry'. This, understandably, tended to produce a breed of book-bound ministers so thoroughly trained in scholarship that they often failed to perceive the needs and interests of the new reading public. WRN was of the second generation of the Free Church following the Disruption, a body of men who, in their taste for more radical theology, "were not of the same mind as their fathers".[25] This difference between the 'fathers' and their 'sons' would grow increasingly marked during WRN's lifetime, though his own father's influence gave him a greater appreciation of past worthies than many of his contemporaries, as well as an insatiable desire to understand the latest views and 'discoveries' of the world of scholarship. The younger Nicoll greatly sympathised with many of the new views, yet he was also aware of the dilemmas and problems presented by scholastic insensitivity to the concerns of ordinary Church members, and so sought throughout his life to emulate the fine balance championed by his father.[26] He could also reflect a sympathy that his father shared with the revival meetings. WRN remembered and said that he owed much to some meetings at Huntly in 1860, to which his father had taken him,[27] where he was impressed by the experience.

WRN moved from Aberdeen Grammar School to Aberdeen University in April 1866 at the age of fourteen. His father had intended his son to have a full year at the Grammar School, but WRN won a bursary that enabled him to matriculate sooner than expected, having sat an examination normally taken by boys a full year his senior. The bursary system of which he was beneficiary was, as WRN himself would later put it, "a link … provided in Aberdeenshire between the parish schools and the University, by which proficient scholars however humble their circumstances, could secure a college training".[28] On receiving the award he "returned to Lumsden in a mood of rapturous exultation, walking the eight miles that lay between the railway station and his home without ever giving thought to the distance".[29] Later in life, WRN reflected on the problems of entering university life so prematurely. He was too young to get the full benefit of his academic studies, as WRN wrote to his friend W. McRobbie : "I entirely agreed that we went too soon to college. We were too young to have a fair chance. The first two years I hardly understood what was going on. It was only in the third session that my mind woke. If I had been a couple of years older it would have been quite different and in every way better."[30] Despite the initial awkwardness brought on by his age, however, WRN soon settled in as a university student. He continued to strengthen the well-disciplined habits gained during a relatively impoverished youth, no doubt encouraged by the fact that, as he later remembered, "[t]he whole atmosphere was one of hard, steady labour. Most of the men were aware that they were having their one chance in life, and if they threw it away, they never could repair the loss. The great majority worked. Very few indulged in sports of any kind. I never remember hearing of any among my fellow students who was distinguished as an athlete".[31] Indeed, it was only by the severest economy that many students could hope to succeed in living on eight shillings a week, which had to cover their entire expenses for board and lodgings, the summers being spent at home.

Later WRN wrote, "[t]ruth to tell, we worked exceedingly hard, for in those days every Aberdeen student believed that the world might be conquered, but only by the sternest concentration of all energy".[32] He did well enough, taking his Master of Arts degree in March of 1870 at the age of eighteen, but achieved no particular prizes or honours in his university career.[33] He had spent much of his time in what was considered 'desultory' reading, passing innumerable hours in the Mechanics' Library acquainting himself with as much English literature as he could.

WRN idolised his father and followed a strikingly similar path through his developmental years (his education having been at Aberdeen, first the school and then the University). WRN skipped only his father's stage as schoolteacher – though he tutored privately and wrote for various local periodicals[34] – and proceeded directly into the Free Church College with the intention of becoming a Free Church Minister. This path was not a peculiar one amongst 'sons of the manse' at the time. Writing about his compatriot W.G. Elmslie, WRN noted that

> [t]he sons of Free Church ministers in those days, however great their University successes might have been generally desired no higher position than that of their fathers. It was, no doubt, the wish of his parents that Elmslie should be a minister, and his inclination fell in with that.[35]

This narrow route trod by many young men seeking to better themselves has been criticised by T.C. Smout in his historical reflections on Scottish life. He wrote that

> [t]he domination of the church was responsible for a large deflection of effort and talent away from the enrichment of secular life. The middle class in particular gave many of its best brains to the ministry, which, in later times, would have been spread more widely in other callings. While there still seemed to be a chance of achieving the Godly Commonwealth on earth there was no shortage of sacrifice of human effort, and what was not poured out to this end was regarded in some sense as profitless waste.[36]

This was a twentieth-century assessment, but the truth was that the Church had an increasingly difficult time recruiting its ministers as the call and opportunities of the secular world of the late nineteenth and early twentieth centuries became more attractive. For WRN, however, there was little doubt as to the desirability of the ministerial life, even though, growing up, he had not been shielded from criticism of the Church. His father had always

> kept pace with the controversies of his time. I heard much of them at the meeting of the Presbytery, where I was allowed to sit quietly in the corner. The ministers of the district were nearly all scholarly men…. These men knew what was passing in the world of thought, and their intellectual interests were of the keenest.[37]

In some ways, throughout his life he remained the boy sitting 'quietly in the corner' and listening to the opinions, views and gossip of others, but he learned to take note and share what he gained. As a child of the second generation, WRN retained a veneration of the Free Church's history and its great heroes. However, he always bonded with his own generation and moved with the attitudes and feelings of the day, which he came to express in his own unique way, always endeavouring to grasp and reflect the emotions and the aspirations of his own contemporaries. Even though, or perhaps because, WRN spent much of his adult life as a Scottish exile in London, he remained true to his inherited love of the Free Kirk, and always remained close to all happenings in his Church and his country.

To suggest that WRN is entirely defined by his father is an over-statement, but any attempt to examine his life without considering that of Harry Nicoll would be incomplete. The love of preaching and the ministry, the deep respect for scholarship and books, the delight in acquiring knowledge, the appreciation of style as well as content, and, above all, the insatiable appetite, termed by some an 'obsession', for the printed pages of books, newspapers and magazines – each of these is a recognisable trait in WRN, but each is also readily found in Harry. Still, WRN developed, in some ways, into a profoundly different man than his father – a man who rebelled, for example, against the strictures of his childhood poverty through striving towards a fiscally successful career. For all the influence of the one upon the other, their fundamental divisions are just as telling as their similarities. Harry was the epitome of the 'eternal student', interested in knowledge for its own sake, but always wary of putting what he had gained into positive action. WRN, by contrast, sought knowledge that he might use, not only for personal gain (though, as Donald Carswell reminds us, certainly for that as well),[38] but for teaching purposes. As his friend, Annie Swan, wrote in posthumous remembrance, "from his own colossal and precious store he so much enriched the lives of others. In that respect he was one of the greatest givers I have ever known."[39]

WRN always appreciated and respected his father, and admired the elder man's contentedness with his life.[40] They enjoyed a good relationship, but to cast it as built upon emotion rather than something far closer to master and pupil would be misleading. WRN once commented that "I always feel that I was defrauded of my youth – there was so little sunshine in it – far too little".[41] WRN belonged to a different generation, one that believed in progress and a world of new and ever-widening horizons. Harry Nicoll, by contrast, was too easily content with ministerial life in the backwaters of Aberdeenshire, combined with the leisurely perusal of his books and magazines. The world of a son not content with a small Scottish parish must certainly have baffled him, WRN's ambitions having far outstripped his father's limited vision before he had even completed his university training. All that followed must have left his father looking on and wondering, but he was always interested in and proud of his eldest son's achievements, the foundation of which WRN would always acknowledge was to be found in the Scottish manse in Lumsden.

2

Ministerial Training and Career in the Free Church of Scotland 1870-1885

In March 1870, WRN was only eighteen as he stood amongst the other aspiring ministerial students ready to enter the Free Church Divinity Hall at Aberdeen. At that time, the colleges in Edinburgh and Glasgow overshadowed Aberdeen, meaning that it was hard for Aberdeen men to gain easy access to good ministerial appointments. Some graduates emigrated to Australia or Canada, where there were opportunities in the expanding colonies. At one time, even WRN entertained the idea of emigrating in response to a call from the congregation of the Chalmers Presbyterian Church in Adelaide, Australia, but his father's distress at the possibility of his leaving was enough to dissuade him.[1]

WRN's ministerial training course was to emphasise a thorough grounding in the Calvinism of the Westminster Confession of Faith. Despite this ostensibly conservative curriculum, however, he began his studies at a time of debate about the orthodox doctrine of the Church, particularly concerning the Bible. For the first sixty years of the nineteenth century, Scottish Free Church Presbyterianism, like many other Churches in Britain, resisted the newer theological per-spectives emerging on the continent and were referred to, pejoratively, as 'German rationalism'. This scholarship critiqued the Bible using literary and historical techniques that were already being applied to ancient non-biblical materials; the aim was to show that the Bible could be 'objectively' interpreted in its original context, and that the historical circumstances could be reconstructed by present-day knowledge and skills. Britain, however, had remained generally resistant to the novel ideas that were fermenting in Germany,[2] at least up to 1860.

Many were suspicious of them, and saw them as intellectual rationalism, potentially leading to deism, as similar rationalism had in the mid-eighteenth century amongst the English Presbyterians. Others, influenced by the Enlightenment and Romanticism, took an increasingly hostile stance in their attitude to the traditional doctrinal orthodoxy of the Bible and the Confession, and the Evangelical Revival put renewed vigour into re-emphasising traditional orthodox doctrine. Theological debate was moving in a more liberal direction, spurred on most particularly by the publication of Charles Darwin's *Origin of the Species* in 1859, and the publication the following year of a collection of exploratory writings by members of the Church of England's clergy, called *Essays and Reviews*. WRN witnessed the intensification of the debate between orthodoxy and liberalism, which began to produce drastic changes in the theological climate in Britain. This intellectual and spiritual dispute caused a very stormy and controversial atmosphere for WRN's generation of Church leaders, although WRN himself was ballasted by his father's influence and attitude and so never seemed to experience any dramatic crisis of doubt, neither in his student days nor in his subsequent ministry. He, alongside many men of his age, felt there was a need to modify their traditional views in the light of 'modern knowledge'. These modifications increasingly seemed to de-pict the older generation of Evangelical leaders as simplistic, naïve, and lacking the ability to come to terms with 'the modern mind'. Amidst this brewing conflict of generations, WRN combined a genuine regard for those leaders with a desire to see the Church move on.

At the same time as this debate was taking place throughout the British Isles, a very particular crisis was waiting to happen in Scotland. The influence of German universities was made apparent via the policy of sending many of Scotland's best students to study at a German or Dutch university. There was a perception that English universities were second-rate and tainted by episcopacy ('prelacy'), even leading WRN to use a Scottish prejudicial quip "As ignorant as a bishop". In England Mark Pattison, surveying the state of theology in Europe in 1857, wrote "It is now in Germany alone that the vital questions of Religion are discussed with the full and free application of all the resources of learning and criticism which our age has at its command."[3] The German Universities "attained something nearer to academic detachment than the English [and Scottish], and contained more chairs of divinity. German professors made many of the important advances. Most of them were free of any desire to defend verbal inspiration, which they saw to be indefensible."[4] In many fields of knowledge, particularly in science and technology, critical study was an advantage and resulted in progress. When applied to theology, however, this enlightened and rational approach could lead to reinterpretations of and a shrinkage in the body of accepted religious truth. Could the divinely revealed veracity of God's Word be established by reason, without recourse to simple acceptance of its truths by faith? The new rationalism and the growth of empirical knowledge seemed to detract from the usefulness and authority of religion in society. Sophisticated hostility began to develop in opposition to simple faith. Skirmishes became commonplace between the 'Modernists' (Liberals) and the 'Traditionalists' (Orthodox), which would become bitter and damaging to the perception of Christianity in the early twentieth century.

The climate of seminary life for students such as WRN was increasingly influenced by the flux of ideas coming from the Continent. The German universities played a key role in the change and perception of religion amongst the educated and growing middle classes, many of whom committed their young men to ministerial training. WRN already had a deep veneration of scholarship which he had inherited from his father, and although he did not go to Germany to study, his father bought the books of the leading German scholars, including those brought out by T. & T. Clark of Edinburgh. WRN paid several visits to the continent, meeting the scholars Kuenen, Delitzsch and Wellhausen, from which he gained a more personal experience of the German theological climate.[5] With his admiration for academicians and his 'youthful' desire for development, WRN was perhaps an ideal student of this new body of thought, and, as a direct result of the atmosphere and concerns in the theological climate of WRN's college days and early ministry, he soon found his Evangelical convictions about the place of the Scriptures in Christianity challenged.

WRN enjoyed his four years at the Free Church College. Although his career was relatively undistinguished, he was a good and conscientious student. Familiar with Aberdeen, he continued the same routine of self-sufficiency that he had established at the University. He secured a bursary and supplemented this with writing and several teaching engagements. For the duration of WRN's theological studies, he was able to write as a regular member of the staff of the *Aberdeen Journal*, producing a weekly column, and contributed frequently to other journals.[6] There were reviews and a column of general notes, and some of his poetry was not only published but won prizes.[7] By these means WRN's income increased to "about a hundred [pounds] a year, and from that time his tuition never cost his father 'a penny piece'".[8] The dutiful son did not want to impinge on his father's ability to enlarge his book collection! Maintaining such a range of commitments, however, meant WRN's programme for the week was arduous: "He started every morning in time to take his English Literature class in a boarding school at nine o'clock. A class in another school followed at ten and a third at eleven. At twelve, he went to the college, where he attended lectures until three. Returning to his lodgings, he dined, and soon afterwards started out for another round of private teaching which continued till six or eight o'clock."[9] Still, he persevered, and was soon able to look forward with confidence to the prospect of a ministerial career and a good supplementary income from journalism.

Throughout this period WRN developed his gift of establishing friendships, his ability to cultivate and maintain which would later be termed 'genius'. His alliance with two local men from University, who both became ministers, lasted through to the end of his life. These were Alexander Rust of Arbroath and William McRobbie of Premnay.[10] Alexander Rust supplied an impression of WRN at this time:

> My home was at Aberdeen, and I met Nicoll for the first time at the Grammar School. I remember that, although he was only fourteen, the English master, Mr Rattray, used to praise his essays warmly. Nicoll devoted much time to 'miscellaneous' reading, although he always managed to come out well in his classes, he seemed to us to devote amazingly little time to the subjects prescribed... but when essays had to be written, Nicoll far outstripped the others.[11]

As this remembrance suggests, WRN possessed a talent for writing, which was also recognised in his winning the Lumsden Scholarship for New Testament Theology. Even as he trained for the ministry, his interest in all forms of knowledge continued to display itself. He was deeply interested in philosophy, and gained several prizes for essays on such subjects as the 'Control of the Will over the Emotions' and the ethics of Spinoza.[12] He was always methodical in his studies and paid great attention to his intellectual development, studying many of the masters of philosophy and ethics as part of a course of his own devising. WRN also learned German in a class conducted by Robertson Smith.[13] He was particularly fond of debates and reading essays at the Students' Association: "Many were the glorious evenings I spent in little attic rooms, discussing and hearing discussions on endless things."[14] WRN's time at both University and the Theological College was far more than preparation for the ministry – his education was wide. He studied not only what seemed necessary but what was interesting, and emerged a well-read individual.

William Robertson Smith

WRN's student years in seminary saw the Free Church College play host to a body of faculty who would, collectively and individually, play significant roles in the greater theological drama of the day. In contrast to the representatives of his father's generation, including Principal Lumsden and David Brown, for whom WRN was always respectful, he gained much knowledge and inspiration from the newest member of the faculty, when in 1870, at twenty-four years of age, William Robertson Smith was appointed as a member of the staff at Aberdeen College, with special responsibility for teaching Hebrew and the Old Testament. Smith was a prodigy of learning and much was expected from him. He had successively taken academic honours at Aberdeen University and New College, Edinburgh. However, though he had interests in both mathematics and science, it was the influence of A.B. Davidson, and periods of study in Germany, that brought him to take up his life work

as an Old Testament scholar and orientalist. Robertson Smith became
a major influence on WRN. Indeed, WRN had likely been aware of
Smith's work from a young age – they were not only neighbours,[15] but
also distant relatives. WRN's relationship with his tutor, however, was
far from straightforward. He remembered Smith thusly:

> Smith's business was to teach the Hebrew language,
> and to lecture on the contents and message of the Old
> Testament. In both branches, he excelled.... He was
> constantly writing new lectures, and these lectures were
> full of depth, freshness, and learning.[16]

WRN further recalled that "[h]e taught us above most things to go to
the original authorities, and not to accept second-hand compilations.
His favourite theologian and expositor was Calvin, who was always
quoted when any difficulty arose."[17] Smith was a great influence not
only on WRN, but also on many others of the second generation of
the Free Church, the sons of the Disruption Fathers, so much so that
the 'William Robertson Smith phenomenon' merits discussion. WRN
appreciated Smith from his first public lecture: "His astonishing range
of knowledge, his masterly intellect, and his frank accessible nature
[which] won him general admiration and good will"[18]. Smith taught
a modified approach to the Old Testament Scriptures known among
Evangelicals as 'Believing Criticism'. Though the real pioneer of
this approach was A.B. Davidson, of New College, Edinburgh, it was
through Smith that it was refined and passed on to WRN. Indeed, Smith
came to be not only an exponent of the 'New' thinking about the Old
Testament he gained from Davidson, but extended the approach by
also accepting the more radical thinking coming out of Germany. He
ultimately developed during his years at Aberdeen Free Church College
into an outspoken advocate of the new perspectives being propounded
by continental writers. Smith, however, prided himself on his efforts
to combine this new critical approach with a pious acceptance of the
supernatural, and a full Evangelical adherence to the standards of the
Westminster Confession of Faith. An American contemporary reader of
Smith's publications reflected that it seemed necessary to

> Warn him that few who adopt his principles of criticism
> will think that they can consistently stop where he stops.
> The Germans whom he follows do not think so. Their first
> principle is that the supernatural is incredible. The very
> aim of their policy in adopting a method so rash is, to
> be able thereby to eliminate this supernatural out of the

> Scriptures. And such will be the tendency wherever such
> methods are used. The result towards which they incline is
> virtual infidelity.[19]

Many in the Free Church felt the same, but they tended to belong to the old Evangelical orthodoxy with whom Smith was increasingly ready to clash.

The controversy over Smith and his views started with some articles he wrote for the *Encyclopaedia Britannica* in 1875. In his article on the 'Bible', Smith openly displayed his acceptance of the documentary hypothesis for the origins of the Pentateuch, the late date for Deuteronomy, the non-Davidic authorship of almost all the Psalms, the non-predictive role of prophecy and the non-apostolic writers of the Gospels. In contextualising this as an issue, N.L. Walker[20] explained that

> To appreciate the condition of things, it is necessary
> to remember that at this time the Free Church had the
> reputation of being perhaps the most orthodox communion
> in Christendom.... It need cause no surprise, then, that
> a violent commotion was produced when a professor
> wrote an article in which no reference was made to the
> supernatural origin of the Bible....[21]

Most leaders thought that Smith's new views were obviously out of step with the position of the Founding Fathers of the Free Church, but a substantial number thought that one of the 'brightest sons of the Church' should in his scholarship have freedom to explore for apologetic purposes. It was in pursuing this freedom that Smith became embroiled in controversy from 1875 to 1881, with both secular and religious newspapers stoking the argument.

A major cause for the growing trouble was that Smith not only advocated the new views on the Scriptures, but also began to attack those defending a conservative position in the Free Church. Smith maintained that, "all theology must advance, if only because the Christ of the gospels so far transcends the theology of any age that to cling to an unchangeable dogma is really to cease to look to Him whom we must ever seek to comprehend more fully, to love more singly, to follow more devotedly."[22] Smith battled with such ferocity that even Principal Rainy's biographer, Carnegie Simpson, was compelled to admit that "In pure theology, he taught his hearers the doctrine of inspiration from the great divines as few had taught it before ... in sheer dialectic he was irresistible.... The Church was trying him but he was educating the Church."[23] The contrary and aggressive elements of his intellectual onslaught did not, however, go entirely unnoticed. WRN was later to observe that "Though Smith showed the most brilliant ability in the controversy, it must be admitted that it did not call out what was best in his nature. He was as keen and sharp as a sword; he was constantly debating with men who, whatever their ability, were not competent to meet him on his own ground, and very frequently he was unable to hide his contempt".[24] Smith thus became a representative for the 'believing critics', who were pulling away from what they considered the rigid and untenable belief in the plenary and inerrant view of the inspiration of Scripture. They tended to concentrate on a personal and subjective experience of God, which authenticated for them the truth in the Scriptural Revelation. Their view was presented as a personal, warm and devotional adherence to Scripture, but the increasing vehemence of the intellectual assault with which they paired this emotive belief soon brought the inherent dissonance of their position to the fore.

With the controversy increasing, various committees at Smith's presbytery in Aberdeen and at the Assembly felt compelled to deliberate, but the unwieldy efforts were more than anything a demonstration of the inability of their cumbersome processes to handle the problem.[25] Excitement reached fever pitch and revealed the gap of the division between Smith's supporters and his opposition. However, in May 1880 the Assembly narrowly opted for a guarded acceptance of Smith, although with an admonishment from the moderator for 'disturbing the churches'. In the midst of his supporter's euphoric celebrations, Smith responded contritely: "I feel that in the providence of God, this is a very weighty lesson to one placed as I am in the position of a teacher and I hope that by His grace I shall not fail to profit by it."[26] Within days of the decision, however, a further volume of the *Encyclopaedia Britannica* was published, including his article on 'Hebrew Language and Literature', which reopened the controversy. In May 1881, at the General Assembly, Principal Rainy of New College, who had originally sought to 'save' Smith but by now had come to regard him as "an impossibility", 'sacrificed' him in order to safeguard the right of colleges to examine and study the latest materials, from whatever source. WRN voted for Rainy's motion, which was carried by 423 votes to 245. Smith was sacked from his position at Aberdeen, but he remained a minister of the Church. He worked at editing the *Encyclopaedia Britannica* and then moved to Cambridge and the Chair of Arabic Studies. Smith was regarded and indeed saw himself as 'a martyr of higher criticism', bitter about being deprived of his first love, serving the Free Church of Scotland.

During the years of the dispute – those following his own graduation from the seminary – WRN ministered at Dufftown and then Kelso. He was not personally involved in the argument, particularly as the 'Smith debate' grew both "fierce and bitter".[27] Smith attempted to clear his name and win the right to speak and publish as a member of the Free Church. This conflict ensured that higher critical ideas were publicised widely, in Scotland and beyond. Some regarded this as an education for the masses, as Smith not only wrote about his case, but also took it to the people in a series of public lectures in Edinburgh and Glasgow. Despite a support for such openness amongst theology students, however, many ordinary church members were perplexed and disillusioned by the controversy. WRN, as a pastor, was one of those who disliked disturbing the Churches, particularly with radical views beyond the grasp of the average parishioner. As a minister he developed a good understanding of the needs and concerns of ordinary church members, and although he eventually came to accept much of what Smith stood for, he was always concerned about how 'new knowledge and findings' were presented to the church at large. Though WRN was, at this stage, doubtful of Smith's trenchant advocacy of his 'believing criticism', he would with time come to largely agree with Smith. It was not, however, to be a sudden conversion – for WRN it was the weight of evidence, the influence of the considerable number of books, and the arguments of individuals such as Marcus Dods, W.G. Elmslie, G. Adam Smith, and James Denney which confirmed his position. WRN later described his stance to A.S. Peake in 1907: "I do not think there is a serious difference between us. I am convinced of the truth of the analysis of the Pentateuch by the converging lines of evidence. It might not be easy to establish it on one line, but the lines converge in an extraordinary manner. I am also nearly convinced that Wellhausen is right in his arrangement, though I easily perceive difficulties."[28] When faced with Smith's far more explosive effort to spread the new doctrine, however, WRN was unable to support his former tutor – he had cast his vote against Smith on two decisive occasions. Smith never forgave WRN and never wrote for any of his former student's publications. Peake remembered that "Nicoll said to me, 'The darkest thing about Robertson Smith is that he won't forgive' He was, I believe, not referring to his general attitude towards those who had deposed him. He was implacable enough there, but towards Nicoll he cherished a peculiar grudge."[29] The 'grudge' was deepened further by what Smith interpreted as another act of disloyalty. In July 1881, WRN went on a tour of Europe and visited Leipzig, where he met Franz Delitzsch and then spent a few days at Greifswald in order to see Wellhausen. His visit to Wellhausen was described in detail to his wife.[30] Their discussions included Smith:

> I said that Smith held the Bible to be inspired and historically true, along with Wellhausen's views, and that he held to the truth of miracles. Wellhausen shook his head and said that while he did not deny that miracles were possible, there was no historical proof for them and that Smith's position was 'sehr sonderbar',[31] but he had no reason to suspect his good faith. ... Smith, he said, was not a good scholar, but clever at presenting other men's theories: scholars were often stupid, but Smith was not stupid at all.[32]

Apparently, Smith got to hear of this report,[33] and wrote to Wellhausen. He received a letter in which Wellhausen tried to explain what he had said to WRN.

> It was almost impossible for me, faced with the insistent questions of my inquisitor, to express myself with necessary distinction and reserve.... In such a situation that is obviously fatal when one has to deal with a man who tries to get statements out of one that suit him.[34]

Since the letter from Wellhausen is undated and WRN was not in any editorial position until 1884 or 1886 to publish the material, it remains a puzzle as to how he had disseminated Wellhausen's comments about Smith sufficiently that Smith might be upset by them. Ministerial 'bush-telegraph', an unknown article by WRN, or Assembly-talk is the nearest that research can currently suggest as a solution.

Regardless of how the information was spread, the trouble over Wellhausen's remarks certainly accounts for the cold resentfulness in Smith's approach towards WRN, for Smith regarded WRN as hostile. However, WRN wrote appreciatively of Smith later, in April 1894, after his early death: "We hazard very little in saying that Professor Smith, in the depth and range of his knowledge, had no equal among living men.... As a Biblical scholar he stood amongst the foremost. He played the chief part in a great revolution of theological thought.... He was, in truth, a very precious and uncommon mind."[35] WRN was nevertheless a disciple of Smith's thinking. He became increasingly convinced by Smith's arguments as a believing critic, though as a pastor, he had reservations about the ways in which Smith had put his case. Were there other reasons for WRN's distancing himself from his tutor? The fact of being neighbouring families could well have stimulated a sense of rivalry in his mind.

The Smith controversy was an important watershed for the Church in Scotland, and for the rest of Britain. It brought an edge of bitterness and a sense of embattlement, which increasingly led to a division of the Church into two hostile camps. There were the liberals or progressives, many of whom sat increasingly light on the doctrine of the inspiration of Scripture, and the conservatives or orthodox, who sought to maintain a high view of the inspiration of Scripture as God's Word. This was the climate in which WRN forged his career, and, although his heart identified with the conservatives, his policy was to try to hold a central position. Even so, his head took an increasingly 'believing critical' stance. WRN would help it to become a dominant position during his lifetime. This policy meant that he perpetuated Smith's legacy in the popular press, in that he appeared to hold a traditional view of Scripture, but at the same time tried to see where the latest research findings would lead. A.S. Peake commented on Smith's influence on WRN: "He [Nicoll] said that if ever I was an editor I should probably have two or three shelves kept for books to which I should often refer. And we went to his own shelves specially devoted for this purpose, and he took down Robertson Smith's *Answer to the Form of Libel* and his *Additional Answer to the Libel.*"[36] WRN was aware of the attacks on the old view of Scripture and its place in the Church, but for him the preacher's new understanding of the Bible meant that though it was still the Word of God, it was only so indirectly. For the Bible was also the word of man, and as such was appropriated as a human book. There seems at best an attitude of disingenuousness on the part of the 'believing critics' for they claimed confidence in the use and preaching of the Old Testament Scriptures, but that this was tenable was doubtful. More accurately, the sense of respect shown towards the Bible had been dealt a powerful blow, and this was slowly beginning to reach the churchgoing public.

Both Smith and WRN were committed to the idea of progress and the need to bring the Church into the modern age, and they were far from alone. However, many came to feel that the Old Testament belonged to the experts, with their knowledge of ancient languages and texts. Others tried to understand it, but could not, and for many Smith's arguments undermined their trust in the Scriptures. It will be demonstrated that WRN's colleagues, who wrote in his journals, thought the same way as he did. This was a significant way in which the Church lost much credibility, because there appeared to be a weakening over the foundation of Scripture and its role as the Word of God for acceptance and obedience.

The 'believing critical' position, at best, appeared as a sophisticated gloss that many failed to appreciate. WRN and his associates genuinely thought they could have the cake of a high view and dependence on the Scriptures and at the same time eat it, in allowing the ideas of errors, doubtful authenticity, and questionable origins to be generally accepted. This was part of a slow decline in the life and vitality of the Church which WRN would be called to struggle with, a pilot in troubled waters.

In 1874, WRN left Aberdeen for the pastorate of the Free Church at Dufftown, Banffshire. He was 'licensed to preach' in 1872 by the Presbytery of Alford, where his father was a member and clerk. "On 12 May in the mission hall of Kinnoir, near Huntly, he delivered his first sermon. Several months later he preached for the first time in a church – it was the Free Church at Braemar – the text being Psalm 110:1 and the subject 'God behind Christ'".[37] WRN spent the summer of 1874 in Rayne, where he was supplying the pulpit, when he heard of his 'call' to two possible churches: Rhynie or Dufftown.[38] He entered fully into the ministry of the Free Church of Scotland and in November 1874 settled in Dufftown. He continued his avid reading habits, but found writing and publishing were becoming as much a passion as his preaching, although he would not have admitted this. Principal Brown of Aberdeen spoke for him at his induction, stating WRN "stood alone among all the other students throughout his course in general comprehension, vigour, intelligence and force of character. I noticed also his extraordinary acquaintance with literature in each of its varied branches and an acquaintance such as I have not found in any other young man and seldom in anybody."[39] WRN's career was gathering momentum; many considered him to have a successful and popular ministry ahead of him.

WRN continued to write articles for *The Examiner* and *The Scotsman*. He later boasted that he had never had an article rejected, for he had a 'strategy': "He was careful to send to each paper only such manuscripts as were almost certain to be welcome."[40] In other words, he did his research before submitting his work. A more substantial literary effort, at this time, was a pamphlet entitled *Reasons for belonging to the Free Church*, published in Aberdeen, which spoke of his sense of privilege at being a minister in the Free Church, discussing in particular its beliefs and pedigree. WRN remained, for all the disputation of the period, a 'Free Church man'. The Free Church of Scotland was formed in 1843 and for about twenty years was prosperous and strong, under the initial leadership of Chalmers and his colleagues. Subsequently, however, there was an inability to sustain the same rate of advance. In spite of its amazing skill at building and maintaining its distinctive witness, it had the problem

WRN at twenty-one

with which strongly held beliefs are confronted: pride in its achievements and a desire to defend the future from views different to its own.

Growing into maturity in the decade following those first twenty years, WRN was part of the second generation who believed they needed to reassess the place of the Church to suit the modern situation. The Westminster Confession of Faith (1647) was the basic standard of belief for the Free Church, its ministers subscribing to it on their ordination, but circumstances had changed between the seventeenth and nineteenth centuries. The Fathers of the Disruption sought to safeguard the standard of orthodoxy with a high view of doctrine and Scripture. Now the second generation of Free Church ministers were feeling pressure to modify their Calvinistic patterns of belief, a move that they believed was the path to strengthening the Church. The 'Fathers' gave their lectures and wrote their books about the necessary standards of orthodoxy. This was particularly true regarding the doctrine of the inspiration of Scripture where the very pronouncements of the Doctors of the Church, such as Cunningham, Candlish, and Bannerman [41], which were intended to form a bastion for orthodoxy, actually gave definitions to be attacked. R.A. Reisen expressed this dilemma of the Disruption Fathers: "Defending the doctrine of plenary inspiration was a much more sophisticated operation than simply believing it, more mined with complication and subtlety than even the staunchest proponents in the middle of the [nineteenth] century could have known."[42] In a fuller discussion of the tension between criticism and faith in the Free Church, Reisen ponders the responsibility of the church's Fathers in stirring up troubles by their very defence of a high view of the inspiration to Scripture.[43]

The doctrinal beliefs of the Disruption Fathers were based on an appreciation of the lofty place to be given to the Scriptures, but from 1860, the theological climate changed dramatically. There was a new atmosphere of reassessment and progress, because Disruption Calvinism was perceived to have "been based on an uncritical interpretation of the Bible.... Part of the explanation of the decline of Calvinism must...be sought in the philosophy classrooms of the Scottish Universities. Men were uncomfortably aware of the need for a rational defence of the faith independent of Scripture."[44] The Disruption Fathers tried to meet the new challenges. According to Reisen, they deployed two tactics. They could simply repudiate the hostile views and argue that the battle was pre-eminently spiritual, that the truth could be seen only by the eye of faith. Alternatively, they could engage the new views contesting every issue on its own ground, and sometimes allowing their position to be vulnerable or even modifiable in order to secure the Bible's defence.[45] WRN responded in both ways, but particularly the latter, which he would pursue in the pages of the *British Weekly* as he and his associates expounded their conception of orthodoxy. This amounted to resolute defences of traditional doctrine, but with a weakened view of the authority of Scripture.

An early 'competitive' attitude led the Free Church to seek to play the part of Protestant Schoolmen, holding their heads up with the best of the academies of Holland and in particular those of Germany.

They wanted to perpetuate the standards of belief which were their traditions, and thought a Church equipped with educated ministers would best achieve this. However, a subtle change took place and the necessity of an educated minister slowly morphed into the veneration of the scholarly minister. This meant that the 'scholars', rather than the ministerial, pastoral-orientated workers of the parishes, increasingly drove the Church. Of course, there were attempts to combine the two roles, which were in keeping with the tradition of the Calvinistic ideal of the scholar-preacher,[46] but there was little doubt as to which role dominated, particularly as questions of biblical criticism became increasingly complex. A later explanation for the decline of the Free Church has been put bluntly: "Not content with opening three colleges, in Glasgow, Edinburgh and Aberdeen, but her theological students would not deem their course complete, or their standing in the Church assured, without a postgraduate course of one or more years in one of the more famous Colleges in Germany. From that folly, the product of spiritual pride, the Free Church was to reap a bitter harvest."[47] The writer was R.A. Finlayson,[48] a member of a group who broke away from the Free Church, becoming known as the 'Wee Frees'. Harry Nicoll, as recorded by his son, gives some partial confirmation. "But there was one class of men for whom he really cared, and whom he treated with profound respect. These were scholars ... the scholar was my father's hero and when he had a scholar in his company he unconsciously behaved as one who had to make the very best of an opportunity that would soon pass, and learn as much as possible."[49] WRN and many of his generation were not far behind his father in his attitude towards the 'scholar'.

WRN was aware of these tensions and felt that resolution was only to be had through action, particularly the evangelistic preaching of the Gospel, for although he was a liberal progressive, he was always concerned about the value and importance of the preaching responsibility of the Church. At the time he began his ministerial career, the situation was partially helped by the evangelistic campaigns of Moody and Sankey[50] that began in 1874. These not only succeeded in starting a new trend amongst the Evangelicals, but also stimulated the ordinary church life of Scotland, which had begun to lag, particularly in the Free Church. D.L. Moody had his own homely and vivid style of preaching, and this appealed to most Christians as something fresh and vital in contrast to the rather dry, academic and passionless sermons of many of the clergy. Carnegie Simpson, in his biography of Principal Rainy, pays Moody a sustained appreciation. "He refreshed in Scotland the religious essentials of the Gospel – the love of God, the freeness of forgiveness, the power for holiness and, it should be added, the Christian call to righteousness and even philanthropy."[51] WRN appreciated Moody as "the most capable, honest, and unselfish evangelist of the last generation".[52] This positive impression came from six months' probation, which he spent at Rayne. "He found spiritual interest strangely quickened all through the countryside. The scattered population gathered eagerly to special evangelistic services, while enduring results were produced in numbers of human lives."[53] This was a reinvigoration of the life of the Church, which Scotland and other parts of Britain experienced from time to time in the nineteenth century. Whilst at Dufftown, WRN published *Calls to Christ*, which began as a series of articles for *The Christian*, an enthusiastic support paper of the revivalist meetings of D.L. Moody. He wrote these articles to seek to "promote personal revival".[54] This action showed that he was impressed by Moody's early campaigns, and that his ministry was broadly evangelistic with an emphasis on an experience of Jesus Christ as a personal Saviour. WRN was one of many who saw the liveliness of faith excited by the evangelists: "The glow and ardour of these experiences left a permanent impress on Nicoll himself."[55] In a preparatory note he declared, "An effort has been made to secure some freshness in the themes and treatment, but there is no novelty in the doctrines taught."[56] WRN's book impressed the publishers Hodder & Stoughton, for he was perceived to be a strong supporter of an orthodox view of doctrine, including the Scriptures.[57] He was an individual with good future prospects, as well as a preacher who would champion orthodox beliefs. Being conservatively minded, he was at home with the publisher's outlook, but his reading and the pressure of circumstances would not allow him to rest there.

WRN's growing reputation was enhanced with his move to the Free Church at Kelso in 1877. Yet he had some pangs of regret, for he wrote later, with obvious nostalgia, "My first house was the Free Church Manse at Dufftown at Banffshire, where I spent nearly three years.... I was alone in my home save for the presence of the housekeeper. During the stormy part of the year, I was practically a prisoner.... I resolved that some hours of the day – the last hours – should be spent in serious grappling with great books, books[58] that would be useless to a hasty reader.... [V]ery soon they gave me great pleasure, so that I looked forward to my evening wrestle with the masters as the happiest time of the day."[59] Harry Nicoll urged his son to stay in Dufftown and enjoy his books, especially during the winter months, but WRN was driven by both greater ambition and a keener sense of service to the wider Church than his father possessed.

The market town of Kelso is in the Border area of Scotland and England, situated between the rivers Tweed and Teviot. With its cobbled streets, elegant Georgian buildings, and the ruin of Kelso Abbey, it only needed Sir Walter Scott to have attended the town's Grammar School and to have called it 'the most beautiful if not romantic village in Scotland', for Kelso's reputation to be made. It was certainly a step up the promotional ladder for the Aberdeenshire lad. At this time, WRN seemed marked out for an even greater sphere of his influence, but he was known to prefer the lot of a country minister, "which allowed him at least some hope of carrying out his literary dreams ... like his poet predecessor, Dr. Bonar, he made time for writing even at the busiest seasons".[60] The church in Kelso had been associated with the ministry of Horatius Bonar,[61] who had been the minister from 1837-1866. In accepting the pastorate, WRN signalled his awareness of what was expected from him: "I am most loyally attached to the evangelical traditions and principles of the Free Church of Scotland. I heartily love them and to the best of my power I shall assert, maintain and defend them".[62] His sister Maria wrote to their father, about the determination of the new minister of Kelso and his extraordinary capacity for hard work: "On Saturday last, he had four meetings, three in the church and a cottage meeting. These cottage meetings are for non-church-goers. In the evening the church was quite crowded they were sitting on the pulpit stairs."[63]

As his ministry progressed, WRN would only go on to further impress and endear his parishioners. Another valuable testimony of the minister of Kelso is found in the autobiography of David Cairns, who gives a vivid picture of him. Cairns notes WRN's rather frail build and strong Aberdonian accent, and then intriguingly describes him as "a mixture of John Bunyan and Murray M'Cheyne".[64] WRN left a memorable impression on Cairns: "One of the amiable features of a rather complex character was his liking for elderly men, and I think he took to my father, and was not infrequently in our manse. We young folk always welcomed his coming, for he was a most interesting talker, of strong individuality and caustic speech."[65] WRN talked about the world of journalism, but also, increasingly, that of politics, even though he always protested that he had no interest in the subject! Here he began to show that, although a Liberal, he was not an uncritical supporter of Gladstone; he could refer to both Disraeli and Gladstone as having 'Jesuitical minds'. "He had little respect for dignities, and was an odd blend of evangelical fervour and clear, practical realism, with a full dash of cynicism. He was a devout, well-informed and amusing young minister. If he was a mixture of John Bunyan and Murray M'Cheyne there was a good deal more in the mixture than that, as the future was abundantly to prove."[66] Cairns' were not the only recollections of the young minister, however – more personal memories were given by Jane Stoddart, a young girl during WRN's ministry at Kelso. She recalled

> His influence was chiefly felt…through the remarkable sermons which, if health and opportunity had permitted, would have placed him on one of the pulpit thrones of Scotland. The Church, which had always been well attended under his predecessors, was even fuller during the eight years of his ministry. I have heard him say that the people he loved best were not those who gave most, or who praised his preaching, but those whom he could see, Sunday-by-Sunday, morning and afternoon, as faithful worshippers in their pews.[67]

As these warm comments suggest, WRN was a hardworking and popular minister with his own distinct voice, and his time in Kelso was, if anything, strengthening the belief in those who knew him that he would go far within the world of the Free Church.

Even as the years in Kelso saw WRN's reputation within the church grow inestimably, they also proved integral to the further enhancement of WRN's nascent literary presence, beginning in the summer of 1878 when he contributed an article on a series of books called 'The Yale Lectures on Preaching'.[68] This met another favourable notice from Joseph Parker: "In this matter of preaching Mr. Nicoll is a man after our own heart. The criticism is frank, sincere and robust, while the temper is most sympathetic and appreciative."[69] In his article he wrote a bold declaration of his Evangelicalism:

> Evangelicalism is nothing unless it is absolutely certain. Conceive the absurdity of singing its rapturous hymns after sermons based on probabilities! It must speak 'ex cathedra', and just because it must it ought to speak from fullness of knowledge and breadth of sympathy. We would not have the Evangelical preacher confront the spirit of the age, but we would have him able to show that he understands it, and has conquered it so far as it is antagonistic in the secret battle-ground of his soul.[70]

The article shows the 27-year-old preacher writing with authority and gravitas, clearly indicating his considerable reading and reflection on the subject of preaching. Tangible recognition of this ever-growing ability arrived the next year, when WRN became a literary adviser to Messrs Macniven and Wallace, who were publishers in Edinburgh. He edited *The Household Library of Exposition*, which resulted in a long friendship with Marcus Dods and Alexander Maclaren. This experience presaged his move towards a professional editorial role, a path along which he would take his next step when the London publishers, Swan Sonnenschein and Company, persuaded him to take charge of a homiletic magazine called *The Contemporary Pulpit*. The first edition was published in January 1884, and the magazine ran for ten years. It sought to promote good preaching by publishing sermons from some of the most outstanding preachers of every age. This was good experience, but, for WRN at this stage, publishing was secondary to his preaching and pastoral work. That active ministry within the church was his priority makes it all the more impressive that the literary accomplishments of WRN's Kelso years continued to grow. The period saw him publish The *Incarnate Saviour*, *a Life of Jesus Christ* (1881) and *The Lamb of God: Studies in the writings of St John* (1883). In these books, WRN was not seeking to give his subjects a scholarly treatment, but to create popular, accessible studies for the average reader. He dealt with his topics in an expository and devotional manner, which left out explicit reference to critical questions, although he clearly indicated how he thought in general terms. In *The Incarnate Saviour*, he wrote about basic Christian truths that became his focus and anchor in his leading articles in the *British Weekly*. In *The Incarnate Saviour,* WRN sought to write about what he called the living reality of the presence of Christ, revealed first in the events of Christ's life and then relived by the disciple-readers of the Gospels. "It is incomplete to say that the miracles justify belief in Christ, and it is equally incomplete to say that it is belief in Christ that makes miracles credible. Christ comes before us as a whole - His person and His work. It is impossible to separate the two and we believe in the whole – that is in both".[71] The conscious choice of language so simple and a subject so important is typical of WRN's work of the period – he stood staunchly by his orthodoxy but sought to explain his treatment as helpfully as possible for ordinary believers, using intelligible terminology and avoiding being drawn into academic niceties.

That WRN maintained a combative and defensive orthodox position on the New Testament and particularly its historicity is unsurprising, given that he published *The Incarnate Saviour* amid the great controversy over the views of William Robertson Smith. He believed that the faith of ordinary members of the Church could – and should – remain undisturbed as the academicians struggled, declaring that

> The difference between law and advice is one appreciable measure of the difference between Christ and human teachers. This is what men needed then and need now. Those who believed in Him first were weary of debating; they were not sure of their own power to thread the labyrinths of reasoning, or resist appeals to passion, and they craved for a solid foundation on which they might build the hopes that were dear as life.... Jesus spoke as a man, for with all these claims He fell back upon God's word. He did not profess to be able to dispense with it, but fed upon it, put His trust in it, and drank out of it as from an ever-living spring.[72]

Soon after the publication of *The Incarnate Saviour*, WRN expanded his published body of work through putting into print a number of individual sermons.[73] One of these was in memory of John Henderson,[74] who had been a senior elder at Kelso. This sermon says much about death, a subject to which WRN frequently returns, but more particularly it shows that he saw himself and was perceived by others as standing in the succession of the great evangelical founding fathers of the Free Church. He exhorts, "I would speak especially to the young, and remind them that as the noble generation of the Disruption passes away one by one, it is for us who were brought up at their feet, have breathed the air made fragrant by their names, to take their places and to follow them in so far as they followed Christ.... Let us serve that great cause which our departed father loved so well and advanced so much, that when we too, like him, lie with our hands folded in their long rest, it may be said of us on earth, that we 'served our generation by the will of God'."[75]

In his study on Scottish preaching in the nineteenth century, W.G. Enright examines the development of sermon construction, as for him the older evangelical sermon (before 1880) was characterised by the content focusing "on the doctrine of salvation, emphasising the atonement".[76] This was generally true for WRN's early preaching, though later the individual sermons he published would not perhaps fit within Enright's analysis. WRN's next book, *The Lamb of God*,[77] did conform to this pattern, taking various texts of Scripture and treating them as fully authoritative and reliable. The sermonic style and origin of the preacher was clear, as he urges the need for a lively awareness of the claims of Christ: "None shall perish that put their trust in Him. Let us trust Him for ourselves – for what we know, and for what we do not know. Through all the awful hazards of the future He will lead us if we cling to Him. Passing the time of our sojourning here in fear, we shall be kept by the power of God, and at the last He will show us His salvation."[78] The manner is exhortatory and Evangelical. WRN was not seeking to give an argument, but the book was nevertheless structured and definite in its doctrinal and biblical assertions.

In WRN's preface to the 1897 edition he wrote "Many, who in this age of unsettled opinions are unable to acquiesce in traditional systems, profess themselves ready to accept a theology, which can fairly be made out of the life and teachings of Christ, apart from all other writings".[79] He then goes on to attack the notion that the Gospels contain a purer statement of Christianity than the rest of the New Testament. "I venture to think, as time goes on, that the exaltation of the Christianity of the Gospels above the Epistles is ultimately fatal to Christianity in every form".[80] WRN's style of preaching would undergo development to a liberal evangelical pattern, which Enright characterises as follows: "… there was a new appropriation of the bible ... as a human book and its message was to be proclaimed in a human way ... salvation was stressed as a matter of character, not of status before God".[81] WRN's growing body of published works was, of course, a testament to his skills with the pen, but because of their shared relation to the form of the sermon, they also provided additional grounds on which to discuss their author as minister – something S.K. Radcliffe would do in his review of Darlow's biography: "One can well imagine from such published works…that the borderers got some hefty discourses illuminated by literary and historical illustrations and these delivered with freedom and power, gave the sermon-tasters of the North the basis for their prophecies about the future of their minister".[82]

Kelso was not only the site of WRN's ministerial and authorial flowering; during his time in the town, he also began his own family. He had married Isa (short for Isabel) Dunlop in August 1878; she was a beautiful, accomplished and supportive wife, particularly known for her musical gifts. Few details are known of Isa, but Jane Stoddart records that she "was twenty at the time of the wedding, had been educated at Maitland House, and lived with her widowed mother near the school. A beautiful and talented girl, she was loved for her courteous ways. Even in such small matters as the borrowing of a pencil, we juniors turned to her."[83] From the same source comes a little reference to the life in the manse:

> "The first seven years at Kelso were a time of unclouded happiness for our minister. A daughter [Constance] and then a son [Maurice] were born to him at the Manse…his study was less remarkable for its book-lined walls than

for the collection of newspapers, magazines and Reviews, scattered on tables and floor. He had ransacked the lending library of Messrs Rutherford in the Square, and acquired new books from many other sources, for he kept up his reviewing connections … literary quotations in his sermons were made at first-hand, and his Bible-class students received constant direction for their reading."[84]

WRN's time in Kelso had seemed to this point almost charmed – he was much loved and respected, able to pursue both the ministerial duties he felt were his calling and the literary work he so enjoyed. He had met his wife, begun a family, and appeared by all accounts wholly satisfied with the direction his life was taking. It was, however, not to last. In 1885 WRN became seriously ill; he caught typhoid while on a holiday break in Norway. His resistance had already been sapped due to a period of stress and ill health caused by the death of his only brother, Henry Nicoll.[85] After many weeks there was improvement, but enough for him to return to his pulpit ministry. The reprieve was short-lived, however, as he then contracted pleurisy, and it was feared that tuberculosis, the illness that had killed his mother, sisters, and so recently Henry, would prove fatal to him also. In his weakness and prostration WRN was advised to give up all public speaking for a long time. He wrote "I went into Edinburgh when I was able, and consulted the two leading men on the lungs, Dr Affleck and Sir Thomas Grainger Stewart. The former most strongly agreed; the latter said, 'Come back in a fortnight.' So I went on Friday, and he said he had not a shadow of doubt that it was my duty to resign, and he took full responsibility."[86]

WRN told his office-bearers at the Church of the recommendation of the doctors, reluctantly resigning the pastorate at Kelso in January 1886. WRN wrote to the Church:

I wish … to express my great regret that I was obliged through increasing weakness to forego meeting with the Presbytery on this occasion, as it was earnestly my desire to do.… I need hardly add how painful it is for me to part with my office-bearers and people – I thank God without one shadow of anything but kindness between them and me.[87]

WRN's decision was sharply and immediately felt. The Rev. D. Iverach, Nenthorn (moderator to the church) gave a tribute to WRN at the time:

We feel we have lost the most brilliant member of our presbytery. His gifts were such as to make him while

2: Ministerial Training and Career in the Free Church of Scotland   49

still young a marked man in the literary and theological world. No one can peruse any of his books without being struck with the gracefulness of the style, the aptness of the illustrations, the thorough grasp of the subject in hand, and the full knowledge of all collateral subjects, which are displayed in them.... He seemed to have a special power in attracting and captivating young people, and over them, he had ... an extraordinary influence. All his gifts he consecrated to Christ. His heart was in his pulpit work … Had it been a matter of choice with him, whatever the loss in reputation or in means might have been, he would not have hesitated one moment in laying aside his literary work. It was to him a recreation; his pulpit work was his life work. He has not been permitted the choice.[88]

It was decided that the Nicoll family were to move south and reside in England, as it was felt that the winters were milder and so less damaging to WRN's weakened lung. Initially departing with Isabel alone, he wrote to a friend that "We have left our furniture in the manse and our children with their grandmother.... It is a great trial to be without a home."[89] He was at this time an invalid, declaring in the same letter that "I do not miss preaching, but that is because I feel so unequal to it."[90] A friend at Kelso noted, "Before Nicoll left he was really very ill indeed.... It would not have surprised me if we had heard of his early demise."[91] In London, he went for further consultations. One of the visited doctors was Lauder Brunton, who informed him that his lungs were all wrong and that he would have to pass the rest of his life at some health resort. This depressed WRN, for his life, let alone his career, seemed to be on the point of ruin. He went for one further consultation to Sir Andrew Clark, who was Gladstone's physician. Clark proved to be more positive and recommended Turkish baths and residence on the heights of Hampstead.[92] Clark added that WRN could easily live until he was seventy: an extraordinary prophesy since he died aged seventy-one and six months! Taking heart at this more optimistic prognosis WRN turned his eyes from the ministry he could no longer practice to the literary endeavours that to this point had been little more than a sideline. He had already made a good start with editing and journalism, and things would really begin to take shape with the help of Messrs Hodder and Stoughton of London.

3

Journalist and Editor at Hodder & Stoughton

With the ministry now closed to him, WRN was quick to turn to the second skill he had honed so constantly throughout the Kelso years – his writing. In 1886 he joined the firm of Hodder & Stoughton, which began life as Jackson & Walford, the official publisher for the Congregational Union. Matthew Hodder[1] had joined the firm in 1844 at fourteen and became a partner in 1861, when "he managed to acquire a third share in the business for £6,335, so to make the firm's name, Jackson, Walford & Hodder".[2] Then in 1868, when both Jackson and Walford retired, Thomas Stoughton[3] joined, so creating Hodder & Stoughton. Stoughton was ten years younger than Hodder, but together they established a successful business partnership. Both were Christians of a Nonconformist persuasion and were already publishing a wider range of genres than just Christian books. "Contrary to later belief, the partners' publishing policy was never limited to religious publications, though they would doubtless maintain that all their books were fit reading for Christians."[4]

Thomas Stoughton was recommended to engage WRN on one of his visits to Scotland, for, "This young minister, newly appointed to Kelso Free Church in 1877, was attracting attention, not only as a preacher but also as a free-lance journalist with articles frequently appearing in a wide range of religious and secular papers."[5] In 1886, WRN saw this as the best option he had for supporting his growing family, and he relished the challenge, but at this stage was concerned that any future career could be undone by poor health. 'Discovering' WRN was an outstanding coup for the firm and a major revolution for the Nicoll household. "Little did the partners realise that the visit of ... Stoughton to the Manse at Kelso would be the first step in a revolution affecting the outlook, the influence – the very future – of the firm which had been started on such a modest scale in 1868."[6] The partners saw WRN's potential from his books and articles, but initially wanted a person with a firm commitment to orthodoxy to meet a particular need with their journal, the *Expositor*.[7] The magazine began in 1875 when the founder editor, Samuel Cox, produced a periodical for ministers with exposition of Scripture as its main emphasis. In replacing Cox, Hodder & Stoughton wished to keep the basic concept of the magazine consistent; meaning the position of editor required someone who could navigate confidently in the turbulent seas of contemporary biblical scholarship. WRN's own style was in line here, but there were also elements of the *Expositor* the partners sought to change. Cox expressed his views about his being replaced:

> I have to announce that the Publishers, who are also the Proprietors, of this Magazine intend to commence a new Series with the New Year, under a new Editor. I make that announcement with unfeigned regret … as both a literary and a commercial venture, The *Expositor* has achieved success. But its proprietors conscientiously object, 1. To 'the loose views of Inspiration' involved in the critical theories of the School of which, for instance, my friend Dr. W. Robertson Smith is a distinguished ornament; 2. To those allusions to 'the larger hope' that occur, e.g. in my own contributions, and to the general tone of thought, which a belief in the ultimate salvation of all men inevitably carries with it; and they feel bound to insist on the exclusion of both these objectionable elements from the pages of this Magazine. It is for this reason and this reason alone, that they have reluctantly determined to place it in what they deem sounder and safer hands.[8]

The partners had received many complaints about material the avant-garde Cox had seen fit to include, and decided on a change of editor. In a letter to Henry Allon, Cox gave his early impression of WRN: "This new editor being a Mr. Nicoll of Glasgow, of whom I know nothing, except that Robertson Smith charges him with having worked against himself in a very underhand way during his long controversy with the Kirk."[9] WRN was to develop his editorial style with the disquiet over his predecessor in mind, as well as the concerns of his publishers. It was likely that WRN did react to the fact that Cox's own contributions had tended to dominate the journal,[10] so he contented himself with editing, and contributing explanatory notes.

WRN was anxious to keep those who contributed for Cox. From them he built up his own considerable body of contacts. His contributors for the *Expositor* in 1885 had a broadly Evangelical look about them – they included Henry Drummond, Marcus Dods, Frederick Godet, Alexander Whyte, Alexander Maclaren and even Benjamin Warfield from ultra-orthodox Princeton. Despite the initial bias towards a more conservative position, perhaps reflective of the need to reaffirm doctrinal orthodoxy, which caused his predecessor's departure, the paper deliberately sought to include a broader representation of views. WRN regarded himself as an inclusivist and sought to publish a wide range of beliefs that were represented in the Evangelical constituency as he saw it. He was always anxious to encourage contributions from younger men, who, in retrospect, usually wrote more radically and in sympathy with the 'newer' views. WRN was open to this more controversial element, seeing it as encouraging a new generation, and promoting the journal amongst the students and ordinands. Still, WRN never allowed the *Expositor* to be consigned to the theological fringe through maintaining a strong body of respected contributors alongside his youthful stable. "Writing little himself, he succeeded in securing contributions from nearly all the leading Biblical scholars in the country, as well as distinguished experts in America and on the continent."[11] WRN had as his aim that his periodical would serve, educate and stimulate the church as a whole, through informing and encouraging the leaders. He had a way with contributors, even those who, like Cox, had reason to dislike him;[12] amongst his few failures, however, was the embittered Robertson Smith, who refused to write for his former pupil.

WRN's first priority was to ensure the journal's success for the partners, so demonstrating his competence to edit, a task which he carried out with a lightness of touch. WRN maintained the overall policy and approach of his predecessor, for he saw the journal as a forum in which writers could express themselves freely.[13] He felt that those who read the journal would be scholars and clergy, who would be able to assess the merits of views expressed. WRN looked back, in his editorial method, to the unlimited access his father had granted him to the family's wide-ranging library, where he had been free to read whatever volumes he wished, then discuss ideas with the older man. This meant that WRN believed firmly in the idea 'that the truth would come out in the end', even though the journey might prove difficult. Willis Glover commented on WRN's editorial style: "Traditionalists and advanced critics contributed to its contents without noticeable editorial discrimination – except, of course, that the general English bias in favour of conservative New Testament criticism and the general English insistence that higher critics be orthodox Christians are reflected in its contributors."[14] Even such minor qualms over WRN's style, however, would be quieted and his approach increasingly appreciated as he maintained and expanded the *Expositor's* readership.

WRN took over the *Expositor* at a time of flux and transition in the world of Biblical scholarship, which particularly affected ministerial students. Willis Glover, in his thorough and valuable study of the period, took the view that WRN's editorship of the *Expositor* at this crucial time helped further the acceptance of the new approaches to the Bible, in fact more than any other agency. "The real effect of the change in editors … was to convert the *Expositor* from a merely able religious journal of homiletical character to the outstanding English forum of Biblical Criticism."[15] Glover was substantially right in his assessment but he dramatised and over-emphasised WRN's role, betraying some disingenuousness in his attribution of almost sole responsibility to WRN. In the company of many fellow churchmen and scholars, he was at the time not simply holding the newer views, but weighing them against tradition, showing a genuine reluctance to change from what was understood as orthodox teaching. Even after such consideration, he did not make a unilateral decision; rather, he sought a consensus of scholarly resolutions, becoming an increasingly convinced member of the 'believing critics' club' only after weighing the opinions of the scholars that wrote for his journal. It was, however, a club aiming at synthesis rather than revolutionary change – many in the group believed that they could hold high standards of Evangelical piety and devotion and at the same time accept the need for radical historical reconstruction of the Old Testament. WRN wanted to be on the winning side, and that meant, for him, tuning in and using the progress and developments of the age, with all the insights, knowledge and discoveries that were becoming available, to help the church cope with the modern environment. The method of innovative Old Testament scholarship he felt most appropriate to the times was that of A.B. Davidson, which had come to WRN's attention during the young man's tuition under Robertson Smith. Davidson's approach was one of extreme caution and diffidence about going to print, which always risked disturbing the 'faithful' unnecessarily – a stark contrast to Smith's impetuosity. It is significant that the scholars that WRN presented in his journals, and counted as personal friends, were mainly Davidson's ex-pupils,[16] and Davidson himself presented as 'the great Old Testament Scholar'.

It is well-documented that WRN's movement towards progressive scholarship was a matter of careful, anxious steps rather than any grand leap, and significant though his eventual patronage of the new thought was, his role as editor of the *Expositor* – and Glover's assessment of that role – needs to be set in the contemporary scene.[17] Chronologically, the dissemination of higher criticism was well advanced before WRN took over as editor of the *Expositor* in 1885. This alone suggests that one must look beyond WRN to understand the milieu he stepped into, and gain any true appreciation of his role in the events of the day. One must first look to the *Expositor* itself, and WRN's predecessor there. Glover's viewpoint does not acknowledge or give due weight to the role of Samuel Cox, who was the founder and in the editorial chair from 1875 to 1885. WRN effectively continued the policy of his predecessor – following his brief conservative turn – as Cox had a definite policy of encouraging the latest views.[18] WRN continued the same format, style, and ultimately content that Cox had set up with the partners and readers accepted this.

Glover also fails to give due weight to other contenders as major influences on the Evangelical Nonconformists. Indeed, the *Expositor* was most popularly circulated amongst Anglicans, and Anglican scholars were well represented in the contributors. Samuel R. Driver, for example, wrote for both editions of the *Expositor*. According to WRN, "He was a teacher of the first rank … he threw himself strenuously not only into books for scholars, but into popular expositions designed to show that the spiritual value and meaning of the Old Testament lost nothing, but gained much, by the fresh constructions of a reverent and believing criticism.... No one entered into a controversy with Dr. Driver and came out of it triumphant. He made no slips either of scholarship or of taste."[19] Undoubtedly, WRN appreciated Driver as an 'English' A.B. Davidson,[20] and certainly welcomed and encouraged Driver's contributions to the *Expositor*. Driver was supportive of WRN: "His spirit was entirely catholic. While most loyal to the Church of England, he regarded with the warmest friendliness Christian scholars of all schools. There was not a touch of bigotry about him or a touch of pride. He invariably put the most generous construction on everything. It was his delight to befriend and succour. The present writer had editorial relations with him for thirty years, and never during all that long period received from him anything but the most cordial help and sympathy … to the *Expositor* has he been a constant contributor for thirty years."[21] WRN saw clearly the role that Driver played in establishing the higher critical position in the theological training of the Colleges, and he proved no less an influence on WRN himself. Other contenders for the title of 'major influence' should include George Adam Smith (who could be truculent in his attitude to the 'old orthodoxy' and yet was a close friend and influence on WRN) and A.S. Peake.[22] They were known for their acceptance of modern criticism, and both publicised the higher critical views, making it something of a personal crusade. However, Glover also overlooked completely the influence of a friend and compatriot of WRN, James Hastings.[23] Apart from a very brief reference to the *Hastings Bible Dictionary*, there is no appreciation of Hastings' influence in disseminating critical views of the Bible and his significant contribution to the acceptance of those views amongst the Evangelical Nonconformists and other churches. Hastings had become,

> Alarmed to find among educated people an increasing scepticism about the Christian faith. He attributed this loss of faith chiefly to the fact that the authority of the Bible had been eroded by higher criticism.... Hastings tried to arrest the continuing decline of faith by undertaking extensive editorial work for T. & T. Clark, publishers of theological literature. This concern was that moderate criticism of the sources strengthened the Christian faith and that it was the misinterpretation of modern scholarship which was undermining faith.[24]

WRN appreciated Hastings' contribution to the theological scene as well as knowing his personal qualities as a friend.[25] He praised Hastings' early issues of *The Expository Times* (from 1889 onwards) in his own paper, the *British Weekly*.[26] Hastings' periodical overlapped with the *Expositor* in content as well as chronology, but whereas WRN's paper was seen as increasingly for scholars, Hastings's *Expository Times* had the widest possible readership amongst the clergy and lay-preachers.

As well as being a fellow ministerial editor, Hastings, as WRN's contemporary, shared the same schooling, university, theological college and church, and their families became close, as is seen in the exchange of visits.[27] The primary difference between them was that WRN was a preacher turned editor and Hastings was an editor who continued to minister. The agreement of their editorial minds can be detected in their common aims. Hastings "sought to educate his colleagues, helping them to come to terms with new discoveries and new ways of thinking: it is as though he saw himself preaching vicariously through those whose ministry he was enriching by his publications".[28] He shared WRN's view that "all true criticism was preparing the Bible for a renewed reign". He believed that "the object of his work was to encourage the church to understand and to assimilate the outcomes of such scholarship, while maintaining a high doctrine of Scripture, since he believed that thereby the evangelistic zeal of the pulpit would be enriched by knowledge".[29] This was their intention, but in the longer term their approach did not meet with the result they had hoped. From the late 90s Hastings' publications began to complement those of WRN, as both sought to publish significant books which supported ministers, and widely disseminated the 'accepted consensus' of scholarship. WRN appreciated his friend:

> Dr. Hastings is a born editor, as he has shown from the very first, when he issued with an obscure Aberdeen firm the first number of the *Expository Times.* But even genius may be cultivated, and Dr. Hastings goes on from strength to strength. His mind is singularly fertile; his interests are unusually wide; above all, he knows men, how to select them, how to induce them to work, how to guide them in the process of their task. He has learned much in the way of arrangement and proportion, and he is particularly strong in bibliography.[30]

Furthermore, WRN saw his own and Hastings' role as seeking to maintain the same objectives, "He held by the great Evangelical tradition, and had no heresy of his own so far as I have discovered. But he liked some presentations of Christianity, and disliked others. He was especially jealous for the doctrine of the Deity of our Lord Jesus Christ ... he was from the beginning in sympathy with what is known as the Higher Criticism, and I remember him saying that Wellhausen had put the whole of the Old Testament before him in a new and surprising light."[31] In over-emphasising WRN's influence in bringing into focus the new scholarship, Glover ignored the work of other men. A better view of the editor of the *Expositor* would affirm that he was not a trail-blazing pioneer, but a journalist/editor who, in developing his journal, knew what the 'modern mind' wanted to read and what would sell. He was one of many other leaders who had to 'think on their feet' as they adjusted to the new theological landscape, and he was very much influenced by the writers he came to know.

As editor of the *Expositor*, WRN made no pretensions to schol-arship; he saw himself as a general reader with theological interests. Rarely writing articles himself, he rightly identified the strength of the journal as defined by its contributors, and regularly invited, pleaded, and pushed the leading biblical scholars to have their say. If he had any distinctive agenda, it would have been that of seeking to hold all Evangelicals together and trying to prevent a widening of the chasm opening between the critics and the traditionalists. Some measure of contemporary success in this regard, may be had through looking to one of the most forceful and watchful of the conservatives in America – Benjamin Warfield. He wrote to WRN on 31 January 1921, not long before he died, able to reflect upon some 36 years of WRN's editorship, "I am enclosing to you a little piece of exegesis in the hope that you find it suitable for use in the *Expositor*."[32] Traditionalist Warfield seemed happy to have his articles published by WRN's journal.

Ever the editor vigilant over his territory, in WRN's letters to individuals, such as Marcus Dods and James Denney, he often reflected on the usefulness of some articles.[33] He had doubts over Henry Drummond, but knew that his name was an attraction for the success of the journal. WRN commented on the success of the *Expositor* to Marcus Dods: "I was rather astonished about the *Expositor*. The circulation has maintained itself with the utmost steadiness. If there is any difference, it is that more of it sells in volumes rather than numbers."[34] WRN was an unashamed populist, in that by allowing the columns of the *Expositor* to contain outlines and reviews of the latest publications he gave space for his readers to hear about the latest ideas. In September 1885, Alexander Whyte wrote to encourage him: "I feel sure you will make the *Expositor* far more interesting and useful than it has been. ... It has been neither truly scientific and scholarly in its papers, nor truly popular. I hope in your hands to see it both – and at the same time deeply and richly Evangelical. There is no theological journal known to me that approaches pleasing me in this respect."[35] WRN genuinely believed that he was fulfilling Whyte's hopes and most welcomed his outstanding efforts. WRN was catering for a breadth amongst Evangelicals, but some disliked the concessions to modern liberal thinking and criticised accordingly.

After WRN's death, James Moffatt,[36] who took over the *Expositor* for a time, reflected on the great editor's achievement:

> He wanted good scholarship, but scholarship good for something ... his sagacity enabled him to make the *Expositor* a medium for bringing fresh and fruitful ideas into circulation among those interested in biblical criticism.... It was an educative influence, in the best sense of the term ... he had an extraordinary perception of what was about to interest the minds of men. Then he steered carefully between the extremes of a technical magazine and a popular, homiletic journal.... Sir William took care

that his young men did not rush in until they were educated.
He had an editorial horror of crudities. But he also saw
that philologists and archaeologists did not monopolise his
pages. It may seem an easy and obvious task, but it was
not easy; it required a trained judgement, and Sir William's
supervision was strict and far-sighted.[37]

Moffatt was appreciative of WRN's legacy and understood something
of the power the editor exerted. He concluded his fulsome tribute to
the man: "He could repress and he could encourage. He wrote very
little in the *Expositor*. But he overlooked what was written, he insisted
on variety and vitality – two qualities of life in any journal; and to his
services for detecting vital issues in religious criticism we owe much,
far more than some of us always realise."[38] WRN enjoyed his editorial
role immensely, but he also believed that he had a job to do for the
benefit of the churches and it was a commercial success as well!

The Birth of the *British Weekly*

The *Expositor* was WRN's perennial connection to the scholarly world
he had reverenced since youth, but it was not to be his only foray
into the realm of editorial duties. He wanted to produce something of
a 'popular' nature and it was with the *British Weekly* that WRN both
found and fulfilled his real ambition, which would prove its quality
in the competitive world of weekly papers. The successive repeals of
advertisement duty in 1853, stamp duty in 1855, and paper duty in
1861 "gave the press legal freedom to do what had already become a
technical possibility".[39] The passing of the Elementary Education Act
in 1870 "created millions of readers by requiring that every child in the
country should go to school. Gradually an immense new public grew up
and began to demand new papers".[40] WRN wanted to launch a paper by
imitating "the new patterns of periodical journalism, and hope for the
necessarily-larger readership needed"[41] to bring success. He perceived
a unique window of opportunity in which he was able "to challenge the
secular press on its own ground, not [just] to fill some special niche as
another religious periodical. But the number of years that such ambitions
were possible was limited, because of further developments in the secular
press",[42] and changes in attitude by the reading public. In founding the
British Weekly, WRN took his opportunity and made the most of it.

One of the many unique features of Victorian society was the
place of popular journalism. Michael Wolff has shown that there

were eighteen thousand periodicals operating over the course of the period, with particular growth in religious journals.[43] Confirmation of the strength of such journals came from R.D. Altick, whose research on statistics of 1864 commented that they showed "that not only did religious periodicals hold their own in numbers of titles, but that they equalled, at that date, the secular press in terms of total circulation."[44] WRN believed he had found a ready market, which would respond to a good product. The time and cost of production were also dropping. When WRN came on the scene, a number of significant technical developments in printing began to emerge: stereotyping, which allowed multiple printing; the steam press; the cylindrical press; continuous paper webs and machine typesetting. All these "combined with much faster distribution methods, to mean that speed of production, frequency of issue, and size of circulation, could increase so much as to change the function, not just the possible influence, of Victorian periodicals."[45] WRN was always interested in new techniques that benefited his papers, and though he disliked science as such, he was interested in knowing anything about the capability of the latest machinery.

WRN had nurtured his ideas in popular journalism for some time, holding a particular admiration for the contribution made by *The Christian World*.[46] This paper, under its second editor James Clarke,[47] came to appeal to a wide readership and reached its peak in 1880 with a circulation of 130,000.[48] For many years the *Christian World* wielded remarkable influence as a pioneer of progress both in politics and in theology".[49] WRN appreciated what was good and successful, but he also noted that some of Clarke's ideas were already out of date in a fast developing industry, and that Clarke's paper "... lacked an aggressive, campaigning tone ... it was too broad in its approach to the questions of higher criticism and the century's liberalising tendencies generally."[50] Facing competition that, while respectable, tended to be somewhat behind the times led WRN to believe that he could make a 'go' of a weekly paper and "soon he fired the partners with his enthusiasm and confidence".[51] There may have been a further stimulus to Hodder & Stoughton's decision in the form of an alternative offer to WRN. G.W. Lawrence, in his study of WRN, cited a letter from W. Pollock Wylie, who was the son of Rev. W. Howie Wylie, the one-time editor of the *Christian Leader*.

> Before Mr. Nicoll resigned his ministry at Kelso my father visited him there, and suggested that the sphere of the *Christian Leader* – then a well-established paper – would

be increased if Mr. Nicoll became its Scottish editor, and my
father returned to London as editor-in-chief. The help of a
great publishing house was to be obtained. Unfortunately,
Mr. Nicoll's health gave way. He went for a lengthened stay
abroad, and on his return started the *British Weekly* himself
on the lines indicated by my father to him at Kelso.[52]

WRN himself had "frequently contributed to a Glasgow weekly"[53]
and wrote at the time, "I cannot understand about the *Leader*. Nearly
two years ago on the editor's earnest and indeed imploring appeal,
I got Messrs Hodder and Stoughton to offer to take it up. This fell
through ... before the *British Weekly* was started. He (Rev. W. Howie
Wylie) wrote me saying he was to bring the *Leader* to London and
asking me to join in conducting it."[54]

Such offers aside, however, it would seem that WRN's true interest
was in founding a new concern, and so he suggested establishing a
high-class journal for advocating 'social and religious' progress. This
concept in hand, he was able to turn to Hodder & Stoughton, both of
whom showed great faith in WRN's editorial abilities by funding the
whole enterprise, although WRN agreed to work for nothing until the
paper paid its way. The new publication was designed to appeal to as
wide a cross-section of Nonconformists [England] and Presbyterians
[Scotland] as possible. WRN wrote to Henry Drummond, seeking an
article and his support for his periodical:

> We mean to try to furnish a paper for Christian Radicals
> which shall be equal in literary merit to the best published.
> As the price will ... be a penny, we must provide popular
> features; so that it will resemble the *Pall Mall Gazette*[55]
> more than the *Spectator* ... a considerable effort will be
> made to float the paper. But if we do not succeed within a
> year, we shall not fight longer. We need 20,000 of a sale, to
> be on a really sound basis, and if we do not get 15,000 in
> six months I should be inclined to despair of the thing.[56]

WRN's own choice of title for the new paper had been *Advance,* but he
was persuaded by Stoughton, who was "a keen imperialist in politics",[57]
to use the name *British Weekly.* Funding and title secured, the first edition
of the *British Weekly* was published on 5 November 1886. WRN had
researched both content and audience well before launching, and the
fundamental nature of the journal was tangible even at this early stage.
There was, however, a necessary period of trial and experimentation
before he settled in to the formula that would prove so successful. "With

THE

BRITISH WEEKLY

A Journal of Social and Christian Progress.

No. 1. FRIDAY, NOVEMBER 5th, 1886. [Registered at the General Post Office as a Newspaper.] Price One Penny.

THE CREED AND THE HOPE OF PROGRESS.

THE creed we shall seek to expound in this journal will be that of progress, and while independent of any sect or party, we shall aim at the ends of what is known as Advanced Liberalism. We are believers in progress because we are believers in the advancing reign of CHRIST. To His appearing, and to the work He planned and did, we trace all that marks the superiority of the new world to the old, and all that is pregnant with growth and improvement yet to come. His day has only dawned, and great as has been the influence on human happiness of the principles of Christianity, we believe that from these principles will yet issue almost unlimited developments, even for the physical life of man.

This is the language of high hope, but we are confronted by the hard facts of a situation at once novel and painful. The hour has come for which all lovers of progress looked with an almost passionate longing—the hour of the emancipation of the people. And it finds us in circumstances little anticipated. We are under a Tory Government, the leading spirit of which has gained his position by means from which an honourable man would recoil; and what is far worse, the Liberal party is rent in twain by an angry feud which ranges on opposite sides those who but yesterday were the truest comrades. For a division in the Liberal party Radicals were not unprepared. One line of cleavage they had long watched, and they waited, if not with desire, yet without disquiet for the separating blow. But this fracture leaves on each side men ever to be reckoned among the best and bravest friends of freedom. So disastrous have been the results, that enemies and candid friends may have been tempted to apply to the party ROBERT HALL's description of Unitarianism —"A headless trunk bleeding at every pore."

But pessimism is always foolish in the advocates of progress. The earnestness of the mind of England, produced by the long political suffering which Reform Bills have palliated, has not passed away, as many imagined it would. The ancient preference for cakes and ale has not prevailed over love for the moralities in the minds of the people. Whatever be the defects and crudities of the leaders they have thrown to the front, and the means these have employed, the movements for temperance and chastity are not temporary crazes, but great uprisings, which any statesman will treat with contempt at his peril. These, if nothing else, might show that there is still in the hearts of the people of Great Britain that which may be trusted in the day of moral battle. But there is more. It is a superficial and false view that the mind of the country is deadened by an incipient scepticism. Notwithstanding perplexities as to doctrine and Church organization, the whole heart of the nation pours itself forth towards the great truths of Christianity. That justice which is the distinguishing characteristic of the kingdom of God is the saving virtue of the democracy, moving at once to the destruction of what ought to fall, and the conservation of what ought to stand. Nor is it an untempered justice, for while the ashes of all other philanthropists and leaders have grown cold, men and women will sacrifice everything that seems to make life dear to serve, in His poor oppressed or fallen brothers or sisters, the Galilean peasant who died eighteen hundred years ago. Nor should it be forgotten that the appeal is now to the nation, and not to a section or a fraction of the community. We may only readily do injustice to those leaders of progress who did our work when it was much harder than it is now. That is not to deny the genuine and self-sacrificing Liberalism of multitudes in all classes. No better Radicals are to be found than those in castles and universities—as it has been said, "No leaves are greener than those which grow upon grey walls." But our trust is in the great heart of the people.

Even in the condition of the Liberal party, the great instrument of progress, there is much to encourage. The Irish party have at last definitely thrown in their lot with the Liberals, and made their appeal to the British democracy. That means much—a great deal more, perhaps, than has been generally recognised. They will best serve their own interest by showing a cordial sympathy with the aspirations of the people of England, Scotland, and Wales, and helping their realisation, as they can effectually do. The main body of the Liberal party must prepare a new programme. Nothing could be more sterile and disheartening than the idea of going to the country with Home Rule and Mr. GLADSTONE's four points. The old programme was never much, and now the Tories have gone far in advance of it. To go back to it would be to complete the reversal of the position of parties. Liberals have been taunting Tories about their conversion to Liberalism; let them take care that Tories have not occasion to taunt them with their conversion to Toryism. But we have no fear of such a thing. Mr. MORLEY has always been sound; Lord ROSEBERY, though he has lost of late by excessive timidity, began as a sturdy Radical, and was, indeed, for a time, the proprietor of the Radical Examiner, in which, if we mistake not, Mr. CHAMBERLAIN made one of his earliest appearances in print. As for the greatest of all, Mr. GLADSTONE himself, why should he not lead us in the new departures? More than twenty years ago it was most truly said by a very shrewd critic that Mr. GLADSTONE had less in common with the Whigs than either with his opponents or his followers who sat below the gangway. He has in him something of the Conservative and much of the Radical, but little or nothing of the Whig. In this also lies the hope of reunion. By their fidelity to their ancient beliefs—a fidelity in many cases well approved in the past—the dissentient Liberals will best show the slender and temporary character of their alliance with the Tories, and hasten the time when all true Liberals will band themselves together for new campaigns against wrong.

OUR RELIGIOUS CENSUS OF LONDON.

THE great undertaking of making an enumeration of worshippers at the two principal services in the churches and chapels of London was undertaken, and successfully carried through, under the auspices of this journal, on October 24th, 1886. While similar enumerations have been made for almost all the greater cities of the Empire, the enormous labour and cost involved in satisfactorily dealing with the problem in London have hitherto proved an insuperable barrier. The only exception is, that a census of the City churches was taken by the St. James's Gazette in 1881. Some 1,500 places of worship, contained within a very wide area, had to be dealt with, and the number of persons employed amounted to several thousands. Thanks to the services of the General Superintendent, Major COLQUHOUN, of Lyons—who had previously superintended a similar, though much smaller work in Glasgow,—the superintendents of districts, many of them well known in the Christian world, and the sub-superintendents and the enumerators who, in the vast majority of cases, did their work with the utmost efficiency, the labour has now been accomplished. The day was bright, though cold, and there is reason to believe there was fully an average attendance. Allowance has to be made for various facts. For example, the West-end of London is to a large extent deserted at present, otherwise the attendances in the churches would no doubt have been much larger even than they are. Then the Church of Rome has several services through the day, attended by different people, and the enumerations of the two services do not give a fair idea of her strength. In the Church of England also, there are often extra services and we hope to be able to give account of these in the future, and to state how they bear upon the general results. Again, in many Nonconformist chapels services for children are held simultaneously with the forenoon services, and these have not been enumerated. Of these also, and of afternoon services, we hope to be able to furnish particulars. Besides, the services in mission-halls, which have greatly increased of late, must be taken into account, and this enumeration will be made. It may be mentioned that the total accommodation in mission-halls was estimated in 1878 as 45,000, but now probably is three times that number at least.

It is also to be remembered that exceptional circumstances in the case of separate churches increased or diminished the attendance for the day. For example, in the Church of England many harvest festivals were held, and in several Nonconformist churches anniversary services were conducted.

Front page of the British Weekly, 5 Nov. 1886

quiet assiduity he mastered the difficulties, which beset all new papers in their early life, and after two or three years had the satisfaction of seeing the paper established as an organ with a note of its own, and with the reputation of having introduced several new and remarkable voices in literature."[58]

To ensure the success of the venture WRN soon began to gather around him a group of writers, many of whom were his friends, who, he saw, could command the interest and respect of readers. At the beginning, however, the paper was mainly derived from his own mind. Later he reminisced to his colleague/assistant Jane Stoddart: "Before you came and when I was quite alone with the *British Weekly*, I wrote the whole of the thing, and with my own hand. For a year the fate of the paper hung in the balance, and it was just a question whether any day I might be informed that Hodder & Stoughton had made up their minds they would close it."[59] Such fears, however, were quite unfounded, and WRN soon became an established character on the journalistic scene, his devotion to work, lingering ill health and strong Scottish accent coming together into what proved quite a memorable figure.

> When the paper began, I was working for its printers, Messrs Hazell, Watson & Viney, in an office adjoining that which Nicoll used to occupy on press-days. His person-ality was a source of continual interest. He always arrived muffled up, and seemed acutely sensitive to draughts. He said very little, but his Scottish accent often puzzled the compositors who brought him proofs. Occasionally visitors would call, but he discouraged them on press-days when his whole attention needed to be focussed on the paper.[60]

The power of the *British Weekly* came to be its 'individuality and independence', for it was not tied to any denominational loyalty. The paper instead owed its character to the persona of its founder and driving force. It was, more than anything, a result of the intellectual openness and methods of thought WRN had cultivated from youth, made manifest through the indefatigable application of journalistic acumen and skilful industry. He declared to Marcus Dods, "I represent nobody but myself; my party is under my hat and will remain so. With all my crimes I am conscious of never having written to please people – often – very often doing the reverse."[61] Darlow eulogises his friend: "He held tenaciously to his own convictions, and never hesitated to proclaim them in trenchant words. But beyond all else, Nicoll glowed and tingled with that precious, indefinable thing which we name personality. He was so characteristically himself, always so fiercely and terribly alive."[62] WRN *was* the *British Weekly*, and readers warmed to his personality. He possessed an excellent memory, an instinct for news and a journalistic skill to present and arrange that news effectively. "He, also, had a kind of editorial second sight; he discerned subjects that were occupying the public mind, and with uncanny intuition he singled out the subjects that mattered most."[63] Beyond these inherent abilities, WRN also quickly developed an awareness of what his readers wanted: "They are not prepared to put up with dullness, incompetence, or belatedness. They demand a certain measure of freshness, life, and vigour."[64] Such comments about the strenuous demands of his readers, however, must be held in balance with his thoughts upon the readers themselves as voiced to Marcus Dods when in the process of setting up the paper: "The fact is we can't please everybody, or say one-tenth of everybody, but if we can only get the one-tenth! We must have 20,000 subscribers, and there is not that number of intelligent people in the country – so we must condescend to weak minds."[65] Whether this jibe is read as playfully cynical or brutally realistic, it certainly suggests that WRN had come to feel even at this early stage a complex blend of frustration with and respect for his public. Regardless of the light in which he held his audience, WRN held no illusions about the significance of his own role in his paper's development and ongoing life. In his view, "a good paper is like a well arranged dinner. There should be substantial food and delicacies to tempt the appetite."[66] He engendered a kind of compulsiveness: "The editor might often annoy people, or even enrage them, but they wanted to see what the editor had to say."[67] His biographer reflected,

> In editing a religious newspaper it is more than ever necessary that the whole range of subjects in which men and women are interested should be dealt with from a frankly and distinctly Christian standpoint, especially now that the secular press inclines less and less to make definite Christian assumptions. On the other hand, the editor knows that readers of a religious journal today expect to find there the same qualities that they find in their secular papers.[68]

In fulfilling this remit, WRN made full use of the skills, abilities and experiences he had developed as a minister. Later he wrote, "I had never even for an hour contemplated a literary career ... I am not in a position to say whether or not I chose wisely in taking up journalism. The truth is I had no choice at all. A minister thrown out of work by a failure of health is placed in a position of the greatest difficulty.... I can now perceive that the training and habits of former years helped me to enter it. I was familiar from the start with the ordinary routine of journalism, though I had much to learn, and though for a considerable time handicapped by weak health, I had more opportunities than most journalists of quiet reading."[69] He was determined to make a success of his *British Weekly*, and he surpassed his own expectations.

Style and Audience

That the *British Weekly* was successful was not a matter of chance – both paper and editor evolved over time to satisfy popular interests, avoiding the staid and formulaic styles of competing religious journals. Though the *British Weekly* was indeed a religious paper, it was also openly political, advocating a Liberal party perspective. WRN clearly set out the *British Weekly's* guiding principles in the leading article of the first issue: "The creed we shall seek to expound in this journal will be that of progress, and while independent of any sect or party we shall aim at the ends of what is known as Advanced Liberalism. We are believers in progress because we are believers in the advancing reign of Christ.... His day has only dawned, and great has been the influence on human happiness of the principles of Christianity."[70] He then went on to espouse strong support for the Liberal party, frank and open about the contemporary divisions then besetting the Liberals after the split over Gladstone's Home Rule for Ireland policy. Yet even here WRN was optimistic, for he saw the *British Weekly* as an instrument for uniting and encouraging Nonconformist supporters/readers. He wrote

> This is the language of high hope, but we are confronted by the hard facts ... but our trust is in the great heart of the people. Even in the condition of the Liberal party, the great instrument of progress, there is much to encourage by their fidelity to their ancient beliefs ... best show the slender and temporary character of their alliance with the Tories, and hasten the time when all true Liberals will band themselves together for new campaigns against wrong.[71]

From the first issue a clear and devoted voice speaking out in support of the Liberal Party was heard, a commitment that WRN would maintain, and which would prove appealing to many Nonconformists as well as useful to the 'grandees' of the party. *The British Weekly* was more than its political bias, however – WRN believed that the journal's leading article should be a unique feature each week, written from an explicitly religious stance. He was deliberate: "his own articles should not be devoted mainly to ecclesiastical, political or literary matters, but to religion".[72] Remembering that WRN had made his mark by a series of expository studies, these articles reveal that he saw religion in a broadly inclusivist way, which embraced social life, culture, and politics as part and parcel of the Christian's field of operations. Certainly, these editorial inclinations contrasted with other leading London newspapers, which Darlow sums up: "Except in one or two cases, there was hardly any condescending to popular taste. In fact, editors and proprietors behaved like schoolmasters. The editors and leader-writers themselves were often dignified and reserved persons, who cultivated aloofness as a sign of superior wisdom."[73] WRN approached his readers very differently; he imbued his publication with a great deal of the personal. In seeking to make his leading article a significant embodiment of the whole of the paper, he followed in particular W.T. Stead[74] in his editorship of the *Pall Mall Gazette* (1883-1889), a post in which he distinguished himself by his vigorous presentation of news. WRN wrote appreciatively of Stead's method:

> His articles were not mixed up with those of others. There was one article each day, and it was put on the front page. Stead appreciated his opportunity, and put his whole heart into his leader. What might very easily have been a dead page was one, which always tingled with vitality. It may safely be said that no purchaser of the *Pall Mall Gazette* left the leader unread.[75]

With his leading article WRN established for himself the prominence of a pulpit, as he took full advantage of the opportunity to declaim upon religious subjects of current interest. He wrote, "I had always thought that religious papers did not give enough direct religious instruction, and that the leading articles should be mainly devoted to this."[76] This instruction, however, was rarely expository or Biblical; WRN instead sought to discuss his religious topics as theological concerns and he wrote in a literary, political, or contemporary in a cultural sense, rather than simply Bible exposition.[77]

Through developing a style so tailored to popular interest, WRN became a skilled practitioner of the broadly devotional, socially aware approach that would prove key to the *British Weekly*'s success, emerging as an effective devotional leader-writer thoroughly at home in the fields of theology, literature and even the latest news, both important and trivial.

Darlow commented: "First-rate devotional writing has always been extremely rare. Nicoll, however, possessed this unusual gift ... nothing else that he wrote cost him so much thought and toil as his devotional articles ... in the *British Weekly* Nicoll never ceased preaching to a great and listening audience until he died".[78] Darlow is quite right to stress WRN's central role in the ongoing popularity of the paper – though on rare occasions others would be invited to author the leading articles, it was as an ongoing platform for WRN himself that this feature became and remained the cornerstone of the *British Weekly*'s identity.

The Contents of the Paper

A list of the subjects WRN explored over his years as editor of the *British Weekly* presents a compendium of varied, but always socially relevant, topics, which also had an element of becoming compulsive reading by being serialised. He began with a series on 'Prosperous Churches and the Causes of their Success'[79] and then 'Books which have influenced me', which gave opportunity for celebrity contributors. When he began a major series, 'The Second Advent: Will it be before the Millennium?'[80] WRN brought in contributions to affirm or to disagree with the question and was able to invite a formidable range of protagonists – who varied in quality – to argue the point.[81] The presentation was gladiatorial, reply upon reply prolonging the debate, with WRN even opening the columns for correspondence. In the end, the ongoing discussion stretched out for just over four months – quite a significant run, and a definite sign that WRN had struck gold in alighting upon an area that stirred great interest among his readers. Another significant series soon followed in the form of 'Tempted London', which began in October 1887, taking the form of a survey of the temptations to which young people were exposed in the capital. He formed a team of able writers, and in introducing the series, he met head on the challenge of 'sensationalising' the topic.

> We have been busy for many months in collecting the necessary facts. We have received help from many sources – from ministers, from the heads of missions, from Young Men's Christian Associations, and especially from young people themselves employed in business. But we have mainly relied on the investigations made by our own commissioners ... we desire to make it sun-clear from the first that we shall have nothing for the love of the prurient – no directory to hell – nothing but what may be read in

> any family.... Our facts are all guaranteed, and we shall
> hold ourselves bound, on proper challenge, to make them
> good.[82]

The series examined firstly the position of 'Young Men' under succeeding topics including 'Drink'; 'Gambling'; 'the Variety theatres of London'; and 'Dancing rooms', before turning to survey 'Young Women in London' under such headings as 'The Flower Girls'; 'Domestic servants'; and 'Factory girls'. The series, lasting eight months, contributed to enlarged circulation figures which WRN always examined each week. Their popularity was widespread and their influence tangibly felt, such that Jane Stoddart commented, "Ministers of all denominations preached upon the 'Tempted London' articles ... the paper on gambling had a considerable effect in closing certain clubs."[83] WRN also reflected on the impact of the series, which, he noted, caused many people to send donations in order that the conditions disclosed might be alleviated. He received scores of letters, sent in to the paper from young workingmen and women thanking the *British Weekly* for bringing their situations to light. The significance of the *British Weekly*'s 'Tempted London' series did not fade following its conclusion – twentieth-century appreciation of WRN's contribution in raising a general awareness of social problems may be found in K.S. Inglis, who wrote, "Nor should one overlook the role of the *British Weekly* and the *Methodist Times* ... without standing for any particular detailed programme of reform, each tried to persuade its readers (most of whom were Nonconformists) to consider the social implications of their faith. And the papers offered a better forum than existed elsewhere for Nonconformists who wished to discuss in public what those implications might be."[84] Even at the onset of the twenty-first century, academic interest in the nature and impact of the series continues. Callum Brown, for example examined the series and interestingly noted that

> Men and women were dealt with separately – men during
> the first thirty articles, women in the last ten. The nature
> of moral weakness in the two sexes was conceptualised
> very differently. The articles on women were organised
> on the principle that occupational exploitation corrupted
> women. ... The men's articles were organised around three
> headings: drink, betting and gambling, and impurity.[85]

Modern gender theory aside, WRN would simply have felt that the series had run long enough, fulfilled its purpose of increasing the circulation figures and made suburban Christians aware of the dangers of the inner-city life to which many of their youngsters aspired. Again, he found that his policies and coverage increased the circulation of the *British Weekly* and sustained his progressive image.

Alongside wide-ranging journalism and a careful attendance to matters of public fascination, WRN also knew the value of 'stunts' to capture the interest of potential readers. Unlike some competing editors, however, he maintained a certain wariness of the device, and perceived that it could be overused, especially for the calibre of reader at which he was aiming. Still, publicity-seeking events were not unheard of; in 1886, for example, the *British Weekly* carried the serialised results of a religious census of Sunday worshippers' survey.[86] The survey had weaknesses which would not conform to modern sociological methodological scrutiny, but it was simply an attempt to see whether there were significant changes since Horace Mann's census in 1851.[87] The interest in numbers can be viewed as an unhealthy need to gauge the church's success in gaining new members, and at the expense of the quality of nurturing new converts. Evangelistic meetings in the late nineteenth century and into the twentieth century were often preoccupied with using statistics as the measure of success. The Survey showed that out of a population of four million some 870,000 attended a place of worship on the day of the poll.[88] Interpretation of the figures provided further 'good copy' for successive editions of the paper, and though some disputed them, a substantial number of readers were appreciative. These included one who wrote "As one of the public Mr Gladstone feels much indebted to the Editor, especially in the present very defective state of our information as to the religious census of London".[89] WRN defended the survey and pronounced it a success, "We have waited until there was ample opportunity for our critics to utter themselves... with what result? Not one single enumeration has been challenged. We were not prepared for this extraordinary testimony to the accuracy of our figures. It will make a deep impression on the public mind".[90] Other, less sensationalistic ploys at garnering both publicity and reader loyalty also featured in the pages of the *British Weekly*. WRN noted, for example, the interest among his readers in contests and competitions. Readers were invited to correspond and asked to give their favourite preachers, hymns, Bible verses, towns or cities, and even holiday resorts, while some contests could require an essay or even a poem on a given subject. These were quite simple in design, never lasting long, and offering prizes such as a guinea for the winner and ten shillings and sixpence for the runner up. They did, however, all have a sustained and enthusiastic following, undoubtedly doing much to cement the role of the magazine within the minds of many of the readers.

Perhaps the most notable of WRN's efforts to keep readers enthralled through publicity-orientated features, however, was his reliance on great 'personalities', another technique borrowed from W.T. Stead.[91] WRN made the interview into a virtually exclusive platform for his assistant Jane Stoddart[92] [Lorna]. His journal carried her interviews of personalities ecclesiastical and political, but also literary, drawing heavily upon the cultural capital of what today is known as the 'Cult of Celebrity'. The realm of 'celebrity' was, however, rather wider than modern minds might think it; he saw preachers, for example, as a completely untapped source of interest for his readers, and they featured prominently amongst the interviews. Adeptly perceiving the nature of the public interest in such figures, WRN moved beyond mere interviews, printing etchings of the celebrities as well, the first of which, a reproduction of 'an unpublished pencil-sketch of Anne Brontë by her sister Charlotte', appeared in the initial issue of the journal. Responding to the popular acclaim with which his mixed media was meeting, he soon expanded from small line drawings to full-page plate reproductions, producing such memorable features as "A Gallery of Pulpit Portraits drawn from life by Harry Furniss, with biographical and critical sketches by Rev. W. Robertson Nicoll MA."[93] He even identified the potential of crossing these popular techniques over into his more academic work, including regular monthly portraits of the scholarly contributors to the *Expositor*.

WRN made use of his *British Weekly* 'Christmas Special Supplement' to present studies of Churchmen and novelists, with an emphasis on the personality and, increasingly, photographs as well, with the likes of J.M. Barrie, S.R. Crockett and Ian Maclaren receiving the 'star' treatment. WRN himself was not above a little self-publicity, as the *British Weekly* for 16 December 1897 presented the Editor surrounded by photographs of 'Some Contributors to the *British Weekly*'.[94] This was hardly the only instance of WRN's marketing of himself as a public persona, for; his 'Claudius Clear Column' was deliberately personal and spun out of his own interests, views and opinions.[95] Through such popular techniques, WRN displayed an ability to seem to get close to his readers, a sense which he actively cultivated through encouraging a perception of his role as something akin to pastor. The *British Weekly* could only flourish if its editor "seemed so conscious of [the readers'] existence as individual persons, and made many of them aware that he felt a certain personal responsibility for them – they belonged to his flock to which he owed guidance week by week."[96]

WRN reached out to the growing culture of celebrity for more than mere publicity, however; the promotion and stimulus of good general reading was always a high priority for him, and from the beginning he saw the need for a strong literary section where the cachet of featured popular authors might benefit, rather than trump, the content itself. To this end, he engaged "writers of distinction such as Robert Louis Stevenson, Walter Besant, Joseph Parker and W.T. Stead."[97] He invited well-known personalities who talked books and demonstrated the importance of good reading as an expected part of the educated and cultured view of life. Fictional stories and serialisations proved particularly popular, a format he began in 1887 with the publication of a serialised romantic story by Annie S. Swan.[98] Though the subject matter struck some readers as strange, the popular acclaim with which the move was met was undeniable: "It may seem strange that a highly intellectual Scots minister should sponsor popular romantic writing. But Nicoll was no ordinary editor."[99] Through maintaining a literary section, the *British Weekly* achieved a number of beneficial ends. The value for a publisher of sponsoring a paper which talked about books and the need to acquire and read them was obvious, but the social significance, advantageous connections and publicity that came alongside featuring well-known authors and discovering new ones also played a marked role in establishing the paper as a true cultural force.

Between the discussion-fostering feature articles, popularly-orientated publicity pieces and the literary section, the *British Weekly* also featured a great deal of more straightforward journalistic fare that its editor felt would prove both interesting and beneficial to his readership. News and opinions were an important commodity for selling a paper, and WRN gave his religious reading public his own style of 'gossip'. 'Notes of the Week', 'British Table Talk', 'Here and there among the Churches', 'Current Chat'; etc., were all designed to keep the readers informed about what was going on, and what people thought was going on. There were also columns for giving brief news that was not sufficient to merit its own article, hence labels such as 'News in a Nutshell', and the 'Minister's Column'. As the *British Weekly* progressed, Church and Ecclesiastical affairs increasingly played a secondary role to political news. Reflecting this, 'Notes of the Week' became almost a place for editorial comment on the events of the week. Less journalistic materials also made serious inroads upon the column space previously devoted to religious topics – journeys and visits to town proved popular subjects, representing a

Some contributors to the *British Weekly*, 10 Dec. 1897

The Editor: WRN. *Lorna*: Jane Stoddart. *Our Parliamentary Correspondent*:
D.C. Lathbury (though various writers fulfilled the role).

speciality in tune with the widening world of holidays and visits at home and abroad, themselves a strong sign of an increased popular focus on leisure-time interests. In addition to ransacking the national press and discussing at length popular subjects such as holiday destinations, WRN listened carefully to the chatter at the London clubs to which he belonged, including The Bath Club and The Devonshire Club.[100]. Indeed, the London club scene had grown into both a notable part of his life and a major source of new stories. As Darlow noted, "He warmed both hands at the fire of life in London, and he especially enjoyed the friendly human fellowship to be found in clubs."[101] Not that he attended all, or found them equally useful or congenial, but when he heard something he thought significant, he would often report back at his office and dictate conversations that he had heard at a club or a dinner – and he would indeed print almost anything that he thought could make good 'copy'. This growing dependence on a blend of legitimate news and overheard gentleman's club gossip was certainly an adept way to sell papers, but, it also represented a secularising tendency in the *British Weekly* which increasingly eroded important distinctions between the religious and the strictly secular press. To what extent WRN was merely following a current trend towards secularisation, and to what extent he was leading it will always be debateable; the reality is likely that in chasing an ever-larger body of readers he followed the paths of other religious editors into secular interest, but in doing so outdid all of them.

Though to discuss the *British Weekly* is in essence to discuss its editor, WRN did not write the whole of each issue himself. He was, however, very discerning in his choice of the writers he commissioned to help him, selecting "his contributors carefully, and then trust[ing] them absolutely when they had been chosen. Unlike certain other editors, he rarely retouched or altered the articles he accepted, beyond correcting any obvious slips of the pen. Nonetheless, he contrived to impress himself indelibly on each periodical he controlled".[102] WRN did rely on his authors to deliver the finished articles, but he maintained a strong editorial hand in offering suggestions, possible subjects, and discussion about the treatment of a topic – even 'nagging' them for a completed article. Even the eminent figure of Alexander Maclaren was not exempt from 'reminders'. Between this careful management of his body of contributors and his own visionary editorship, WRN was able to craft the *British Weekly* into a journal not only reflective of contemporary concerns and interests, but one so eminently successful that it quickly became the masthead of Hodder & Stoughton's magazine division and a major cultural force in its own right.

The Business Side

Given the innovative and commercially successful editorial approach WRN brought to the *British Weekly*, it is not surprising that he enjoyed a good working relationship with both of the partners; it was business-like, loyal, at times robust, but always mutually respectful. "Many records confirm that Mr. Hodder and Mr. Stoughton were no sleeping partners. Not only was their watchfulness known to the senior managers and to their fellow partners … every member of the firm was also conscious of their joint presence behind the two roll-top desks in the room on the first floor at St Paul's House."[103]

The partnership was built upon more than personal friendship, however, and the two businessmen had to learn to handle WRN. As a journalist and editor, he had ambitions that were continually being fuelled by his considerable achievements. While not a problem at the best of times, on occasion these ambitious flights were fired more by frantic overwork than rational thought, and could reach such heights that he would threaten his resignation unless he got his own way. Handle him they did, however, learning to brace themselves when WRN had been too long without a holiday, and in the end succeeded in fostering so strong a business relationship that their star editor remained firmly and loyally in Hodder & Stoughton's employment until his death in 1923.

However strong their working partnership, WRN was aware that Hodder and Stoughton were older men who often viewed publication possibilities in old-fashioned ways, so he was particular in his attentions to the next generation, cultivating a close, special relationship with the Hodder heir and the firm's future 'chief', Ernest Hodder-Williams.[104] Hodder-Williams was a compulsive reader who also shared the propensity to overwork of his future partner at the *British Weekly*. "Nicoll, who understood the younger generation so well (also knew more than most about overwork!), recognised the tendency immediately he met the boy, and persuaded Mr. Hodder to give his grandson a year's further education at London University."[105] When he did join the firm, he was 'apprenticed' under WRN's tutelage. "There was, indeed, an immediate mutual attraction for Nicoll, as he had demonstrated in his Kelso-days he knew how to inspire enthusiasm in the young and how to teach them."[106] WRN began by employing Hodder-Williams on the retrieval and placement of advertisements, for he saw him as a journalist in the making, possibly as the future editor of the *Bookman*. "Soon Ernest was to be found writing reviews and paragraphs for Nicoll's literary monthly, getting contributions for it and supplying it with new ideas. Hodder-William's relationship with WRN meant that he soon became the liaison officer in matters between the editor and the partners. For this, he developed the skills of interpreter and more particularly that of diplomat. Hodder-Williams' aspirations were higher than just being editor of the *Bookman*, and these were realised in 1901 when he took his grandfather's place as a partner of the firm. All this took place at a time when WRN's own interests and ambitions took on a heightened concern for the field of party politics.[107]

This shift in the political scene and the accompanying change in WRN's focus benefited Hodder-Williams, providing the opportunity to assert himself at the firm and take on more editorial control at Hodder & Stoughton without too much interference from his 'teacher'. WRN maintained his role as editor of the *British Weekly* – indeed, it was most important for his new political 'friends' that he did. He was not, however, overbearing in his presence. What may have developed into a clash between the established and the rising editors was also defused to some degree by a recent change in locale. The offices in Paternoster Row had become increasingly over-crowded, and in October 1906, Stoughton organised the move to St. Paul's House, Warwick Lane. This meant that, though WRN saw Hodder-Williams when he visited every Wednesday, the press day for the *British Weekly*, any sense of two strong personalities in conflict over office dominance was happily avoided. That the men were able to maintain the closeness that had long characterised their personal relationship is evident in the older man's concern over Hodder-Williams' health, an ongoing subject of particular interest to the perennially infirm WRN: "I was very vexed to receive your long letter which shows that you are exciting yourself very much on matters of business. The only chance of recovery is to put all these things out of your mind until you come back. Read good novels and talk to people and keep your mind easy, or you will not get well."[108] The existing correspondence[109] between the two men shows something of how they coped from day to day in the turbulent world of contributors' fees, writers pressing for more recognition, relationships with the printers, new printing machines from Germany, the availability of paper stock, and, most distressingly, distribution problems such as the lateness or the non-arrival of journals. WRN was aware of his friend's obsessive, even dark inclination towards depression, often brought on by his acute sensitivity to European and world affairs. The counselling and encouragement so important to their relationship, however, was mutually shared and appreciated, and would prove a sound basis for WRN's years with the firm.

In 1911, on the death of his grandfather, Hodder-Williams became the *de facto* head of the firm[110] and WRN's role changed from that of mentor to trusted adviser. Hodder-Williams first significant step was to separate book publishing from journals in the accounts structure, forcing the two mediums to prove themselves in financial terms without support from the other. This followed an expected threat from WRN to resign, but he did not. "Steps were taken for his workload to be eased and his remuneration increased. The first was achieved by reducing the number of journals handled by the firm … *Woman at Home* was sold to Newnes. This freed the editorial staff – above all Jane Stoddart – for the service of the three papers that Nicoll really loved – the *British Weekly*, *The Bookman*, and the *Expositor*. Meanwhile, Nicoll was also given a financial interest in the *British Weekly* profits, of which he received 33.33%."[111]

Hodder & Stoughton was undergoing change: "the sales organisation of the firm was renovated and extended; a new and clear-cut editorial policy was moving away from the confinement of Evangelical boundaries; a smaller, but profitable journal commitment, with *The Bookman* celebrating its coming of age in 1912, was paying its way."[112]

From around 1910, WRN found Hodder-Williams becoming concerned about German ambitions for power and the possibility that war would eventually break out. He dismissed these fears as part of Hodder-Williams' obsessive worries. "Ernest saw much more clearly than Nicoll that the Liberal government's pursuit of social reform … was hiding from the common man the inherent danger of the German power game."[113] Later, when the First World War had come, Hodder-Williams wrote of WRN's resolve to survive the war, "He told me of his faith, of his determination to see it through – 'You and I together', as we had seen through many fights in the past. 'Never fear we shall win – in the end.'"[114] In 1916 Hodder-Williams wrote for the war effort two personal stories of courage under fire; One Young Man, and Jack Cornwall VC.[115] In peacetime, Hodder-Williams continued to make his contributions to the *British Weekly*, particularly travels and the Victory Parade in London.[116] He, like his predecessors, knew how to handle WRN, and in his twilight years, Hodder-Williams arranged for St John Adcock to edit the *Bookman*, and brought in J.M.E. Ross to be groomed as WRN's replacement on the *British Weekly*. Both were honoured by King George V in 1921 and in the October Sir Ernest and Lady Hodder-Williams hosted a seventieth birthday celebration for WRN. In tribute after his death, Hodder-Williams wrote,

> I can find no words for my sorrow. I started to work for Sir
> William when I was a young boy, and I worked with him to
> the end. He was my ever-affectionate friend. I was through
> the years, even after I became his publisher and, as he
> would smilingly say, his 'proprietor was still his boy'. Our
> relationship was so intimate, the sad, the happy memories
> are so personal, so sacred, that I would I might pay my
> tribute in reverent silence.[117]

That the firm of Hodder & Stoughton continued trading following the
effective end of its first incarnation with the elder Hodder's death is
attributable almost solely to the joint efforts of Hodder-Williams and
WRN.[118] Their leadership saw the firm grow larger, more wide-ranging
in subject matter, internationally aware, and economically sound; a
considerable achievement.

A Faithful Assistant: Jane Stoddart

Miss Jane Thompson Stoddart (1863-1944) was for many years WRN's
indispensable assistant editor, and she described herself as having the
privilege of being his trusted "marshal". WRN had the male leadership
view that accompanied his age and yet he was very encouraging to
female talent and endeavour. Whether 'Sir William's' preferences
about 'a woman's role' had effects on her it is impossible to say, but
she remained nevertheless a valuable and valued part of the Hodder &
Stoughton journal staff throughout her mentor's tenure, and long after
he passed away. Indeed, in the years after WRN's death, it was Stoddart
who helped to maintain the standards of the *British Weekly* under
successive editors, always seeking to keep the publication to the level it
had achieved in the 'golden years' under 'Sir William'. Stoddart's ties
to WRN ran far deeper than mere editorial camaraderie – she came from
Kelso, where her family had long attended the Free Church.

> My first personal contact with [Nicoll] occurred at an
> evening meeting for young people in the Foresters'
> Hall … he asked, 'Is there any girl here who can repeat the
> answer to the question, 'What is effectual calling?' Though
> I had failed with the proof-texts, I was familiar with the
> noble language of the Shorter Catechism, and, rising in my
> place, I recited the answer without a break…. He was quick
> to discover any kind of promise, and his net was widely
> thrown. Verse writing was in those days my favourite

> pastime ... Mr. Nicoll knew their many faults, and their
> fatal imitativeness, yet he encouraged me to persevere.[119]

Indeed, it was this love of literature that was the base of the empathy
between Stoddart and her minister:

> With the coming of Mr. Nicoll...the manse, where his
> sister Maria reigned as a gracious hostess, was open to
> all in whom he discerned a genuine love of books. He
> led us to the poetry of William Morris and D.G. Rossetti,
> choosing certain pieces to be committed to memory. There
> was magic in his soft, crooning tones as he read aloud
> *The Blessed Damozel,* or one of the Morris ballads. With
> that critical instinct which the after-world recognised as
> almost infallible, he diverted our minds from the cheap
> and second-rate in literature.[120]

Stoddart initially trained as a teacher, including some time in Germany
where she became competent to teach the language. After a number of
teaching positions in 1887, she moved to London where she combined
some tutoring with helping WRN, who was trying to start the *British
Weekly* and needed assistance "in the preparation and editing of a largely
planned series of homiletic volumes.[121] She became a familiar figure
at the British Museum Reading Room[122] and research was one of her
main occupations at first. Working in the vicinity of WRN and the other
established journalists contracted by Hodder & Stoughton at the period,
however, gave her the opportunity to absorb a great deal about the trade,
and she made her first written contribution to the *British Weekly* with
an obituary entitled 'A Good Congregational Layman', signed simply
as 'S'.[123] The piece was well-received, and, a career change being
advised, she left teaching in 1890 and became a full-time journalist.
"Mr. Nicoll...thought I might waste my best years in poorly paid work
as a governess.... I once heard him compare teaching with journalism
in these words: 'The teacher's path lies straight and dusty to the grave,
while in journalism one never knows what may lie round the corner.'"[124]
WRN continued to give advice to Stoddart and helped her define her
role: "Mr. Nicoll did not think shorthand necessary or even useful, as
part of a journalist's equipment. He discouraged me from learning it on
the ground that I might sink into dependence on other minds, through
trusting to notes rather than observation."[125] Stoddart was also useful to
him as a translator, given her facility with German, and in return for her
diligence and loyalty he encouraged her in her career through assigning
to her the 'celebrity' interviews which were occasionally printed next

to the leading article.[126] "She was never parochial. Her appreciation of people and reviews of books were always tolerant: and if she had a fault it was that, she was too kind to impute any faults to them.… She was an invaluable assistant editor.… She liked interviewing people and people liked being interviewed by her."[127]

In 1893, Stoddart first used her familiar pen name 'Lorna' for her regular feature, 'The Woman's World'.

> While she could talk theology with the theologians and politics with politicians, Miss Stoddart also became an authority on subjects particularly appealing to women. When she was once complimented on her interest 'in the world of domesticity and fashion', she admitted that she could hardly remember the time when she did not find pleasure in dress.… This also enabled her to be practically the editor of *Woman at Home*.[128]

Her journalistic abilities growing increasingly evident, both WRN and Hodder-Williams encouraged Stoddart to write books in her own name. She tried fiction, publishing *A Door of Hope* (1886) and *In Cheviot's Glens* (1887), but did not feel encouraged to write again. Biography became a more successful field for her skills, and here she published an impressive number of studies.[129] Here it is not hard to see the advice of her friend and mentor who employed her considerable talents as a journalist, commissioning her to investigate particular religious groups,[130] including examples in politics, such as 'The Terms of the French Disestablishment Bill' (1905), *The New Socialism: An Impartial Inquiry* (1909), and *Against the Referendum* (1910). Stoddart, was encouraged to make her own contributions to *The Clerical Life: a series of Letters to Ministers*, and held her own with Marcus Dods, John Watson, T.C. Edwards, James Denney, as well as WRN himself.

Stoddart assisted in most of WRN's enterprises, gaining recognition as a fellow collaborator.[131] Stoddart even proved that she was capable of running the paper for a time. This impressive ability to assist her editor wherever he may have needed it enabled WRN to maximise his time for pressing on with all his interests and projects. Wherever it was manifest, her assistance proved invaluable to him – his body of work would likely have a quite different appearance taken as a whole were he to have lacked so constant a professional companion of the calibre of Jane Stoddart. His comment in *Princes of the Church* is typical: "The selection is due to my friend and colleague, Miss Jane T. Stoddart, who has also helped me generously in the revision of the proofs."

The Other Side of Hodder & Stoughton: WRN's Books

Though his major work with Hodder & Stoughton was in the realm of journals, WRN did involve himself on occasion with the book-publishing side of the firm, to which his most significant contribution was editing the various volumes of *The Expositor's Bible* series. He was anxious to bring together first-class scholarship of the Bible with the best qualities of good literature, seeking to achieve continuity of narrative, readability, warmth of devotional engagement, literary style, and above all a conviction that the Bible was a living word. Darlow notes that the scheme was already in WRN's mind when Stoughton visited him in 1884 at Kelso: "There is no work I would more gladly try my hand at: it would be my monument. Seriously, in capable hands, this is an enterprise of great promise."[132] Eventually the series was published in eight groups of six commentaries, lasting from 1887 to 1896. The partners agreed to finance the project, which eventually amounted to fifty volumes of commentaries covering the whole of the Bible. Over half the volumes were written by friends and contacts north of the border, such as Marcus Dods, R.A. Watson, James Denney, and W.G. Blaikie, which led John Attenborough to describe it as "a triumph for Scottish theology". Attenborough also noted that "One of the volumes was George Adam Smith's *Isaiah* [2 volumes] which established the separate identity of First and Second Isaiah and represented a theological discovery of world interest. It proved to be a best-seller, sufficient to carry the whole gigantic project."[133] This 'discovery' was certainly not new in the world of scholars, but WRN had determined to make the series accessible and informative for educated lay folk as well as clergy. Scholars of repute who engaged with the text of Scripture wrote the series, but in doing so sought to highlight applications for contemporary preaching and living.

The new views WRN sought to encourage discussion of were not radical, by any means, rather reflecting a transitional stance on the matter of Higher Criticism:

> Reverent [believing] criticism resulted from the practical necessity of relating Evangelicalism to the Bible of criticism before the principles of such a relationship had been worked out. In some cases, as in G.A. Smith's *Isaiah* or Skinner's *Ezekiel*, the results were surprisingly good. But the Biblical scholarship of the period was marred by the forced and mechanical way in which rational criticism and Evangelical theology are mixed. The criticism does

not rest on assumptions provided by Evangelicalism, and, on the other hand, the theology is not derived from the critical interpretation. Instead there is a mechanical alternation of passages of criticism with passages of Evangelical exhortation.[134]

WRN deliberately selected as his contributors scholars who could preach a little, as their brief was not to write critical commentaries for the scholarly community, but to be a help to preachers. A.S. Peake reflected on WRN's role as the editor of the series: "Nobody but an editor knows what the trials of an editor are.... Nicoll was sorely tried in this particular venture, as he told me ... writing on 3 December 1894, he says: 'I have had the utmost difficulty in producing *The Expositor's Bible*, owing to contributors not keeping to their dates, but I think now I am within sight of the end.'"[135] Whatever difficulties he may have faced, however, he achieved a remarkable degree of success, and the commentaries proved a valuable part of his attempt to stabilise the confidence of the Church in difficult times.

Particular highlights of WRN's book-editing career beyond *The Expositor's Bible* included *The Expositor's Greek Testament*, which was considerably admired in its day, though some contributions were felt to be more important than others. Again, WRN had trouble in keeping the contributors to datelines, and the series dragged out longer than he had anticipated. His concern for the ordinary minister's needs was reflected in the series *The Theological Educator* [15 volumes], which, begun in 1887, was an ambitious series designed to educate students and experienced clergy in understanding and awareness of the questions facing the contemporary Church. In 1888, WRN followed this with *The Clerical Library* [12 volumes] which was designed to stimulate and support clergy from all churches. Beyond these more ambitious endeavours, WRN was also always thinking of books that would appeal to the popular market, and so he brought out *Little Books on Religion*, a series of small books designed for general readers of the *British Weekly*.[136] Some of the titles were suggested and commissioned by WRN, with those by P.T. Forsyth proving particularly popular. Also aimed at a popular audience were *A Book of Family Worship* and, not long after, *Sunday Afternoon Prayers*, each a series of readings and prayers that had been first published in the *British Weekly* and were designed as a tool for readers in their personal and family worship. WRN was always concerned to facilitate and strengthen the Christian devotional life, regardless of the ongoing secularisation of his periodicals.

In addition to his own editorial and authorial exploits, WRN was also interested from the earliest days of his ministry in fostering the burgeoning skills of young writers. As his prominence in the publishing industry waxed, sympathy for the younger generation and encouragement of future writers grew apace. It remained a feature and a policy in all his journals, which often proved launching points for new voices both journalistic and literary. In the *British Weekly,* he designed a column entitled 'Our Young Men's Page', covering a full range of topics about contemporary issues in Church life and intended to provide a forum for promising young writers without other avenues of publication. His search for talent was constant, sponsoring literary competitions and scouring the local papers in hopes of spotting a new writer of note. "He kept a sleepless watch for fresh writers, and was eager to enlist able recruits from the ranks of the new journalism ... the editorial instinct is undoubtedly the thirst for new blood."[137]

Unsurprisingly, this fostering of new writing led to a growing reputation for WRN as a figure of great significance on the literary scene, including the 'well circulated' rumour that WRN was a major 'log-roller' or 'wire-puller' in promoting or terminating prospective authors. In his 'Claudius Clear Column', he tried to meet this head on.

> To the charge of writing in praise of certain authors in daily and weekly papers, I plead guilty, and I have no compunctions of conscience on the subject. There are two classes of critics, both necessary and useful. One class guard the passes to fame; they suspect and scrutinise every new author, they never give praise freely until the author is past the need of it, and their supply of cold water never runs out.... There is room for another set of critics, who as a rule, leave writers of established fame alone, and devote themselves to those who are appearing. It is their business to watch for promise, to hail it wherever it appears, to impress a reluctant public with the sense of new names and new achievements.... I for one mean to indulge in the 'noble pleasure of praising' and to enjoy the triumphs of my friends to the last laurel leaf.[138]

A similar, if more amusingly conceived picture of WRN as the great – and friendly – critic was penned by Andrew Laing for the *Morning Post*:

> Will nobody boom me?
> Oh Robertson Nicoll!
> My prospects are gloomy,

> Will nobody boom me?
> With sword, they review me,
> With pen points, they pickle.
> Will nobody boom me?
> Oh Robertson Nicoll. [139]

That aspiring writers may have felt that their avenues for review were shrinking is understandable, if one considers the degree to which WRN had begun to loom over the whole of the industry. In light of his ever-growing reputation for literary acumen, he was often asked to write reviews of current books, particularly the latest novels – in addition, one must remember, to the ongoing forums he held in the *British Weekly* and the *Bookman*. In May of 1899, Conan Doyle, decided to take issue with him on the subject of 'multiple reviewing'. Doyle made a complaint in the *Daily Chronicle* concerning WRN writing reviews of the same book in different journals. After mentioning WRN's editorial roles in the *Bookman* and the *British Weekly*, he wrote,

> Turning now from these more serious papers to their somewhat frivolous contemporary the *Sketch*, we come upon a column of literary criticism signed by yet another symbol, 'OO'. Yet, incredible as it may seem, the opinion of 'OO' is still the opinion of 'Claudius Clear,' of 'A Man of Kent' of the critic of the *Bookman*, of the critic of the American *Bookman*, and of the critic of the *British Weekly*. This, I hold, is not legitimate criticism. And now when I add that this same critic frequently expresses his opinion of any important new book in the anonymous columns of a daily paper, and thus adds a sixth to his possible methods of influencing public opinion, I think that I have said enough to show that a protest is needed. [140]

Of course, as a journalist, WRN was always interested in book publication, and he certainly used his articles to 'push' or 'puff' particular books – often those published by Hodder & Stoughton. As such, giving up the opportunity to push what books he would in such a variety of publications was quite opposed to his own interests, and so in replying to Doyle he was unsurprisingly defensive:

> Criticism is to me the merest aside in a very busy life. It is no pleasure to me to denounce a young writer. I do not remember that I was ever guilty of the crime. I have never worked in connection with any other critic, and have never

made the slightest endeavour to bring any individual round to my opinion of a book. In rare cases where I have written several reviews of a book, the book has been invariably one which I have had no connection, direct or indirect. Only in the remotest sense have I any pecuniary interest in the success of any book, and not a single sixpence I possess is invested in publishing. Nevertheless, I do review very occasionally, and hope to continue in that way. There are pleasures in criticism, though the profits are very small. I have no doubt that Dr. Doyle has received more for one novel than I have ever received for all the criticisms I have ever written.[141]

This was an expected defence, for WRN, with his position of great influence, was an obvious target in the cut-and-thrust world of publishing. It did not change anything, but he always went out of his way to humour protagonists if it was at all possible.[142] The event was reflected in a stanza from 'A Picnic on Parnassus', which appeared in the New York journal the *Critic*:

Then Doyle was heard complaining, with resentment and surprise
That Nicoll put his finger in too many of the pies;
But Nicoll, with a weary smile, still sampled every course, And wondered Doyle should pass him such a quantity of sauce.[143]

Even *Punch* carried a bulletin: "DISTINGUISHED PATIENTS: Dr Robertson Nicoll remains in a very critical condition. He complains of plurality and congestion of the organs."[144]

WRN achieved a high status in editing and publishing through his long-term connection to the multi-faceted firm of Hodder & Stoughton. The opportunities this gave him, along with the ever-trumpeted public support of the firm's partners created an unassailable image of the man as amongst the greatest talents in the field. This was not the case of some behemoth of the publishing world selecting a new face and shepherding him to prominence – as much as WRN benefitted by his connection to Hodder & Stoughton, the firm owed him more. When he joined the partners, Hodder & Stoughton was still a concern of relatively modest proportions; it was, as much as anything, through his indefatigable and innovative labours in promoting and expanding not only *The Expositor*, the *British Weekly*, and the *Bookman*, but drawing in new authors and raising public awareness of Hodder & Stoughton that the company grew into one of the premier publishing houses of the day.[145] He came to hold the aura of a 'panjandrum'[146] and he was not at all displeased with the role, playing along in public, though debunking it with family and friends. Such was his reputation that WRN found his name a 'marketable commodity', even within so competitive an environment, which was rich in individuals with extraordinary talents. Such prominence does, however, complicate a historical assessment of the man – people deferred to him and could be deliberately kind when reviewing his personal publications. WRN's American friend and colleague, George Doran, assessed something of the 'Nicoll Phenomenon' in writing that WRN was

> A vital force in the religious, social, and political life of Great Britain – if not of the entire English-speaking world. For forty years … I witnessed the flow of books of distinction resulting from his acute perception and discovery. These books were in all departments of literature, represented by theology, religion, philosophy, fiction, biography, and belles-lettres. He was not only an indefatigable worker himself; he had all the qualities of a great executive who compelled others to work along the lines of his conceptions and ideals.[147]

Despite the breadth of positive reactions to his work and career, it is worth noting that WRN has always had his detractors as well, which is inevitable if one considers that he achieved success at a time of great competition, and, perhaps more impressively, sustained that achievement throughout the rest of his life. WRN was always his own man, aware of what he liked and he was prepared to encourage and praise such work regardless of its perceived commercial 'quality'. This meant that some doubted his real power to discriminate and evaluate literary work. S.K. Ratcliffe wrote "What Nicoll took for criticism was simply the downright assertion of what he liked and did not like. I doubt whether he ever thought about principles or methods. Hence his judgments were often staggering, as when he calls Balzac the greatest Christian novelist."[148] A more recent writer has repeated this assessment, suggesting that "Nicoll had, by today's standards, a narrow cultural range. By our standards, too, he was often tremendously wrong (he thought Barrie a genius, but George Eliot 'something else')."[149] That WRN made mistakes and had his share of failures, however, is hardly evidence of mediocrity in taste or ability. He also demonstrated rare insight, practical business sense and a great deal of knowledge acquired through his wide reading. Indeed, it was this unique blend of financial acumen and decisive, if arguable, literary tastes that led A.S. Peake to offer up in an anecdote what proves to be as vivid a summary as any of the root of WRN's success in the public realm:

> He had a fine literary taste.... He was one evening at the dinner of some society, and in the smoke-room a publisher's reader said: "I have something to show you. It is the finest volume of poems I've had through my hands for a long time." Nicoll took the manuscript, ran down page after page with his lightning swiftness, and in a few minutes handed it back to his friend saying, "I quite agree with you. It is the finest volume of poems I have seen for some time – and you won't sell two hundred copies."[150]

4

Becoming Established in England and the Halcyon Years
1885-1910

WRN's literary career in London spanned several decades, but in order to appreciate fully its progress one must understand something of his life as an individual and a family man. In the winter of 1885, WRN travelled to England with his wife, initially spending some weeks in Dawlish, Devon; eventually, however, they sent for their family and furniture and settled in their first home at 'Glenroy', Highland Road, Norwood, South London. To his friend M'Robbie he wrote, "The place is within five minutes' walk of the Crystal Palace. I have always preferred this suburb: it is so high, with so much open country and such splendid views, and the air is the purest and most bracing in London."[1] During these years, the family acclimatised to its new situation and, although WRN's health remained a matter of some anxiety it underwent a very slow improvement.

WRN made the most of his contact with Hodder & Stoughton, and from the autumn of 1885, his life began to revolve around the offices in Paternoster Row and the production of the *British Weekly*. His invalidity made him appear frail, even in later days of relative good health, but WRN tended to downplay any infirmity, and he always worked with the mental vigour of a far healthier man. Annie Swan reflected: "They settled at Norwood, and he gave himself up entirely to literary work... and wherever he was, in whatever state of body, his mind seemed able to function unceasingly. He wrote all kinds of 'stuff', to use the common name to journalism, but his heart was inevitably and almost entirely in religious journalism."[2]

The bustle of the London journalistic scene was something new for someone from rural Scotland; there was certainly no dearth of outlets for his desire to work. Indeed, it was a very different world, with very different opportunities: "he found many doors opening to welcome him or left ajar for him to enter, and he made his way through them all. He discovered that to be at home in a library and a pulpit was quite different from being at home in Fleet Street and in the club-land".[3] Far from daunted, however, he seized this change in circumstances and, as Darlow noted, "Gradually his whole outlook broadened, his judgments grew surer, he gained more actual grasp of affairs, while his personality and power as a journalist soon developed so as to command attention".[4] WRN established a reputation for his methodical work, thorough research and shrewd assessment of colleagues. He was motivated by the need to support his family.

From its launch in October 1886, WRN had watched diligently over the growing success of the *British Weekly.* As he felt the paper secure, WRN reflected,

> "It is surely right that a man should continue in the work that Providence has assigned to him so long as he can and this was the course I took. When one door is closed to him, he has to consider whether another door will open. I am thankful that the door opened for me and I can now perceive that the training and habits of former years helped me enter it."[5]

With this ongoing concern occupying his working hours, the ensuing years were busy and successful, but WRN wanted to realise another dream and relocate from south of the Thames to the more desirable suburbs of West London. In March 1889, the Nicoll family moved into Bay Tree Cottage, Frognal, Hampstead; "a Queen Anne House with later additions, standing back in a garden, with a little lodge at the gates and stables and a cottage at the back".[6] This was to be their London family home until WRN's death in 1923. Hampstead, a cultured and literary suburb of North-West London, was well suited WRN who not only loved exploring the Heath and its surrounds, but also found in the area a rich collection of personalities about which to write. He loved its literary associations, and believed that his own house had been the home for a time of Dr. Johnson, though this was no more than wishful fantasy.[7] With his new home established much of 1889 saw WRN not only pursuing his regular journalistic commitments, but also labouring on his first biography. Finding the history of a fellow Aberdonian journalist, James Macdonell,[8] to be inspirational and full of good practice, he set out to document that life in print, writing, "Mr Macdonell never lost his belief in the press as a great influence

... he never wearied and wasted himself in personal disputes. The most magnanimous of men, he had no room for small grudges, envies and resentments. If he thought himself unjustly treated, he had to put the thing out of his mind – and he succeeded".[9] The book absorbed a great deal of WRN's time throughout the year, and when he completed the manuscript in late November, his wife recorded in her diary, "Tonight Willie finished the last chapter of his book. I am very glad, for it has been troublesome to him"[10] – and, no doubt, to the rest of the family. Such relief was to prove short-lived, however, for in the same month he finished the Macdonell text, WRN's friend and mentor Professor W.G. Elmslie[11] died unexpectedly, and WRN felt compelled to immediately set to work on a biography[12].That he was able to pursue independent projects at this pace was, given the volume of his journalistic work as well as his editorial work, was an extraordinary accomplishment. Now he turned his attention to a number of other literary projects, making these years the most productive of his life. He seemed to be full of ideas for new columns, books, and even entirely new journals, many of which were good. Although he did over-reach himself at times, these years saw the birth of a number of successful ventures, including the *Bookman* and the *Woman at Home*.[13]

WRN did not, however, limit his endeavours to publishing; never willing to sacrifice entirely the world of his youth and first career, he maintained his connection with the Free Church of Scotland, acting as their unofficial public relations man in England. His great interest in Free Church affairs meant an occasional visit north of the border for speaking engagements, even outside the customary family holiday break of the summer months, particularly as his health became stronger.. He kept an eye on the changes taking place within the Denomination and the occasion of the Free Church [Fiftieth] Jubilee in 1893 was an opportunity for assessment. WRN felt provoked by the Moderator of the General Assembly, William Blaikie,[14] who delivered a nostalgic commemorative reflection, which drew an ireful response from him. He criticised its reactionary and unrealistic call for a turning back of the clock:

> No doubt, there are some who think that the whole movement of thought and criticism, during [the] fifty years has been a futility.... We cannot believe it, nor can we believe that the new views of Scripture do not shake the faith of the people ... the teachers of the Church cannot but carry a grave burden of difficulty and responsibility. It is

Bay Tree Lodge, Frognal, Hampstead

> not so easy to be sure who is for us and who is against … it checks exuberance and self-confidence to be compelled to say often, 'I do not know; I am waiting for light'".[15]

In crafting this deliberate and pointed reply, WRN was particularly concerned about encouraging the men that were then at work in the ministry.

> "The question is – Are the men of today as willing to dedicate what they have to spend? We believe they are. The Free Church has had hard tasks … she had to bear first among the churches the brunt of the great Biblical problem, and had to sacrifice her most brilliant and accomplished professor. She had to face the unrelenting hostility of the literary class. The most powerful newspapers in Scotland have daily held her up in derision … of how she has been treated by the man[16] who was her political idol nothing need be said. She has committed mistakes about which we can afford to be silent, since so many are eloquent. Yet today she abides in undiminished strength, with growing numbers, and a revenue of some £620,000 a year, a band of ministers and missionaries unsurpassed in any church, and numbering

some of the most eminent names in Christendom".[17]

It is clear from his apologetic article that WRN was proud of his contemporary 'progressive liberal' generation and could mount a robust attack on a nostalgic view of the past. However, he also knew that his Free Church was on a course that would change it into a more liberal structure, in which minorities would feel themselves forced to secede. Even as the majority were negotiating to unite with the United Presbyterians, WRN, like other contemporary liberals in theology, really had no way of knowing how much they would have to concede in the future, but optimistically thought they could hold their present position.

Triumph and Tragedies

Such labour as that to which WRN committed himself was not, it must be said, without its rewards. In March 1890, WRN received the degree of LL.D. from Aberdeen University, which was welcome recognition for his work. His wife recorded in her diary, "This honour is all the greater as it was in no way solicited. Three professors had his name on their lists".[18] This growing professional success and recognition, however, was counterbalanced by an ongoing rash of personal pain. 1888 had seen the deaths of both WRN's mother-in-law and his infant son, Louis Dunlop, aged eight months In October 1891 WRN's father died, at the Old Manse in Lumsden. Harry Nicoll had lived quietly and long, although as he became frailer he needed a live-in assistant to relieve him completely of his pastoral duties. He was not, however, entirely an invalid – he still preached on occasion and continued to read and buy books right up until his death. WRN later committed to write a filial biography,[19] and the Old Manse, inherited by WRN upon Harry's death, became the summer home for the family, remaining in the hands of descendants for several generations.

The family was soon to begin grieving a loss far less expected and with a much greater impact. Just when the Nicolls had fully settled into their Hampstead life, making connections with the neighbours and slotting themselves into local society, tragedy struck as WRN's wife, Isa, died in June 1894 aged only 36. This was not only emotionally devastating, but also left WRN with two young children to bring up. His wife's death was sudden, for though she had undergone an operation in November 1893, she had recuperated sufficiently by Christmas to be able to spend the holiday with her husband and children at Shere. However, in February and March her health fluctuated and she spent Easter at home in bed. By May she seemed stronger, but ominous symptoms set in, and her diary for June 1st contains the following entry: "I am leaving for a private hospital to undergo a grave operation … I do not feel hopeless, for God's love and mercy have preserved me, and surely goodness and mercy will continue and follow all my days. But when I think of the possibility of my not recovering, it is indeed Gethsemane. May God bless and keep my dear ones – and if not here then above [grant us] a happy reunion … I feel so much for Willie – it is harder for him than for me". With those words, her diary breaks off. The next day she was dead.[20] WRN wrote,

> "We had no thought, nor had the doctor, of the state of things … he got the chief specialist in London, and they agreed that the operation was necessary. We knew it was a grave one, but were very hopeful, and you know how it ended.… All sixteen years of her married life, she was full of sunshine. There was never a more radiant nature, and it was so to the last."[21]

That WRN would need help in order to maintain his family and work schedule was certain, but, despite the undoubted strain, he somehow managed to keep up with his professional duties, Jane Stoddart noting that "He was only absent for three weeks from the regular duties of his office."[22]

Death and bereavement were increasingly a part of WRN's life experience, and from 1890, he had begun to explore them within the context of Christian faith with a series of articles.[23] He had not initially planned to write a book, but as the series continued, he began to feel that the issues he was discussing were important. The collection of articles that emerged, named *The Key to the Grave*, was published just before his wife's death. In writing it, WRN was reflecting on not only the frequent tragedies of recent years; the numerous familial deaths he had learned how to deal with over his life[24] as well as the loss of a number of mentors and colleagues. William Elmslie's death was followed by those of Charles Spurgeon, Andrew Bonar, Robertson Smith and R.W. Dale. This cavalcade of grief understandably left him yearning for relief, and in his preface to *The Key to the Grave*, WRN addressed the lack of a published frank discussion of the topic from the Christian perspective which had resulted in his own volume. "The papers would never have been put together had it not been for an incident that showed that there are not many books written directly for those who are discovering, by actual experience, what bereavement and death really are."[25] In answering the need for such a work, WRN drew comfort from seeking to expound what the Scriptures taught. Difficult though it must have been, his efforts proved fruitful, and both his work and personality led those who came to him during their own bereavement to note, "In trouble he was a matchless friend. While others were searching for the fitting word of comfort or hope, he had spoken it. He was a great comforter."[26]

The rending apart of his family, however, required practical resolution as well as spiritual. The most pressing necessity was making provision for his children, who had for the moment been sent for their usual Scottish holiday at Lumsden while WRN himself remained behind, noting that "It was a great trial for me to part with the children, but I felt Lumsden was the place for them, and I could not face the North this year".[27] Soon securing his late wife's cousin's agreement to help with their day-to-day care at Bay Tree Lodge, WRN was able to return to work, throwing himself into it. Even after a year WRN was still deeply affected. As he wrote to his friend M'Robbie, "It is trying for me to see the anniversary [of his wife's death] come round, and yet I am thankful, deeply thankful, that the time has passed. On the whole I get on better, but have intervals of black depression. As to the future, I do not see anything clearly. ... Don't you feel very old – as if your life was largely behind you? I do, and yet it isn't quite a reasonable feeling".[28] Throughout his profound personal grief, WRN not only maintained his journals, but he actually added to them, bringing out another collection of *British Weekly* articles, entitled *Ten-Minute Sermons*.[29] Work and more work was his strategy for coping.

Success and Some Failures

The year 1895 saw WRN emerging from beneath the weight of the previous year's troubles, engaging with his work at least as much as he had before Isa's death. Perhaps the most notable of his ventures at this stage was his collaboration with Thomas J. Wise,[30] whom John Attenborough suggests that WRN first met in connection with the *Bookman*.[31] Their project was the first of a proposed series of some ten volumes entitled *Literary Anecdotes of the Nineteenth Century*, intended to contain 'odds and ends' that would be of interest to readers of recent literature. A second volume appeared the next year, but then the series abruptly stopped, for what were at the time reasons unknown. It would appear, however, that WRN simply went cold on the project, and it is now known Wise was a fraud, which may well have been an aggravating factor.[32] While *Literary Anecdotes* ran, however, WRN was the senior collaborator in the project, which involved ferreting out details on the background of literary figures. The idea was to create a journalistic space where 'gossip' overlapped with 'interesting information'. Despite the demise of their shared project, however, Wise soon became a familiar contributor to WRN's magazine, and used its columns to further his own enterprises – the over-valuation of forged 'antique' books in which he had some financial stake. Attenborough observed,

> "The *Bookman* provided just the opening Wise needed. It is almost unnecessary to add that Robertson Nicoll, as also the proprietors, Messrs Hodder & Stoughton, were unaware that the *Bookman*, emanating from the same highly respectable office as that popular religious paper, the *British Weekly*, was being utilized to boost the values of publications that were to be proved forgeries. Had they known, oh the groans in that peaceful square off Warwick Lane!"[33]

Wise perpetrated this 'scam' essentially undetected, and WRN, along with many others, was taken in. The contributions from Wise to the *Bookman* first began to appear in 1892. "Then, in 1893, Robertson Nicoll proudly announced that Mr. Thomas J. Wise, the 'well-known collector and bibliographer', had undertaken the 'editorship' of their 'Recent Book Prices' reports, and that he added, 'out of the fullness of his knowledge and experience,' his comments are 'particularly valuable to Book-buyers and book sellers.'"[34] As for *Literary Anecdotes of the Nineteenth Century,* WRN seems to have left the editorial work largely to Wise, but contributed, along with his name, his influence with the publishers, and a number of anonymous articles. That he embarked on the work in the first place is unsurprising – WRN had a life-long unfulfilled ambition to write a history of nineteenth-century English Literature, and was vulnerable in this area not least due to his pride in his reputed expertise. It also has to be acknowledged that Wise was a convincing, even, a consummate, 'artist', and was not exposed as fraudulent in the majority of his activities until the 1930s, long after his death.

Third-party reflections upon the Nicoll-Wise partnership have varied in tone. Attenborough, for example, offers a rather judgmental analysis of Wise's role in *Literary Anecdotes*:

> "The first two [volumes] appeared in 1895 and 1896. Then the series suddenly stopped, and it may well be that WRN had discovered that many of the anecdotes were bogus (as demonstrated by Carter and Pollard).[35] But the unhappy

connection did not stop there, for [an intermediary], who remained WRN's lifelong friend, told him that Wise could lay his hands on some original Brontë letters, held by Charlotte's family in Ireland. WRN determined to buy the copyright and publish an edition of the Brontës … Alas for these hopes! Nicoll [was] double-crossed by Wise, and the Brontë edition, lacking all unpublished material, died a quick death."[36]

After Thomas Wise was exposed, his work became 'fair game' for many a literary detective. WRN knew nothing of the dealings of his collaborator, but it is intriguing to wonder why WRN pulled out from the partnership.

Darlow's biography, by contrast, simply reports the arrangement with Wise in a factual way: "Nicoll collaborated with Mr. T.J. Wise, who has unrivalled knowledge of the lives of modern English writers, while his famous library of their autograph MSS is a wonder and envy of other collectors."[37] Darlow also quoted WRN writing to Marcus Dods, displaying his early enthusiasm for the project: "I am very busy indeed, and hope to get the first volume of my book out in October … it will not be history but a useful collection of [documents] to scan for a history".[38] Even just after Christmas of 1895, he could write to James Denney, "I am quite satisfied with the reception of the 'Anecdotes'. There was a thoroughly intelligent review in the *Chronicle* yesterday, and we appear to have sold about 600 copies."[39] That he was so quick to transition from enthusiasm at this stage to the outright abandonment of the project shortly afterwards suggests that something – perhaps the Brontë letter fiasco – had warned WRN off. While this would certainly have aroused his publisher's concerns, they would have had little recourse but to stifle their groans and say nothing, for a display of discernment and judgment on their part would have shown up WRN, becoming the occasion for much amusement among their rivals! WRN was supported by an understanding and generous partnership, and would often quote Matthew Hodder's words, "What is past, is past. What is done is done. Learn from the past and go forward to the future".[40]

Other awkward situations cost the partners considerably more. In the early years of the *British Weekly*, for example, WRN had "run the firm into a libel suit with the Sunday School Union over a Sunday School lecturer whom he believed to be bogus".[41] More spectacular was the fate of *Success*, a newspaper launched by WRN in 1895, which he based on the style and format of the magazine *Titbits*. WRN was

WRN at forty-five

playing a hunch for, "Naturally Matthew Hodder and John Stoughton had very little liking for it! That was without doubt the reason why it did not bear an H & S imprint or address! It ran several sensational items, e.g. £1000 prize and a mystery to be solved with another prize."[42] Attenborough recorded the basic facts: "An editor for the new venture was found, articles of educational interest were commissioned, prizes and competitions invented … but as the Partners wryly put it 'Success proved a failure'."[43] WRN wrote of both the partners, "they were excellent losers. Neither was ever heard to make any reference to any failure".[44] Though journalistically adventurous, WRN was not one to ignore the lessons of experience. From this point onwards, he curbed his speculative ventures yet still gave the partners some notable publishing triumphs.[45]

One of those triumphs was occurring at virtually the same time as *Success* was floundering. It was in 1895 that WRN edited a series of *Little Books on Religion*. This became an extensive series with contributions from a wide range of contemporary scholars: Dale,[46] Dods,[47] Forsyth,[48] Adam Smith,[49] Denney[50], Whyte,[51] etc. Some of the contributions had already had an airing in the *British Weekly,* as had WRN's own volume in the series, *The Seven Words from the Cross*.[52] In these studies, which initially appear to be straight exposition, WRN used the Biblical statements more as devotional exercises for believers than in trying to understand the meaning of the Passion of Christ. For example, in the fifth chapter where he expounded the saying "I thirst", he saw this as 'Our Lord's Knowledge of Holy Scripture'. "That the Scripture might be fulfilled, He said, 'I thirst'… A deep and intimate knowledge of Holy Scripture is the foundation of an enduring and stable spiritual life".[53] The series was well received and WRN had colleagues in the press who could give him a good write-up, as he was known to do for others, but one review in particular stood out:

> Perhaps no finer appreciation of the sublime significance of Christ's last words has hitherto been given in the whole scope of religious literature. The book must be classed as one of transforming power … to the reader in any way acquainted with its author's many-sided work it will reveal how far the mind may keep above the thronging duties of the work-a-day experience. These pages have about them the atmosphere of unclouded thought, such as is found in the works of few writers.[54]

That should have had them all queuing up in the streets to buy their copy! Of course, such recognition was far from the norm – WRN always wrote well, but not this well. In 1896, WRN published, *When the Worst comes to the Worst*,[55] a short book in the 'Tavistock Booklet' series. For once, these three chapters[56] had no previous life in the *British*

Weekly. He wrote encouragingly of the need to persevere in the trials of life, and ended in his typical style: "The trouble may come back again worse ... what then? At the very worst, the memory of the past will help us. We shall retrace the slow, difficult way to peace; our trust in God will be deepened, and we shall realise that, after all, the range of sins and sorrows is limited, though the sea of troubles may roll its white-crested billows as far as the horizon. What are truly numberless are God's mercies. What is truly infinite is God's love."[57] Strangely WRN, given his astuteness with using his lectures as mainstay articles, did not use this material in his papers.

The autumn of 1896 saw WRN spending six weeks in the United States with Mr. and Mrs. J.M. Barrie as travelling companions.[58] The men saw the visit as both pleasure and work, for they were booked to give a number of lectures. The firm was furthering its connections with American publishers and WRN was interested in seeing the American scene at first hand and affirming many of his contacts there. Jane Stoddart quoted from "a series of letters published in the *British Weekly* [in which] Dr. Nicoll gave his impressions of this American journey"[59]. Interestingly Darlow, by contrast, used a number of letters written to Miss Catherine Pollard to which he became privy after 1923 – and which, in addition to outlining the trip, quite clearly show that WRN was moving towards matrimony.[60] As an amusing aside, in reading the two accounts it is clear that WRN reused particular passages to do two jobs, showing yet again that he was never usually one to miss an opportunity to make good copy serve more than one purpose. The party spent most of the time in New York, but made excursions to Boston, Massachusetts, and New Orleans.[61] Their visit coincided with the Presidential election battle between William McKinley and William Jennings Bryant, which WRN enjoyed, even though it turned out to be, as was generally predicted, an overwhelming victory for McKinley. He also had time for being a tourist and even heard the odd preacher.[62] When WRN returned he conveyed his evaluation of his visit, writing to Marcus Dods: "Barrie made the best and kindest of travelling companions, but I was very sorry to find him so frail. We saw the American literary society thoroughly well and were received with great kindness. Of church life, we saw very little, though I could have done so had there been time. I formed the impression that the nation was suffering from a kind of febrile irritation, which led to petulant outbursts not really of deep significance".[63] As well as being both interesting and, one must imagine, a welcome break from the constant struggles of editorship, the American trip allowed WRN the opportunity to gauge his transatlantic experience. On that last count it was quite a triumph, as his comments give the impression that he returned from abroad with the sense that his editorial ventures were receiving increasing acknowledgement as an international hit. It seems that while in America, WRN took a number of speaking engagements, the experience of which encouraged him to continue to do the same when he returned to Britain. Using his inherited Aberdonian inflection, he was able to speak in some of the largest preaching venues in the country. The worry of sheer physical inability laid to rest, WRN's American visit had fired up his mind with 'ideas and possibilities' for his own and the firm's publishing future, not all of which landed on British soil without stirring up dust. There was also the return to the strain of the London office as he resumed working at an incredible pace and intensity, especially when he came to complete the papers for publication. The partners were accustomed to WRN's ambitions, his fertile mind brimming with fresh ideas and his tendency to use the threat of his resignation[64] as a strategy to get his way. However, this occasion seems to have been out of the ordinary[65] and there were further factors that need appreciating in order to understand WRN's concerns. He was conscious that the firm had just had two very successful years with books, largely from that growing pool of his 'discoveries', so he thought he had earned the right to have a more dominant part in organising the total book-publishing business. Further,

> Nicoll felt it was essential "to have a literary man with a tolerably free hand who will look out for writers, suggest subjects, conduct negotiations and do what he can to make the transaction straight between the author and publisher." If the partners wished to do all this themselves, Nicoll would confine himself to the editing of the firm's periodicals. "Since coming to London," he added, "I have had at least seven offers from publishers to become their literary adviser."[66]

The partners graciously, but firmly, called his bluff. They replied by reiterating their appreciation of his work, but thought that their 'discovering' him must have helped his literary career. They then made it clear, "That they wanted Dr. Nicoll to continue as the firm's literary adviser, provided he could accept that 'they reserve to themselves independence to use their own judgment, experience and convictions' in relation to their literary adviser's multitudinous ideas. If that condition were unacceptable, Dr. Nicoll. was 'perfectly free to work for another publisher.' The partners then added a nice touch to the effect that they had just negotiated additional space for the editor and his staff.[67] Undoubtedly somewhat chastened, he accepted the partners' terms and got on with his work, for he appreciated the secure base that Hodder & Stoughton provided for his many activities. He also welcomed the freedom they willingly granted him, allowing him to have Continental holiday breaks in winter and the summer in Aberdeenshire. Attenborough insightfully commented, "The truth is that, at this time, Nicoll was often in two minds as to where his own future lay. Sometimes he felt overwhelmed by his work for the periodicals, sometimes by his work as literary adviser. In 1898, for example, he agreed reluctantly to serve for seven more years as editor of the *British Weekly,* 'though he felt he should give way to a younger man under 50.'"[68] The partners were not fazed by WRN's mode swings and he was secure in knowing that they appreciated having him on board.

Home and Family

At the beginning of 1897, WRN had a particular pleasure in seeing his new library/study take shape at Bay Tree Lodge. The influx of cash his professional success engendered, had inspired him to improve his home, and he settled upon adding a new upper storey to the wing of his house centred around a room fifty-one feet long, able to house over 24,000 books. "It [was] divided into two parts and arranged somewhat on the plan of Mr. Gladstone's library at Hawarden".[69] This became WRN's sanctuary, and though there was much hard work and many challenges ahead, he had his library. It operated as both his retreat, and his 'command centre'. His assistant, Jane Stoddart, recalled, "Our working-nest was at the far end of the room, where his armchair, on the right of the hearth, faced at almost every season a blazing fire.... Newspapers lay thickly on the floor and a carved chest for manuscripts, known as the ark, stood behind his massive writing-table. Except for a few chairs and photographs on and above the mantelpiece, books in their open cases were the only furniture. I never saw him seated at his writing-table; all his dictating was carried on from the fireside."[70] WRN's habitual delight was to saunter among the shelves and then have a good read, but he also liked entertaining visitors who were full of conversation.

> No visitor to that wonderful chamber will forget its long vista of crowded bookcases.... Between these, a narrow winding rivulet-track of rugs led up to the armchair of the owner, dimly seen amid a cloud of tobacco by the fire. You

had the uncanny sense of a vampire brain crouching in its corner, having sucked the life-blood of innumerable books and absorbed half the souls of their authors. For Nicoll's memory was preternatural. He knew every scattered volume, where to lay hands on it, and almost the page on which a needed quotation lurked. There, for a quarter of a century, he read and wrote and brooded and dictated.[71]

His books had been chosen to serve a purpose, and writing in 1915, he had no illusions about the possible value of the library's contents: "I am writing in a library, which at the present moment contains from 23,000 to 25,000 volumes ... the library is only a journalist's library. There are no rare books in the number, and if the whole were sold by auction, the results would be disappointing. Nevertheless to me the collection means something."[72] This was WRN's place for work, reflection, and study; it was his hobby, his hideaway, and his delight – the place where most of his friends and visitors remembered him – a place for a 'twasome crack', if one was invited in. However, WRN also knew that he and his children needed not only a more accommodating home, but also a new lady of the house, and it was a call that would soon be answered.

Not long after beginning these improvements to his home, WRN embarked upon a far more significant change to his life in the form of his second marriage. His relationship with Miss Catherine Pollard began in June 1896, when WRN was first introduced to her and developed as he corresponded with her during his American trip. Absence had made the heart grow fonder, and on returning to Bay Tree Lodge, WRN wrote to her,

> It flashed upon me that people were always asking me to do things for them – to give or lend them money – to hear their confidences whether of grief or joy. It occurred to me that all my leisure and much of my money were bestowed on others.... Yet I think there is a want in life – the want of some one who would not be always asking, but would sometimes give – who would remember that I had my own sorrows and struggles and failures and despondencies and illnesses, and who would watch for them and give me a steady quiet sympathy and would say, "*I* do not care for you merely when you are prosperous, but when you fail and are down. I care for you all the more, and I am yours to help you."[73]

A wife was needed at Bay Tree Lodge, as much for the owner as for his growing children. As a friend commented, "a more utterly helpless

WRN in his library

being in household affairs could not be imagined, and after a run of acute domestic difficulty and discomfort, he married Miss Catherine Pollard... who by her grace and sweet kindliness, quickly restored the atmosphere of home to Bay Tree Lodge".[74]

Their engagement was announced in January 1897, and they were married in early May. Possibly, there were a few raised Nonconformist eyebrows at the announcement: "On May 1 1897, at Shillington Church, near Hitchin, the wedding took place of Dr. Robertson Nicoll, and Miss Catherine Pollard, daughter of Mr. Joseph Pollard, of Highdown, Herts. The ceremony was performed by Bishop Mitchinson, assisted by Rev. J.A. Bonser, Vicar of Shillington. Sir George Douglas, one of Dr. Nicoll's oldest friends, acted as best man."[75] Here was the Free Church minister and the editor of a premier Nonconformist paper, being married by a Bishop in an Anglican Church![76] Doubtless this was completely in deference to his bride. Darlow comments, "His second marriage opened a fresh era in Nicoll's domestic happiness. For his children, as well as for their father, Bay Tree Lodge became a true home once more under its gentle and gifted mistress, and in 1898 the family affection was deepened and enriched by the birth of a new daughter [Mildred]."[77] From her personal knowledge, Jane Stoddart confirmed, "through the tender and constant care of his wife, a great improvement soon became manifest in his health, and he was able to undertake occasional preaching and platform work".[78] It is an interesting reflection that WRN, with his old-fashioned views about women and opposition to women's suffrage, was nevertheless very dependent on two ladies, each necessary in their respective spheres of his life. His new wife proved herself a very competent organiser of the family and his home, arranging everything round his needs and preferences. She later observed, "I think I soon adapted myself to my responsibilities and the regular routine of the house ... punctuality was essential. Assistants and secretaries were coming and going and their time was of value. We knew the day of the week by that day's programme."[79] At work, he had trained Jane Stoddart to be his assistant, and she was quite capable of taking control of an edition, which she did when the editor was absent or on holiday. It must be appreciated that WRN's achievements were to a great extent dependent on the calibre and competence of those around him.

With his health becoming more reliable and his family life stabilised once more, WRN took increasing opportunities to speak, for he found many such doors were opening to him. If drawn up in its entirety, an itinerary of his addresses, lectures and sermons would show that he was able to speak as much as he wanted: the list included Carr's Lane, Birmingham; the National Free Church Council; City Road Methodist Chapel, London; The Jerusalem Chamber, Westminster Abbey, London, not to mention opportunities north of the border and even in Ireland. His articles in the *British Weekly* reflected these appearances, and, quick as ever to spot an opportunity to reuse material, reappeared in his books, such as *The Return to the Cross* (1898) and *The Lamp of Sacrifice* (1906). These are all 'Sermons preached on special occasions,'[80] and demonstrated that he was in demand as an acceptable and honoured speaker.

WRN's ever-growing influence with his readers translated well to a higher-visibility public persona, leading him inexorably towards an increasingly active involvement in politics.[81] Amongst the first steps in this progression was, unsurprisingly, an issue that bridged journalism and public advocacy. In March 1899, the *Daily Telegraph* announced the intention of producing a Sunday edition. Before long, Alfred Harmsworth's *Daily Mail* stated its intention of doing exactly the same thing. There followed a short 'press war' which sounds extraordinarily quaint to the modern ear. To WRN, however, it was alarming, and he was determined to stop what he termed 'Seven-Day Journalism'. In his 'Notes of the Week' (30 March) he informed his readers of what was happening, and on 20 April he launched a lead article on the subject. "The battle is fairly on us now, and it is perhaps the most serious battle that Christianity in this country has had to fight during the century.… It is not too much to say that it will be in the end a battle for life and death.... The effect is this – a completely materialised society and civilisation, a society that has lost its ideals, lost its faith, and considers that nothing in life is worth having except money."[82] Though his cause in this instance may have been doomed in the long-term by the marching columns of secularisation and commercial interests, WRN's efforts on its behalf provide ample evidence of his ability to rouse a 'crusading' spirit in his readers. This tactic was to be perfected in the struggles and causes ahead, when WRN would prove that he could not only rally the troops, but map out campaigns with which ordinary Christians could – and would – identify.[83]

Future endeavours aside, in the battle of the moment WRN found support with his audience; some felt quite certain that seven-day journalism would never catch on. The following week, he noted in his leading article, "We are glad to find from the newsagents that the Retail Newsagent and Bookseller's Union are intending to do all in the power of the trade, supported by the clergy and ministers of all denominations and backed by the unions of labour throughout the land, to prevent the introduction of the seven-day newspaper into the country".[84] For the moment, WRN's minor movement culminated in success. He glowed,

> As we go to press it is announced that the *Sunday Daily Mail* is to cease. This is described as 'a frank concession to the religious feeling of the public.' It is further said, 'We bury it without regret,' and it is owned that the resolutions of protest from the country have assumed gigantic

proportions. All's well that ends well, and we are the last persons to press a victory. Nevertheless it must be pointed out that this is distinctly a victory.[85]

There had been bitter things said but WRN was confident that good relations could soon be re-established between the press, the newsagents and the public. When the *Sunday Daily Telegraph* soon followed the *Mail* and ceased publication, he could tell his readers: "The victory is complete, and the experiment of seven-day journalism has been buried, we trust never to revive".[86] WRN had felt a real sense of the power of a popular movement; though ostensibly still within the journalistic realm in which he had made his name, he was in truth notching up his first success in another field – politics.

The Free Church Dispute and Increasing Circulation

WRN's expanding public persona meant he was increasingly regarded as a useful speaker, especially north of the border. On 31 October 1900, WRN travelled to Edinburgh to witness the Synods of the Free Church of Scotland and the United Presbyterians processing together to a specially fitted hall in the Waverley Market. Negotiations for the union of the churches had been occurring since 1897, and he had kept his readers informed of the progress. WRN covered the event himself:

> The event will be hailed as one of rich promise and historic importance through all the Christian world…. Is it not certain that the chief cause of the great alienation from the Christian faith, which we see in our land, is very largely due to the bitterness of contending Churchmen?… If we are filled with the Holy Ghost our faith will send us out eager to do anything for those living in the gloom outside, and it will make many who live in that gloom gaze wistfully as to a new source of light, and come out to meet us.[87]

His tone was devotional, optimistic, and even euphoric. However, the negotiations had resulted in some fracturing to the Free Church, as some were implacably opposed to the union and saw the Union of the Churches as the culmination of a liberalising movement that had been at work in the Free Church over the previous years. Both Churches had passed Declaratory Acts that loosened their unreserved subscription to the statements of the Westminster Confession of Faith. This was a battleground in the Free Church and the passing of the Act brought the first secession in 1893 – The Free Presbyterian Church.[88] Then in

1900, twenty-seven ministers of the Free Church refused to join the Union. They "were strongly conservative in their doctrine and Church principles, holding to an uncompromising Westminster theology and to the hallowed Scottish Presbyterian belief in the recognition of Christianity by the State through an established Church. They regarded the union as an abandonment of these principles."[89] This minority and their people, mainly from the north west of Scotland, took out a long-threatened legal action for the payment and transfer of the property of the Free Church to them, as the true and rightful successors of the principles of the Disruption of 1843. This produced a legal dispute lasting some years. WRN was at first relatively unconcerned, but when the minority group took their case to the House of Lords, he foresaw there could be problems with prolonged litigation and made himself an expert on the details of the case.

WRN was always interested in surveys and statistical evidence and in 1902, the *Daily News* published a survey of churches, in which it was shown that the non-Anglican groups were more than equal in church-going population to the Anglicans. Though the Anglican communion remained the largest single group, it was certainly true that the two were comparable, and that Anglicans no longer constituted a true majority Of the total attendants, the percentages by denominations ... read, 43% Church of England, 38% Nonconformists, 14% Roman Catholic, 5% Salvation Army & mission services".[90] Furthermore, Stephen Koss has pointed out that there was a contemporary upsurge of numbers and morale amongst Nonconformists from the impact of the Welsh Revival of 1904 and the successful evangelistic rallies of R.A. Torrey and C.M. Alexander, which were held from 1903 to 1905.[91] This period would prove to be high tide for Nonconformist power and influence. WRN, as other leaders, thought that this would be a movement that would surge on and they enjoyed the success, though much of the rhetoric about what would be possible proved to be unsustainable and illusory.

The ephemeral nature of Nonconformist prominence was due not least to the ongoing internal dissent ravaging the communion. WRN found that events of the Church dispute in Scotland had moved on, for in the courts of Scotland a minority who were against the merger with the United Presbyterians claimed to represent the principles of the original fathers of the Free Church. Known as 'the Wee Frees,' they met continual rebuffs to their demands to be recognised as the true Free Church of Scotland, and therefore the heirs to its property. They appealed to the House of Lords, who considered the 'Scottish Church

Case'. The verdict pronounced on 1 August 1904 was, controversially, in favour of the minority Wee Frees. The author of the biography of Principal Rainy summed up the situation:

> The effect would have been to make the very name of justice both a laughing-stock and a scandal. The entire property of the Free Church of Scotland, which was a Church with some eleven hundred ministers, three fully equipped theological colleges, and a missionary organisation which ranked second or third amongst the Protestant missions of the world, was given over – to a Church with a score and a half of ministers, one professor with (it was said) three students, and not a single missionary.[92]

WRN was not alone in feeling dumbfounded, but he mastered the details of the situation. He was able to explain the case as it penalised the majority:

> The effect of the decision, if carried out, will be to put in the hands of the Minority a property, which they cannot possibly administer, and to deprive the Majority of the power to carry on their work. The vast Free Church organism has been the growth of sixty years. The machinery has been created by constant and willing sacrifice on the part of the dead and the living.... Apart from the public confusion and the paralysis of Christian work, there will be private miseries and anxieties that are beyond reckoning. These will affect every part of Scotland. It is not, however, of their own personal suffering that the ministers and members of the old Free Church are chiefly thinking. What concerns them above all is the future of their work for Christianity.[93]

He sought to demonstrate that, when the Lord Chancellor said he was basing his verdict on his understanding of the minds of the donors, "'or what we are to infer would be their view if it were possible to consult them'"[94], he was offering fundamentally flawed reasoning. The Lord Chancellor's effort to act on the behalf of a body not available for questioning was a spectacular failure, not least because, "as it happens, very many of the donors are now alive".[95] He concludes with a personal reference,

> I have remained in association with the Free Church and have contributed according to my means not only to the ordinary income but to the building of churches and

manses ... our money has been taken and violently diverted to purposes which are hateful to us. Should we not have a right to demand it back? Is there not a clear case for restitution? I make the appeal to all fair-minded men.... Is there not an urgent call for immediate redress in the interests of common justice as well as of Christianity?[96]

WRN made every effort to impress in his presentation of the Majority's case, particularly south of the border. He detailed his activities after the House of Lords' decision to his wife who was at Lumsden:

"Mr. Donald, the editor of the *Daily Chronicle,* came round to take me to his office to write the leader ... the quickest bit of work I have ever done. The article seems to have made an impression ... I also 'inspired' the *Westminster* and the *Daily Mail*.[97] It is the best that ever I could do, and I hope I may never have to [do] such a job again. I do not feel depressed. This will work for good and come right in the end. I only feel concerned about my own duty in the matter."[98]

The following week he wrote in an upbeat way,[99] viewing the decision as God's providential leading, for he was convinced that the members of the United Free Church were more united than they ever had been. On this issue, as many others before, he gave selections of the letters and encouragements from ministers who had spoken of their support, though he allowed statements from both sides. The Government was forced to intervene and introduced its 'Churches Bill', (Scotland) on 7 June 1905 generating a compromise which was generous to the smaller claimant, but – as it was bound to be – controversial. WRN felt that his articles that had appeared in both his own paper and others had maintained pressure on the Government. The debate went on for some time, but there was in the end an equitable division of the property, though it remained, some would say, generous to the minority. The United Free Church passed an Act in 1906, which was designed to state that the Church had freedom to revise her constitution and rules so that it could never again be challenged in a civil court.

WRN quietly continued at his post editing and in 1906 brought out another volume of sermons/articles *The Lamp of Sacrifice*.[100] This was unique in the sense that all of the pieces had been addresses or sermons that WRN had given in the previous eight years.[101] This was something he could not have foreseen when he was forced to leave the ministry and was proof that his career as a preacher was not completely forgotten. He was always fully orthodox in his doctrine, but his style was more concerned with apologetics than simply expounding Scripture. He still took a text of Scripture, but it was usually a peg on which to hang his discourse.

Meanwhile, still recovering from the legal wrangling, the Free Church community suffered a blow of a different kind towards the end of 1906, when the great Free Church leader and architect of the union of the Churches, Principal Robert Rainy,[102] died. Though Rainy had always been controversial, and continued to be so after his death, his liberal approach to evangelicalism was a significant influence on WRN. Reflecting on the career of Rainy, a man he knew well if not closely, WRN wrote,

> Superbly prosperous in winning his own men, he was very much less successful in obtaining the confidence and overcoming the hostility of those who were outside and opposed to him. Perhaps there was no ecclesiastical leader more bitterly attacked[103] and more sincerely disliked than Dr. Rainy ... Dr. Rainy was satisfied with the Free Church. He was not even anxious to promote reconciliation between the Church and culture.[104]

WRN reflected further on Rainy when Carnegie Simpson's biography was published in 1909,[105] noting that Rainy "never had an atom in him of the gossip, and his correspondence is notably free from all those trivial personalia which have so much attraction for some minds."[106] WRN thought that Rainy had made unwise decisions in his time of leadership and felt that there should have been more probing of the wisdom of some of the decisions made by him.

> He [Simpson] is in full sympathy with Dr. Rainy throughout his public action … he is persuaded that Rainy chose in every one of his controversies the best course open to him in the circumstances. Mr. Simpson shows historical insight in judging Rainy's action not by the condition of things as they are, but by the circumstances in which he played his part. And, so judging, he vindicates him from end to end of his great career.[107]

This was quite wide of the mark in WRN's view. He also maintained that Rainy was not a great orator, and quoted Λ.B. Davidson's comment that Rainy could preach best and worst of any man he knew. Neither did WRN believe that Rainy would impress posterity with his books. It was as 'leader' of the Free Church Assembly that he would be remembered: "Principal Rainy was primarily an ecclesiastic, but he was an ecclesiastic of the great type! The term has not worn well!"[108] Rainy could work well with committees and seemed to come fresh to each controversy. There were aspects of Rainy in WRN, not least his commitment to liberalise evangelicalism as a strategy for the Church coping with the contemporary scene. K.R. Ross concludes a biographical study of Rainy with a reflection that could apply to WRN. "It may be that his serene confidence in the integrity of the reformed faith, born of the Evangelical buoyancy of the early Free Church, prevented him from seeing how undermining the movements of biblical criticism and creedal revision might be. Certainly, he seems to have been too easily satisfied with building a consensus within the Free Church, when something more prophetic was needed."[109] Very reluctantly, WRN would have agreed.

Amidst the ongoing drama of the fracturing Free Church, WRN found himself caught up in an entirely different brand of theological conflict when, early in 1907, he found that one of his protégés, R.J. Campbell, then minister at the City Temple in London, had developed heterodox views. WRN had long been supportive of Campbell, but suddenly found that he not only had to sack him from the *British Weekly* team, but was also left with little choice but to plunge boldly into the brewing dispute.[110] More unexpected news came in May 1907 when John Watson (Ian Maclaren), WRN's friend and protégé, died while on his third speaking tour of America. Watson had enjoyed fame as one of WRN's 'Kailyard Novelists',[111] and had been a regular writer in the *British Weekly* writing under either of his names. Between the loss of one apprentice to radical new theories and another to death, WRN was by this stage feeling as though he was more survivor of a past phenomenon and generation than a man at the forefront of theological journalism, as he had grown accustomed to being.

By the end of the first decade of the twentieth century WRN had become established and respected as an editor and publisher of the front rank. He was knighted in October 1909 for his services to politics. In fact, although church life was still important to him at this point, his centre of gravity had moved more towards the political area. WRN presided over a well-oiled mechanism which produced his papers and he continued to write topical articles and comment on the news as it unfolded and so maintained the church's witness to the volatile times. WRN continued resolute in his conviction that the orthodox Christian truth had great relevance for the particular problems of the period. There were times when he thought he might retire and live a quiet life, but neither his temperament nor events would allow this to be a serious option. WRN did not slow down – he maintained his routine, strenuous though it was[112], and added 'political advisor' to his schedule. WRN still took on lecturing and preaching engagements, fulfilling two appointments in Edinburgh in October 1910: he delivered 'Thomas Chalmers: a Reconsideration' before the University Theological society, and then on the Sunday he preached in St. Giles Cathedral to over 2000 members of the Students' Representative Council. He responded to concern for him that was shown by his nephew, Innes Logan: "That sort of thing [lecturing before 2000 people] doesn't worry me. What does worry me is my spectacles, my papers, and my bands. They are perpetually getting lost."[113] Of course, WRN was able to get leading articles out of his engagements,[114] and though that meant he also had to commit time for research and preparation, he was loathe to give it up – the task remained 'meat and drink' to him.

5

Relationships with Key Church Friends and Leaders

Journalism is an industry that requires of its pre-eminent figures not only great skill, but a large and varied web of connections across the full societal spectrum. WRN always enjoyed people, especially those who had something to share and quite simply people fascinated him. Many were useful to him for his work, but there was a smaller group with whom he enjoyed the stimulus and recreation of his relationship with them. WRN had a 'genius for friendship', which enabled him to be methodical in cultivating a large number of friends whom he used effectively, not only in establishing his periodicals, in maintaining their success, but also, in giving them a platform to display their capacities. His relationships are an important key in seeking to understand WRN's own achievement and appreciate his warm humanity. However, because of the size and complexity of his networks, there are difficulties in assessing WRN's thoughts about others. Selection is difficult for WRN had opportunities to appreciate many of the key figures of his day and these were in different fields of interest. This Chapter looks at some contemporary Church figures with whom he engaged; they are selected from a virtually endless list of colleagues and acquaintances who figured in WRN's life. The following studies are from WRN's own point of view. Consistency cannot be guaranteed in all cases, for at times WRN could be partial, forcefully demanding, warmly supportive and, occasionally, wrong. He had learnt to be 'all things to all men', especially if he wanted a contribution from that person for his papers.[1] So long as such concerns are borne in mind, however, the fact remains that WRN possessed shrewd insight into the character and motivations of those he read about and observed – sometimes at close quarters. Through exploring his relationships, one can come at a far greater understanding of the man himself, his work, and his motivations and attitudes. It will be seen that more Scottish than English relationships

Andrew Bruce Davidson

have been selected and this simply reflects the fact that WRN had more – many more – Scottish friends.

A number of historians have assumed that **Andrew Bruce Davidson**[2] of New College, Edinburgh taught WRN during the younger man's tenure there.[3] This mistake highlights the important influence of Davidson on WRN's views of the Old Testament. His admiration was derived from W.R. Smith, who, at Aberdeen, taught in a 'Davidsonian' way, in both style and content. Davidson was an enigmatic figure who worked quietly and conscientiously, influencing a whole generation of ministers and scholars at New College between 1858 and 1902.[4]

WRN's affinity was with Davidson's approach to criticism and the older orthodoxy. Davidson believed and practiced a patient approach to change, rather than the 'revolutionary' stance of his 'brilliant' pupil, but he also had a real respect towards those who maintained the older orthodoxy. Davidson had more of the pastoral insight and sympathy that Smith lacked. WRN discerned this; it appealed to him as he judged it sensible, and he sought to employ the approach as an editor. Davidson himself grew quickly into both inspiration and major editorial asset – not only did WRN feature Davidson in the *Expositor*, but he also kept Davidson before the readers of the *British Weekly* with an occasional sermon and, most frequently, extracts from Davidson's articles.[5] A typical inclusion was Davidson's review of a book on Old Testament criticism: "Professor A.B. Davidson, in his incisive manner, gives some cautions to the more reckless among the critics. He warns them that the argument from language is in danger of being carried to excess … the sober practitioners of the higher criticism are finding their chief enemies now not among the traditionalists, but among those on whom the critical spirit has acted like wine".[6] WRN kept the work and influence of Davidson before his readers and Davidson's significance as a thinker did not cease upon his death. WRN played his part in maintaining that influence when the project for a biography of Davidson was suggested. He saw the potential in this area of discussion, drawing as it did necessary attention to understanding that there was a development in Davidson's mind as he sought to come to terms with the challenges of higher criticism. His encouraging presence can be detected in Strachan's biography[7], even though it did not turn out to be satisfying biography. WRN saw Davidson as the ideal evangelical scholar; painstaking in research, thorough in knowledge, quick to grasp a topic, conciliatory, and ultimately reluctant to engage in controversy and as he learnt from Davidson he wanted others to learn as he had.

Charles Haddon Spurgeon was one of WRN's heroes and in his early days in London, WRN had often visited him at his home in Northwood. Spurgeon[8] was an acclaimed preacher and leader amongst the Baptists, but also appreciated by the church at large. In the 1880s, he became increasingly alarmed at the spread of unorthodox views – even heresy – within his own denomination, and came to represent a defensive, orthodox wing of the church, facing off against more innovative liberal thinkers.

Spurgeon also proved an early journalistic patron, and the *British Weekly* published some short summaries of his sermons during its early days. This friendly arrangement, however, was not to last; though initially Spurgeon seems to have thought the younger man saw things as he did, WRN was in truth a different breed of Evangelical, far more open to innovation. As Spurgeon felt provoked by a significant number in the churches, he became more vocal in his defence of conservative theology, but WRN came to take a different view of the state of the contemporary church, and indeed may have been one of those who unwittingly contributed to Spurgeon's final sense of isolation and loneliness. Within the first year of the *British Weekly's* run, the Downgrade Controversy burst on the scene; though WRN attempted to remain on the sidelines at first, his involvement – and the inevitable rift – was not long in coming. In March and April of 1887, articles[9] appeared in Spurgeon's magazine *The Sword and the Trowel* that drew attention to a 'downgrade' in doctrine and faith that he perceived in the contemporary Church. WRN noted Spurgeon's concerns in the *British Weekly*, saying that Spurgeon had commented in his magazine saying that many were trying to unite the church with the stage, cards and prayer, even dancing with the sacraments. "Too many ministers are toying with the deadly cobra of 'another gospel', in the form of 'modern thought'... when the Gospel is concealed and the life of prayer is slighted, the whole thing becomes a mere form and fiction".[10]

This was interpreted as Spurgeon throwing down a gauntlet. Although WRN admired Spurgeon's writings, he came to believe that Spurgeon epitomised an old orthodoxy that had to give way to a new order.[11] Though they shared common Evangelical beliefs, their mindsets, training, and understanding of modern society were very different. Whatever his intentions, WRN continued throughout the controversy to cover the preacher's movements in the news columns of the *British Weekly*, realising that whatever Spurgeon did or said was potentially newsworthy for a journalist[12] and his readers wanted to know.

Initially WRN took a stance of sympathetic neutrality, but as the Downgrade Controversy raged on, he committed his journals to attack the position taken by the Baptist preacher. In 'The Coming Battle', WRN summarises the position taken "in the judgement of the vast majority of scholars",[13] choosing his ground carefully but writing in a way that could intimidate many ordinary readers:

> The real battle is over the Old Testament. Thoroughly to
> understand the arguments that weigh in this question is by
> no means easy, and this is why the people, and many of

their teachers, do not yet apprehend the real seriousness of the situation.... But the argument for the new view of the Old Testament is complex, and can only be followed by those who are willing to take the pains. Perhaps it can hardly be understood without some knowledge of Hebrew…the historical part of the Old Testament is largely untrustworthy, and parts of it, such as the Book of Chronicles, are 'written with a purpose'. Such are a few of the results reached.[14]

Forced into decisive action by the polarisation of the church, WRN moved openly towards the position of the believing critical school of his old tutor, William Robertson Smith.

In the same article, WRN focused on Spurgeon, pointing out what appeared to be an inconsistency: "Mr SPURGEON lately condemned the Old Testament Revisers for not going far enough in reconstructing the text, stating that from the point of view of verbal inspiration the original text was necessary. Yes; but does Mr SPURGEON go through a delicate critical operation before he ventures to preach on an Old Testament text?"[15] WRN, as did others, felt that the liberal view of the Scriptures was carrying the day. Yet reassuringly he ended his article: "We do not believe that there is reason to feel alarmed. We are sanguine that there will be a settlement of the doctrine of Inspiration as final and satisfactory as that of the doctrine of the Trinity. But before that time, much must be thought and unthought, said and unsaid. And what concerns us is that orthodox scholars and theologians should study and face the serious difficulties raised".[16]

Despite these evident leanings, at the end of August, Spurgeon wrote hopefully to WRN seeking his support in his protest:

> I wish you w[oul]d come out most decidedly, & whole-heartedly. I shall be pleased to see you if you call round. I would not say a word to silence or hinder you if you are not on the right side; but believing that you are so, I should be very sorry to say half a word to vex you, or hurt your paper. I will write you a note which you can print if you like; or in some other way, if wiser, will let all men know whom it may concern that I judge your article & not you, when I said 'of a neutral trust'.[17]

WRN did respond, writing some comments challenging extreme critical views, very likely trying to maintain at least the partial illusion of a balancing or mediating position. His points bear repeating and at this stage show him trying to maintain a balance: "All this pulling to pieces does not give us the Book we have … The Old Testament lives and it is a unity." Then, "… the new critics are continually obliged to find 'interpolations' in the Bible in the shape of inconvenient passages; they say whenever a text militates against them, 'Oh, it is the work of a late editor and did not belong to the original form of the document'", and, again, "Above all, we have to face the relation of Christianity and of JESUS CHRIST to the Old Testament.… Whatever JESUS believed about the Old Testament, we must believe."[18] However, in the same issue, WRN began to publish the results of a survey in which he asked leading figures from amongst the Nonconformists to comment on the statement, 'Are Nonconformists departing from the Faith?' The overwhelming response from the correspondents was that the Churches were full of lively Evangelical faith. WRN then went on to show there was clear water between Spurgeon and himself.

> Mr. Spurgeon is aggrieved because we described his recent charges against Nonconformist ministers as "unduly pessimistic" and "vague" … for our part we could only speak on such evidence as was in our possession.… We do not close our eyes upon light. To fight against the light is simply suicide … and having said this may, we suggest that the term "modern thought" as a description of rationalism and infidelity be wholly dropped? … We believe in the fullest study and in the most careful reflection, and are confident that the result will be an ever-deepening attachment to the great verities that circle round the Christ.[19]

The survey in the *British Weekly* continued over several weeks. There seemed to be overwhelming evidence that there was no departure from the faith to be observed.

Spurgeon wrote four letters of protest in his *The Sword and the Trowel*. WRN found reporting these 'grist to the mill' for he was seeking to establish his 'new' paper; indeed, he quoted and commented on Spurgeon's published views throughout the whole period of the controversy. Though WRN realised from his survey the strength of the opposition to Spurgeon, and turned reporting on the increasingly controversial figure's ongoing argument into a convenient way of expanding his readership, his paper did not lead the charge against the older preacher. This was done by the *Christian World*, which published a 'liberal manifesto' on 1 September 1887.[20] When Spurgeon seemed to dismiss the evidence of *British Weekly's* survey, however, WRN felt he

Rev. Charles Haddon Spurgeon in the Metropolitan Tabernacle

needed to be more active in dissociating himself publicly from Spurgeon's position. In the *British Weekly* for 7 October, he quoted Spurgeon's latest articles under the front-page title 'The Case Proved', saying that *The Baptist* and The *British Weekly* had invited correspondence on the state of the churches. Of the results, he said, "there has been a considerable number, which may be roughly summarised as declaring that it would be best to let well alone, and that the writers see little or nothing of departure from the faith among Baptist and Congregational ministers. This is reassuring as far as it goes; but how far does it go?" WRN said that Spurgeon regarded those ministers as seeing the controversy in a completely unrealistic way and denying serious departures from the truth. WRN reflected on Spurgeon's attitude:

> As to doctrine, we have no dispute with Mr. Spurgeon. Nor
> do we dispute for one moment that there is a very large
> and threatening amount of unbelief in all the churches. To
> combat this is the main business of this journal. We are
> also at issue with Mr. Spurgeon as to the manner in which
> charges of heresy should be brought.[21]

That WRN had a greater tolerance of modern thought than Spurgeon
is certainly true. A greater difference, however, was his ability to hold
newer ideas in suspension, believing, as he did, that the truth would
win out in the end. Though inherently indecisive, this route meant that
WRN could take considerable notice as to where the majority of his
readers stood; carefully treading the route least likely to impinge on
his editorial success while continuing to trust that the correct end point
would eventually be reached. Considered from this angle, it is difficult
not to see a certain disingenuousness in his attitude to Spurgeon.
Opportunism was not, however, the only reason spurring WRN towards
more open confrontation. Spurgeon had been making protests against
the state of things since at least 1883,[22] and the terms in which he was
doing so were growing increasingly fervid: "The language in which
Spurgeon sought to convey his warning was unrestrained and devoid
of theological precision and argument; it reflected his sense of outrage
and determination to overcome the silence that had engulfed his earlier
protests".[23] Friendship aside, WRN was trying to run a successful
periodical, and as Spurgeon grew more adamant, siding with him would
have been to commit editorial suicide.

WRN noted that at a Baptist Union meeting, "not a voice was
lifted to echo his [Spurgeon's] sentiments… Mr. Hugh Price Hughes
[Methodist] in his powerful speech pointed out that Mr. Spurgeon
had not been supported by a single leader of religious thought in the
country".[24] Disappointed at the tide rising against him, and desperate to
draw attention to his position, Spurgeon became convinced that it was
time to take action and he seceded from the Baptist Union.[25] The *British
Weekly* reported the news:

> He states what in his opinion essential matters of faith
> are: (1) the vicarious sacrifice of Christ; (2) the plenary
> inspiration of the Scriptures; (3) the eternal punishment of
> the lost; and he finds himself unable to remain in a Union
> which contains men who reject any of these opinions.[26]

WRN then sought to rally the troops to stay loyal to the Baptist
Union:

> We think we understand Mr. Spurgeon this time, but we
> cannot follow his argument in the least. It appears to us
> a reductio ad absurdum of all organisations in creedless
> churches. Suppose the Baptist Union consisted of one
> thousand orthodox men. Suppose that into this body there
> came a heretic. According to its constitution, it could not
> expel him. But according to Mr. Spurgeon he could expel
> them … we say no, and we appeal to evangelical ministers,
> for the sake of the truth that is dearest to them, for the sake
> of the kingdom of Christ, for the sake of Nonconformity in
> this crisis of her fate, to stand by the Baptist Union.[27]

In blending a discrediting of Spurgeon's attempts to assert moral
authority with a calm support for the integrity of the Baptist Union and
the efforts of its ministers to hold the line against the splintering of the
denomination, WRN was acting strategically – and he prevailed. This
son of the 1843 Disruption Fathers, who had seceded from the Church
of Scotland, could not see Spurgeon with any Chalmers' mantle: "We
rejoice to see an all but universal agreement in our view of Mr. Spurgeon's
secession".[28] The controversy did not abate with the resignation of
Spurgeon; there were meetings of supporters and opposition and
WRN kept up a watchful comment in the columns of his paper. There
was much activity – deputations, meetings and articles tried to bring
Spurgeon to reconsider his decision. Nothing came from these attempts
and WRN announced the fact to his readers in his leading article on 27
January 1888: "We hardly know how to write of the severance between
Mr. Spurgeon and the Baptist Union. All efforts and hopes for peace
have been in vain. To minimise the significance of this event would be
folly. No one who knows the immense influence of Mr. Spurgeon will
fail to see in it a crisis for Nonconformity in England".[29] WRN had
come to turn his back on the old world order that Spurgeon typified, and
was concerned to lead his readers into the brave new modern world.

Now firmly established in the first rank of the forces gathering
against Spurgeon, WRN continued to produce leading articles in which
he sought to maintain the broad Evangelical common ground:

> A man is evangelical in the true sense that glories in the
> Cross. We fight against the tendency to belittle the great
> redemption. We believe that sin broke the order of the
> Divine thought, and that Redemption came in to repair
> it. We believe that this Redemption is through the death
> of Christ … these truths remain unaltered by the progress

of the years and the labours of the human intellect. They
cannot be shaken by any progress of knowledge, and do not
need fear it. The policy of obscurantism and denunciation
is doomed. Science must be studied; the Scriptures must
be studied; all light must be welcome; we must take heed
not to slander or crush any prophet of God.[30]

WRN supplemented these bombastic general articles with an aggressive
response to Spurgeon's decision to publish Gaussen's *Theopneustia*,[31]
and intimated in a preface that there "was enough argument in the book
to convince any open to conviction; over others he can only mourn
and pray".[32] WRN ridicules the book: "we have never been afraid of
being accursed from Christ because we were unconvinced by irrelevant
arguments and obsolete books".[33] As the weeks rolled by, he showed
little sign of relenting, returning to the attack in June with, 'The Apology
of the Narrow Minded' in which Spurgeon's stance and arguments are
likened in their usefulness to a modern general issuing 'quantities of
bows and arrows' to his troops. WRN ended with an assertion of his
convictions: "The moral we draw is this; traditional beliefs will be
modified without irritation and passion when it is made clear that the
new creed conserves the spiritual and moral forces of the old."[34] WRN
and Spurgeon were singing from very different hymn sheets.

W.B. Glover, in his evaluation of the Downgrade Controversy, wrote
that Spurgeon "seems to have expected that the majority of English
Baptists and perhaps of other denominations would rally around him
in opposition to pernicious influences ... but Spurgeon had underestimated rather than over-estimated how widespread the heretical taints
were. Even real evangelicals were theologically confused".[35] WRN's
contribution was to calm the sense of crisis – albeit in favour of the
modernisers – and to reduce the impact of Spurgeon's concerns. Such
efforts could never be a true resolution; they merely masked a serious
problem, which seemed to be growing steadily worse. However, also
WRN maintained his opposition to Spurgeon, even he allowing Joseph
Parker to write his infamous 'Open letter' which just coincided with
Spurgeon's conference in April 1890.

Viewing the relationship between WRN and Spurgeon solely
through the Downgrade Controversy is tempting, but doing so gives
an incomplete picture. Though WRN considered Spurgeon's views
reactionary and unhelpful in both theology and culture, he appreciated
the man and his achievements. After Spurgeon's death he wrote critically
and bluntly in 1892 to his friend Marcus Dods, "Your paragraph about

Spurgeon really vexed me ... I never knew a sign that his immense popularity turned his head. Rather the other way – it made him often very melancholy and depressed. As to his bigotry – yes, and I had my share of his abuse. But think how slowly the critical light has broken – think what most of us did and said in the days of our darker ignorance – think how incomprehensible it necessarily was to him.[36] Spurgeon's death seemed to make WRN more objective and appreciative, and he continued to correct his friend Dods: "I never knew any character that impressed itself so deeply on the whole English people – and he was regarded with a most unaffected respect and trust by men of all creeds and none. I believe him to have been as sincere and humble a Christian as has ever lived".[37]

WRN went even further when writing about Spurgeon's sermons in July 1917: "there are a great many things in these sermons which show that he was not all the narrow and illiterate bigot that many people think him. On the contrary, he had great breadth of mind. He made serious concessions to the new spirit, and was far better read and far more able and powerful intellectually than most people think."[38] Indeed, WRN had a genuine appreciation for Spurgeon, the man and his published sermons, but it seems for WRN, "There was certain monotony in his beautiful voice."[39] Despite all the equivocation and argument, however, there was at one point a serious suggestion that WRN should write a biography of Spurgeon, probably because he had written about his feelings of dissatisfaction with the biographies that had been published. However, WRN knew his limitations and although he admired Spurgeon's sermons, particularly his volume of sermons on the 'Song of Songs', he suggested that a good biography should be, "written by one who knew intimately his manner of living and his way of thinking. [However] most of his old students who have written about him failed entirely to do justice to the deeper and finer element in his mind and culture".[40]

Positive remembrances aside, one cannot escape the question of whether WRN exploited Spurgeon's position for the interests of the paper. A later biographer of Spurgeon, Dr. Carlyle, wrote that "Spurgeon's articles ... appeared at the time described in journalistic circles as the 'the silly season', when editors run short of interesting copy ... and numbers of irresponsible writers added fuel to the fire."[41] Was WRN seeking the acceptance of more modern views of the Bible by attacking a pillar of orthodoxy in Spurgeon? The truth of the matter is probably that none of the participants realised the full extent of the feelings that would be unleashed. Certainly, the battle over the Downgrade injured Spurgeon, and many, including Mrs Spurgeon, held that it brought about his early death in 1892. Though the fact of WRN's involvement is unavoidable, the true details of his role are difficult to draw out, leaving more questions than answers. He was protective of his new readership and carefully chose his own ground for viewing the controversy. Probably, there was a mixture of motives, including the fact that he saw this to be the 'stuff' of popular journalism, especially if it produced good 'copy'. WRN admired Spurgeon as a man and as a writer of great sermons, but Spurgeon also represented the 'older view' of Evangelicalism and Nonconformity that was suspicious about the modern world of scholarship and culture. In short, WRN appreciated and understood much about Spurgeon, yet thought, genuinely, that the future of Nonconformity lay in a more realistic engagement with the world of modern thought. This was the contemporary world, WRN had grown comfortable with it, and it was in this direction which he patiently and deliberately directed his readers.

When WRN was at college in Aberdeen, he formed many valuable friendships, including one with **Alexander Whyte**.[42] In 1872, when WRN was the president of the Students' Missionary Association, he invited Whyte to preach. Later WRN remembered an address by Whyte in the General Assembly of 1875 as "the finest piece of pure, true, genuine eloquence I have ever heard; the effect produced was electric and eternal".[43] Whyte came to play a key role for WRN and his journals, and in turn, Whyte's reputation was boosted by his exposure in the *British Weekly*. In August 1887, Whyte began his contributions, an arrangement which lasted for over twenty years. Mainly Whyte submitted as articles his evening sermons in Free St. George's Edinburgh.[44] WRN valued Whyte's ability and was perfectly happy to serialise his contributions over the years, as they fell in with his own wide-ranging tastes and reading. In writing for the *British Weekly*, Whyte was able to show a tremendous width and catholicity of interest: not only consecutive Bible characters, but also 'The Mystics' and 'Great Autobiographies',[45] subjects which always intrigued WRN.

Whyte's biography contains surviving letters and there was a pronounced display of his indebtedness to WRN: "I shall never be able to tell you what I owe you for taking me up into your unparalleled pulpit. Your influence is immense, and you have given me some share of it. God bless you and yours".[46] Although by the time of Whyte's death, WRN himself was feeling his frailty, he nevertheless led the appreciations of Whyte in a memorial issue of *British Weekly*. "On thinking over our long association, it becomes clear to me that his main characteristic was his intense humility. He might seem austere, and he was austere at times. The burden of the world lay more heavily upon him than it lies on most, and before men, he could at times denounce sin with terrible emphasis ... [yet] if he thought he had been carried away in some access of passion he humbled himself to the dust before the man whom he thought he had wronged. Evangelical humility is the note of all he preached and wrote".[47]

Whyte was an essential part of the reason why the *British Weekly* became popular, his articles embodying their author's extraordinary breadth of literary and spiritual enthusiasms,[48] which were shared by the editor. Whyte was expressing those areas and interests that WRN enjoyed personally and displaying in his papers.

WRN's friendship with **Marcus Dods**[49] was not quite as old as that with Whyte, which began around 1886, the time of Nicoll's enforced retirement from ministry. He felt in need of encouragement, and Dods was able to bolster WRN's confidence. As their friendship, which lasted until Dods' death in 1909, developed, they helped and supported each other, WRN never forgot Dods' counsel at such a critical stage in his career, and so it is quite unsurprising that when he found that Dods had a wide range of practical interests and a facility with the pen, they were quickly put into service. Dods was a Free Church preacher, perhaps epitomising the 'educated scholarly minister', being cultured, knowledgeable, and possessing considerable erudition in many kinds of literature. These very strengths, however, also mean he can be seen as a tragic example of a type of sophistication that led to a decline of the faith amongst many of the educated leaders on both sides of the border. That WRN used Dods so extensively in both his main journals would seem to argue that an influence in the direction of this new sophistication was encouraged in some of his readers.[50]

Dods was the son of a stalwart of the Evangelical movement, who began his ministerial career as a staunchly orthodox Evangelical,[51] but increasingly modified his views in the light of the higher critical theories. Dods supported Robertson Smith, acquired the Chair of New Testament Exegesis at New College, and defended himself successfully against heresy charges in the 1890 General Assembly. He provoked such attacks by making aggressive liberalising statements, a modern writer tends to feel that Dods was misunderstood, "The case against Dods seems to have rested on his large-hearted tolerance for the positive things said by those with whom he actually disagreed".[52] Be that as it may, Dods' exposure in WRN's papers and his support from the editor helped the

cause of 'believing criticism' considerably – his motivation, as WRN's
own, was to help the Church readjust to very changed circumstances.
Indeed, such was the progression of life in the liberalising movement
that Dods' radical views came before long to be regarded as rather
conservative! When Dods accepted the role of higher criticism in the
study of the Scriptures, some felt that he saw "the real enemy of the faith
as being the traditional, non-critical view of Scripture".[53] Certainly, this
gave Dods a 'suspect' reputation amongst the conservative section of the
Free Church, particularly as represented by the Highlanders. WRN was
aware of the feelings in the far North, but he identified with his friend,
and stood by him through triumphs and trials. WRN bought into the fact
that, his friend's defence of criticism was a classic enunciation of the
position of the believing critics and openly displayed how large the gulf
was between liberals and conservatives. They not only disagreed on the
methods of criticism, but on the purpose of criticism and the validity of
the critical approach. "As Dods commented at the time of his 'trial' by
the Free General Assembly in 1890, wearily if not bitterly, 'no theory
of Scripture promulgated at present by me would be at all likely to find
acceptance'."[54] Dods viewed the attempts to deny Scriptural errors as
'disingenuous' and 'thoughtless', arguing that it really just produced
new questions in the place of the original ones. Although Dods was often
depicted as an ecclesiastical savage by his opponents,[55] he understood
their position, despite considering it wrong.[56] WRN not only supported
his friend, but encouraged him to express his views in his periodicals.

The question of whether Dods had motives beyond merely helping
his friend is difficult, the answer to which is greatly complicated by
their similar objectives. He addressed the question of biblical inspiration
head-on, and worked to bring his views into general acceptance in the
Free Church of Scotland. WRN trusted Dods and gave him an eminent
place in his papers, asking him to write several commentaries in the
Expositor's Series, including 'Genesis'. "As editor of the liberal *British
Weekly*, Robertson Nicoll was never going to be a favourite of the
conservatives in the Church, and this [Dods on 'Genesis'] was merely
another example of what they saw as the liberals working in concert
to foist their pernicious convictions upon the Church at large".[57] Later,
Dods was able to give his own assessment in a letter to WRN "On
looking back over the last twenty-five years I see how very much I
am indebted to you for giving me the opportunities and encouragement
without which I should have addressed a very much smaller audience."[58]
Dods was a methodical and dependable writer, who shared WRN's own
believing criticism for the theological progress needed in the Church.

Though his skills as writer and promulgator of the new thinking were much trumpeted, of no less importance to Dods was his role as teacher. In his study on Dods, Sterling Edwards commented that he heartily disliked participation in church courts, yet for a considerable period of his adult life he was involved in ecclesiastical controversy. "He always showed shyness and reserve towards men of his own generation, but young men claimed him as their own because of his ability to speak to them openly as friend and comrade.... He was one who had a natural affinity for teaching, a deep delight in young men, and a growing interest in the subjects he taught".[59] WRN caught this aspect of Dods in a series he commissioned for the *British Weekly*, 'Teachers of Young Men':

> "Dr. Dods fully understands the importance of personal intercourse between professors and students. He cultivates the acquaintance of his classes, and invites them to his house. It is a proud moment for a young student when he first sets foot in the Great King-Street library, or walks up the Mound with the professor, or sits beside him at the common table. A new life seemed to breathe through the College from the day that Dr. Dods was appointed".[60]

This focus upon Dods' skill in relating to his charges as people is not mere flattery – for all his championing of believing criticism as the way forward for his students, he knew that they would have tough times ahead of them in ministry. In an address delivered at New College, not long before his death, he seemed to be rather pessimistic – or perhaps realistic.

> "It is in a time of transition such as this, when every old belief is called in question and when the traditional moorings are sunk, that men feel their need of guidance and the expert finds his opportunity.... Now it is useless to protest against new ways, and to suppose that having done so our whole duty is discharged and our hands are clean. These new ways have come to stay; they are, if not an essential part of the progress we are making, at any rate so associated with it as to make it impossible for us to object to them in the mass. Our business is, so far as conscience permits, to adjust ourselves and our methods of promoting Christ's kingdom to the new conditions".[61]

This pragmatic attitude has been caught in the *Later Letters of Marcus Dods*, which WRN commended to his readers. He was able to share with

Dods his literary ambitions, as part of the necessary progress and cultural width the Church needed for moving into the future with confidence. Dods was an example of one who found that literary sophistication and cultural deference to 'the modern mind' could undermine an individual's spiritual faith and confidence. In 1902, Dods wrote to a friend, "The churches won't know themselves fifty years hence. It is to be hoped some little rag of faith may be left when all's done".[62] Even in 1898 he had written, "I am a backslider. I used to enjoy prayer, but for years, I have found myself dumb. Of course, one can always make a prayer, as I do every morning for my class, but prayer in the sense of asking for things has not been in my case a proved force. The things I have chiefly prayed for all my life I have not got".[63] In 1906, he wrote to WRN,

> Our ecclesiastical affairs here are in a disgusting mess –
> no one satisfied with anything. What is to come of it all I
> know not? Happily, I enjoy my own work, and have good
> times with the students. I fear some of my moroseness and
> pessimism is due to age. I hope so, and that this generation
> is better and not worse than the last; but I do not envy those
> who have to fight the battle of Christianity in the twentieth
> century. Yes, perhaps I do, but it will be a stiff fight, and
> will require great concessions to be made.[64]

Dods seemed to think that concessions to the 'mindset of the modern reader' would give the Church firmer ground. If so, it was a sad illusion.

Dods' support and style continued to be a regular feature of both the *Expositor* and the *British Weekly* up to his death in 1909. Then WRN wrote, "It is impossible for me to write anything like an estimate of Dr. Dods. He was the best friend and the most Christ-like man I have ever known. He was in his daily work and conversation a living evidence for Christianity. There were many who have never lost their joyful confidence in Christ, and they owe this to him as much as to any".[65] This contrasts and is at variance with Dods' own feelings reflected in his letters and yet even in an emotional and overblown obituary written just after Dods' death, WRN insightfully reflected, "He was a scholar as distinct from a bookman. He was willing to read almost anything, but he carefully sifted his library, and he studied the enduring books. In this way, his mind was nobly built up. On the strange fortunes and destinies of the Christian church he looked with interest and hope".[66] It seems that Dods, in spite of his concern to help the church change, became a victim of his acquired scholarship and his well-meaning sophistication about the place and value of the Scriptures to undermine his spiritual confidence.

Marcus Dods

His influence via both the *Expositor* and the *British Weekly*, let alone upon WRN himself, meant that he unwittingly furthered a main strand of decline in the form of the Church's veneration and dependence on its own Scriptures, particularly in the estimate of those of the younger generation who turned their backs on the Church. Though all he did was in the name of progress and seeking to find firm ground for the future of the Christian faith, he was ironically a major figure in the erosion of confidence in the Scriptures, a part of that broader process known as 'liberalisation' which in some cases, led to extreme infidelity.[67] WRN would have been appalled at such a statement, but then he shared Dods' aspirations, cherished his friendship, and embraced aspirations beyond those presented by his theological beliefs – the worlds of culture and politics.

Another Scot, **Professor Henry Drummond**,[68] was a phenomenon. WRN described him: "No one we have ever listened to impressed us quite in the same way. His words were the effortless utterance of a man with a message ... perhaps his main characteristic both as speaker and writer was his brilliant and untiring freshness. You might agree with him, or you might not, but you could not choose but hear and remember".[69] WRN was not a close friend to Drummond, but he was important and WRN used him to good effect in initiating his own editorial reign with both the *Expositor* and the *British Weekly*.[70] In 1882, Hodder & Stoughton had published *Natural Law in the Spiritual World*, and within five years of publication it had sold a sensational 70,000 copies. Drummond was at the height of his popularity and WRN made use of his name in his journals, in spite of his finding Drummond one of the few that he was antipathetic towards.

Drummond was an enigmatic figure who sought to reconcile his Christian faith with the theory of evolution. He was also a supporter of, and worker on, D.L. Moody's campaigns in Scotland. WRN used him extensively, though, according to D.W. Bebbington, Drummond, "composed no systematic exposition of the Scriptures[71] and accepted biblical criticism without reserve.... It seems that Drummond, though living through the critical reappraisal of the Scriptures ... emerged with a renewed zest for the Bible ... he had come to believe in progressive revelation, an understanding which, he held, made the Bible as impregnable as nature".[72] Needless to say, many of the conservative orthodox mistrusted Drummond, but he proved to be an effective evangelist. WRN even defended[73] Drummond from the censure of his Kelso predecessor, Horatius Bonar, who had denounced Drummond "as an atheist, pantheist and we know not what, and had called his teaching 'poison'".[74] WRN strongly resented this use of 'poison' for Drummond's teaching, by noting the acceptance made of Drummond by D.L. Moody. Professional and theological sympathies aside, truthfully WRN was not really a fan of Drummond. However, WRN always noted that Drummond was an effective evangelist and his books and papers sold well, as people wanted to read him.

WRN was not the only one with a use for the controversial but effective Drummond – Moody employed him to counsel the young men[75] who responded at his evangelistic meetings. He had a great power and influence over individuals. Drummond kept up "a constant confessional ... [and] the success of his work was obviously dependent upon his presence, ministers and leading laymen ... look[ed] to him as their chief, the sense (right or wrong) that the Christianity of the next

Henry Drummond

generation in these places might largely be determined by the work he had charge of".[76] David Fountain, in his biography of E.J. Poole-Connor, regarded Drummond's influence upon the next generation as pushing them towards a full acceptance of higher-critical views of the Scriptures, and thereby weakening their grip on Evangelical Christianity.[77] Others thought Drummond had something to say to the Evangelical Church as it sought to handle the challenge from Darwinism, and the (perceived) hostile world of science. "Drummond was known as a practitioner of science who enjoyed the confidence of the competent authorities. Although in most disciplines except geology he was no more than a 'gentleman amateur', he could be said to possess a certain reputation in scientific matters".[78] So many Evangelicals saw Drummond as one they could trust confidently on scientific matters.

Given these quite controversial credentials, WRN took a calculated risk in using Drummond's writing to the extent that he did, but he viewed the direction of the Church as becoming progressively liberal, and therefore needing to move away from the conservatism represented by the Highland Free Churches in Scotland and Spurgeon amongst the English Nonconformists. Drummond was neither frightened to advance his own beliefs, nor so frenzied in his protest as to turn his tongue and pen upon unnecessary targets – as WRN wrote, "Criticism did not in the least trouble him. He was not affected by any dogma on inspiration. Large parts of the Bible he was content to leave alone."[79] Taken in that light, not employing Drummond's influence to further his goals or popularity and circulation figures would have been to forego an eminently useful tool.

Amongst the preachers of London, WRN was a well-known figure. Only a small number of them, however, would claim to have been a friend of his. **Joseph Parker** was one of them. He was prized by WRN, whose character, style of preaching and personality fascinated him. Parker remained fundamentally a conservative in his theology, but in light of the growing furore of the day, he proved quite open to the progressive ideas that were coming into the church. He did not accept the new views of Scripture, but he supported the need for continued scholastic studies and research. Parker was a leading London Congregational preacher and 'reigned' at his church, the City Temple on London's Holborn Viaduct.[80] He became a master of dramatic, dynamic preaching and ejaculated unexpected statements, which was admired by many as a fresh and vigorous style of ministry. His career saw him begin as a radical and republican, then as he came more into contact with rich and influential people he developed into a defender of the social and economic establishment. "He seems to have been intent on creating a united Nonconformist Church that would eventually embrace all denominations and be able to compete for social and religious pre-eminence with the Church of England. In his development, he embodies the ambition to transform dissent into a powerful movement that would be socially respectable, morally influential, spiritually prophetic, and politically powerful. It was to be an unfulfilled hope".[81] Parker admired WRN and valued 'his genius and his friendship'.[82] The relationship was, however, hardly one-sided: WRN used Parker as a writer, and reported regularly on Parker's conferences, visits and tours,[83] effectively speeding the preacher's growing status as a celebrity. Darlow summed up their mutual respect: "For Dr Parker, in spite of his idiosyncrasies, Nicoll felt unbounded admiration as a unique pulpit genius. The two men became drawn into common friendship, which grew more intimate when the great preacher had to mourn over his wife's death."[84]

Parker was a complex figure, simultaneously conservative and open, innovative and appreciative of tradition and as a personality appearing in public as an egoistic 'drama queen', but in himself rather shy and sensitive. WRN came to understand Parker better following the death of his wife in 1899, remaining close to the man until his death. This closeness meant WRN was able to reveal something about the private and unknown side of Parker. He saw that although Parker was friendly, he did not have many close friends. WRN regarded Parker as essentially a loner who enjoyed the close support of his wife and her relatives.[85] This public sense of Parker as a private man uninterested in society seemed contrary to whatever many people thought of him as an extroverted and sensationalistic preacher. Parker was, according to WRN, extremely sensitive,

> "He greatly lacked self-confidence, and lived in a constant need of encouragement. The occasional brusqueness and egotism of his manner was in reality a mask for shyness … he was often taken for an enormous egoist, and in a sense that was true ... no one was more vulnerable to unkindness, no one was more easily shaken by a breath of adverse criticism".[86]

That he was able to penetrate the façade of a man so formidable in public, yet so self-consciously fragile in private life is a testament to WRN's unique skill and sensitivity in appreciating the inner lives of his complex acquaintances.

Private difficulties aside, Parker was a significant force in the church during his day. WRN assessed him as a leading figure amongst the Nonconformists:

"Dr. Parker, through his entire career, was firmly and
consistently evangelical and Nonconformist ... With works
of systematic theology he had little acquaintance, but he
was mighty in the Scriptures, and never was the Bible read
more earnestly and believingly than by him. By his own
study and thought he had worked out independently all the
main conclusions of evangelicalism, and he never moved
away from them. In the same way, he was a convinced and
consistent Nonconformist ... On the great questions that
have divided Liberalism in the last twenty years he wavered,
changed his views from time to time, and latterly he shrunk
wisely from committing himself. He would take up a cause
and grow weary of it, and turn to something else. On all but
the great subjects his mind was restless, and he would seek
for premature and impossible reconciliations".[87]

In perceiving this blend of forcefulness and indecisive wavering, WRN
managed to capture Parker's deeper patterns of motivation, which were
hidden to most people. That Parker never emerged as a true figurehead
of any particular Nonconformist faction was likely a mystery to many,
but if one turns to this brief summary, the sheer impossibility of his
doing so emerges in clear tones.

It was as preacher that Parker truly made his mark, and in that role, he
cast a tremendous shadow.[88] He was a giant of the pulpit in an age of great
and formidable 'pulpiteers', one of a small group whose public displays
of skill drew broad crowds. In Parker's case, however, artistry trumped
content – people came to experience the phenomenon of his ministry, and
could thereby grow to think of their religion as an experience primarily
received rather than performed, consequently failing to mature and
progress in the Christian life for themselves. Parker's rival 'over the river',
Spurgeon, was just as mighty in the pulpit, but Spurgeon was concerned
that Christians worked out their faith in displaying it in the world at large.
Spurgeon encouraged every kind of work that displayed the reality of the
faith and thrust his people out in building churches, preaching, teaching,
colportage work, missions and orphanages. Ironically, Parker's world
was much narrower than Spurgeon's, though Parker would never have
believed it and was to write his infamous 'Open Letter' telling Spurgeon
to widen his view! WRN admired both men, and though his relationship
and personal preference put him closer to Parker, he knew that Spurgeon's
contribution to Christianity in the nineteenth century would outlast that
of Parker's.

Dr and Mrs Parker

Dr John Clifford,[89] an outstanding Baptist preacher who exercised a popular ministry in West London, was a liberal Evangelical who believed, "Our first business is to make men see Christ".[90] WRN saw Clifford as a good model for contemporary Nonconformity. He selected Clifford's Church as the second example in his series 'Prosperous Churches': "Dr. Clifford's teaching [is] sound to its very core, and full of blessing to those who listen to it. Powerful sermons of the dogmatic order may cause a desire on the part of the hearer to go home and think over them; the usual effect of a Westbourne Park sermon is to create the purpose of putting its substance into practice."[91] As well as displaying a theological position held up as ideal by WRN and his allies, Clifford was widely thought a moral and personal model. He has been described as a fighter, and a fighter against no imaginary foes. "It would be to misread history to belittle the results of his life-long battle for liberty and justice as embodied in a hundred gallant causes. There were times when he was feared and even hated by his adversaries ... Clifford was a fighter for sixty years – and he was the one man on earth, one sometimes imagined, who had never cherished a thought of real enmity against a single fellow creature."[92]

In the period during which WRN knew Clifford, the heft of this renowned fighting spirit was aimed towards bringing the church – and British society along with it – into the modern world. Clifford was committed to the church getting involved in practical out working of the gospel in better wages, better schooling. Yet he was a pacifist, in favour of the women's suffragist movement and a supporter of the League of Nations. "His axioms of faith were Religious freedom and equality".[93]

All this chimed with WRN; 'Dr. Clifford' soon found himself highlighted in the *British Weekly's* 'Our Young Men's Page', particular attention being drawn to his ministry success with the young.[94] This professional respect and readiness to make use of one another's skills should not be mistaken for any particular personal closeness – the two were comrades-in-arms more than friends, and as with any such situation, were equally prepared to oppose one another if it appeared necessary.

The beginning of their lengthy, if intermittent, relationship is to be found in the midst of the Downgrade Controversy, with WRN taking the point of view of Clifford and the Baptist Union against Spurgeon. He carried a full report of Clifford's address to the Baptist assembly, which was able to avoid a mass secession.[95] This success led to a period of co-operation on a *British Weekly* debate on 'Are there Errors in the Bible?' and 'Inerrancy'. WRN allowed Clifford, who had just written *The Inspiration and Authority of the Bible*, not only to put his case for a guarded Evangelical openness to reverent [believing] criticism but also to sum up at the end of the debate. Clifford states quite clearly, "Certain I am that we gravely imperil the welfare of men by advancing and upholding the unnecessary and unsustained theory of the 'absolute inerrancy' or verbal inspiration of the Bible."[96] Clifford was only an irregular contributor for WRN, and usually when there was some particular issue.

Common causes continued to appear: they were shoulder to shoulder in their opposition to the Education Bill of 1902 and were

Dr John Clifford

together in calling for Passive Resistance, though Clifford sustained his commitment, even after the First World War, WRN saw the Electoral success of 1906 as a fitting end for the Passive Resistance strategy. They were also together in their support for Lloyd George and the Liberals, though Clifford joined and wrote tracts for the Fabians. Their respective lifetimes of service were recognised, as both received the award of

Companion of Honour in 1921 and subsequently both died in 1923.

The most significant points of contention to be found in their relationship revolved around the topic of war. Speaking generally, WRN was careful to maintain the Liberal Party's line on such issues, while Clifford was more staunchly pacifist, though willing to concede the necessity of arms in times of extreme duress. The South African War, for example, saw Clifford strongly opposed, while WRN held to the main Liberal imperialist position and reluctantly supported the War. They both stood by the call to arms in 1914, but Clifford was opposed to conscription and supported the conscientious objectors. This was something that WRN was completely at variance with, for in his judgment it undermined the needed unity of the War effort. They shared much in common, so that it is strange that Sir James Marchant's biography of Clifford made no mention of WRN. One reason could well have been WRN's quickness in dropping 'Passive Resistance' in 1906 before anything had been achieved – a sign of the undeniable significance of their differences, however broad their similarity.[97] Those differences must be borne in mind; the men were two very different warriors, but despite those differences, they found themselves united by many common causes and a similar basic attitude towards the future of the Nonconformist church. Clifford paid a warm tribute to his colleague in 1923: "Sir William was a powerful and penetrating journalist, whose influence upon the Free Churches of Britain and through them on the world it is impossible to exaggerate".[98]

WRN had been very dependent on the skills and labours of Marcus Dods, and as Dods declined, another Scottish connection met his need for both a personal confidant and a source of authoritative input for his various journals. WRN developed a very warm working relationship with **James Denney**.[99] Denney first showed his incisive mind and literary abilities when he exposed the fallacious analogies used by Henry Drummond in his best-selling book: "*Natural Law in the Spiritual World* is a book that no lover of men will call religious and no student of theology scientific".[100] WRN saw Denney's great potential and encouraged him to write, firstly for the *Expositor*, then commentaries,[101] and finally in articles for the *British Weekly*.[102] After Denney's death, WRN reflected,

> "I certainly have a certain mournful pride in thinking that I
> did something to induce him to come forward as an author.
> At that time his mind was fully made up, his future was

> foreseen, he was to preach the Cross of Christ – on the one
> hand its power to save, and on the other its sharpness and
> self-denial. From this preaching of the Cross, he was never
> moved, but as time went on, he became more and more master
> of a style, which did justice to the great thoughts".[103]

Like Dods, Denney had a wide cultural knowledge, and could write a
variety of useful articles and reviews, as well as theological studies.
In the autumn of 1906, WRN even proposed that Denney write more
regularly and help him with the demands of writing the leading article.
Denney modestly replied, "I have thought over your proposal about the
BW, and concluded to give it a trial. To be quite candid, I have no such
fertility of mind as can be depended on to produce interesting matter
regularly. I don't need to tell you that; but between books and other
things I dare say I might relieve you once a month and it is a pleasure to
me to think that you have been willing to ask me".[104] The arrangement
lasted for the rest of Denney's life, but their correspondence became an
even more vital part of their lives following the death of Denney's wife
in January 1908 and WRN's loss of Dods the following year, leaving
the two sharing a need for encouragement and stimulus. Denney held
the same progressive Evangelical viewpoint as WRN, and their letters
sparkled with their similar concerns. Denney wrote sympathetically after
WRN had published his worries about New Testament scholarship:

> "I ought to have acknowledged at once the *Church's
> One Foundation*: it is very good of you to send me the
> book…What troubles me is not how to blow the trumpet,
> or sound an alarm, but how to teach in detail, and persuade
> people who are alarmed not to close their minds in
> impatience, but to face the kind of questions criticism
> raises, and to meet them with the composure of intelligence,
> as well as the assurance of faith".[105]

WRN always wanted good copy for his journals, but he was also wary
of any radical view that might appear to be eroding basic pillars of the
Christian faith. WRN's sensitivity was combined with an awareness of
what his average Evangelical readers would tolerate. An example of
WRN's help and advice is seen in the publication of some lectures that
Denney delivered to the Chicago Theological Seminary in April 1894.[106]
In particular, Denney ploughed his own furrow on the question of Biblical
inspiration, and from the correspondence with WRN, it can be seen that
Denney was given help in preparing the final publication. Denney believed
that formulas and doctrinal statements that sought to demonstrate Biblical

inspiration were neither right nor helpful. For Denney the Bible was a limited, if not closed, book to all except believers. For they alone felt and therefore accepted the truth or reality of the Scriptures as God's Word. "It is as we use Scripture, without any presuppositions whatever that we find it has power to lodge in our minds.... This, I am confident, is the only rational and experimental way of reading and stating the truth".[107] Denney was convinced that the experience of inspiration was sufficient to be able to guide people to the reality of the value of the Scriptures. J.R. Taylor, in his study of Denney's theology,[108] wrote, "There are those who feel that this is an insecure approach to the matter and that what is required is a doctrinal statement concerning inspiration, which will serve as the foundation upon which Christian faith can be built. This approach would first seek to prove the inspiration of the Scripture and on basis of that would construct Christian doctrine, this was popular under the patterns of the older orthodoxy and some men still seek to cleave to the appearance of security that it seems to offer. Denney's feeling is that such an approach is exactly opposite to what we know in our Christian experience."[109] Taylor cites Denney's statement "We do not use the Bible because of an antecedent conviction that it is inspired; we are convinced it is inspired because it so asserts its authority over us, as we read, that we cannot but use it in that way".[110]

WRN was wary and concerned about his friend's presentation: "You cannot but see that you have a very special responsibility, partly arising from your official position, and partly from your personal qualities. I have thought recently that you were more inclined to give way to the current of criticism than formerly".[111] He wrote to Denney about 'the Bible chapter' on 7 August 1894: "So far as it goes, I agree with it – but I think its tone is hesitating as compared with the other lectures, and it is not clear like them. Writing from memory I cannot put criticism properly, but will venture a few rough suggestions".[112] The original form of the 'Chicago' lectures was unknown,[113] but it can be seen that Denney took note of his friend's counsel by including some of the points raised; so Denney commented in his preface, "They [the lectures] are printed as they were delivered, with one exception. The ninth lecture ... has been rewritten; not with the view of retracting or qualifying anything, but in order, as far as possible, to obviate misconception, and secure a readier acceptance for what the writer thinks true ideas on the authority of Scripture".[114] Certainly, Denney included an extended consideration of the attitude of 'Christ and the Old Testament', emphasised the Canon, the witness of the Holy Spirit and confidence, "on the surest of all foundations on this revelation of

James Denney

God".[115] Taylor reflected, "Denney is thought of today, more or less, as a conservative exegete and interpreter. It is not a reputation which fits him altogether, nor is it one which would have altogether pleased him. In his lifetime he was regarded by many as being too liberal, particularly in his handling of Scripture ... Robertson Nicoll, who was far ahead of the body of the Church on this matter, was nevertheless fearful of his friend's advanced positions".[116]

Much of the correspondence of their friendship can be found in *Letters of Principal James Denney to W. Robertson Nicoll (1893-*

1917)[117] and in Darlow's biography. Both men spoke their minds confidently and, at times, with the considerable forcefulness that a sound and respectful friendship allows.

Denney was the evangelist theologian who sought clarity of thought that was unambiguous and true to the Scriptures. He wrote to WRN stating his view of the Church as the instrument of God's purpose in reaching out and proclaiming the Gospel of the love of God in the Atoning work of the Cross of Christ,[118] which WRN would have affirmed. Given this closeness of thought, it is unsurprising that the two men's professional relationship proved as fruitful as their personal one: Denney made good his promised support with substantial contributions to the *British Weekly* and the *Expositor*, some of his articles being republished in book form. Taken as a whole, his work for WRN demonstrates an impressive range of interests.[119] WRN gloried in the success his friend's work received and in his own contribution towards making Denney better known.

WRN so valued Denney's friendship and usefulness and at the time of Denney's death in 1917, wrote this of him:

> "There is no doubt that he sacrificed himself. The zeal of God's house had eaten him up. Not content with his work as student, professor, and author, he undertook the charge of the Central Fund of his Church, moved by a deep sympathy with the needs of his brethren, and to that noble cause he gave himself continually … he preached incessantly, generally twice every Sunday.... He slipped almost insensibly into a large share of ecclesiastical work. His pen was always ready. He gave us in the *British Weekly* such help as no other man could, and over a period of many years, I never remember him refusing any request. Thus, he was continually spending himself, and all of us seemed to take it for granted that he was capable of any labour. Also he thought so himself. But alas! We were all wrong."[120]

George Adam Smith[121] was another young Scottish prospect befriended by WRN. Smith shared WRN's 'believing critical' view of the Old Testament Scriptures,[122] and Smith wrote many articles for Nicoll's journals, particularly the *Expositor*. Smith was a dynamic preacher and it seems likely that WRN heard some of his series on 'Isaiah' during his ministry at Queen's Cross Church in Aberdeen. Whether he heard it or not, word of Smith's mastery of the topic clearly reached him, for he gave Smith the task of writing a commentary on 'Isaiah' in the *Expositor's Bible* series.

George Adam Smith

His two volumes became the bestsellers of the whole series, and Smith later added two volumes on 'Minor Prophets'.[123] Certainly, the novelty of Smith's critical views drew readers. He was a preacher and his passion and concern for contemporary application proved popular with many of them. Smith enjoyed his commissions from WRN. He produced very readable work, but later Iain Campbell critiqued, "At the same time... Smith's work is noticeably characterised by a paucity of critical engagement with other scholars. That may be a sign that he is truly a pioneer; it may also, however, reflect a desire to be less critical of contemporary scholarship in the interests of a more devotional approach".[124] Certainly, Smith saw himself as a moderniser, in many ways taking over the mantle of his namesake [W.R. Smith], and he sought to use his ability to interpret the pages of the Old Testament for the contemporary scene by using the new critical approaches to the Scriptures.

Smith gave the Yale Lectures on Preaching in 1899 and he chose for his subject *Modern Criticism and the Preaching of the Old Testament*, which was subsequently published in 1901. WRN reviewed it in the *British Weekly*: "We take leave of one of the best contributions to Christian literature that has been published for many years, a book full of truth, tenderness, reverence and wisdom".[125] Praise Smith though he might, however, WRN was certainly not above crossing swords with him – he took issue with Smith's slight use of archaeology and impatience with the allegorical method of interpretation, though he did appreciate his treatment of vicarious suffering and the question of immortality. Regardless of its reception elsewhere, however, the book did get Smith into serious trouble in the General Assembly of the United Free Church of 1902, where an attempt was made to indict Smith on an ecclesiastical charge.

For Smith the evolution of Israel's history led upwards from primitive barbarity, through the ethical prophets, and culminated in the work of Christ. It was his acceptance that critical ground was proven that so alarmed many. As Carnegie Simpson reflected, "He himself described these views as 'revolutionary in respect of methods of interpreting Scripture hitherto accepted among us'… [yet] with all this, the Christian and even evangelical motive of all Dr. Smith's book was unmistakable".[126] WRN also saw the contemporary situation in theological scholarship as the progress from old orthodoxy to the new dynamics of believing criticism. He would have agreed with a later evaluation of Smith's work:

> "Development, for Smith, was apparently a kind of law to which all phenomena, including the origins of Scripture and the story of revelation, must conform. At least, it was a principle, which to Smith made sense of these particular phenomena. But ... the point is that Scripture is seen in the light of this principle rather than itself enunciating the principle, although to be sure, Smith was convinced that the Scriptures gave clear evidence of it".[127]

Assessing Smith, and therefore WRN's support for him, raises difficulties; firstly Smith did not establish his case well enough, and certainly, he never treated views as theologically as he might. Like WRN, he thought he could hold the transitional use of criticism in reconstructing the Old Testament, but failed to anticipate or allow for the same tools being used on the life and the message of Christ himself. Secondly, Smith did not "discuss the allied problems of the relationship of faith to knowledge, that is, how one gets from (criticised) Scripture to the God of Scripture".[128] Smith and Nicoll tried to balance faith and criticism, but to others it appeared as little more than "a kind of gymnastic feat, an intellectual prank, possible to men of trained intellect, perhaps, but impossible to children and the poor, to whom the gospel is preached.... Who do not comprehend the fine distinctions by which acute or philosophic minds can reconcile a sceptical and severe criticism of the Word of God with a simple faith in underlying truths"?[129] In short, Smith, in spite of his good intentions and considerable skills as a preacher, did not contribute to a halting of the overall drift from the Faith; rather, through his inclination for intellectual competitiveness over popularly intelligible discussion he embodied one of the reasons that furthered a general process of decline.

WRN had high expectations for **Reginald J. Campbell,**[130] although he was always a preacher rather than a scholar. At the suggestion of his friend Darlow, WRN first went to hear Campbell at the Union Street Chapel, Brighton in 1897. He was impressed, and wrote,

> He is apparently young, not more than thirty, and his striking head is abundantly covered by hair already turning grey. His eyes are peculiarly sympathetic, and his voice clear and sweet. Mr. Campbell does not use a note, he gesticulates freely, and his voice is a very pleasant one to listen to, with sufficient rise and fall … thus he held the attention of perhaps 800 people for a whole hour … I had no thought of criticising, and my heart was full of joy as I returned homewards.[131]

Was this the new Spurgeon? Campbell preached well and without notes, a style which always impressed WRN. His readers were soon informed all about the rising young star as he began a process of promoting his new find, and, in passing, gave some of his comments about preachers and preaching: "admirable as the Sunday morning sermon was, I am sure Mr Campbell would have done better to preach at about half the length and with half the material".[132] It appeared as though WRN was

putting Campbell forward as the new voice of Nonconformity, an
embodiment of the modern view on matters of faith. This voice was,
however, so intoxicating in its fresh modernity that WRN and others
failed to listen carefully enough to the actual content of Campbell's
sermons. With time, significant differences between the two men began
to emerge, and, though WRN showed distinct loyalty and supported the
younger man far longer than one would expect given their theological
dissimilarities, an eventual break was inevitable.

Following Joseph Parker's death, the City Temple gave an enthusiastic call for Campbell to succeed him. WRN shared this enthusiasm and
spoke at Campbell's recognition service in May 1903; he saw Campbell
as having the same potential for usefulness as Professor Elmslie. He
even gave Campbell his own column in the *British Weekly*, and it
was hoped that Campbell would pioneer a new progressive dynamic
pattern for the next generation of Nonconformists. The young preacher
and now columnist would indeed try, but before long WRN found that
Campbell could go too far. Anthony Deane, a local Hampstead vicar,
was prevailed upon by WRN to get to know and encourage Campbell in
his early days at the City Temple. Deane wrote,

> At this time, though still quite young, he was in the front
> rank of celebrities. Twice a week he filled the City Temple
> with huge congregations. He was invited everywhere, his
> 'fan mail' was enormous ... In part, Robertson Nicoll and
> his *British Weekly* had built up his reputation assiduously;
> they were unmatched at this business. But in part, his
> sermons were welcomed for a better reason; always their
> theme was directly spiritual, always they preached the
> Gospel – whereas just at that time most of the eminent
> Nonconformists were preaching ceaselessly about the
> Education Act and 'passive resistance'. Above all, though,
> it was Campbell's personality, his transparent sincerity and
> goodness, which, aided by his striking appearance, brought
> his message home to his congregations.[133]

As Deane suggested, WRN had done much to 'puff' the Campbell
phenomenon in its nascent stages. Despite such support, however,
Campbell observed in retrospect that he knew he was not of one mind
with WRN:

> His purpose in making contact with me was to ask me to
> become a regular contributor to his columns, specialising
> in the spiritual needs and difficulties of young people. It

Reginald J. Campbell

would be disingenuous to refrain from confessing that I did not run well in harness with Robertson Nicoll. Looking back, I am astonished that he bore with me so long. His

neo-Calvinism was not for me, neither then nor now; and
when he protested, as frequently he did, against my stark
latitudinarianism he was, from his doctrinal standpoint,
thoroughly justified.[134]

There was a separation of minds that WRN, at first, was unaware.
Despite this divergence, however, the two men's collaboration had
been a relatively long one – Campbell's column ran for a full three
years, from 1903 to 1906, drawing throughout that period a great deal
of attention to the magazine.

Publicity, however, can have its problems – as it turned out, Campbell
was not all he seemed nor what he was expected to be. In an attempt
to deal with what he saw as the perceived 'irrelevance' of the church,
Campbell began to preach with some disturbing emphases. Among these
were a stress on divine immanence, a rejection of original sin and the
necessity for social reform and moral action. Arthur Porritt, who knew
Campbell well, felt that he was a man at war with himself: "A writer
once said of Mr Campbell that the Reginald in him was always in raging
conflict with the John, and that the spirit of 'the house' (Christ Church,
Oxford) was eternally battling with his Methodist upbringing."[135]
Gradually, feelings about Campbell changed and alarm was expressed.
The main question was whether Campbell was in truth an orthodox
Evangelical, the inevitable answer being that he simply never was an
Evangelical, in the usual meaning of the term. Again, Porritt shared
WRN's growing concerns:

> At the request of Sir William Robertson Nicoll...I
> searched through Mr. Campbell's published sermons at the
> time of the controversy to see if we could find a single
> authentic utterance that brought him definitely within the
> radius of evangelical orthodoxy. But the search was made
> in vain. For two years before the furore, Mr. Campbell had
> been preaching a theology with an underlying monistic
> philosophy. 'Jesus was divine; but so are you', he told his
> congregation at the City Temple long before sermon tasters
> scented heresy in his teaching. He was cutting sharply
> across Pauline theology long before he defiantly declared
> that 'Paul's opinion is just Paul's opinion and not binding
> on you and me.[136]

The storm finally burst on Campbell in 1907 with the publication of a
series of sermons in the *Christian Commonwealth*.[137] In plain language,
it seemed clear that Campbell had thrown over the Doctrine of the

fall, the Pauline Plan of Salvation and other basic beliefs deemed essential to the orthodox Evangelical faith. Shock and disappointment accompanied the violence of the reaction to Campbell. In January 1907, WRN employed the editorial 'cannon' of the *British Weekly* to attack what he called 'City Temple Theology',[138] passionately denouncing Campbell's 'Pantheism' and its implications. In March, Campbell issued his defence, *The New Theology*. "The questions at issue caught hold of public imagination, and were debated for months in both the secular and the religious press".[139] Later John K. Mozley referred to Campbell's book as,

> A reinterpretation of Christian theology under the influence of the idea of divine immanence. Especially did it appear as though the incarnation itself were regarded by the author as no more than the supreme example of God's indwelling, and the distinction between God and man was obliterated through a comprehensive Pantheism. If this theology were to be accepted as not only new but true, it was obvious that the theological tradition of the English Free Churches was gravely defective.[140]

Soon other leaders, some orchestrated by WRN, assailed the 'New Theology' position. Dr. Fairbairn called the book a "farrago of nonsense"; James Denney wrote about 'The New Theology'[141] in the *British Weekly*, but it was P.T. Forsyth (also writing in the *British Weekly*), and writing[142] as a fellow Congregationalist, who took Campbell's book to pieces and exposed its errors: "It was like a bad photograph, underdeveloped and over-exposed".[143] Far more important to Forsyth was the idea that, for him, "New Theology represented the culmination of an insidious tendency in modern Christianity, a tendency to evacuate its objective, historic core and to lose sight of ... 'the cruciality of the cross'".[144] The controversy caused a strain within the Congregational Union, which met in conference on 9 June 1910, but after much discussion, it failed or refused to condemn Campbell. He was invited to speak at a meeting in Nottingham in 1911 to explain his views. The *British Weekly* noted that Campbell explained his theology and particularly his relationship with Christ in orthodox-sounding terminology, so that even Dr. Forsyth declared the controversy between himself and Campbell to be at an end. The *British Weekly* went on, "The chasm that in recent years has rent Congregationalism still remains uncovered; but the event at Nottingham is interpreted as meaning that a bridge has been thrown over the chasm to establish friendly relations between one side and the other".[145] However, Campbell was not comfortable within Nonconformity and in 1915 he left the City Temple and Nonconformity to join the Anglo-Catholic wing of the Church of England. His convictions changed and he withdrew the circulation of his book *The New Theology*. In later life, he became an active yet a quieter Canon in Winchester. After his resignation from the City Temple and acceptance into the Anglican fold, he wrote *A Spiritual Pilgrimage*.[146] WRN reviewed it: "His secession from Nonconformity and his re-ordination in the Church of England were a foregone conclusion. Nothing could be franker than his confession that he was never a Nonconformist at heart. 'Nonconformity will forgive me for saying that no one of their number has ever touched me at all from first to last, and I am not conscious of owing anything of my religious life to Nonconformist influences'".[147]

WRN could make mistakes, even in the realms where he was proud of his discernment – doctrine and preaching. However, he felt betrayed by one for whom he had held such high hopes; indeed he had bolstered and encouraged him. The Campbell affair brought out the fighter in him, yet it seems ironic that his position in this business seemed to some to be opposite to that which he had taken in the 'Downgrade Controversy'. The affair hurt WRN personally, and not just his pride in his discernment. Campbell had been one of a number of young men that he had tried to encourage, but WRN the journalist knew that what he had built up he could also knock down. The episode left its mark on the faith of the churches and on the younger generation in particular. It was, perhaps, a sign that this new generation was becoming less and less predictable to him. The whole 'New Theology' affair seemed yet another knock to the reputation of the Christian Church's credibility, and Nonconformity in particular. It was not long after the Campbell affair that WRN began to appear more interested in the world of politics than that of theology. Precisely why this shift occurred is a matter of conjecture, but it does not seem unreasonable to ascribe it in part not only to the defection of a protégé, but to a sense of growing distance between himself and the young men who would lead the church where they felt it should go, rather than where WRN and his peers had led it in the past.

James Moffatt[148] was a capable Scottish New Testament scholar who had an encyclopaedic mind and was versatile enough to be able to write acceptably on literary as well as theological subjects. Moffatt had been a friend to James Denney, and his friendship with WRN only really flourished in 1917, following Denney's death. Initially, WRN had reservations about Moffatt because his *The Historical New Testament* (1901) was deemed too radical. WRN felt Moffatt had conceded too much to negative criticism. He asked Denney to write a review of Moffatt's book[149], while he voiced his own reservations:

> I look upon Moffatt's book as a landmark, not for anything
> in it that is important or new, but because he first among
> the Presbyterians of our Church calmly yields the crucial
> points on the New Testament, and makes the admissions[150]
> as if they were of no consequence.[151]

WRN certainly perceived the ability of the man, even though he didn't appreciate all his views.

On the recommendation of Marcus Dods, WRN commissioned Moffatt to write *The Golden Book of John Owen* (1904). From then on, he pursued a positive relationship with Moffatt and in 1906 invited his contribution to a series of three articles on the Sermon on the Mount. Later Denney observed, "Moffatt's article was the one I was most curious to see, and the one which did interest me the most: it struck me as mighty clever, but so impalpable that only another man as clever as the writer would see all that was in it."[152] WRN was clearly pleased, as he later invited Moffatt to write on the book of 'Revelation' for his *Expositor's Greek New Testament*. Again, Denney appreciated it, and it seems that he was helping WRN in getting to know Moffatt better, "Moffatt's 'Revelation' is by far the best."[153] From 1907 to 1911, Moffatt became the minister at Denney's old Church at Broughty Ferry, in 1911 publishing his *Introduction to the Literature of the New Testament*[154] and becoming Professor of Greek and New Testament Exegesis at Mansfield College, Oxford. Denney reviewed Moffatt's book for the *British Weekly*, and wrote to WRN, "the one thing for which I value it is, that at every point, whether you agree with him or not, it suggests questions to the mind. It is not that everything is in flux, though for him this is too much the case, but that you become aware that there is something further to be investigated and to be learned on every point."[155] During his time at Oxford Moffatt published his *Modern Translation of the New Testament* (1913)? There is reason to believe[156] that it began as a result of a challenge thrown out by WRN to a class of students that they should try to translate a New Testament book into everyday English – a challenge to which Moffatt was the only one to respond. Of this,

> "The Establishment was predictably critical, especially
> about Moffatt's rendering of the Gospels, for he

deliberately translated the market-place Greek of Asia
Minor into the plainest of English, garnished with some
good vernacular Scotticisms. It was sacrilege to lovers
of the Authorised Version. Yet few could find fault with
the accuracy of the translator whose work … was a direct
translation from original texts, not an inspired paraphrase
in modern English … In no time at all, 'Moffatt' was being
reprinted on both sides of the Atlantic. No criticism could
stay demand."[157]

WRN loved it and so successful was the effort that Hodder & Stoughton
later persuaded Moffatt to translate the Old Testament and so complete
the 'Moffatt' Bible.

During the First World War Moffatt assisted WRN with the *Expositor*,
and even wrote occasional articles for the *British Weekly*. There was an
expectation that he would take over the editorial chair, but though he did
so for a time, it was neither congenial to him nor something he could
sustain. Moffatt, with all his gifts, could not in the event occupy WRN's
shoes, leaving the *Expositor* little option but to cease from publication.
After Moffatt's death in 1944, it was Arthur Porritt who summed up
Moffatt's life, in an almost Nicoll-like manner: "Dr Moffatt's versatility
often staggered me. His learning was prodigious. It was said of him, as
was said of Robertson Smith, that he might have filled with distinction
any chair, except that of science, in any university. With all his learning
… he was wholly free from pedantry. He did not even look like a
professor … anything in fact, but what he was … I never found a book that
I had read and he had not, or told him a story that he did not know. He
carried his learning lightly and was the most unassuming of men."[158]

Conclusion

WRN had contact with most of the leading preachers of his day.
These were important individuals, but they are only samples of the
broad spectrum of contacts that enabled him to keep his finger on the
pulse of affairs in the churches. A more ambitious list would have
included Robert F. Horton, John Henry Jowett, Alexander Fairbairn,
Arthur Peake, Dinsdale Young, F.B. Meyer, G. Campbell Morgan and
others who wrote odd articles for the *British Weekly*. Spurgeon has
been given special treatment because of his influence on WRN's view
of preaching, but more particularly for demonstrating where WRN
differed from the older man in the contemporary understanding of what

it was to be an Evangelical. The Downgrade Controversy played the role of both catalyst and major crisis, enabling WRN to find his own path through the issues, emerging in a markedly different place from Spurgeon. Through looking at Spurgeon, Campbell and the others, an image emerges of WRN as an intelligent, eminently capable man striving to balance the myriad forces at work in contemporary society.

Of course given his effectively forced removal to London, it is hardly surprising that WRN retained an emotional connection to the land he had left behind. The friendships he maintained with his Scottish peers were always particularly close, to the degree that he often relied upon them as his nearest confidants. They provided great personal support, and also proved an invaluable body of contributors to his many ongoing enterprises. WRN was always his own man in the choices he made. When he wrote his obituary articles he always sought to remember and honour the best and the most positive of the attributes of his colleagues and friends. His evaluation and sympathetic studies of the humanity of his subjects underscores those values he admired and prized most. Yet at the same time he was always wary of the economic factors of 'readership', WRN was ever striving to encourage and embody his liberal principles in both religion and politics, but never to lose the stance and attitude of an orthodox Evangelical, which the widest audience respectfully needed.

6

Culture, Biography, *The Bookman* and 'Claudius Clear'

Harry Nicoll instilled into his children a love of reading and an appreciation of good literature, including classic novels. He also gave his son an interest in literary style: "My father was a connoisseur in style, and used to talk much on the subject. He disliked high-flown writing…what he asked for in a writer was clearness, limpidity, [and] short sentences. His favourite stylists were Hazlitt and Newman".[1] These adjectives came to characterise WRN's style. It was not merely in this that the literary tastes of the father shaped the life of the son; Harry also encouraged his son's love of poetry, of which WRN published an anthology, *Songs of Rest* (1879) WRN continued to write verses until late in his life. It was his particular activity for Sunday afternoons. It gave him sensitivity to the poetic parts of the Bible. WRN was not only drawn to the well-known poets, in his anthology he was concerned, "to include poems less known".[2] WRN's favourite poets, from whom poems were taken for his anthology included[3] Browning and Rossetti, but also George Macdonald, Alfred Norris, and Dora Greenwell. The popularity of his anthology, as shown by the number of reprints, gave WRN much satisfaction.

WRN's literary knowledge and early teaching experience almost made reading him feel like taking a course on English literature. One beneficiary wrote,

> Those who had no real width of literary knowledge could gain from him an introduction to both the classics and to the contemporary writers. As editor and publisher's adviser Nicoll made keen fiction readers out of people…who had been brought up to look on fiction as sinful and altogether remote from their own experience. They were astonished by what seemed to them the clarity and truth in the picture

> portrayed by Barrie and Ian Maclaren of the world they
> knew. Their womenfolk sat up far into the night to finish
> an Annie S. Swan.[4]

WRN brought this enthusiasm for reading with him to England, where, through his journals, he tried to present literature as a positive force to his legions of Nonconformist readers. Integrating the literary into religious journalism was not breaking new ground, for Alexander Strahan and Norman Macleod had pioneered serialised fiction in an Evangelical paper in *Good Words* in the 1860s, but WRN achieved a popularity entirely new.

To indoctrinate culturally the Nonconformist reader of Evangelical journalism was no insignificant feat. Historically speaking, Nonconformity was not viewed by those outside of it as a bastion of culture. To a man as culturally educated as WRN, this was a delicate topic and he took seriously the criticisms of Nonconformity made by Matthew Arnold in his *Culture and Anarchy*, wherein Arnold attacked the 'Philistines', the great middle class, especially in "its main stronghold, the Puritan or Dissenting connection – now the most influential section of English Society".[5] Basil Willey, in his *Nineteenth-Century Studies*, commented: "Puritanism, by which Arnold usually means Protestant Dissent, is of two types, the bitter and the smug: both of them thwarting 'the full perfection of our humanity' ... [for] its ideal of perfection is narrow and incomplete. It has 'Hebraism', the principle of conduct, but not Hellenism, the principle of sweetness and light".[6] This is not to suggest that WRN disagreed with Arnold's survey of how things were, but rather that he refused to accept that they must be so. He took on board Arnold's opinions, and had his own feelings confirmed on moving south in 1885. Some of his early experiences of Nonconformist services in Dawlish were noted:

> "Sundays are worst. Dissent here is nowhere … the ministers
> get about £80 a year, and are quite uneducated … still if I
> had to stay here, I should be forced to go to the English
> Church. No educated man could stand the Dissenters".[7]

He was determined to bring some 'sweetness and light' into Nonconformity's social and cultural life.

In 1887, WRN wrote, "Faith and culture need each the other. It is high time that Christians should frankly acknowledge that light is a thing always to be welcome – never to be feared. Intellectual fear on God's behalf is stupid impiety".[8] Darlow commented, "When Nicoll began the *British Weekly* … it was with the conviction that 'much more might be done in the way of uniting religion and literature' and that 'the Nonconformists had too long behaved as exiles from the world of culture.' He recognised what a great advantage it had been for the High Church party that men like Keble and Newman dealt frankly with imaginative literature instead of trying to put it down, as the Evangelicals did to their sore discomfiture and shame".[9]

As his journalistic influence increased, WRN sought to bring an educational programme into the lives of his Nonconformist readers. Many of his contemporaries certainly appreciated this in their aspirations for cultural respectability. For WRN, Arnold's statement: 'He who knows only his Bible knows little of that', could almost be written down as his motto. It was, however, a balancing act – he wanted his readers to buy his papers, and, at the same time, he wanted to benefit them. WRN wrote, "I thought that much more might be done in the way of uniting religion with literature, believing that Nonconformists had too long behaved as exiles from the world of culture".[10] He was responding to a generally perceived need amidst Nonconformity's elite, yet even here he had to act with care, for, although Nonconformist leaders felt an obligation to the gospel to be part of the wider world of English and Imperial life, ironically, amongst Nonconformists generally, there was a very real fear of too much education, especially if it led to Oxford or Cambridge Universities.[11] "An incessant stream of the sons of our wealthy laymen feed[ing] the ranks of the Anglican Church"[12] and the rearing of Nonconformity's young warriors, who "under the shadows of a 'Trinity' or a 'Balliol', amid the luxuries of the political establishment, will be emasculated 'ere they fight".[13] WRN was aware of the fear, which rose to a particular head when Mansfield College, an institution for the training of Congregational ministers, was opened at Oxford in 1889. A.M. Fairbairn,[14] its first Principal, wanted it to be not only a theological college, but also a centre of learning. On this, Fairbairn and WRN were of one mind about the future for the Free Churches. He wrote, "There need be no fear of the alienation of youth and culture … it is this work – the sending forth of students thoroughly trained, who will use the most finely-tempered instruments of modern culture in the proclamation of the ancient Gospel which Nonconformists have found so quick and so powerful – that we expect from Principal Fairbairn. Let him be cordially upheld".[15] Indeed, so inclined towards cultural knowledge and integration was Fairbairn that WRN would later find himself striking a conservative pose, voicing some criticisms about the quality of student spiritual life at Mansfield College.

From the beginning, the *British Weekly* featured literary news, book reviews, and extracts from books. WRN would tackle head-on such topics as 'Is our Literature declining?' In which he wrote, "In what may be called non-imaginative literature there is surely no decline ... in the world of imagination the situation is wholly different ... in fiction our plight is worse, for the masters of the Victorian period went early".[16] It should be stressed that his sole approach to culture was through literature. Quite simply WRN did not appreciate or enjoy music, the theatre, or painting. He enjoyed, traded and lived for his books and sought to convey his enthusiasm to a new generation. In 'What can books do for us?', he built his homily solely on the reading of books:

> They will loosen the hard tyranny of time and circumstance by taking us in to the radiant-coloured world of fancy. And they will engage us. After all, though we work hard enough, the great vice of the country is idleness. We do our routine work – too much of it – but we sink into lethargy outside of it, and are defenceless in the hour of greatest peril. We want something to rescue the mind from vacancy, to stimulate and interest, and so diminish the temptations to sensuality. And they will help to deliver us from narrowness, blindness, and uncharitableness, by showing us how great is the world of thought and learning.[17]

WRN was particularly interested in the ethical and moral effect of literature, and it was out of this concern that in April 1887 he introduced Annie Swan,[18] who had by this point been writing for some time, to the readers of his paper. WRN commended her as "a popular writer of religious fiction, and who is to contribute the next serial to the columns of the *British Weekly*".[19] The association began with the appearance of *Doris Cheyne: the story of a Noble Life*, the first of many serialised novels that she wrote for the paper. Through Annie Swan and others like her, WRN sought to encourage a particular brand of religious and ethical fiction, satisfying what he felt was both a niche in the market and a moral necessity, particularly amongst the younger generation.

The same year as he introduced Annie Swan, WRN wrote 'Can English Literature be taught?' Again, he stressed the importance of inculcating the habit of reading, giving the paper the tone of a 'crusade'.

> The subject is one of immense importance. We see no way of preserving young men[20] in great cities from demoralising amusements save by imbuing them with a love of reading. Our columns lately have borne witness to the monotony of the life to which many thousands are condemned. Escape from it they must have, and is not the escape to the world

of Walter Scott or Charles Dickens better than the escape
to the public house or the music hall?... We have heard
it said that reading is the idlest of human occupations,
but... Johnson was right when he said that if a man would
read anything four hours a day, he would by-and-by grow
wise. Books will fit a man for his work; they will teach
him large, noble, merciful thoughts; they will widen the
horizon about him; they will help him to understand the
spirit of the days.[21]

In the *British Weekly* he included columns such as 'Literature' and 'New
Literary Anecdotes', in order to make his readers think about the world
of books, a world which he thought it was vital to know about to lead
a cultured life.

Though the *British Weekly* provided a valuable forum for a particular
brand of fiction, it hardly satisfied WRN's passion for English literature
and books. It was a desire to expand his scope from the Evangelical
to the purely literary that led him to start *The Bookman*,[22] which was
first published in May 1891. Apparently, he had the idea just after he
launched the *British Weekly* and wrote to Marcus Dods,

> I have an idea of a magazine which I may carry out yet.
> I would call it something like this – *The Bookman: a
> Magazine for Book readers, Book buyers, and Booksellers.*
> I would give in each number a certain amount of popular
> matter – such as lives and portraits of living authors – gossip
> – literary anecdotes – advice to aspirants, etc. Then I would
> give a complete classified list of all publications of the
> month. Each class would be under a special co-editor with
> me, who would briefly characterize in a line or two all the
> good books, warn against pretensions and ignore rubbish.[23]

Jane Stoddart knew about WRN's requirements for the new periodical:
"Dr. Nicoll has aimed at providing the four essential requirements which
he himself once said he expected from every periodical, (a) Thrills; (b)
News; (c) Sense; (d) Pastime."[24] WRN kept his friend Marcus Dods
informed:

> I hope to make a fair first number. One of the features will
> be a map of [Thomas] Hardy's 'Wessex', with his and the
> real names of places. This he has supplied. I have seen a
> good deal of Hardy lately and [I] am much taken by him.
> He is certainly the most winning literary man I have ever

> met – shy and silent in company, but in private remarkably communicative and interesting. He used to be a fiery Evangelical – now he thinks Christianity utterly dead, save for surviving moral fragments.[25]

This enterprise pushed WRN's capacity for hard and sustained work to higher standards: "I have by twelve hours' work a day steady for a fortnight got the *Bookman* into shape, though the first number will not be what I hope to make it. Still, now that the compilation of lists, etc, is done, I wait the event serenely".[26] The first number[27] of the *Bookman* appeared on September 25 and, as WRN informed his friend, proved popular from the start: "The *Bookman* has been a great success. We sold the first day 6,000 copies, now we have only 100 copies left of the whole large edition [of 10,000], and we hope to print another edition… the press notices too have been numerous and generally friendly. The only adverse criticism of which I recognise the justice is that two or three articles are too long. But I wanted not to make it too snippety".[28] Indeed, the reaction was startlingly favourable. Positive reviews were widespread, and not only did the articles please, but the early numbers impressed many with the rarity and beauty of their plate portraits and photographs. It gave WRN particular satisfaction that he had created a purely literary periodical, which had become a commercial success. Others had tried and failed, but the *Bookman* prospered.

WRN was able to entrust much of the running of the magazine to a number of able assistants, which meant he had enough time for his first love, the *British Weekly.* The timing had been right for a growing literary awareness had followed the improvement in national education, so the nature of the paper virtually ensured its ongoing success. The venture established WRN as a major figure in the literary as well as the religious world, and soon increasing numbers of aspiring writers began to emerge who looked to WRN for help and 'very' occasionally to 'puff' their literary efforts. The 'Young Authors' Page' became very popular and Jane Stoddart commented,

> The editor's idea was that, while it is unreasonable to expect hard-working publishers, journalists, and literary men to spend time and trouble on the consideration of manuscripts from perfect strangers, the literary aspirant would often be benefited by a little judicious counsel at the beginning. In this department, all manuscripts were examined and criticised, and hundreds of young writers have taken advantage of the assistance offered.[29]

He was continually on the lookout for fresh talent. As to what established writers regarded as talented, WRN admired many; with some, he had a particular affinity and others he sought to encourage by recommending them to others. He always liked the Brontës and the less well known George Gissing. However, he placed before the reading public others, and particularly those whom he saw as reflecting a Nonconformist heritage. George Eliot was a favourite of his; however, he felt that her depiction of chapel life was rarely in a positive light. WRN was fascinated by the literary work of George Meredith,[30] whom he regarded as enigmatic. The fascination in this case was more than purely literary, however – when discussing Meredith in his 'Claudius Clear Column', he seemed to be more interested in the man than his writings, and more concerned to list fellow admirers than to say why *he* appreciated particular works.[31] WRN approved of the depth and intellectual power he felt reading Meredith, but did not recommend him as he did 'Mark Rutherford'. In 1901 he wrote, "Great as he is, one is almost afraid to recommend him to the average reader, who is first bored, then wearied, by an author whose calibre towers so far above the ordinary level that one need to be educated up to a certain literary pitch before understanding it. Better to leave Meredith alone, than to read without understanding".[32] This certainly made a change from WRN's customary policy of recommending with unbridled enthusiasm.

WRN had first written about Charles Dickens as a student in Aberdeen,[33] but his appreciation of the man was somewhat checked by the problem of Dickens' very unsympathetic treatment of Nonconformity. Dickens was too significant a figure to ignore on such grounds, however, and pieces did appear, such as *The Problem of Edwin Drood*, WRN's study of Dickens' unfinished novel in which he examined the various suggested solutions before presenting his own. In his preface, he wrote, "Those who believe that Dickens is the greatest humorist and one of the greatest novelists in English literature, are proud to make any contribution, however insignificant, to the understanding of his works".[34] The book met with considerable approval, with the *Times* noting "Robertson Nicoll proves himself a literary detective of no mean capacity." In 1923 a selection of WRN's essays on Dickens from his 'Claudius Clear Column' were published,[35] showing that his attitude was not one of blind idolatry, for he writes with a keen sense of the faults in Dickens' character and work alike. Inevitably, amongst WRN's major concerns in the collection was that of why Dickens held such a dislike of Nonconformist ministers. He examined the question, but had little choice but to confess in the end that he had no answer. Indeed, insightful though he was and given his capacity for ferreting things out, WRN could find no reason for Dicken's antipathy in his life and his respect for literature was such that he did not seek to pose as one possessed of any special knowledge of the nature of authors. As Darlow reflected,

> "In appraising authors Nicoll always insisted upon the mysterious elemental distinction between genius and talent. He recognised that we have many gifted novelists, with imagination and insight and style and dramatic power. Yet 'a man of very high talent may write a book which is a model of all the canons; but if that light golden flame which we call genius does not play upon its pages, the book will not live.'"[36]

Rare though that 'golden flame' may be, there was still a reliable cadre of men writing in England at the time whose possession of it WRN acknowledged, including Charles Dickens, Thomas Hardy, and Rudyard Kipling.

Impressive as English authors were, however, WRN was unashamedly biased towards all things Scottish and he regarded it a coup when he managed to get Robert Louis Stevenson to contribute an article to the *British Weekly*.[37] He always took an interest in Stevenson, identifying with his necessity to travel south for the benefit of his health. He wrote,

> "The personality of Stevenson is strangely arresting … he was by nature and training religious…. Yet he was by no means 'orthodox,' either in ethics or in religion. Much as he wrote on conduct, there were certain subjects ... on which he never spoke out. On love, for example, and all that goes with it, it is quite certain that he never spoke his full mind – to the public at least."[38]

Interestingly, Stevenson's article for the *British Weekly* was acclaimed, but WRN ruefully remarked to his friend Marcus Dods, "I am glad you liked R.L. Stevenson, but these articles make little difference to the sale. It is personal matter that people like. Don't you think there is something sickly about RLS – perfume at best – opium at worse? I think Mark Rutherford a much greater master of English style".[39] Scotland's contribution would truly come, in WRN's assessment, with the entry of the 'Kailyard School' of Scottish novelists.

Value though he did the contemporary giants of literature, WRN was no less fascinated with many of a lesser-known, but to his mind no lesser-skilled, group, including the mysterious figure he judged so much better a stylist than Stevenson – 'Mark Rutherford'. This was the pen name of one William Hale White,[40] a discovery WRN took much delight in, achieved as it was through his personal detective work. Jane Stoddart noted White's impact on WRN, from the time in 1881 when he bought *The Autobiography of Mark Rutherford*:

> I was at home from school at the time and vividly remember that evening in his study when he read aloud to me the preliminary poem, in which the writer anticipates death. He lingered on the verse:
> For I was ever commonplace,
> Of genius never had a trace,
> My thoughts the world have never fed,
> Mere echoes of the last book read.
> 'I believe,' he said, "that is how one might feel if one were dying," and added the opinion (which he never changed) that William Hale White was a master of English style."[41]

WRN wrote much about White, saying how he had never seen a style quite like his: "A style translucent in its simplicity, and yet incapable of any amendment. Nor was the matter less noteworthy. Many have written of Dissent, some foolishly, some ignorantly, some spitefully; but this writer wrote not only with knowledge,[42] but with insight, and he dealt with life, laying bare its secret places, and especially rendering with consummate skill the miseries of its darkest hours."[43] In time, the two men came to know one another, "though never intimately, and we had occasional personal intercourse and correspondence for some twelve years. He was very reserved and dignified in appearance, but essentially kind and modest. His great interest was in books – books as makers and helpers of life. He was a singular exact student, mainly of the English classics".[44] WRN recommended White to his friends and readers, even from the early days of the *British Weekly*,[45] and yet as Munson observes "White develops those favourite Victorian themes: the decline of faith, the rise of doubt and the construction of a new, more 'rational' faith. His world is that of the lone intellectual seeking truth regardless".[46] White's demographic was that he identified with intelligent, educated readers who were finding their old context of life as members of Nonconformist churches increasingly unsatisfactory.

> "His appeal to intellectual readers in 'search of truth' has continued although he himself warned ... 'we think too much of ourselves' and cautioned against 'spiritual misery'. He came to feel that 'speculations on the why and

> the wherefore, optimism, pessimism, freedom, necessity,
> causality, and so forth, are not only for the most part loss
> of time, but frequently ruinous'".[47]

However, WRN enjoyed White, writing, "He wrote many articles for the *British Weekly*, some of which were not signed. He was also a frequent contributor to the *Bookman*, and latterly to the *Nation*, in which his last papers appeared".[48] His enthusiasm for White glowed: "If there are any books of this generation better than *Mark Rutherford* I do not know them. The author is like the painter who can produce a perfect circle".[49] WRN believed that White's novels gave a sense of integrity to the Nonconformists, but was that picture created by both Eliot and White truly representative of life within Nonconformity or simply a view from those who attained a more sophisticated attitude and reflected this in their creations? Their books were not positive in their appreciation of Nonconformist life and were part of an unhelpful presentation of doubt, creating problems for the credibility of the central beliefs of the Christian faith. The result was not to help many gain a stronger faith, but quite the opposite – those who accepted wholesale the tenets of authors such as White and Eliot were faced with the necessity of modifying their faith or else jettisoning it completely. WRN's apparent immunity to this effect was far from the norm; he was able to enjoy their books as literature, but not all his readers could do the same.

Woman at Home

With the success of his general literary periodical, WRN was growing increasingly open to innovative journalistic concepts. He spotted a similar opportunity to plug a market gap through producing a journal for women, entitled *Woman at Home*. This too followed his basic premise of giving the buyers what they would want to read. It was unashamedly consumer driven and built around the story-telling talents of Mrs Burnett Smith (*nom de plume* of Annie S. Swan).[50] The combination of romantic stories, domestic advice, drawings and photographs, fashion, and celebrities gave the journal popular appeal. Its remit reflected the leisure time available for such light reading among middle-class women, and the widening of the horizons of Nonconformist interests to a broader social and cultural appreciation. Jane Stoddart, the first editor of the paper, wrote, "The age of popular monthlies was beginning and I little thought that within a year I was to be closely identified with one of them. Dr. Nicoll believed there was room for 'a female *Strand*', and the title he chose was suggested by that of another magazine, the *Sunday at Home*".[51] Alice Head, who succeeded Jane Stoddart as Editor, wrote of the first editorial team: "The regime of Sir William Robertson Nicoll, Jane T. Stoddart and Annie Swan was one of exceptional brilliance, and provides an example of editing, on the literary side, that is an inspiration to this day".[52] Beyond her narrative acumen, Annie Swan also proved to be a gifted 'Agony Aunt' in her column, 'Over the teacups'. When her husband became the Nicolls' family doctor, they became close friends of the whole Nicoll family and part of the Scottish colony of Hampstead. As well as providing much of the bedrock upon which *Woman at Home* was erected, she wrote regularly for the *British Weekly*, including many serials that later came out as very popular books. As well as writing under her own name, she adopted multiple pseudonyms – 'David Lyall'[53] was a name employed in the *British Weekly* as a 'mystery writer' to be guessed, and her work was also to be found under 'Evelyn Orchard' and her married name Mrs Burnett Smith. Later she wrote a number of reminiscences of WRN,

> My friendship with Sir William Robertson Nicoll and his family covers the whole period of my life in England, over thirty years. During that time there never has been a break or a cloud upon our intercourse with one another. Our children grew up together, shared walks and plays, and sometimes nurses.... [H]e was very encouraging to me … although a trenchant and merciless critic, he had one quality, which, I think, is rare in editors – at least I have never met it elsewhere. When satisfied that you could do the work required he left you in peace to do it, and accepted what was submitted, believing you had done your best.... Commenting on this comforting quality of his once, all the answer he gave was: "When you know your business you do not need to be taught it." I have never forgotten that.[54]

The family connection remained close and later WRN's youngest daughter published a volume of Annie Swan's letters.[55]

J.M. Barrie and the 'Kailyard School' Writers

By this stage, WRN had established the type of cultural influence that allowed a man to define trends through the mere fact of their support; though the extent to which he was aware of this is doubtful. He exercised an influence when, between 1890 and 1900, he helped to orchestrate a phenomenon in the literary world of Britain and America. There was

Annie Swan in 1884

an extraordinary popularity of books written in Scottish dialect, with very little plot; just simple domestic tales of ordinary people. It was known as the 'Kailyard School', which was a pejorative term for the 'Kailyard,'[56] which was the name for the Scottish manse garden or 'cabbage-patch'; it suggested a trivial or limited domesticated range of the novels subjects. Indeed, George Blake, no friend to this school of novelists, says that they presented to,

> The English and the American reader with a picture of
> their country as a sort of collection of picturesque rural

parishes peopled by 'pawky' and/or 'nippy' characters.... Their work was genteel, patronizing: really a queer sort of toadying to the old traditions of Toryism, in which 'the lower classes' are the honest, feckless, delightful friends of their superiors in education and financial resource. They held up their fellow-countrymen as comic characters for the amusement of the foreigner.[57]

However, the Scottish social historian, T.S. Smout, argued that they were excellent commentators on social life because they had, "come to life, not as pastors but as intelligent gentlemen sowing clover, speculating on ornithology, applauding the new linen work or a new road, agitated over the expense of poor relief, nervous of the effect of rising wages on rural virtue and watchful for any signs of idleness among the labouring classes".[58]

WRN's contribution was to part-create and certainly promote (called 'puffing') them.[59] These novels caught the mood and imagination of the general public, not least through the novelty of the Scottish dialect. They were never demanding reading (except for those who needed a translation), and the sentimental tales with their moral side became a popular craze. WRN fanned the fire while it lasted and no doubt had considerable personal nostalgic pleasure in doing so.

The first member of the school to score a hit was James M. Barrie,[60] who had come to London in March 1885 when Frederick Greenwood, the editor of the *St James's Gazette*, helped him by taking an interest in his Scottish stories. However, it was Barrie's contact with WRN that brought him outstanding success, for he had first seen Barrie's work under the name of 'Gavin Ogilvy'. WRN and Barrie formed not only a good working relationship, but also an enduring friendship. Barrie wrote,

> Greenwood invented me... in time, however, I found another paper, the *British Weekly*, with an editor as bold as my first (or shall we say he suffered from the same infirmity?). He revived my drooping hopes, and I was again able to turn to the only kind of literary work I now seemed to have much interest in. He let me sign articles, which was a big step for me, and led to my having requests from elsewhere; but always the invitations said, 'Not Scotch – the public will not read dialect.' By this time I had put together... from my drawer-full of rejected stories this book of 'Auld Licht Idylls', and its collected form it

> again went round … then on a day came actually an offer
> for it from Messrs Hodder & Stoughton. For this and many
> other kindnesses I had the editor of the *British Weekly* to
> thank.[61]

From many there was praise for Barrie's Scottish tales, but there was
also criticism, which developed into an attack on the whole group of
novelists who were said to have followed Barrie's lead.

> Outside Kirriemuir, the acid criticism of the books had no
> personal note in it, but was an expression of rage at what
> was considered to be a slur on the national Scots character
> in general. It came from reviewers, from schoolmen and
> other professional men, and it was to lead to a widespread
> dislike – among at least a literate and realistic minority –
> of the Kailyard School, of which Barrie was accused of
> being the founder.[62]

However, WRN and the firm knew how to push Barrie's books,[63] even
to the extent of producing "a sixteen-page, illustrated supplement [in
the *British Weekly*], entitled *J.M. Barrie, A Literary and Biographical
Portrait*.… It showed how, with all his masterful and practical methods,
Robertson Nicoll could remain a very faithful friend".[64] It would seem,
however, that Barrie felt that WRN could be a little too possessive, so he
gave the rights to publish *The Little Minister* (1891) to Messrs Cassell
& Co. and a biographer comments "For all his real gratitude to Nicoll,
he may well, from what we know of him, have hankered for more
freedom and independence".[65] Barrie's career went on successfully and
after 1900 he became more interested in writing for the stage. However,
even before that, Barrie's success had priced him out of the range of the
usual contributors to the *British Weekly*. WRN appreciated his friend:
"Of Barrie's career I need say nothing except this, that nothing in it
has surprised me in the least. From the day I first knew him I never
doubted that he would come to the first place and that he would keep
it".[66] Barrie had struck a vein of gold in the reading public, and WRN
wanted to exploit this commercially as much as he could. He continued
to appreciate Barrie when he moved on to fresh triumphs in a successful
career as a playwright. Their friendship had survived the trip to America
(1896) and Barrie referred to the successful and happy memories of this
time in his last letter, written before WRN died. "In my mind, I have
many adventures with you still and embark once more on our lugger for
USA. Again I see us driven from place to place as your room became
uninhabitable through the size of the Sunday editions in it, or we ran

lest be hauled before the magistrates for burning so many writing tables with your cigarette-ends."[67] In the wake of Barrie's success, which caused him to move on, the value of the 'Kailyard School' did not dissipate – WRN was able to find two other writers who were skilled in the 'Kailyard' idiom of Scottish dialogue and who imparted something of a moral favour to their books, which was part of the formula that he looked for.

The first, the Rev. John Watson,[68] was the minister of Sefton Park Presbyterian Church in Liverpool, and it seems that when they first met, WRN was not overly impressed. He wrote to his friend Marcus Dods: "He stayed with us three nights and was very pleasant, but somehow I did not take to him so much as I expected: he was too cynical for me."[69] He was aware that Watson had worked steadily in Liverpool, and had built up his Church in fifteen years, but he was not known outside his circle and had not written anything. The initial contact was to interest Watson in writing for the *Expositor*, but then,

> I was so much struck with the racy stories and character-sketches with which Watson regaled us, and I suggested he should make some articles out of them. The idea had never struck him and at first was unwelcome. But I kept on persuading him… then he sent the first four chapters of what is now known as *The Bonnie Brier Bush* complete, and I knew on reading them that his popularity was assured.[70]

Watson took the nom de plume 'Ian Maclaren',[71] which was simply the Gaelic form of his Christian name paired with his mother's surname. The effect of the publication of *Beside the Bonnie Briar Bush* in October 1894 was to make Watson one of the best-known men in the country and in America. His timetable became crowded every day with requests for his services,[72] and WRN noted, "The circulation of the *British Weekly* rapidly increased. 'Even the critics had to confess that the articles made them cry, and the power of drawing tears from readers, though many people do not believe it, is one of the rarest given to the author'".[73] Watson became a regular contributor to the *British Weekly*, of both articles and sermons. He was invited over to America for speaking tours, and in 1896 he combined this with an invitation to deliver the Yale Lectures on preaching, which became his book, *The Cure of Souls*.[74]

After Watson's semi-jubilee in February 1905, he resigned from Sefton Park, Liverpool and in January 1907 he and his wife sailed for America, where he kept up a punishing schedule. He went to Iowa Wesleyan University to lecture, but tonsillitis turned into blood poisoning and he died suddenly on May 6. This stunned all his friends and no one more so than WRN: "It seems but the other day when he was with us in that abounding and rejoicing vitality which terrified those of a feebler make … the blow fell suddenly, and in the turmoil of thought and feeling which it has evoked, we scarcely know how to write about him".[75] WRN reflected on the life of his friend:

> The temper of his life was eminently joyful, though, like every Celt, he had intervals of deep depression … when we look back we can see better than before how he strove to encourage others, how he would not allow his occasional melancholy to cast a shadow, how he cultivated joy as the purely Christian temper of life. In any and every company, he gave himself largely and freely.[76]

WRN wrote the biography of his friend, which was published the following year, in which he also defended 'Ian Maclaren' over the charge of 'sentimentality' that was levelled at his 'Kailyard' novels.

> No doubt, a disproportionate space is given to descriptions of deathbeds. The feelings are deliberately and cruelly harrowed by an accumulation of pathetic incidents and words. Watson himself was well aware of this. All he had to say in reply was: "We ministers rarely see the brighter side of life. We are tolerated at weddings I admit; we are more at home at funerals. People do not ask a minister to share family festivities. He most often hears painful disclosures, and meets death from day to day. This is apt to have a very sobering effect on his mind".[77]

WRN's put his friend's novels on the same level as Rousseau![78] WRN's second replacement after Barrie was Samuel Rutherford Crockett:[79]

> "The first time I saw Mr Crockett he was occupying the pulpit of the Presbyterian Church in Hampstead. Nobody who once beheld him would easily forget his appearance. Somehow, his sermon did not interest me till he came to the end. Then he read musically and with obvious feeling one of Ruskin's loveliest passages."[80]

Although WRN gave no date, it was at the time that Crockett was contributing a series of sketches to the *Christian Leader*. "I was attracted by them, and wrote suggesting that he should collect and publish them. This very trifling service was immediately and most warmly recognised.

I never knew anyone so ready not only to acknowledge but to impute a kindness as S.R. Crockett".[81] This was *The Stickit Minister*[82] and the year 1893. "*The Stickit Minister* speedily laid hold of a public which had been prepared to relish Scotch stories by two predecessors".[83] His high-water mark was 1894, in which he published *The Raiders* and *The Lilac Sunbonnet*, and had a tour of America. Riding on this success, he resigned his Church, which caused a minor sensation. WRN was concerned, but philosophical about it.[84] "Crockett did right to resign, whatever happens. When he felt his main interest elsewhere, it was not for his soul's health to keep a pastorate. What he will do and where he will turn 'being let go,' is a serious problem; but I hope for the best."[85]Crockett and his family became friends of WRN's family, with Lady Nicoll particularly remembering his visits: "We often had a visit … from S.R. Crockett on his way through London to or from Spain or France. He was a man of wide and deep sympathies, and a born romancer."[86] Crockett identified with the Kailyard School, but his range was much wider. WRN reflected over Crockett's career:

> He discovered that he could turn anything into a story. What a discovery that was for a mind stored like his…. When the great and sudden rush of popularity came to him, when his income in one year was multiplied by twenty and thirty times, when from all parts of the English speaking world he received invitations to work, can it be wondered that he wrote too much and too fast? He had no fear for the future.[87]

However, there are those, then and subsequently, who have pointed out that Crockett's books were very limited and, as novels, "suffered from excesses of coy whimsicality and sugary sentimentality".[88] Crockett had a modestly good career, but he had promised more.

WRN succeeded as both editor and champion with all three writers; he not only saw the potential in Barrie's initial stories, but he had the means of marketing them. He had attained a standing and "his approval was sought, and ... he soon became, and for more than thirty years remained, the Grand Panjandrum of popular literary journalism".[89] WRN was, according to George Blake,

> An alarmingly good cook, [who] saw that his recipe must include a swatch of fiction, no doubt to please the ladies of the manses. We may never know whether he bought his stories and serials to please himself or to satisfy his own acute sense of what comfortable liberal Nonconformity

would be like. Bearing in mind the real acuteness of many of his judgments, particularly in his private correspondence, one inclines to conclude that he was mainly a shrewd merchant.[90]

All this has some truth in it, but Blake surely misses the main element that led WRN to build up the Kailyard School – nostalgia. He was a deep-dyed Scot, one of those who refused to lose their accent, but, above all, he was a Scotsman living in the alien land of England. The stories of dialect appealed to him personally, very probably before he saw the commercial possibilities of the books – the good businessman in him merely settled the matter.

The overwhelming popularity of Barrie's stories initially surprised WRN, but they conformed to two of his criteria: they were sympathetic to the Christian Church, and they had a positive moral to them. Certainly, the novels would give the view of life from the manse window, for two of the writers were ministers of the Free Church of Scotland, and Barrie drew on his memories that he associated with his mother, who was a faithful churchgoer. Blake was right in his verdict about WRN: "One cannot think that there would ever have been a Kailyard School without him".[91] A more relevant problem for assessment and posterity than WRN's inarguable role in the rise of the genre is the fact that WRN presented and promoted these books as 'great literature', and at times compared them favourably with, or even asserted their superiority to, some of the English classics. The literature caught a passing interest, which fitted into a popular appeal. However, this meant that not only did this product have a definite sell-by date, but it also presented an unhelpful image to the increasingly literary public, which was becoming more discerning. Furthermore, being the subject of an intense but passing fad, they would cease to be in demand when the public taste moved on to a new interest or craze. John Buchan attacked the influence and worth of these novels:

> Idylls of humble country life have lately grown upon us thick and fast; charming pieces of literature many of them; nigh perfect in their narrow sphere ... but some gentlemen of the press, whose interest it is to puff such books, do not let the matter rest here. These unpretentious and delightful volumes are gravely set above work with which they are scarcely even comparable.[92]

Buchan was 'gunning' for the Kailyard School, whose virtues were often rammed down the throats of the Presbyterian young. Chief among the critics who 'puffed' them was WRN of the *British Weekly*, favourite reading in Scottish manses. Buchan's stings drew blood. "Robertson Nicoll retorted in the *British Weekly* that Mr. Crockett had more strength in his little finger than Mr. Buchan in his whole body."[93] Such combativeness was largely bluster, however; WRN succeeded in getting Buchan to write a few things for him and continued to enjoy his niche in literary history.

However, WRN could also spot and promote more durable winners and John Kent thought that the novels of Arnold Bennett provided a more representative model for understanding church life in what he calls 'a late nineteenth-century Nonconformist renaissance'. Kent suggested that many writers have allowed Matthew Arnold's strictures to colour their estimate of Nonconformity. He called for 'a new model of late nineteenth-century English Nonconformist history', which Kent saw in Bennett. This has its merits but it is not only very debatable, it also seems to secularise the impact of the Evangelical Faith and regards its interaction with society, as simply sociological changes. For Kent, the need was to see the changes in Nonconformity in an optimistic way. "One may see a return of the human as the subject of value, a humanism which might employ some Christian imagery, but might equally resist the cramping effect of some religious systems and institutions on the human personality. This Nonconformist renaissance was not parasitic on Anglicanism, nor particularly anti-Anglican; its existence did not necessitate images of decline."[94] For Kent the Liberal Christianity represented by "C.J. Cadoux, R.J. Campbell, John Oman and A.S. Peake...mediated between orthodox protestant evangelicalism and a new, more liberal Christianity."[95] Interestingly, WRN, who tried to hold a bridge between the newer liberal and the older orthodox view of the faith would not have been adverse to this view, and he appreciated the strength of Arnold Bennett's novels, doing his bit to popularise them.[96] At the time, he certainly did not see any deeper significance in Bennett's work, but perhaps he was too much a part of the scene to appreciate the distinctive portrait Bennett was creating.

Nicoll and Biography

WRN had a particular love for biography, which he often wrote about: "My biographical collection is tolerably full, numbering at least 5,000 volumes...many people will think that I have wasted much time, which is no doubt true, but I have found [it to] my account in the reading and do not for one moment regret it...for the journalist who knows how to use them, biographies are a rewarding study, and meanwhile I do not propose to part with mine".[97] He read everything he could and not only wrote some substantial biographies himself, but turned his obituary articles and his comments on published biographies by others into veritable mini-biographies, displaying his own insights, occasional prejudices, and adding details that he had come by. This was especially true of personalities that he had known, but he was also capable of drawing attention to imbalances or distortions, as he saw them, in authorised biographies.

WRN shared, along with his contemporaries, an interest in studying the inner workings of an individual. He had a passion to know as much as he could about people's personal lives and so be able to assess their motivations and individual psychology. William Enright in a study on preaching in the nineteenth century noted that sermons became increasingly concerned with the human characters of the Scriptures, their lives and their situations. "The biblical writers were human beings. The situations to which they originally spoke were human, historical situations … the preacher approached his text psychologically, attempting to probe the mind and motive of the author".[98] The root of the interest in the personalities of the Bible was an effort to appreciate their humanity. Enright says, "George Matheson of St. Bernard's Parish Church, Edinburgh, Marcus Dods, George Adam Smith and Alexander Whyte were all masters of the character sermon",[99] and all these men also wrote for WRN's journals, strengthening his own approach to biography. WRN shared this concern with bringing out the human interest in his biographical studies, but he did not extend this approach to his own preaching. However, in his biographical articles he felt that a study of how individuals handled issues of life threw light on their motivations, and gave a better appreciation of their achievements. WRN collected much material throughout his life, but his concern could be open to other interpretations. George Blake recounted how he felt unhappy about some things in WRN's collection:

> It was a queer experience for a young man to deal with the private papers of a leader in journalism, and it was indeed an extremely curious collection of material (in both the general and the special senses) that thus passed through my hands. It was clear that, in his most influential position, Nicoll had been lent or been able to borrow all sorts of documents bearing closely on the private lives of famous literary persons, and had been canny enough to keep

typewritten copies of them all.... I was more fascinated by
a wholly blameless collection of autograph letters, dating
from the early 'eighties, in which all the great British
literary figures of the day, Stevenson included, confided to
the young Free Kirk minister at Kelso the general intentions
of their works and their methods of writing.... They were
of singular bibliographical interest, and I feel that their
preservation over so many years, if merely prudent, was
still the not unpleasing mark of Nicoll's passionate, real
interest in the mechanics and *personalia* of writing.[100]

What Blake had seen was the fruit of the preparatory research of
WRN's great, unfulfilled dream – a 'Literary History of the Nineteenth
Century', a project which needed considerable data, but Blake regarded
the depth of detail revealing WRN's over-concern to amass personal
details as being more than what was necessary to better understand the
writings of a particular author.

WRN's interest in the biographical form began early; what
biographical articles the young student wrote for the Aberdeen papers are
unknown, as most of his early newspaper work did not carry the name
of the writer, but his first book with biographical content was a study
of Alfred Tennyson, written under the pseudonym 'Walter E Wace'.[101]
Tennyson had been a favourite of his father, and WRN visited Horncastle
and Somersby for research. Darlow simply remarks, "Nicoll brought
together by far the fullest collection of personal facts regarding Mr.
Tennyson and his works that had hitherto been published. The facts were
gathered with great labour from many sources, public and private".[102] His
next known foray of significance into biography appeared in 1884 when
WRN gave a published lecture at Free St George's, Edinburgh,[103] one
of a series given by different individuals as an attempt at the popular
level to reassure the faithful that the Evangelical roots and aspirations
of the Free Church were unchanged, healthy, and in safe hands. His
subject was 'John Bunyan', on whom he wrote authoritatively, though
he acknowledged that he was indebted to "the chief living authority
on John Bunyan, Dr. John Brown".[104] This was his pattern – either to
study the best books on his subject, or consult the best authorities, and if
possible he would do both. For WRN, Bunyan's place in the Evangelical
Succession was located in one main area: "He teaches the priceless value
of a true spiritual experience. He preached and wrote what he himself
had gone through.... If Evangelical preaching is to retain and increase its
power, it also must rest on an original and definite experience on the part

of the preacher".[105] He wrote to the formulated pattern of the series, but felt that it gave him scope to say things that were pertinent and applied to the contemporary situation. He discovered in his reading lessons of life, and his wish to address ethical concerns found concrete examples in biography and history, which drove and encouraged WRN to use the life illustrations and examples in his biographical writing.

WRN's first full biography was *James Macdonell, Journalist*,[106] written in the summer and autumn of 1889. There was considerable personal interest in this subject as Macdonell also hailed from Aberdeenshire before making his reputation in London. Through sheer ability and hard work he became the leader writer on the *Daily Telegraph* and then the *Times*, before dying at the age of thirty-seven. WRN stated his purpose in writing the book: "I was anxious that some record of his life should be written for the sake of journalism – a profession which has many heroes who die unknown; for the sake of the increasing multitude of thoughtful and able young men who are looking forward to that honourable labour as their life-work, that they might learn in how great a spirit it may be pursued".[107] When he described Macdonell's characteristics, the first he would not have applied to himself: "The work in which his strength was spent was the work of his choice".[108] However, subsequent traits could have been applied to the biographer as readily as his subject could – though, of course, what qualities were inherently true of him and what he took on board from his study as a master of good practice is impossible to say, only speculate.

> Of old friends, he kept tenacious hold: he prized especially the affection of his relatives, without which, he said, life would be poor and weary.... He was a born journalist. First among his qualifications, we reckon his natural communicativeness with the pen.... The characteristic which most helped to secure for him his rapid success in journalism was his special knowledge. He perceived very early that nothing could be done in that profession by a man who possessed merely the average knowledge of a subscriber to a daily paper... he made a study of special subjects... to this store of knowledge he was continually adding.... This consciousness of power gave his articles a ringing clearness, a genial freedom, a confident mastery of tone, which carried his readers away.[109]

Punch reviewed WRN's book: "It is what it professes to be, the life of a journalist – 'perhaps' he claims, 'the only life of a journalist pure and simple ever written'. The materials are arranged with great skill and the story is told with simplicity of style, which seems so easy till you try to reproduce it."[110] This piece of work encapsulated WRN's method of working – he had found his example of good practise and was determined to learn and emulate all the best practical lessons.

In November 1889, William Elmslie died, and WRN felt constrained to collaborate with A.N. Macnicol to bring out a biography.[111] Elmslie had written regularly for WRN's journals, and WRN had enjoyed his friendship and entertained high hopes for Elmslie's leadership potential amongst the Nonconformists. He empathised with Elmslie, who was frail in health and shared a similar vision about educating a new generation, particularly with regards to believing criticism. WRN most admired his preaching gifts:

> He loved preaching and freely accepted invitations to appear not only in the churches of his own denomination, but in other places, notably among the Congregationalists.... His great purpose was to write a book that should carry the message and meaning of the Old Testament to the people and for this much needed service no one perhaps was equally qualified.[112]

WRN was generous in his appreciation: "the advantage of personal intercourse with him was unspeakable. I have never learned so much from any other human being."[113] This was very much a tribute to a friend, "a perfect picture of the man and his life-work",[114] but it was another sad loss for WRN. He was conscious that though well-received, this study was rushed. With this in mind, he later republished the biographical material without Elmslie's sermons and addresses,[115] instead adding materials from friends, who wrote their appreciations in the *British Weekly*. WRN always tried to capture as full a picture of an individual as possible, and it was with the second edition that WRN felt satisfied.

Over the next twenty years, there were no substantial books of biography from WRN. His time was occupied with his many projects, but he always continued to read biography and give his readers the benefits of his studies. He took special care when he covered the death of some notable person, and the *British Weekly*'s Memorial Issues became an expected feature, satisfying to WRN's biographical interests and, happily, also good for the circulation figures. The special issue covering the death of Spurgeon[116] called for considerable reprinting to cope with the demand. WRN's contribution was the leader, which headed up the tributes, together resulting in an issue to be kept and treasured by contemporaries and posterity. He had a special ability to say something not only worthwhile, but also appreciative. He was always able to bring out an individual's unique contribution to life. Where the *British Weekly*'s Memorial Issues focussed upon the eminent of church and state, WRN included biographical studies of literary figures in the *Bookman*. Here he enlisted the help of G.K. Chesterton for a derivative series of *Bookman Booklets,* offering as his own single contribution a study of Robert Louis Stevenson.[117] More regularly, commemorations would consist of a memorial sketch composed by WRN himself, accompanying other appreciations of the individual and possibly some writings of that individual. He was called on to give his appreciation to many memorial productions, as well as his work in the *British Weekly*. Henry Drummond's *The Ideal Life* carried a memorial sketch,[118] as did *Hugh Price Hughes as We Knew Him*, in which WRN contributed a personal reminiscence. "Mr Hughes was among the kindest of the kind. He took frequent occasion to mention the paper in his addresses and in his own journal, and I have never ceased to be grateful".[119] Other admirable examples are his introduction to a life of John Clifford,[120] and the *Memoirs of the Late Dr Barnardo*.[121]

WRN's biographical skills were not employed solely in commemorating the lives of recently deceased luminaries. He called on his extensive knowledge of English Literature – and its authors – to write introductions to a number of editions of classic novels.[122] His projects in this realm were extremely varied; his name, for example, was given as the co-writer of *A History of English Literature*, although "The main part of this history has been done by Mr Thomas Seccombe".[123] This publication appeared to be an excuse to issue some very basic text with lavish photographic plates of portraits and illustrative paintings. To the production, WRN contributed his considerable editorial advice and literary expertise, but the most likely reason for his involvement was that his name was 'marketable' in matters literary. Biography and an appreciation of literature gave him the opportunity to contribute to the *Chamber's Cyclopaedia of English Literature* (1906), in which WRN wrote articles on the Brontë sisters and Thomas Hardy. Indeed, such was his recognised expertise that WRN's presence came to be felt throughout the industry. Darlow was to intimate later, that, "it is no secret that he contributed to the *Times* and to the *Times Literary Supplement*".[124]

Though celebrity begets the most successful and widely known of biographies, it has never been an art practiced exclusively in honour of the well-known. WRN's father died in 1891 and some years later he felt 'provoked' to write a brief appreciation of his father's life. He read Edmund Gosse's *Father and Son* (1907), sent to him by the author, and commented later to his wife that he felt that Gosse gave an "account of the severe religious training which his father subjected him to and which made him an infidel. It is well written and has moved me a good deal. I think I will write an article upon it describing my father's way with me as a contrast".[125] Increasingly, WRN felt that Gosse's book was an unmerciful attack[126] and an exposure of a 'puritan' upbringing for the gaze of sceptical minds. So in 1908 he published, *My Father: An Aberdeenshire Minister 1812-1891*, which was dedicated to Lord Rosebery, who had encouraged him to write. In the event, some of WRN's friends thought that he was far too kind to his father. However, he wanted to study "the religious and literary training in a puritan household of the strictest type",[127] and to show that, for him, there had been a very different outcome to that of Gosse. WRN describes his father with respect and warmth, but it is just a sketch of the man and contains little about their interaction. James Munson sums up what most readers have felt:

> Unfortunately this book has never had the appeal of Gosse's. It lacks the tension brought about by the growing conflict between two powerful personalities, one young, one old.... As an author, Nicoll was too detached and respectful. His is an affectionate memoir, not a penetrating story of a struggle which has an appeal to readers because it reminds them to some degree of similar struggles in their own lives.[128]

Annie Swan remembered; "I heard him say more than once that Gosse had been too ruthless in that revelation, that there had been too little tenderness and covering up".[129] WRN wrote a touching tribute to his father – that was how he wanted to remember him, and so he chose not to reveal any of his own personal thoughts.

As the years passed, more and more of WRN's friends would succumb to illness, leading to an ever-expanding body of biographical work. In addition to *My Father*, 1908 also saw WRN publish a biography of Ian Maclaren, entitled *Ian Maclaren: Life of the Rev. John Watson*, following his death. He wrote, "For the friendship with which he honoured me and for the love I bore him, I have done my best. There is nothing in this book that is not based on indisputable authority. I have thought it my duty to set him forth as he was, and to give his own views as nearly as possible in his own words."[130] WRN's biography was met with approval from friends and peers: "An ideal biography. No one else could have written it. Whilst recognising the lighter qualities of Ian Maclaren, paying full tribute to his ever-bubbling humour, Dr. Robertson Nicoll reaches down to the depths of a character that endeared Dr. Watson through a long succession of years to an overflowing church congregation."[Sefton Park, Liverpool][131] When another close friend, James Denney[132], died in 1917, WRN published a volume of his correspondence as *Letters of Principal James Denney to W. Robertson Nicoll*. This 'labour of love' sold well. WRN received a letter from a relative of Denney.

> You will understand that to me the letters themselves are the chief interest. They are so alive, so full of his prompt good sense, his honest wisdom that never required to wonder what he thought or how he should say it, that it is hard to believe he is not speaking or writing within our reach. This not without a touch of envy, I see from [them] how much of him I was shut out by my own defects of knowledge and character. That you were his intimate and trusted friend I always knew, but these letters have made me know more fully than before: they warm my heart towards you.[133]

George Adam Smith, a colleague and friend of Denney, sent an appreciation, "It is a work of real piety, and I thank God that our friend so fully opened his heart and his convictions and opinions to you, and that you have been moved to preserve his letters with such care, and now to let his friends and the public share them with you."[134] WRN sent copies of his books to friends and interested parties, and kept their letters and notes of appreciation. Alexander Whyte dashed off a typical pencil appreciation: "Your volume is an incomparable footnote to all of Denney's books. The long and deep sorts of all his life work are found...what a volume of truest criticism is here!... Penetrating, illuminating, radiating criticism".[135]

In 1921, Hodder & Stoughton published a volume for which WRN wrote the following preface: "Since the *British Weekly* was founded in 1886 I have been in the habit of writing tributes to notable figures in the Christian world. Out of a large number the present book has been made up."[136] The volume was *Princes of the Church,* a selection of his obituaries, which Jane Stoddart helped her ailing Editor select from amidst his considerable oeuvre. That WRN had amassed a large body of biographical work is inarguable, and that he wrote authoritatively, and with a personal sensitivity most prominent in the appreciations of those, he himself had known. Despite this closeness to his subjects however, he always maintained a detachment that enabled him to assess objectively an individual's life and work. His study of biography had taught him how to write meaningfully about someone's struggles and achievements. WRN's skill in the medium can be seen in this collection of distinct and appropriate tributes.

The 'Claudius Clear' Phenonenon

WRN wrote a great deal of biography, but he also developed his own column that gave full rein to his literary and biographical reading. The column began in the fifty-first issue of *British Weekly*. Jane Stoddart recalled the origins:

> When the idea occurred to him, he went to the British Museum to find a name. Searching in the obituary pages of the *European Magazine,* he came upon the life-record of one Claudius Clear, and chose this signature for the correspondence. His intention was not to write regularly, but to get friends to write to him … it was found difficult to keep this up, and for many years past the 'Claudius' letters have been written by Dr. Nicoll alone.[137]

WRN wrote under many other pseudonyms, but the 'Correspondence of Claudius Clear' became a literary phenomenon. He saw that there was a great interest in personal reflections in the manner of Oliver Wendell Holmes.[138] The column gave WRN the opportunity of covering many different aspects of life as they appealed to him. He could be light or heavy, humorous or serious, but as long as he was neither dull nor uninteresting, he could be sure of a band of devoted readers.

> Men professing no religious belief whatever will read these essays, especially when a solemn note is struck, who would not think of reading the front-page leaders? I believe they have guided many into sound lines of thought and have been a liberal education to others who have been familiarised with some of the best literature of the day through these columns. Decidedly, Claudius Clear is a personal force in journalism.[139]

Darlow described 'Claudius Clear' as showing WRN's 'broad humanist side', and it certainly was broad. It seemed that WRN could write on anything, taking after the vast range of Jonathan Swift:

> 'Claudius Clear' ranged over an immense variety of
> topics.... Nicoll's versatile mind found sermons in stones,
> tongues in trees, and copy in everything. A Proverb or a
> paradox, the home of some famous scholar or a weekend
> in some quaint country town, an article in some forgotten
> review, or a problem of everyday conduct, or the habits
> of a pet cat – they were grist to his mill ... often he would
> discourse about some writer, ancient or modern. But,
> with all his own ardour for reading, he was too vividly
> concerned with actual men and women ever to become
> bookish.[140]

WRN's reading and travels were prominent, and he wrote with the
homely style of a letter from a friend. "He contrived to make them
feel that they had always believed what he was telling them, though
they had never seen it put so well in print before. Pascal used to say
that the best books were the books which every man thought he could
have written for himself".[141] In his 'Claudius Clear' essays, he showed
a fertile mind, stored with the fruits of his wide reading in theology,
philosophy, literature, but mainly in biography. As he wrote to his friend
Rev. McRobbie, "You get all that I am thinking in my articles, and all
that I am doing in 'Claudius Clear'.[142] When the *British Weekly* took a
simple poll amongst its readers, to find the most popular regular item,
'Claudius Clear' won by a large majority.

Such was the popularity of 'Claudius Clear' that four collections of
articles were gathered and published: *Letters on Life* (1901) "Contains
a store of shrewd wisdom in regard to matters that we idly call
commonplace. Again and again, it touches the primary fibres of human
nature. It deals with those elemental axioms which govern men's daily
lives".[143] William Hale White wondered if it should be better entitled
'Letters *from* Life'. *The Day Book of Claudius Clear* (1905) "Is full
of 'humanities,' treated with real catholicity and expanse of view. It
included fine biographical tributes to men like George MacDonald, and
R.H. Hutton of the *Spectator*.... Best of all, however, are those papers
which deal with the conduct of life, written with benignant sagacity in a
style that fits the matter like a glove and often twinkles with humour".[144]
In *The Round of the Clock: The story of our lives from Year and Year*
(1910) WRN divided human living into five periods of existence, and
"illustrated from hundreds of well known persons the stages of experience
from childhood on to extreme old age. It is a survey of the milestones of
life".[145] *A Bookman's Letters* (1913) was a personal favourite of WRN's:

"I think the best of my 'Claudius Clear' articles were published in that volume."[146] Some pages are included from contributions to the *North American Review*, *Blackwood's Magazine*, and the *Contemporary Review*".[147] Darlow notes, "It consists of causeries about books and men, pervaded with the writer's wide knowledge and intimate sympathy. The sketches of Frederick Greenwood – 'the greatest journalist of our time' – and David Masson, and 'Mark Rutherford', are masterly studies in the psychology of men of letters."[148]

WRN kept all reviews of all his books and included in appreciations on his 'Claudius Clear' articles were those from America, such as, "These papers are the work of one who has a wide knowledge of literature, who can quote aptly from authors of the past who are forgotten, and writers of today who have barely emerged. Like every true moralist, he looks on the present in the light of the past, and is not seduced by the glitter of fair seeming into the laudation of men and events that his conscience condemns".[149] Another wrote,

> The writer has a comforting way of putting himself on the level with the reader who still has the hill of difficulty to climb and proffering suggestions out of his own abundant experiences. The preaching is uppermost in these essays, which is no charge against their excellence. Dr. Nicoll is a kind and helpful preacher to sit under. His freedom from cant, his literary knowledge and breadth of experience make these sermons on everyday ethics most pleasant reading.[150]

Readers appreciated WRN's style, and he struck a popular chord for his contemporaries:

> His is not a great, easy, and smiling spirit, but an alert, sure, and intent spirit. He jokes without difficulty, but never without purpose. His limitations are plain, but so, within them, is his power ... his counsels are for live men and women, whose capacity for being alive and useful he wishes to increase. Attention to life, interest in life, order and efficiency in life, are his ideals in these essays. He has gravel for the fool, the half-baked man, and the half-asleep man ... we can commend the book to anyone who wants a Monday morning moral shake-up. And who does not?[151]

WRN even brought out a series of 'Claudius Clear' entitled 'A Library for Five Pounds' which was serialised in the *British Weekly* for six weeks and brought out as a small book for reference purposes, for those serious about their reading. They, obviously, took at face value WRN's claim that "everyone who faithfully goes through these hundred books or so will be much more cultured, much better educated, than the vast majority of men and women".[152] Sadly, WRN's 'Claudius Clear' has proven with time to be only of passing worth, possibly because the style, though clear was stilted and easily dated and was not ranked amongst the great essayists. As a phenomenon of its time, however, the column stands as a valuable testament to the interests of author and readers alike.

In discussing WRN's cultural significance, one must begin by making a basic distinction between his impact in a broader sense, and the degree to which he achieved his more focussed goal of introducing a large amount of cultural capital into the otherwise empty world of the Nonconformist life. That WRN did succeed in making a significant contribution to the cultural attitudes within his readership is fairly clear, as testaments such as that of David Cairns suggest:

> Nicoll and the *British Weekly* did a lot for us younger people. It brought us into touch with a new world of current literature. Nicoll had an extraordinary knowledge of minor Victorian literature. He rarely entered into the world of the great masters. But he did know thoroughly all about the little fishes and the shallow waters of literature, especially of the Victorian age.... In short, Nicoll and his work brought a lot of life and interest into our leisure hours and helped to bring us all into the midstream of what was going on in the world.[153]

How far he played the role of propagator of culture in a wider sense, however, is a more complex issue. WRN's contribution to reading culture calls for reflection on the extent to which sales figures indicate quality literature. Good figures do not necessarily indicate good literature. He sometimes seemed to speak in terms of revenue from sales rather than the merits of the book. However, he knew that quality was not necessarily demonstrated by profitable sales, and often he was content with a popular 'good read', as, after all, he loved books.

In considering WRN's impact on the culture of popular reading, then, it helps to remember he thought of popularity as a legitimate goal. Darlow assessed WRN's contribution: "Nicoll exercised immense influence upon the development and expression of Evangelical religion during the last three decades [1890-1920], and it was an enlightening and humanizing influence … he quickened their desire to read, he guided inexperienced readers, he helped to popularise the best books".[154] John Clifford appreciated Nicoll's achievement: "His genius has worked and is working in the Free Churches of Britain and the world to secure 'a synthesis between Nonconformity and culture which refutes Matthew Arnold'. He won for it a high place in literature, broadened its sympathies with art and science, and made it a share in all the real wealth of the modern mind".[155] After WRN's death, a fellow journalist summed up the success of the *British Weekly*: "It has done great things, in uniting Nonconformity and culture; indeed, it is due in no mean degree to the *British Weekly* that Nonconformists are no longer looked upon as without the pale of serious thought and literature".[156]

These achievements could become ends in themselves, and certainly, there are clear signs that he could worship at the idol of popularity. Such a concern was never his exclusive objective, but to understand WRN in his role as arbiter of literary taste it is necessary to be aware of it. There was always much more to WRN, but the duelling purposes of his literary emphasis and fundamentally religious outlook could encourage a division in the minds of his audience. The educated and more literarily sophisticated lives which he encouraged amongst his readers seemed to move away from the important spiritual issues of religion to the degree that, in some circles, WRN could be viewed as having a 'secularising effect'. There seems to have been an unwitting tension between what WRN wanted to achieve – in his own mind, at least – and the popular secularisation of reading culture to which he contributed. There was a slow decline in the essential dynamic of personal living-faith commitment, both in wider society and within WRN's readership, and this was in spite of his own intended emphasis on this very thing. The truth is perhaps best seen in WRN's recommended novels, which not only prominently featured Nonconformity [Mark Rutherford] or the Free Church of Scotland [Kailyard School], but all were narrowly focussed upon the past, ignoring the present, and did not display the kind of atmosphere that would inspire excitement or even positive feelings about the Church and its future. For all his drive and perseverance, WRN's work and concern in maintaining orthodoxy in doctrinal belief and an awareness of personal commitment to the Christian Faith was undermined and negated by his commitment to cultural education and consumerism. This latter drive purveyed a more interesting realm of fantasy and fiction as an alternative to the strife-ridden world of theology and belief, a means of escape that proved, for many of his increasingly well-read audience, impossible to resist.

7

Preaching and Apologetics

Preaching was a lifelong fascination for WRN. From childhood he had wanted to be a popular preacher, and even after his forced career change and had come to London to pursue journalism, he never lost his interest in the calling, nor with the men who were exponents of it. Much of what he wrote was as both editor and minister, for the benefit of his fellow preachers and educated church members. He was anxious to do what he could to stimulate and help preachers, both his peers and the new generation who were coming through the colleges. WRN's lifetime saw the end of the age of Victorian Pulpiteers and as a transitional figure, he had warm memories of those giants of the pulpit, his heroes. He reminded his readers of the great preachers of the past, and yearned for a new generation of champions of the pulpit. His function as a preacher had been involuntarily forfeit in exchange for an editor's chair. WRN sought to maintain a role for himself in church life through advising others, establishing himself as an authority on the art of preaching. It is strange that T.H. Darlow's official biography of his friend, though thorough and admirable, failed to do WRN justice on this major element in his life. Darlow did show that he was not altogether ignorant of this side of WRN, mentioning preferences amongst the preachers, but an understanding of the scale of his fascination with preaching is vital in order to appreciate the man's motivation and the emphasis of so much of his work.[1]

WRN had many he regarded as his preaching heroes, as Darlow writes,

> For sheer, overpowering eloquence he placed Dr. Herber Evans[2] above every other preacher he had heard. But as a minister, to listen to regularly, he would have chosen Principal T.C. Edwards[3] ... to the end Nicoll persevered in his admiration for 'the rare mystical genius' of the Rev. S.A. Tipple[4] of Norwood. In 1912, he told a friend: "There

have been two men in my life whose preaching I could
have listened to twice every Sunday and these two were
Parker and Tipple. I did that with Tipple for years and I
never heard him preach a poor sermon".[5]

However, this was as far as Darlow explored WRN's interest in
preaching.

WRN developed his shrewd skill in analysing sermons from an early
age, recalling enough of his father's approach to his pulpit ministry so
as to analyse it,

Though he spent much time and pains on his sermons,
he did not cut a channel between them and his reading.
This was partly due to his theory of preaching. He never
told anecdotes, very rarely used illustrations, and made
it a principle never to employ the first personal pronoun
or to relate any experiences of his own. He had no poetic
quotations, and he abhorred perorations. His sermons were
clear, able, and deeply reverent expositions of Evangelical
theology.[6]

WRN's own style was very different, but in the essential seriousness
of preaching and its great responsibility – father and son were at one.
When WRN began his ministerial career, he looked before all else to
Spurgeon, studying and emulating his concentration on expository
preaching and tendency to focus upon expounding and applying the
text of the Scriptures. This influence is particularly visible in some
cards of his original Dufftown sermons which remain in the collection
of his papers now held at Aberdeen University.[7] The brevity of these
cards, a testimony to Spurgeon's influence, is itself indicative of WRN's
preaching style – though he prepared his sermons by writing out a full
outline, all he took into the pulpit were one or two postcards.[8] At this
stage, WRN was against taking any detailed set of notes with him. The
strategy clearly worked, giving him considerable freedom in his delivery
so that he acquired something of a reputation as a popular preacher.[9]

From the late 1870s, WRN rarely allowed his work in the realm
of preaching and the study thereof to lapse. In 1877, he published a
short collection of his sermons, entitled *Calls to Christ*, and in 1878,
honed his analytical skills by writing an extended review of 'The Yale
Lectures on Preaching'. He was thorough in his appraisal, beginning
with the contributions of Henry Ward Beecher:[10] "They are in many
respects incomparably the most important contribution ever made to
homiletics. In matters of detail they are less valuable than many, the

author's individuality being far too pronounced to render his experience a safe guide for ordinary men".[11] For another American preacher, Phillips Brooks,[12] WRN had sustained praise, "His lectures form a permanent and precious addition to the best literature of the subject.... [W]e miss in them the fullness and frankness of self revelation which we find in other volumes; but a nature so rare and fine as Mr. Brooks' must almost of necessity be shrinking; and there a charm in his reluctant shy confessions which we do not find in the more ample and candid disclosures of the others".[13] However, a book by R.W. Dale was given a detailed and critical scrutiny. Dale's style,

> Has all the merits and the vices of the popular lecturer; and vices are more conspicuous in this volume on preaching than in any of his other works ... it will hardly be believed by those who have not examined the book, how much of it is written in [a] thoroughly vicious style of distressing amplification. At least one-half of it might be cancelled without being missed, and a considerable portion of the other half might have been much more briefly and directly expressed.... Still the book is frank and honest; it is a distinct gain to have read it; but more was to be expected of Mr. Dale.[14]

That this was WRN's comment on Dale's lectures speaks to the sometimes merciless severity of his critical eye, however, when he came south to England it was Dale's thinking on progressive liberal evangelicalism that he was to expound in his journals.

This early experience with criticism highlighted for WRN precisely what he felt was central to the preacher's art. He soon launched into an extended discussion about the importance of extemporary preaching. For him, at this stage in his career, extemporary preaching was the true and natural method of preaching. "It is only in extempore speech that the highest exaltations of the mind can be reached. The stimulus of audience raises a man to points of vision and power never to be reached in the still air of the study".[15] To place too much weight on WRN's preference would, however, ignore the fact that, coming from the Highlands and having had his early ministry experience in Dufftown, WRN inevitably identified with the Highland stance that a discerning sign of spiritual maturity in a preacher was to preach without notes. Though WRN's early tendency to preach from a brief outline evolved following his move south to Kelso to the use of a complete manuscript, he always retained a preference and admiration for those who preached without notes.

> Extempore preaching admits of at least as much preparation
> as the other kind, though not in the same way. Any one,
> who adopts the method from laziness, is not fit for the
> work of the Kingdom of God. Allied is another objection
> that the language of unread preaching does not admit of the
> same polish as that which can be given to a manuscript....
> It is unquestionable that a man is surer of doing uniform
> justice to his reputation by reading than by speaking. But,
> whilst this is true, it is also true that a man rarely can reach
> the highest point of efficiency by reading.... The power
> of extempore speech seems to such to be a gift bestowed
> upon few, and to be used by them thankfully, but not an art
> to be acquired by study. The most determined advocate of
> speaking, as distinguished from reading, will admit that a
> very large class are constitutionally best fitted for reading,
> and could never by any process of training become expert
> in the other manner.[16]

His critique showed promise, and demonstrated that he had a clear idea
of what qualities he admired in the effective preaching of others.

WRN's earliest books were mainly concerned with his preaching,
but from the time of his resignation in 1886, his priority was learning
about journalism and establishing his new career and periodicals. A
change of life circumstances, however, does not necessarily indicate a
complete reversal of interests – immediately following his illness and
move to England, he edited a series of theological books on preaching
and ministry.[17] The series was aimed at providing practical assistance to
preachers – an unsurprising subject, given that the first editions, such as
The Clerical Library, were begun before leaving Scotland. This early
editorial project was a strikingly appropriate bridge for the still young
WRN, linking a life he'd been forced to leave with that he'd stumbled
into not only thematically, but in practical terms – it was during work
on *The Clerical Library* that Jane Stoddart, WRN's stalwart assistant
editor through the remainder of his life, was first brought onboard.

WRN wrote as a minister to encourage other ministers. An early
example was 'Is Preaching Doomed?' in which he struck a forthright
note: "We hope much that passes for preaching *is* doomed. By this, we
mean not only the philosophising on one's own account, which often
usurps the name, but all preaching, however orthodox, that is slovenly
and unstudied. Preaching must interest hearers, or it will certainly go".[18]
Then he counselled,

> No rule is without exception, but is it not almost universally true that effective preachers have been men of wide reading? We do not mean scholarship. We refer to English Literature … the preacher need never fear to appeal to the interest of his hearers in the Bible and the profound reverence and belief with which they regard it … No! Preaching is not doomed ... not until men are transformed and the earth empty; not until then will the work of the Christian ministry cease.[19]

It was quite apparent that the preacher in him was alive and active when the subject featured in a further two articles in 1888: "We propose a brief survey of the present-day pulpit, dealing now with preachers who are in full maturity and fame." The following week, he continued his brief survey.

> We fully believe that a host of men are rising to maintain and extend the sway of the British pulpit, but of necessity many of these are unknown, and the more prominent have yet so much of their careers before them that criticism is dangerous and inexpedient.… [B]ut we have room only to point out that all these know that Christianity is nothing if it does not lift from off the ground – if it does not save men from sin and raise them into holiness.[20]

His emphasis was emphatically on an Evangelical transformation of lives and WRN displayed his capacity to appraise preachers, and succeeded in conveying his genuine sympathy and concern for his colleagues in ministry. At the same time, his general readers felt that they were being kept in touch with progress in the wider church scene.

WRN gained such good feedback from his readers that he was encouraged to publish selections of his leading articles. Though strictly speaking these newspaper articles were not sermons, since he usually dictated them, they certainly had a sermonic style and flavour. This 'preaching' style contrasted with his more intimate and personal approach for his literary essays such as 'Claudius Clear'. Nothing of WRN's was entirely divorced from his deep interest in the preaching arts, however – it was in this latter column that WRN drew attention to his favourite preachers and their preaching, such as S.A. Tipple of the Central Hill Baptist Church, Upper Norwood.[21] In writing to his friend M'Robbie, he simply stated, "He is a very venerable old man, and we like his preaching very much".[22] He had first written of Tipple when he disguised him under the name of 'Rev. Eli Julius':[23] "Mr. Julius never uses a note, is very simple and quiet in manner, has a sweet low voice, and allows the sermon itself to prescribe the manner of the delivery. He preaches short sermons, but, as he never says anything twice over, there is a great deal in them".[24] In a later article, WRN gave several quotations from Tipple's sermons, noting that

> Mr. Tipple's printed volumes convey no adequate impression of his power. This is always so, I suspect, when the preacher does not use manuscripts, and in his longest and most elaborate quotations to this day the preacher does not need so much as a word on paper. But that his printed sermons have always been fresh, thoughtful, and suggestive, the twelve printed in this little book abundantly prove.[25]

Tipple was hardly known for his Evangelical orthodoxy and yet the usually doctrinally astute WRN enjoyed his preaching. The contradiction is resolved when it is remembered that Tipple imbued the sermon with a sense of occasion, his flow of suggestive thoughts were most often of a literary nature *and* he preached extemporarily, which always drew WRN's admiration. Further, WRN loved finding and listening to speakers from the smaller chapels and denominations in England; to him they seemed to have life and conviction, but he was, and would remain, an 'establishment man' – wedded to his Free Church of Scotland.

WRN's love of preachers and preaching increasingly made him regret the passing of the age of the great preachers, though he remained convinced about the need and importance of preaching for the Church. Nevertheless, his literary and stylistic taste in sermons saw WRN develop a greater breadth and tolerance than might have been expected from his orthodox Evangelical pedigree. He, like many others, believed that Evangelicalism could and should come to terms with 'the mind of the modern age'. He affirmed that the position of 'believing critics' gave confidence to the preacher in his use of the Old Testament. The truth was that his published sermons and articles show that he had all but abandoned the Old Testament. For, far from 'believing criticism' giving him confidence, he personally hardly ever preached from the Old Testament, and if he did he did not expound, but used the text in a poetic or mystical way. A confirmation of this occurred when WRN preached at Viewforth Free Church, Edinburgh in October 1899 upon Isaiah 60:8, the sermon ultimately becoming the lead article in the *British Weekly*.[26] He saw his text from Isaiah as a 'motto' and spiritualised its meaning with no reference to the historical context of the prophet. The occasion was made even more interesting by the presence in the congregation of "Professor A.B. Davidson and the popular Wesleyan preacher, the Rev. George Jackson [both known for their acceptance of the critical views of the Old Testament]".[27] At the outset, WRN did not hide his intention and indicated the path of presentation for his sermon:

> I propose to say some simple things about the characteristics of the next revival of religion. Most of them apply to every revival of religion, for the Gospel does not change. But some are special. Let us take as a motto the beautiful questioning words in the Prophet Isaiah, "Who are these that fly as a cloud and as the doves to their windows?" … It would be absurd to dissect critically such a text as this. Poetry must be treated as poetry. The picture given to us is that of a multitude flying to their stronghold with a rush of glancing wings.[28]

Then using the picture of the dove returning to the ark in the account of Noah's ark, says that in the same way

> Do the Saints fly to the Wounds of Christ … to which they repair and where their peace is found… But the broad idea of the passage is unmistakable. It is of a great revival. It is not the language that any of us is talking at this moment; however, we may long to speak it. Rather do we say, how many pews are empty, how few conversions there are, how stinted is the growth of Christians, how little is given to the cause of Christ, how thankful we are if we can just hold our own.[29]

He then recalled the revivals of 1859 and 1874, and gave his points on the characteristics of 'the next revival'.[30] What the illustrious listeners in his congregation thought of the address is not known; it contained much that was memorable and stimulating, but this was no advertisement for confident preaching from the text of the Old Testament. This lack of assurance is discernable in his books. In 1894, WRN published *Ten-Minute Sermons*,[31] the title of which shows the way WRN constructed his works in a manner that supports the present writer's contention that he viewed himself as a preacher. Furthermore, in practising and becoming very proficient in the art of dictation, he ensured there was an oral element involved in the creation of his leading articles, albeit a rather tenuous one. The 'sermons', being essentially 'freestanding' or independent works, also provide progressive evidence of development in WRN's compositional style. Gradually he developed a more 'literary' approach, which meant that his addresses became more thematic than expositional, but with WRN 'old ways' could resurface – particularly his stated preference for expository preaching.[32] Moreover, the 'sermons' within the collection were not ordered in any way.

WRN constantly affirmed that in Evangelical preaching, there needed to be a lively awareness and experience of the personal presence of 'Living' Christ – this was, for him, the Gospel that the Church was privileged to proclaim to the nations. He therefore jealously guarded the approaches to the New Testament, particularly if there was any threat to its historical reliability. WRN believed, with others, that the work of the Cambridge Trio of theologians (Hort, Lightfoot and Westcott),[33] in their defence of the New Testament, would hold back much of the challenge from the extremes of the radical reconstructions of Christian theology and history coming from the continent.[34] They had endeavoured to defend the Christian castle's 'Keep' [the historicity of the New Testament documents and witness to the reality of Christ]. WRN had, of course, as other 'believing critics', conceded the outer walls and fortifications (the Old Testament), which meant that he was all the more determined to defend the Keep as inviolate. However, this was but a phase in the continuing conflict between traditional Christian orthodoxy expressed in the great creeds, and the inquiring pressure coming from the university colleges (of Germany in particular). For a time their stance on Scripture seemed, to the 'believing critics', the sensible and only realistic course of action to be propagated for the maintenance of credible and tenable Christianity. This was certainly how WRN liked to see himself.

WRN's editorial apologetic for the preacher's 'living message of the Gospel' was influenced by the views of Robert W. Dale.[35] Dale was regarded by many of his contemporaries, not only as a successful minister of Carr's Lane, Birmingham, but also as a progressive thinker who sought to develop, even reconstruct, Nonconformist Evangelical thinking. Dale led by example, not only through his involvement in Liberal politics, but also in some of his theological reassessments. WRN appreciated Dale's approach, as shown in his writings, and he made use of and even propagated Dale's views. WRN did not know Dale personally, but Dale appreciated his paper. On occasions, Dale either wrote or was the subject of several leading articles such as 'Dr. Dale's Theological System'[36] and 'Dale on Calvinism'.[37] He was also included in the 'Teachers of Young Men' series, where Dale's sermons are described:

> For sonorous and lofty rhetoric, there are no sermons in our time equal [to] Dr. Dale's.... Dr. Dale has no uncertainties.

Robert William Dale

He scorns the attitude of the halting apologist. His thoughts move as in a triumphal march. Like Bossuet, he is a preacher for the thoughtful. Those who listen to sermons with their minds only half awake will think him difficult and perhaps too long ... he scorns the suggestion that religious worship can be divorced from the intellect ... he will take infinite trouble that no hearer shall miss his meaning ... his preaching ranges exclusively among great themes.[38]

WRN was anxious that the *British Weekly* was seen to reflect Dale, as one of the leaders of progressive thinking amongst Nonconformists.

When Dale died in 1895, WRN wrote,

> He had borne the brunt of the controversies … he saw
> what was coming, and he steadily endeavoured to place
> Christianity beyond the reach of all such assaults. To show
> that the Christian religion cannot be judged from any
> standpoint but its own and that all true theology must in
> the end be the interpretation of the truths revealed in the
> experience of believers living and departed.[39]

He followed Dale in making concessions to the 'modern mind',
although he did not always agree with everything Dale advocated.[40] One
particular agreement and point of concurrence between them, however,
was the acceptance of the Bible as 'fallible'. In 1890, Dale published
The Living Christ and the Four Gospels, and his son wrote

> His contention was that faith in Christ is trust in a person,
> not belief in a book. That we believe in Christ, not because
> we believe the Bible to be supernaturally inspired, but
> that we believe in the inspiration of Scripture because we
> believe in Him. That the ultimate foundation of faith is
> personal knowledge of Christ, and its originating cause
> the personal testimony of those who in our own time and
> before it have trusted in Christ and have found their faith
> verified in spiritual experience.[41]

Dale tried to combat what he saw as a tendency to set the Bible in
the place of the Living Christ. He had maintained this stance for over
twenty years and he appreciated that WRN was on his wavelength,[42]
and, in turn, WRN thought that Dale's approach was right for the
contemporary situation. Dale had sought to steady the 'ship of faith':
"Uncertainty with regard to the authorship of the Four Gospels,
uncertainty with regard to the dates at which they were written, is
not to be regarded as the sign of faltering faith in Christ".[43] Dale
set a basis for faith that was not dependent on the scholars' latest
thinking. Many grabbed at this seeming safe haven in the reality of an
individual's experience of Christ, but others felt a problem in basing
their sense of certainty, or assurance of faith, on a felt, subjective
experience. Moreover, that experience was itself increasingly seen as
dependent on the very 'faulty' Scriptures, which revealed that there
was an experience to be had.

The problem was that WRN and Dale, with others, were endeavouring to change the image of the Nonconformist Churches, but

without the help of firm ground upon which to build. Instead they faced a landscape where the distinguishing marks of biblical certainty were becoming less and less easy to determine. Their motive was to help, but their achievement was to add to the confusion and difficulties, for many people were not able to discern the reliability of the Faith. In the end,

> Dale bequeathed no theological school, nor did he leave behind him a group of disciples. His theology, more a mixture than a synthesis of old and new elements lacked a strong unifying theme to act as a handle by which contemporaries and posterity could grasp it.... In his theology Dale engaged valiantly with the difficult problems of the century but failed to blaze a trail through them: never thus succeeding in becoming a theological leader.[44]

WRN consciously chose to popularise many of Dale's views for he valued and admired a hero and regretted his passing,[45] but Dale was not ultimately the reliable or successful guide that he had hoped.

A Return to the Pulpit

It was in 1896, two years after the publication of *Ten-Minute Sermons*, that WRN made his return to the realm of public speaking with his first preaching and lecturing engagements since 1885. This change of situation was reflected in his next collection of sermons and articles, *The Return to the Cross*.[46] These addresses were, most often, delivered in theological colleges or church anniversaries. His interest in theological issues and the equipping of the next generation of preachers for their work was a concern, was one which continued to be his emphasis throughout the period. One of the addresses was given on his tour of America in 1896,[47] where WRN had felt encouraged and strong enough to do more public speaking at home. He responded to invitations to speak and his addresses to colleges show a high level of theological content that would be appreciated by the staff, if not by all the students. In one article 'The Wisdom of God in a Mystery', WRN draws attention to the usefulness is of Christian Mysticism, which had become a recurring theme.[48] This emphasis was also noted in an address given at Bala Theological College,

> It is the union between man and Christ that makes Christ the propitiation, and without such a union we could not have the remission of sins. It is also through this union with Christ that we attain his likeness. ... It is not on our

own resources, enriched as they may be through divine
grace, that we rely, it is a deeper depth; a depth to express
which language is taxed and exhausted.[49]

WRN's unashamed orthodox Evangelicalism was observed by his
Northern friends:

> It is not a volume of sermons, but it contains more vital
> theological teaching than the majority of modern sermons.
> It is more than a mere volume of essays, though it has
> much of grace and charm of the true essay. It has in
> addition much matter calculated to make men think on the
> highest subjects, much that will linger in the memory and
> influence the life ... if we go to church to hear sermons,
> then the sermons must be worth hearing and where they
> are not we are absolved.[50]

WRN's next project was *The Clerical Life – a Series of Letters to
Ministers*,[51] a composite book, with each chapter discussing particular
questions about church life. Its topics and styles were mixed; some of the
articles were humorous, but all had serious concerns to bring out. WRN
used them to good effect in the *British Weekly* and then edited them into a
book.[52] The writers wrote in an accessible, popular style as they enjoyed
their topics, which ranged over different aspects of church life. Wit and
insights abounded: "However much we may bewail it, it cannot be denied
that this age is not favourable to the making of great preachers. It produces
critics and criticism; honest thought it may-be means doubt, but preaching
implies faith. The great critic is seldom if ever a great preacher, at least,
not before he wins his way into the light."[53] WRN wanted to instruct and
inform, but chiefly to stimulate the next generation of preachers.

Around 1900, WRN became alarmed by published statements about
the reliability and trustworthiness of the New Testament. He saw works
like A.B. Bruce's sceptical comments in *The Encyclopaedia Biblica*
and then James Moffatt's *The Historical New Testament* dropped onto
his desk. WRN thought highly of Moffatt's abilities and saw him as
representative of the next generation, but his book distressed WRN due
to the number of concessions being made to sceptical criticism. He was
even critical of Denney: "Now, if you professors think that Christianity
or the Church will survive in any form after these admissions, you are
entirely mistaken. The Old Testament business is ... different [to] the
New Testament. The historical Jesus Christ is the article of a standing
or falling Christianity".[54] The degree of WRN's concern is measured
by the fact that ordinarily he had the same veneration as his father for

'scholarship'. He was a conservative, cautious liberal and this produced tensions, but he was determined to maintain his Evangelical belief that there was a vital core of Gospel truth which needed defending.

WRN believed that good preaching was based on the 'verities' [certainties] of the Gospel, and saw that advanced scepticism on the reliability of the New Testament endangered the necessary Gospel confidence. Interestingly, sometimes the tension between his conservative theological 'heart' and his progressive, believing-critical 'head' is seen in his correspondence. On one occasion, he wrote to the Primitive Methodist scholar, A.S. Peake: "Some questions are closed, else how can we be set for the defence of the Gospel? We are not set for the provisional acceptance of certain views and the candid consideration of everything urged against them. I see many things that more or less disquiet me".[55] Another time, he wrote to Peake, "I think criticism very dangerous unless it is accompanied by a strong and positive element of teaching".[56] WRN developed his own line in Apologetics and used what knowledge and skills he had to defend the Gospel. Again he wrote to Peake,

> I am convinced of the truth of the analysis of the Pentateuch by the converging lines of evidence. ... I am also nearly convinced that Wellhausen is right ... though I easily perceive difficulties. Of course I am not speaking from the standpoint of an expert ... but I have followed the controversy more or less closely through many years.[57]

WRN was cautious of venturing into print, for he did not want to be 'shot out of the water', which had been the lot of others. As he reflected, certain lines of thought had developed and he discussed these with his circle of friends and colleagues. He wrote to Peake,

> What I am trying to make out is that there may be a consensus of critics, and a rightful consensus of critics.... [T]hat until the materials are complete it may very well turn out that the critics are all wrong, not because they are dishonest or stupid, but because the case is not fully before them. This will not go very far in answering the case about the Pentateuch, but I feel sure it would throw into doubt a great many confident conclusions as to other parts of Scripture.[58]

WRN was seeking to hold the tiller of the Nonconformist Church steady in the choppy waters of controversy and avoid the rocks of 'obscurantism' and the sceptical conclusions of advanced critics. He always appeared orthodox and conservative, even when he was allowing his paper's columns to inform about the latest theories. WRN tried to hold the divergent views together in his own mind, and also saw this as the breadth and scope of the readership of his journals, which he wished to keep. He genuinely held the intermediate position as his own personal stance and recommended it to other preachers, yet at the same time he exhorted them to preach with the old certainty and confidence in the Gospel.

WRN's Defence of the New Testament

WRN's apologetic concerns came to a crisis in 1901 when he wrote a series of articles for the *British Weekly*, later collected as a book in *The Church's One Foundation*. These pieces sought to defend the historical integrity of the New Testament. His main approach was summed up by his title page quotation from Robertson Smith: "There is in the Bible above all the personal Christ, a personality which men could not have imagined; a personality which must be historical and which must be divine".[59] WRN worked avowedly to produce a popular book that would be accessible to the plain man. The questions he would discuss were 'too important to be left to the experts', for they concerned the very existence of the Church. "The critics have to be met. If they are not frankly encountered, the door of faith will be closed on multitudes".[60] He was out to write a popular treatment, as an editor and journalist, though he was looking over his shoulder at his 'scholarly' friends. His introduction was a call to arms, for the need to defend the historical integrity of the New Testament:

> The battle turns on their truth or falsehood. It does not turn on the inerrancy of the Gospel narrative. It does not turn even on the authorship of the gospels. Faith is not belief in a book, but a belief in a living Christ. If there is no living Christ to trust to, Christianity passes into mist and goes down the wind.[61]

The substance of the book could be said to be a series of robust comments on different spokesmen who were negative in their criticisms and in WRN's estimation were undermining the truth of the Gospels. His treatment is necessarily episodic (they were successive articles); however he does marshal his material as an apologetic contribution, fending off the attacks of extreme sceptics on Biblical Christianity. From the outset, WRN grappled with some of the modern protagonists of the conflict. He wrote of his reluctance to engage in criticism because both T.K. Cheyne[62] and A.B. Bruce[63] had written good things in the past, but now he accused them of being deniers of miracles and the supernatural. He was less severe with James Moffatt, but noted that he seemed to adopt positions that lead to naturalism, as he 'dropped vitriol on the pages of the New Testament'. WRN's style was denunciatory and generalised and motivated to avoid there being a repeat of the bitter struggle over the Old Testament.[64] He tended to illustrate his points by denouncing departures from the mainline positions of the traditional view of the New Testament. WRN did not explain his contentions in detail, but called the faithful to be aware and know what was at stake.

Believing that Christian believers should have a personal relationship with the historical Christ, WRN echoed the writings of Dale. He insisted that the New Testament account of the life of Christ retained its power, for in the eighteenth century when some 'learned' men had come to regard the testimony of the Gospel as wholly discredited, then an Evangelical revival had broken out and a new witness to the Gospel was declared to the world. WRN believed that, "The vast mass of Christians are unable to follow the arguments of scholars about early Christian history … nevertheless, their faith is not shaken by the varied assaults on the Christ of history because they know Christ by faith … knowing this, they do not become independent of the Gospel history. They do not set it aside. They do not say that inquiry as to its source and meaning is impiety".[65] WRN was affirming his conviction that the truth would triumph in the end, and the believers who knew the presence of Christ in their lives would be content that when criticism had stated its last word, the Gospels would have been found to preserve the true earthly history of Christ.

WRN looked at some 'primary assumptions', which he expected his readers to share. In particular, there was the question of miracles and the supernatural, for he maintained that if these are assumed incredible, then the whole Gospel history was incredible. Again, Robertson Smith is cited, writing about criticism of his own methodology: "if they could show that in any step of his argument he assumed the impossibility of the supernatural or rejected plain facts in the interests of rationalistic theories, he would frankly confess he was in the wrong".[66] WRN's point is that the 'Church's best apologists' had accepted the miraculous element "as the fit accompaniment of a religion that moves and satisfies the souls of men, and that asserts itself to be derived directly from God".[67] Something distinctively WRN comes out when he writes, "Mr Moffatt speaks contemptuously of 'amateur critics' who find great difficulty in following the conclusions of him and his school. We venture, however, to say with great respect that those who have studied the problems in English

Literature will be the first to hesitate as to the legitimacy and validity of the methods adopted by many Biblical critics".[68] WRN prided himself on being an informed 'amateur', who nevertheless had 'professional' knowledge of problems in English Literature – problems of a type that could require comparable skills as those needed for scriptural studies, and which he felt ought to make Biblical critics more cautious.

Further on WRN begins to examine the historical portrait of Jesus found in the Four Gospels. "Everyone is called to judge: the materials are accessible to all. What the experts possess in addition to what people possess is of comparatively small account. Experts may wait for the latest paper-covered book from Germany ... which is going to make a complete end of historical Christianity".[69] He appealed to "unbiased readers of the Gospel" to consider "the wonderfulness and originality of the character of Christ",[70] but he does not examine in any detail the particular challenges being made by the critics. One of WRN's main concerns was 'The Sinlessness of Christ': "Was our Lord without sin, as He claimed and His apostles testified, as the Church has believed".[71] Here his thrust was that, "One thing at least is certain, that a sinner cannot save sinners. The Gospel for mankind is not merely a recovery of man from his moral weakness, but a deliverance of man from his guilt. Till the consciousness of sin and guilt is present in the heart, much in the revelation of Christ will remain inexplicable".[72] Here, clearly, the 'preacher' asserts his view with the emotional warmth of an Evangelical doctrinal declaration, rather than producing a strong and persuasive counter argument.

WRN was orthodox in his affirmation of the historical reality of the Resurrection; to put it simply, for him this was the bed-rock of what he understood as New Testament Christianity. Then, WRN returns to the witness of the reality of Christianity from the 'living experience of Christ'. "The experience of Christ's delivering power in the soul is more than sufficient for all who know it.... [Yet] experience ... is no argument for the outsider, but if the transforming power of Christ manifests itself in outward action, the outward result can be stated as a proof. The phenomena of Christianity are not hidden from the world".[73] He cites 'the long-roll of Christ's captives' from Augustine to Bunyan, and Thomas Scott and claimed that each conversion was the consciousness of a vision of Christ and with it a revelation of His love. This, he maintained, was the sign that the supernatural is the native air of Christianity, and that Christianity is primarily a converting and sanctifying force. Though the book consisted of ten chapters, it is best to view the first nine as a progressive, largely cohesive argument, and then the remaining chapter was an added exhortation. Read in their original, discrete form, the articles felt disjointed – they needed to come to more of a conclusion than just an exhortation to be faithful, however legitimate the historical critique. Once collated into book form, however, their nature changed. There were repetitions, which showed clearly the chapters' origins as a sequential series of *British Weekly* pieces, essentially unedited between their appearance there and their collation into book form, but WRN's concerns were strong, and he wrote with skill and conviction. He concluded chapter nine positively and with a rallying call to his readers:

> It has been a great refreshment and reinvigoration of faith to spend so much time as we have done with the great champions of unbelief. Christianity has never appeared more wonderful than in the light cast upon it by those who cannot receive it because they cannot receive the supernatural, and therefore begin with an assumption, which makes faith impossible.[74]

The tenth chapter stands in some contrast to the rest of the book. Where the first nine chapters present an interesting critical analysis of the historical basis for Christianity, here WRN presented an exhortation to guard and keep the old faith: "What right have we to think we can keep it if we do not live in communion with God, his Word, and His saints?"[75] Typically WRN ends with a flourish, "It is the duty of spiritual guides to know the difficulties of their time, that they may help others, but for themselves they should seek to die as deaf to the reviling and mocking around them as Christ was when he sank to His last sleep on the Cross".[76]

The book probably read better as articles in the *British Weekly* than as an apologetic statement. It was a highly subjective way of arguing and depended on the reader having the same experience and interpreting the wider testimony of the Church at large in the same way as the author. Articles can catch a reflection of a moment and move on, whereas a book should trawl at a deeper level with a greater emphasis on the quality of reflection. WRN's approach was a series of 'exercises in caution', for in no way did he seek to defend the truth of New Testament Christianity based on the text of Scripture. Most of the book is the well-tried format of presenting the need for the integrity of the experience of Christ at conversion and in the Christian walk, with just that hint of the mystical that WRN was increasingly anxious to commend. The fact that both the theology and the experience which he proclaimed were inevitably based on the trustworthiness of the Scriptures did not come within his view. Nothing pleased WRN better than to bring out the relations and reactions between the authors of different periods, whether they dealt with morals, poetry, metaphysics, romance, devotion, dogmatic belief and to show how each author in turn had been infected, coloured and moulded by other writers. Looking back on WRN's work one finds it both idiosyncratic and at times eccentric, but he wrote as he saw things – that is, in the way he felt would convince himself and his general readership. Yet surprisingly, he gives several footnotes quotes in Greek, Latin and German, all without translation, a gesture that could hardly have been aimed at an average audience. Was there an element of ostentation? Did WRN want to appear scholarly? Was he looking for approval from 'experts'? Certainly, this would have detracted from the power of its effectiveness for his 'ordinary readers'.

Whatever the purpose of the erudite notes, with the strength of the on-form publishing machinery of Hodder & Stoughton behind it, many spoke of the book's usefulness. Whatever its popularity, however, it had been an exercise of trying to hold back a flood, and in the end amounted to only a barrier of sand. Despite the general trend of academia and public interest alike, however, WRN was not to be ruffled. Ever maintaining his reassured editorial stance, he declared, yet again, that in his view the situation was not cause for alarm: "The living interest in the Bible steadily grows ... there never perhaps was a more extended appreciation of the moral power and spiritual value of Christianity. There never was a greater yearning after its succours. For Christianity no substitute, ethical or other, has been discovered".[77] This conclusion was from WRN's overview of the theological scene during his tenure in the editorial chair of the *Expositor* in 1906. He considered that in 1885, most British scholars rested securely in a conservative view of the New Testament. WRN fought hard to maintain the historical reliability of the New Testament, but he had already conceded significantly on his doctrine of Scripture. Many bought into his position and hoped that he was right, and that this much orthodoxy was defensible. However, more extreme liberal views asserted that his position was an impossible 'staging post' to hold and defend. While others affirmed the restating of orthodox doctrine, they also felt that there was an undermining of the Evangelical doctrine of Scripture, and so, in their view, the strength and vigour of Christianity itself was compromised.

WRN himself, continued to preach with certainty and conviction, urging ministers to be gripped by the importance of preaching. An example of his emphasis was seen at Bloomsbury Chapel at the closing session of the Baptist Union Assembly in 1899.

> If you will forgive a personal reference, I have been made
> increasingly to feel that ministers do not sufficiently believe
> in the power of preaching. So little is said about sermons. A
> man may pour out his heart's blood for years and practically
> hear nothing of it. He is tempted to conclude that he will
> do his best work in visitation and in organising. It is not so,
> believe me. Though hearers say little, they feel much. Those
> who have to fight a hard battle through the week come to
> church on Sunday starving for the Bread of Life. It affects
> all the week to come if they miss it. If they are fed they do
> their work more easily, more happily, more bravely.[78]

However, it was 'Bread' from a flawed source, for although WRN exhorted
preachers and his listeners to read their Bibles,[79] he seemed, despite the
great efforts expended in producing *The Church's One Foundation* and
similar works, to be unaware of a credibility gap that had opened up
between the need for certainty in preaching and confidence in the basis of
it – the Scriptures. John Clifford summed up WRN's contribution:

> Gripping with the utmost firmness the evangelicalism
> of the New Testament he aided in liberating the soul of
> the Free Churches from the inherited prejudices of the
> past, pioneered its acceptance of the established results
> of investigation into the origin and up building of the
> structure of Holy Scripture. In that necessary task Sir
> William gave most invaluable aid … translating the truth
> in the older theologies into the living language of the hour
> and illustrating his teaching from the marvellous stores he
> carried of the literature of the world.[80]

In the light of posterity, neither Clifford nor WRN proved altogether
satisfactory pilots in the troubled waters of turbulent ideas, for their
approach did not succeed in defending historical confidence in the Bible,
rather they promoted a liberal approach, which damaged the engine of
the ship of faith by weakening confidence in the Scriptures – the source
of spiritual power for the Church.

Christian Mysticism

WRN regarded Christian Mysticism as a helpful way of enabling
the contemporary church to handle its doubts over the doctrine of
Scripture, and, furthermore, mysticism was in his genes. As Lady
Nicoll remembered, "My husband would give utterance to some

thought in his mind, as if thinking aloud ... I remember so well driving
through Bordighera once when, where that beautiful range of snow
peaks comes into view, he suddenly exclaimed in tense, earnest tones –
'Behold, I stand at the door and knock: If any man hear my voice, and
open the door, I will come in to him and will sup with him, and he with
me.' They are at supper within; they are making so much noise they
don't hear Him. – He is knocking at these big hotels – at Monte Carlo
– they are so busy they don't hear. He is not knocking at the solitary
places – the people living lonely solitary lives can hear Him. To how
few people do we 'open the door ... He will be our guest and we shall
be His' ...It was spoken so expressively in his gentle flexible voice,
as an unquestioned reality."[81] WRN wrote about his father, reading
"Upham's [Life of] *Madame Guyon* to his young wife when she was
dying and she liked nothing so well".[82] WRN always maintained that
he was a Christian Mystic[83] and that his excursions were always in a
Christian frame of reference.

Mysticism implied the possibility of an immediate personal
intercourse between the human soul and the Divine Spirit, but for WRN
it sharpened his focus on the need for the individual to have a personal
experience of the Living Christ and saw it as the way of increasing the
believer's sense of certainty. He wrote, "In the first place, mysticism
teaches the entire dependence of the spirit of man on the Spirit of
God ... the mystics teach that delight in God is the happiness of life.
In manifold forms they proclaim that all the happiness or misery of all
creatures consists only in this, that they are more or less possessed of
God ... the object of mysticism is indeed a closer union with the divine".[84]
Interestingly, WRN always denied being a true mystic and confessed,
"I am merely an amateur in the subject",[85] and he preferred to maintain
that he was 'mystically inclined'. He had some strong reservations
about 'mysticism' in general and none as strong as over the place given
to the atonement. Then there was his concern as to whether mysticism
was practical; for example, "It is not clear in what sense the mystic
believes in the specific answer to specific petition. Is it that the mystic
gains such an insight into the mind of God that he offers prayer and
supplication for what God desires to give and will give in His time"?[86]
WRN regarded mysticism as a needed tool, or helpful attitude in the
present crisis over the Bible: "The higher critic seems to the orthodox
to destroy the authority of the Holy Scripture, and in many cases he
himself believes he has done so. But I think the Christian mystic would
smile at this. He would be neither on the one side nor on the other; or
perhaps he might be on both sides."[87] He was fundamentally opposed to

any form of sectarianism and his mystical emphasis underlined the fact. As Darlow recorded,

> "Once when he heard religious men of a very different school sharply criticized, he quietly quoted the words, 'He appeared unto them in another form.' He realised the immense orthodoxy, which underlies all our differences. He claimed and cherished his fellowship with Christians to whom he stood in acute ecclesiastical opposition".[88]

WRN regarded Christian mysticism as strengthening the Evangelical assurance in a personal awareness of Jesus Christ as Saviour and Lord, and therefore this was important for preachers of the gospel.

WRN was far from the only adherent of Christian mysticism at the turn of the century. He was, however, discriminating on the topic of fellow thinkers and writers, finding some useful, but criticising others. He found Robert Vaughan's *Hours with the Mystics,* is an extraordinary achievement but the writer unsympathetic, even hostile. His position may be judged by his definition of mysticism: "Mysticism is that form of error which mistakes for divine manifestation the operations of a merely human faculty".[89] Even Dean Inge's Bampton Lectures were censured as "less unfriendly, but the tone is vigilantly critical throughout". One writer that WRN approved of and appreciated was Dora Greenwell.[90] Darlow notes carefully that WRN's own spiritual meditations were written with a poetic fervour of phrasing, and not only was this impassioned religious writing "a new thing in journalism", but that he "seems to have learned it from Dora Greenwell.... Both for matter and manner [he] set her far above the other Englishwomen who ventured to deal with the deep things of God".[91] WRN not only delighted in her books, but also considered that he had learnt more theology from Dora Greenwell than from any other teacher. He believed that the mystery of union with Christ was the ultimate mystery and experience of the Christian Faith. WRN doubted whether this highest spiritual truth could be ever expressed in words, "just as it has been said that the most poetical region of all is that which is incapable of taking the poetic form ... some things are impossible to utter, and other things it is unlawful to utter. Over such truths the Spirit wanders brooding till it becomes vocal, and that is the utterance we have from the mystics."[92] However, he found this approach helpful for coming to terms with the contemporary scene and particularly the attacks on the Scriptures.

WRN's contribution began when he examined the topic in some lectures given at a Summer School of Theology in Glasgow (1905). After an appearance in the *British Weekly*, he published them with other articles as *The Garden of Nuts*, having already encouraged his friend, Alexander Whyte, to preach a series of sermons on the mystics at Free St George's in Edinburgh, which were reproduced as Whyte's ongoing contribution to the columns of the *British Weekly*.[93] In his own lectures on Christian Mysticism, WRN acknowledged his dependence on Arthur Edward Waite[94] and believed that his approach would help the Christian preacher.

To begin with he was concerned to show that to the mystic all the universe is an omen and a sign and therefore everything exists as an outward expression of an inward thought of God. He held that God was the great symbolic teacher, he taught by signs, but there was a veil hanging between ourselves and God. However, the veil was "thin and penetrable, and mysteriously inscribed on the side shown to us".[95] He then discusses what he calls the believer's attachment, which for WRN was, "The creation of an attitude of perfect correspondence with Christ".[96] By this he meant a conversion experience, or "the gradual satisfaction of the hunger and thirst after righteousness that is awakened in the soul".[97] As a mystic WRN saw Christ as the repairer of the Fall and his work was to reunite us to the living act of the Divine principle. His thought is that the individual Christian must live through the experience of Christ in a union so close, "that each step of the redemptive process, the life, the death, and the resurrection, are repeated in the believer".[98] WRN was seeking to concentrate on the need for there to be a deep, even profound, awareness of the individual relating to his Lord and Saviour.

Of course WRN signalled up the difficulties that would be experienced when following this pathway. He talks about 'the night of the obscure illumination', which was called 'The Dark Night of the Soul,' stating that this was a "time of aridity, weariness, temptation, desolation, and darkness".[99] WRN saw this as a time when individual souls seeks after a great affinity and closeness to Christ and bemoans their sin, even doubting their own value to Christ. Such would be the sense of dissatisfaction at any level of supposed attainment in the Christian life. In the *Garden of Nuts*, WRN was setting out his stall with a theoretical approach to the benefits and also the dangers of mysticism for the Christian and there is an inherent weakness from the fact that the author fails to give any personal illustrations of how this looked or felt in his own life.

WRN wanted to answer the question, 'What can the mystical view offer the Christian Church?' His answer was that he ceases to become so focused on the mundane and the petty and is taken up with the transcendent glory of being in relationship with his Lord and Saviour: "When the element of mysticism is in the mind of the theologian, he will avoid dialectical victories, and not attempt to stone his antagonists to death with texts".[100] WRN examined the area of atonement and pleaded for an inclusive, expansive, and profounder view. Here he quotes Spurgeon, with obvious approval: "I try to explain it as a substitution, and I feel that where the language of Scripture is explicit, I may and must be explicit too. But yet I feel that the idea of substitution does not cover the whole of the matter and that no human conception can completely grasp the whole of the dread mystery".[101] WRN never retreated from a full Evangelical view of the atonement, but he felt the mystical awareness gave it depth and breadth and a true grasp of the importance of the Atonement of Christ was the basis to WRN's idea of Christian mysticism.

This emphasis upon mystical awareness trumping analytical argument was then carried over into a debate for which WRN felt it was particularly well-suited – the doctrine of Scripture, so ravaged in recent years by the drive towards critical accountability: "The Christian pulpit can never be strong so far as it depends on nervous and inaccurate estimates of the present trend of German theological thought, measured in most instances by summaries of periodical articles".[102] The mystic would know that the time for decision on many questions had not yet arrived, indeed it might never arrive. Then WRN specifically comes to the contemporary situation regarding the Scriptures: "Criticism has changed, and will change, but to the mystic the Word of God remains. In so far as the higher criticism is dangerous, he meets it with the highest criticism".[103] For WRN saw no benefit to being hostile to historical criticism, rather for him historical criticism must ever be of secondary importance; it was the revelation of God that must be full of signs and wonders in the individual's person experience and only then would they be well assured.

Having established the pre-eminence of mystical understanding, WRN concluded with an assertion of the necessity of obedience to and trust in one's own brand of Christianity, which he labelled as the 'Doctrine of the Holy Assembly'. He regarded this as, "A doctrine sorely needed in these days of fierce and bitter sectarianism". [104] To WRN it was the duty of every Christian to connect himself to a community or church. Once the community was found then that person "should remain in the church in which he was born, unless driven out by the gravest necessity".[105] Here WRN took Paul's word to the Corinthians as a literal principle: 'Each one should remain in the situation which he was in when God called him'.[106] WRN practiced what he preached and he celebrated the differences between various groups and counselled folk to stay loyal to their 'originating' Church, a necessary corollary of promoting implicit trust over against a questioning divisive spirit. The earlier WRN would have been more inclined to speak of the work of the Holy Spirit rather than a mystical awareness promoting true and lasting fellowship between Christians.

In the last two thirds of *Garden of Nuts*, WRN repeated and attempted to clarify his earlier arguments through demonstrating what he meant by the 'mystical' exposition of the Scriptures. He felt that, "The mystical interpreters expounded the phrase 'the garden of nuts'[107] as pointing to the prophecies, allegories, parables, and poetry of the Old Testament".[108] WRN used the title for his book for a brief series of articles on what he believed to be an old, true, precious, and divinely sanctioned method of interpretation. He did not intend to revive the purely mystical and allegorical reading of the Bible. His firm opinion was that, "Whatever disparages or sets aside the historical record of redemption, whatever turns the Bible into a set of fantastic puzzles, dishonours it, and makes it of none effect".[109] WRN was certain that believers were in danger of losing a helpful key to the understanding and appreciation of Scripture.

It is quite clear that WRN's apologetic purpose was to stir up a fresh interest in preaching from the Bible – particularly the Old Testament – as he was well aware that the younger generation of preachers were inclined to move away from the practical use and importance of preaching from this source.[110] His apologetic concerns attempted to hold together his readers, who were inclined to polarise over the new style of criticism. He counselled that the work of the critics when it is sound, must be good, but when, "they are engaged in mere processes of destruction and dissection, there can be nothing but trial, but trial patiently and bravely borne will in the end be for the confirmation of faith".[111] WRN's was for a great revival of interest in the Bible, but felt that at present time for many, the Bible was a curious book and many were bewildered. He felt confident that by studying the mystical interpreter, then much Scripture, especially in the Old Testament would receive the illumination of the mystic fathers and come to the aid of a younger generation of preachers. Specifically WRN thought that, "the method of interpretation we seek to expound moves in a region which criticism does not touch. It is above and beyond criticism, and when criticism has accomplished all its work amid the complete unanimity of the experts, it will be as much in place as ever".[112] This was WRN's laudable hope and his optimistic forecast, but his advice was largely ignored and here, he proved to be a less than an accurate prophet.

In concluding, WRN reflected on a certain 'world weariness', for there were 'battles against the odds' and things happening in life that are 'mysterious and defy easy explanations'. In combating the analytical bent of so many young churchmen, WRN encouraged, in an exhortatory manner, following the pattern of life shown by Jesus: "The more Christ-like the cause is, the harder it may be. With what stress and vehemence of hate did the evil power attack Christ!… Nothing is easy; things will not go as we fain had hoped. There will come mortifying disappointments, checks and desertions, but all these things are only sent to discover our manhood …But the victory is sure because the leader is Christ".[113] WRN's intentions were good, and there was much helpful truth in what he said. He wanted to write further on mysticism,[114] although his appeal was limited to a narrow range of people and critics were far from rare – Elliott-Binns, for example, critiqued this influence:

> "Mysticism and reliance on spiritual intuition, though they might bolster up the faith of those who were religious by temperament or upbringing, were of little avail to common men and women for whom traditional religion, received on authority, had had no personal verification. It was all too vague and subjective and alien to their experience of life".[115]

Elliott-Binns felt that there was a lack of realism with the apologetic of mysticism for the ordinary church members. He pointed out that writers, like WRN, might appeal to some well-read, culturally sophisticated people, but ordinary folk found nothing in the mystical experience to help them with their problem of authority and credibility of Christianity. "Confused and disquieted, many abandoned religion, as a matter beyond their comprehension and sought, by ceaseless occupation, to shut out anxiety over the inevitable mysteries which surrounded them. There was, in consequence, a steady drift towards indifference and agnosticism".[116] WRN's concern was to help the preacher cope with presenting the truth of the Bible in a vital and living way, but with an awareness of the great mystery of the Scriptures in the modern context.[117] He sought only to recommend the methods of thinking and stimulus that had been of help to him. Unfortunately, as Elliott-Binns noted, those methods were fitting only for a man with a 40,000-volume library, and WRN's success was limited to those of like mind with himself.

Conclusion

WRN's apologetic work must be seen as an attempt to be a steadying influence, an encouragement for Church leaders and particularly ministerial students who he knew were in various states of apprehension about the intellectual and theological climate of the time. As a preacher, he was always concerned about the quality and the dynamic impact of preaching. His apologetic was not aimed at those outside the Church, for his thought-forms and vocabulary would be understood by 'in-house' Christian believers. This was understandable as he was writing a Christian newspaper. He stressed and believed in the total dependence on a living experience of Christ for an understanding and appreciation of the Scriptures.

> Not till the first advent was the Old Testament to be fully understood, nor till the Second Advent will the New Testament be fully understood … it is Christ alone who can interpret the Scriptures. It is He only who possesses the key to the Scriptures, and the key to human souls. It was under His teaching that the disciples discerned His way and His kingdom in the Old Testament. No man can say that Jesus is Lord but by the Holy Ghost, neither can any man, save by the Holy Ghost, say that the Scripture is the Word of God.[118]

However, this was not the same as the traditional Evangelical doctrine of the inspiration of Scripture to the Old Testament, for with that part of the Bible, he would use his 'believing critical' and Christian mystical approach to draw out the meaning. In a sense WRN's advocating the usefulness of Christian mysticism only fudged and added to the confusion of those who wanted to know how the Scriptures were the Word of God.

WRN continued to preach when he could, generally to groups who, churchgoing or not, understood his position and could enjoy it. Though WRN had a simple and usually direct style that the uninitiated could listen to, the content of the material he chose to discuss was fine for theologically attuned mind, but not generally appropriate for any audience lacking a well-versed knowledge of theology and Scripture. He assumed a high level of knowledge, and his sermons were thick with doctrine and Evangelical culture and history (e.g., Arianism, Socinianism, etc). Limited though his audience type may have been, WRN preached in a wide range of venues, and was heard with much acceptance. By this stage of his career, preaching was a matter of desire rather than necessity -- he felt a compulsion to proclaim vocally the good news of the gospel, and the effect of the human voice over a crowd of people continually fascinated him, even when that voice was soft and frail due to a damaged lung. Indeed, he was masterful in his articulation, which enabled him to be heard distinctly in days well before any amplification systems. Arthur Peake gave his impression of WRN as a Preacher:

> His style was probably better suited to Scotland than to England. I also heard him give the address on the Annual Day of the Baptist College, Manchester. His immense admiration for Spurgeon came out on that occasion. ... he told the students that if ever any of them invited him to preach they must never dare to let him come and find no Spurgeon on their shelves…speaking of preaching, he said that in his early days he found it difficult to get enough matter to fill his sermons, but at present he had the opposite difficulty.[119]

One insightful assessment of WRN in 1925 frankly states, "His first love and his last would appear to have been the pulpit; one can see that his dearest ambition was to be a great preacher".[120] The writer, in reflecting on this feature of WRN's life, says that, "he lacked the mental qualities necessary for great preaching. He had an acute, vigorous, and active mind, but it was of the discursive, not of the illuminative kind…he belonged to the type that builds up businesses rather than to that which discovers new ideas".[121] E. Hermann published an interview with WRN about the prospects of the Christian ministry. In it WRN said,

> I do not believe that one can fix upon any one type of preacher as most likely to meet the present situation. Every preacher does it in his own line, provided he has worked out a message for himself and presents it in the best way he can. Every man [only] really that meets the situation in part, and none of us can do more than just meet it in part. Speaking personally, I prefer expository preaching to any other kind, but nothing is more difficult. It is easy enough to give a dry explanation, a kind of running commentary saying a little about each verse; but nothing is more wearisome and jejune than such exposition. To give a unified impression of a Scripture passage and to light it up is very difficult, and good preaching of this type is exceedingly rare.[122]

WRN concluded, "The great thing for a preacher is to be entirely free from any kind of affectation; to be real and simple".[123] Interestingly, however, by his later career this preference for ex tempore speech and a lack of pretension had given way to a more grandiose style – his published sermons show that he became more thematic and had a tendency to fill his sermons with literary allusions.[124]

Preaching was important to WRN throughout his life, and enthusiasm and commitment to the Gospel message became a deep and abiding concern. He actively promoted preaching that engaged with the contemporary scene, proclaimed the Evangelical Gospel and possessed awareness of the cultural progress being made amongst the generality of church members. He always sought to remind preachers to look for conversions to 'the living Christ of all history'. He not only thrilled to listen to great preachers who could weave their extraordinary power over the people, but he also sought to practise what he wrote about in his journals concerning what, for him, made good preaching. Given his early forced abandonment of the pulpit, WRN was unsurprisingly delighted with his second chance to preach and give literary lectures, but when he turned sixty and his energy and stamina were even more limited, he became something of an after-dinner speaker. He had enjoyed and had been confident as a preacher: "I was never nervous in the pulpit. The only thing that makes me nervous is when many in the congregation are not hearing me. I have sometimes felt a little nervousness in after-dinner speeches".[125] Needless to say, he carried this opportunity with success, acceptance and much appreciation. WRN's interest and belief in preaching remained with him to the end of his life. For him, preaching was the passionate personal expression of God's Gospel of love for humanity in the life, and more particularly, in the Atoning Sacrifice of Jesus Christ. He revelled amongst the great 'pulpiteers' of his age, longing to see and hear an incandescent flame of eloquence coming through particular personalities. However, latterly [after 1910], Nicoll felt that the age of the Great Preachers was over and lamented that passing. In looking for a new generation of preachers, he was forced to turn with the world to secular society and the oratory of politicians like Lloyd George.

However pleased WRN had been to return to the pulpit, the world and the church alike had changed a great deal in the intervening years. The encroaching forces of biblical criticism had laid siege to the sanctity of the New Testament, and those older men who sought to stand astride the line as peacemakers appeared as little more than reactionary digressions from the true discussion. Though, like other contemporary leaders of Nonconformity, WRN could appear radical in persuading the church to come to terms with the contemporary situation, he was essentially a conservative in temperament and core theological beliefs. In his broad accommodations to the new ideas, he intended not to usher in new thought, but hoped to limit damage and stimulate fresh hope in the vibrant truth of the Gospel message from a mystical rather than analytical perspective. His attempts at apologetics were neither substantial nor generally successful in the long term, although, in his day, many complimented him on his efforts. His work here was always idiosyncratic, being mainly of a literary, theological variety, and often operating at a subjectively mystical level which did not appeal to all. He fought with other men's weapons in ideas and did not personally engage with the text of the Scripture, instead proving accommodating on that most central of subjects and thereby unwittingly undermined the very truth he was seeking to establish and defend. This flawed attempt to bolster the defences of the embattled Christian faith amounted in the end to a contribution to the liberalisation of the Evangelical Church.

8

Politics, the First World War and the Peace
1900-1920

WRN was a Liberal; he founded the *British Weekly* to be an instrument for promoting 'advanced Liberalism', and after 1900, took an even greater personal interest in politics. The very success of the *British Weekly,* which by 1902 had built up to a circulation of over 100,000 copies, was regarded as influential over a considerable constituency of voters, and, therefore, useful for those who sought to gain and maintain political power. WRN had worked at his declared mandate, and the success of the *British Weekly* made politicians appreciate that he was not merely responsible for the policy of his papers, but that he seemed to embody them: "He was less an editorial spectre than a physical presence whose contributions defined the newspaper."[1] WRN's views about political involvement were similar to those of many of his peers amongst the contemporary Nonconformist leadership, but they also reflected his Scottish Presbyterian background, rather than the pietistic tendency towards non-involvement found within some English Nonconformity. He maintained his 'mission' to educate Nonconformists into their responsibility of playing a full part in the affairs of the country. WRN, like other contemporary leaders, saw this as part of their entering the 'promised land'[2] of power and influence as the once-despised 'Dissenters'. He was one of a number of leaders who advocated a greater Nonconformist presence in the political arena, following the thinking of R.W. Dale and actions of John Clifford and Silvester Horne.[3]

WRN's interest in the political scene was to view politics and social affairs from an openly Christian standpoint. Like other Nonconformist leaders, he welded his Christianity to the Liberal Party.

> Because of these convictions his editorial chair enabled
> him to bring to bear on the Churches and the nation a
> persuasive and powerful Christian influence that in time
> made him one of the most potent forces in public life. He
> was not an infallible judge on all occasions, nor did he
> always pick the winning side, but throughout his career he
> could be depended on to have a very sure instinct as to the
> trend of political feeling among the Nonconformists.[4]

He was capable of having personal fancies, but the greater part of his
convictions, were carried out for real benefit to his country.

WRN followed his early 'mentor' R.W. Dale in seeing politics as a
legitimate and necessary interest for the Christian. However, he ignored
Dale's later cautions that the church which seeks to grasp political
power would dissipate its power and vitality: "I have the gravest
fears of what will come from the present passion of some excellent
persons to capture Christian churches and change them into political
and municipal caucuses. It will compel a serious reconsideration of the
true idea of the church".[5] WRN was also aware of the strong pietistic
element amongst Nonconformists, which was against any practical
involvement. The Nonconformists divided in three basic ways over
their attitude to politics. First, there were those who distrusted politics
completely; these were the 'pietists' who advocated non-involvement
with the 'world's systems'. As one exponent of this line wrote, "Let me
exhort the believer, then, to surrender all interference in politics. 'Let
the dead bury their dead!' Your concern is the Kingdom of God, your
city the one to come, your citizenship in heaven."[6] WRN was furthest
removed from this type of thinking.

Second, there were the 'activists' who were inclined to let their
politics take over their religious view of things. This was to be an
increasingly secularising factor amongst the younger generations of
Nonconformists. In 1926, Stanley Baldwin addressed a meeting of
Methodists: "I find there [in the House of Commons], especially among
the Labour Party, many men who fifty years ago would inevitably have
gone into the Christian Ministry. They have been drawn into political
life from a deep desire to help the people … on this account I feel it to
be so important that a church like yours should send its quota of young
men into politics to-day".[7] These found more sympathy with WRN, but
they were, in his judgment, inclined to hang loose or even abandon their
faith commitment. Thirdly, there were those who sought to display their
Christian convictions in their political involvement. This, they believed,

was 'Rendering the things that are Caesar's to Caesar, and the things that are God's to God'.[8] WRN declared his convictions plainly,

> We believe in the close alliance of the three [Faith, Politics, and Culture]. Faith is the one thing needful, and comes before the rest. But faith without works and without influence is dead. We believe that between faith and politics on the one hand, and between faith and culture on the other, there ought to be the most intimate and friendly relations … let politics alone, say some Christians; faith has nothing to do with such earthly subjects. If so, there has been a change since the time of the Hebrew prophets.… The problems that are coming up are largely ethical – questions of right and wrong.[9]

WRN was convinced that Nonconformist involvement would show vibrancy of the Christian faith to a new generation, though he was careful to pick his battles. As one of the architects of this politically motivated Nonconformity, he remained publicly silent on some issues: "One such issue was that of Women's Suffrage which, with its violence, created widespread attention".[10] Here WRN generally contented himself by inviting others to contribute to the debate on the subject,[11] carefully keeping his personal views from public display.

WRN was in journalism at a time when there were a number of newspaper heavyweights,[12] all participating in politics, some practising their concern to show Christian involvement, and more than a few were Nonconformists. These included figures such as Hugh Price Hughes of the *Methodist Recorder*, who caught the headlines in 1890 over the Parnell affair, with his call that Parnell had to 'go'. These were times of emotional outbursts and strong feelings, particularly over the Irish question and Home Rule. In such circumstances, WRN was more restrained and careful about which issues he would lead from the front. He was content to follow the paths of others, employing the relative shelter of predecessors to snipe at such targets as Sir Charles Dilke. It had been in 1886 that a court accepted Dilke's adultery as grounds for his wife's divorce. Here W.T. Stead was the main protagonist, which led to the blighting of Dilke's political career. However, "the waspish editor of the *British Weekly* … kept up the harrying. When Tom Ellis, the rising young Welsh MP, appeared on the same platform as Dilke in 1891, WRN wrote to him a stern letter of rebuke. He wanted to know if Ellis had anything to say in extenuation, before, as he put it, 'publicly

William Ewart Gladstone

condemning you'".[13] WRN was maintaining ranks with those seeking to signal the need for the highest standards of moral integrity for those who aspire to public office.

From his Aberdeenshire days, WRN always enjoyed an interest in politics and social concerns. He heard and marvelled at the oratorical power of William Gladstone:[14] "If I had not heard Gladstone in the Midlothian I should have lived and died without the faintest conception of what human speech can do. At that time, Gladstone simply maddened his audiences. He welded them into a unity, wild with passion, ready to follow him even to death".[15] Though he became critical of Gladstone, he retained a respect for him. In his obituary article, WRN wrote,

> For ourselves we can say that we should have never known,
> never even have remotely conceived, what the power
> of speech might be unless we had heard Mr Gladstone
> then.... He could rouse the most unemotional Scots to
> the highest pitch of passion, and the wonderful thing was
> that these orations did not end in a grandiose or confused
> glory, but took practical shape and issue.... His absolute
> fearlessness always impressed his audience; no difficulties
> ever daunted him, no enemy made him quail, from first
> to last he believed that a righteous man, trusting in God,
> could do anything.[16]

It was as a Christian that he remembered Gladstone: "His own
Christianity was itself a great argument for the faith".[17] WRN promoted
Party unity by loyally supporting the leadership of the party, and
the partners Hodder & Stoughton also held this conviction. Though
Gladstone was WRN's early hero, he came to feel that the 'Grand
Old Man' overstayed his usefulness[18] and was rather less than 'a true
friend' to his Nonconformist supporters. Reflecting after the death of
Joseph Chamberlain, he wrote,

> I cannot understand how anyone who has studied
> Gladstone's career can fail to see that he regarded
> Dissenters with something like loathing. He knew that he
> was mainly indebted to them for his political victories; he
> knew that they took his side and made it possible for him to
> prevail in causes that lay nearest his heart. Under extreme
> exigencies, he would even compliment them, address their
> meetings, and tolerate their company. But he never made a
> real friend, so far as I know, of any Dissenter.[19]

Gladstone was not the only controversial figure from whose example
a youthful WRN drew lessons. When younger, he was something
of a 'radical' and was attracted to the style and policies of Joseph
Chamberlain.[20] He "was the political idol of my youth. I learnt more
from him, and received more stimulus from him, than from any other
statesman".[21] Before the founding of the *British Weekly*, there was a
possibility of WRN supporting Chamberlain. He remembered:

> I wrote and told him the circumstances, and said that if the
> thing materialised I should like to have a monthly review
> of political affairs ... this was before the Home Rule split.
> I suggested that he should write the review. He replied

with an invitation for me to come and visit him and talk it over and of course, I went. I found him most genial, and friendly, and interested … he said that he did not profess to be a writer. He had written some things at the request of his friend John Morley, but he felt that his forte was speech. "However," he said, "I shall always be willing to give you my help. You can come to me at any time and I will tell you my views on the situation, and I daresay you can utilise them." When I was leaving him, he put his hand on my shoulder and said, "You can take notes and can you keep a secret?" I assented to this, and he said with a smile, "that is all you will have to do".[22]

WRN paints a dramatic picture of the powerful influence that Chamberlain held over the younger radicals like himself:

I have no power to show adequately how much his early political teaching meant to young Nonconformists scattered about often in lonely and difficult places, and longing for a champion to make vocal their inmost thoughts. Joseph Chamberlain did it as no other did, and as no other could. He brought into English speechmaking a new and victorious style … he could state a certain number of facts and arguments and infuse them with the vehemence of his own soul … behind all his speaking there was that vivid and quickening personality with which no man came in contact without being influenced.[23]

Whether the partners interfered is not known, but WRN gave his support loyally to the mainline policies of the Party rather than Chamberlain's Unionists. His articles and comments showed that he was always aware of other points of view, and this enabled him to appear as a peacemaker in seeking to unify divergent factions when differences arose. He would be loyal to the main party leadership, but at the same time give space and attention to dissident ideas within the party.

When Chamberlain broke with the Liberal Party, WRN came to see another side of his former hero. He later reflected on Chamberlain, "As time went on it became apparent that he had for good or evil the dominating quality. He must be the master … he could conduct negotiations up to a certain point, but he believed in reality that the remaining members of any board at which he sat must be instruments of his … both for happiness and for unhappiness he had a very strong will".[24] WRN subscribed to the view that Chamberlain could not have worked with Gladstone, even if the Home

Rule question had not arisen. He used his knowledge of Chamberlain's speeches to good effect when called to attack his inconsistency over issues like the Education Act of 1902.[25]

The young editor's political savvy did not end with Chamberlain. WRN came to know and be impressed with Lord Rosebery, who was Prime Minister from 1894 to 1895. He left no overall assessment of Rosebery as he had other leaders, for Rosebery outlived him by six years,[26] but as a popular Scot, he admired his oratorical skills and thought that he would provide the Liberals with good needed leadership.[27] In 1895 the Liberals lost the election and Rosebery resigned from leadership, having been 'bitterly assailed' in the recriminations that followed the defeat. Interestingly, though the Liberals lost in 1895, James Denney felt that WRN's campaigning at the election had increased his personal reputation: "I congratulate you, in spite of the result of the elections, on the place you have made for the *B W* in the political as well as the religious world. You are quite an authority in places where you might hardly expect it, thanks to your candour and principle, not to mention the other things needful to command attention".[28] WRN and the *British Weekly* continued to support Rosebery "as decisively superior to any rival in the field"[29] until the arrival of the 'Welsh Wizard'.

WRN dined with Rosebery from time to time, and found these occasions useful because of the quality and interest of the discussions on literary and political matters.[30] There was one occasion in 1905 when the conversation turned to the relationship between Gladstone and Chamberlain. Rosebery was much interested in the topic: "He stood up for Gladstone – said he was as high-minded a statesman as there ever was. But he admitted that Gladstone never forgave Chamberlain for his unauthorised programme. In this, Rosebery thought Gladstone right. It was a gross breach of discipline".[31] WRN would not have agreed on this point, but, in the early days of the twentieth century, he, like many other Liberals, expected more from Rosebery and in the hope of forwarding Rosebery's popularity, he encouraged his assistant, Jane Stoddart, who admired Rosebery, to write an illustrated biography of the Earl in 1900.[32]

The second Boer War became a divisive focus in Britain at the end of 1899, and this was particularly so amongst Nonconformists. WRN could identify with those in the Liberal Party leadership who were reluctantly in favour of the war, but he had no great sympathy for the war, for as a rural Aberdonian Scot, he had sympathies with the Boers. However, like his partners, he believed in the importance of party unity. This ambivalence enabled WRN to reflect party divisions and write

> Never was a war contemplated with more reluctance
> and misgiving than this. It is not too much to say that
> it is hated and loathed by all sensible and right-minded
> people … [moreover] in all the long chapter of bungling
> there have been no worse blunders than those committed
> lately. There are dark shadows hanging over the Jameson
> Raid,[33] shadows that may yet be lifted. Whatever may be
> the result, we have evidence enough that Mr. Chamberlain's
> proceedings have been eminently unwise and eminently
> unpacific.[34]

However, WRN felt that the Government had tried to be conciliatory
and reasonable, and that the Government's proposals[35] contained
nothing offensive. The terms were rejected and President Kruger
sent his ultimatum to the Colonial Office, which gave Her Majesty's
Government 36 hours to remove all British troops quartered in territory
that immediately bordered the South African Boers, to recall extra
troops that had arrived and not to send any more. WRN printed the text
of Kruger's ultimatum, and assessed the situation "Sober minded people
must deeply regret the necessity for war, but the overwhelming majority
of them feel that war is now a necessity which cannot be evaded".[36]
WRN felt convinced that if the Government were to give way on any of
their main points, this would result in an even more intense struggle and
put Britain in an impossible situation in the area. He saw the rejection
of government terms as a challenge to the British resolve to take action
over the matter.

WRN took the view advocated by the Liberal leader Campbell-
Bannerman that they were not disposed to refuse the Government, the
money and the power necessary for a swift conclusion to the war. He
believed that in war there was a duty to unite behind the Government
against a common foe, yet he admired the Boers and kept up contacts
with ministers of the Dutch Reformed Church, as well as other subjects
of the Boer States. In this way, he remained in touch with a considerable
number of Liberals, who for reasons relating to conscience were openly
hostile to the war.[37] A series of leading articles[38] in the *British Weekly*
sought a positive and yet purposeful approach to the situation.

The War began disastrously for the British when they suffered a
number of defeats between October 1899 and January 1900. This was
not altogether surprising, as the Boers were far more prepared, whilst the
British not only had to gather themselves together, but fundamentally
underestimated their opponent's quality as soldiers. WRN faced the

reverses with the call "We are baffled to fight better",[39] commenting, "The nation should be as one – above all recriminating and taunting. Do the next thing that is our business and let it be done in the true British spirit".[40] WRN had an ability to encourage and galvanise a country and a party that were going through difficult times. He seemed to have the capacity to maintain the Liberal agreed position and at the same time keep in touch with the dissidents.[41] "To this patriotic resolution he held firm till the war reached its welcome close in June 1902".[42] He employed this rapport with all sides of the debate through continuing to seek reconciliation between the Liberal Imperialists and the anti-war Liberals.

In the euphoria of the eventual victories of the British troops in South Africa, especially following the early disasters, the Salisbury Tory Government called an election. WRN knew that the Liberal divisions would keep them from regaining power. He tried to rally the Nonconformist vote in support of the Liberals with his leading articles, as he wrote "In one of his pregnant political remarks Tennyson said 'In a war we English do not listen to argument until we are victorious.' Victory, if we are to believe the telegrams, is already ours in South Africa, though it must be noted that our 220,000 troops still appear to be needed in that war".[43] Then again in his leader for the following month:

> Are these deep wounds to be cured by fanatical and virulent imperialism? Already we have seen in high quarters exultation in the misery of the Boers, a disposition to triumph over and trample the fallen enemy. Macaulay used to say that this was never one of the besetting sins of English men, and we hope that it might be possible for him to say it now.[44]

After the election he noted that in fact the Liberals did better at the polls than in 1895, assessed the lessons to be learnt, and provided space for a Liberal spokesman, R.W. Perks, to give his assessment of the election defeat.[45] The 'Khaki' election triumph for the Conservatives had still left some encouraging signs for the Liberals, particularly in the Celtic fringe of Scotland and Wales.

The turn of the century saw WRN's involvement in politics increased[46] alongside the national resurgence of the Liberal Party. He saw "the 1902 Education Act, which Balfour presented gratuitously to his opponents that transformed ... the Nonconformist commitment to Liberalism from a vague sentiment into an active electoral alliance.[47]

Free Churchmen in the House of Commons, who had been inclined to subordinate religious to party interests, now saw them as identical".[48] This single event pulled together the divisions and sectional interests that plagued the Nonconformist support for the Liberal Party. Strangely, their unity arose out of their shared opposition to a piece of legislation, which R.C.K. Ensor has stated, "Ranks for England and Wales among the two or three greatest constructive measures of the twentieth century".[49] The reason for concern was that Nonconformists were required to contribute, through the rates, to help support Anglican schools. In some rural areas, the Anglican school was the only school for Nonconformist children to attend, but Nonconformist teachers were often barred from them by tests, and three-quarters of the training colleges were also closed to non-Anglican members. To WRN, and others, the insult was compounded when state-help was also extended to Roman Catholic schools. He saw the 'Education Issue' as an opportunity to fuel Nonconformist demands for recognition of their status in society. For the same year (1902), the *Daily News* had published a survey of Churches, in which the Nonconforming groups were equal to the Anglicans; this meant that overall the Anglicans were in a minority position. "Of the total attendants, the percentages by denominations ... read, 43% Church of England, 38% Nonconformists, 14% Roman Catholic, 5% Salvation Army & mission services".[50] WRN noticed a remark of George White, Member of Parliament for Norwich, about the need for a campaign of passive resistance,[51] and in his leading article for April 3 1902, he advocated for the first time a national policy of passive resistance.

> In these things, however, Free Churchmen will, we venture to think be compelled to resist. Alderman George White, MP, has expressed his opinion that the one effective way of fighting the battle is to bind ourselves by solemn pledge to pay no school rate ...we as ratepayers must allow our property to be seized for the school rate, but we cannot conscientiously pay for it.[52]

As the passive resistance movement spread over the country, it gradually seemed to absorb every other issue. WRN committed himself to addressing meetings at Manchester, Liverpool, Birmingham, Sheffield, Leicester and everywhere he received a "rapturous reception from great audiences".[53] A flavour of these speeches is caught in his articles:

> It may be said without the smallest exaggeration that Nonconformity in England has now reached the greatest

crisis of its history. The Government has defied it in
the plainest and directest manner. Mr. Balfour was
uncompromising in his reply to the Free Church Council
deputation ... the Nonconformists are plainly told that there
is nothing for them but unconditional submission.[54]

WRN rallied his readers: "There can be no resistance except the refusal
to pay rates. This is a passive resistance. They can come and take what
we have; they can send us to prison if our possessions are not enough
to satisfy their demands."[55] He met opposition from papers such as the
Daily Telegraph and the *Christian World*, but increasingly he identified
with the cause and found himself in the national limelight. Others felt
that the crisis on Education was misconceived and unhelpful. Arthur
Porritt, a journalist who had worked for WRN, believed that 'Passive
Resistance' was a mistaken policy.

Nonconformity sacrificed much of its salutary political
influence when its opposition to the Balfour Education
Acts took the form of 'passive resistance'... a very large
number of responsible Free Churchmen however refused
to be stampeded by Dr. Clifford, Dr. Robertson Nicoll,
The Rev. C. Silvester Horne, and the other Nonconformist
leaders into defiance of the law. [56]

Supporters rallied round to challenge the Bill, including politicians
like Lord Rosebery,[57] and Lloyd George.[58] In the early days of the
Education Bill, Lloyd George had approved of many of its measures,
but gradually, for tactical reasons as much as from deep convictions,
he changed. "By July 1902, Lloyd George had come round to WRN's
view, conveyed privately as well as in the columns of the *British
Weekly*... to this end, he invited Nicoll, Clifford, and Hugh Price
Hughes to consult... the proposal portended a growing correlation
between the political fortunes of Lloyd George and those of radical
Nonconformity".[59] WRN spoke at many public meetings, but his
real contributions were his leading articles,[60] which sought to keep
the focus of his readers on the issues of the Bill. The real champion
speaker of the cause was John Clifford, who not only spoke all over
the country, but also gave a personal lead with his own identification
in 'Passive Resistance', which he maintained[61] right through the First
World War.[62]

Many Nonconformists rallied to the cause of 'Passive Resistance',
but there were definite, if subtle temptations for the advocates of such
civil action.

> Few of [an advocate's] hearers had come to listen to a reasoned exposition of the case; the minds of most of them were already made up, and they had come to rejoice in the strength of their cause and to hail the approaching day of its triumph. Their appeals are couched in the language of moral idealism. Every political issue becomes a sharp cleavage between right and wrong. They use the whites and blacks and avoid the half tones ... political questions can be very complicated, and sincere and informed Christians may disagree about the practical answers to them.[63]

Porritt has pointed out that all through Nonconformist history they had respected constitutional methods of agitation for the redress of grievances in their struggles for religious liberty and equality, and noted Churchill's verdict on 'Passive Resistance' was a 'pantomimic martyrdom'. "Passive resistance virtually ceased when a Liberal Government came in to office in 1906. I have always felt that this lapse of respect for the law and order set a precedent for the violent defiances which followed in the Women's Suffrage campaign and the Ulster Rebellion against Irish Home Rule".[64]

Later in the 1920s there was a reaction of distrust against the use of 'crusading oratory', which affected both politics and religion. By then even pulpit oratory would be viewed, by many, as somewhat insincere and theatrical. However, WRN had died before this reaction came about.

Of the landslide Liberal victory of 1906, WRN wrote exultantly: "Mr. Balfour's appeal to the country has been answered by an avalanche.... For the friends of freedom the dark hour of despondency is past, and it has been succeeded by a general feeling of hope for the future".[65] However, "There were some Nonconformist clergymen who thought that the pulpit and the denominational press had become too blatantly partisan ...[and complained] of unscrupulous divines who led their congregations in prayer for the defeat of the sinful Tories".[66] The Nonconformists were part of a great victory, with WRN playing his significant part. Ruling, however, was not to prove easy – they not only found political objectives difficult to turn into legislation, with the House of Lords vetoing their attempts at changing the Education Bill, but also faced internal dissent as many came to believe that they had sold their spiritual heritage for short-term political gain. The Nonconformists' crusading style was often interpreted by their opponents as motivated by 'self-interest'. "Nonconformists tried to stamp their own standards of behaviour on public life, but encountered a barrage of criticism for allowing their political views to be shaped by self-interest or the interest of the party".[67] There was a political necessity that most Nonconformists found impossible – the need to compromise. As David Bebbington reflected, "Compromise was essential if Nonconformists were to gain the substance of their aims, but the whole inspiration for Nonconformist political effort was the belief that with unrighteous policies there could be no compromise. The resulting tension was a fatal flaw in the politics of the chapels".[68] The sight of their soundly supported Government being rebuffed by the House of Lords caused disillusionment to some, but for others, like WRN, it only increased their determination to fight.

During the early years of the Liberal Government, WRN, it seemed to some commentators, was expecting a mention in the honours lists and as there was a delay in delivery of this expectation, his criticisms of the Government, occasionally had a sharp edge.[69] However, he had come to value Lloyd George as the best representative of Nonconformity in Parliament, and so they formed a close relationship. A.J.P. Taylor observed,

> Lloyd George used the press, and the press used Lloyd George. The two grew great together. Lloyd George had never cared much for the society of other politicians. Now he built up a group of advisers drawn almost entirely from the press. The chief of these were Riddell, who owned the *News of the World*; C.P. Scott of the *Manchester Guardian*; and Robertson Nicoll, editor of the *British Weekly*.[70]

WRN became an advisor to and chief cheerleader for Lloyd George's advancement in the Government.[71] WRN's admiration for Lloyd George was partly due to his gift of public speaking with colour, power and fluency, the kind that he looked for and admired in his preachers. In turn, Lloyd George appreciated WRN and his paper, and a mixture of genuine regard and old-fashioned, even blatant, flattery kept his support: "Will you allow me to tell you how much I enjoyed and appreciated your ringing and rousing article on the Budget in last week's *British Weekly*? It is so opportune – a real battle cry and will help us enormously at this juncture".[72]

WRN became increasingly caught up in the radical programme of social improvements that the Government were proposing. In 1908, the Government passed the Old Age Pensions Act, and, with Lloyd George's enthusiastic drive, began a radical programme. WRN admitted to James Denney,

> We are now in the thick of the fight about the Budget. The
> main point is the taxation of unearned increment on land,
> which is being fought by the moneyed classes with fury.
> On this point I am wholeheartedly with the Government,
> and have even found a kind of pleasure in writing political
> articles – a thing I almost always detest … we shall have
> lively times to look forward to. I am glad of it, for I like a
> good hot controversy if I am sure of my side.[73]

He committed the resources of the *British Weekly* to support of the
Government and rallied his readers in 'One Fight More'. Tensions rose,
and the House of Lords finally rejected the Lloyd George 'People's
Budget' in November 1909.

At this time, George Riddell[74] of the *News of the World* became a new
friend to both WRN and Lloyd George. He wrote in his diary in October
1908, "I have struck up a friendship with Robertson Nicoll, Editor of
the *British Weekly* and famous 'literary gent'. He is a remarkable old
boy. His memory is wonderful, and he is a brilliant talker. He has great
political influence and is much sought after by Liberal ministers".[75]
Riddell was one of a circle of advisers that Lloyd George gathered from
the Newspaper editors, and he certainly seems to have been one of the
most active and skilful. He could even use his influence to help WRN;
Riddell's diary entry for 9 November 1909 was "Have been urging
L.G., Pease and others to recommend WRN for a knighthood. Today it
is announced. The old boy was very pleased".[76] WRN was knighted in
recognition for his political and social services in November 1909, after
being one of those on a list drawn up by Prime Minister Asquith, which
might have been needed in order to swamp the Lords with Liberal Peers
during the Constitutional Crisis.

Colleagues and friends showered him with their congratulations,
and his family were justifiably proud. Formally, the *Daily Chronicle*
acknowledged the honour and noted some of the reasons for it:

> Sir William Robertson Nicoll has thoroughly earned
> the distinction conferred upon by the King. In addition
> to being a consummate journalist, he is one of the most
> scholarly and versatile of our literary critics, and certainly
> our greatest bookman. As both a speaker and writer, he
> has been looked to for guidance by the Free Churches.
> [He] has shown great capacity and acumen as a writer on
> political affairs. These articles have not only been marked
> by literary distinction[77] but have also all the fervour and

force of an enthusiast. It is no exaggeration to say that they powerfully influenced public opinion.[78]

WRN had earned his honour not least through his loyalty and support to the Liberal Party, which had been marked and significant. As both a colleague and a former editor, D.C. Lathbury summed it up: "No one had a better claim to it than you did on that ground. The amount, the variety and the quality of your work are a constant marvel to me".[79]

In the Constitutional Crisis over the reforming of the House of Lords that followed, WRN battled for the return of the Liberal Government, which was achieved twice, though with reduced majorities and a dependence on the Irish Nationalists. Darlow noted that WRN's secretary said that in her judgment he had "never worked harder than during 1910".[80] To James Denney he apologised for not writing, because his time was "eaten up with political talk".[81] To his friend he intimated that he had felt the strain and been prompted to indulge thoughts of retirement from the *British Weekly*. However, after a judicious pay increase and annual holiday in the South of France, the editor was back at his desk, revelling in the work. WRN supported the Government in the two elections of 1910, and they were successfully returned, but the old enthusiasm was missing. Not only was their substantial majority reduced, but ominous cracks were appearing in the superstructure of political Nonconformity: "One ran horizontally, separating clergy from congregations; another vertically separating the denominations".[82] It would seem that the clergy[83] were more enthusiastic about political involvement than their congregations, which was reflected by speakers at denominational conferences. Further, there was the beginning of a discernible change from religious to class motivation as the determining factor in political commitment: "The relation of class to religion was also changing. The Liberal Party with a firm base in the chapels gave way to the Labour Party based on unions. Though religious conflicts before the war had a class basis, the class conflicts of the post-war era were fought without religious labels.... People now defined themselves more by class and occupation than by religion".[84] Times and old societal landmarks were changing, giving WRN a sense of having lived through the best years.

Many Nonconformists were moving over to support the emerging Labour Party. Increasingly Liberal politicians used the columns of the *British Weekly* to make their particular case. WRN showed interest and concern about the advancement of the Labour Party, and commissioned his assistant to research '*The New Socialism: An impartial inquiry*'.[85]

Lloyd George in action

He commended the resulting book and contributed his own thoughts in the *British Weekly*.[86] The rise of the Labour Party must be partly attributed to a disappointment with the Liberal Party in truly representing the workers' interests. Its early leader Keir Hardie was an avowed Christian, and Arthur Porritt said of him "No one I have ever met took Jesus Christ quite so literally as Keir Hardie. 'The Sermon on the Mount. was practical politics to him".[87] There was a feeling that the affluent and social achievers amongst the Liberals and Nonconformists had forgotten the deprived masses of the nation. The early leaders of the Labour Party were almost all from Nonconformity, and learned their public speaking skills in the chapels, often as lay-preachers.[88] Given the new party's Nonconformist credentials, WRN was all but obliged to examine Labour's ideals, even attending a Conference; he stood by his old loyalty, yet liked to appear open for the benefit of the range of his readers. Though his party succeeded in holding on to power, the world was still changing; the old guard continued to disappear and the contemporary political, social, and international atmosphere grew increasingly wrought with strikes and strife.

In 1912, against the background of socialism, syndicalism, and strikes, WRN wrote four articles presenting a Christian viewpoint that did not toe a party line. In 'The Church and Labour' he believed that:

> As the labour situation changes, the duties and oppor-
> tunities of the church have definitely increased. The way is
> clearer than it once was. Unless we are wholly mistaken,
> there is a disposition on the part of people to grow weary
> of abstract discussion. Controversies on Socialism may be
> carried on without issue and without end.

WRN continued the following week, in 'The Massing of the Masses', "The power of Democracy has been manifested on a tremendous scale. Within the last 25 years we have been told that the day of Democracy has come." The sense of the need to take the responsibility and the opportunities continued, in 'Faith and Changes':

> Change is the most familiar element in life, and we must
> not forget that change is welcome ... it may well be that
> in the new order of society the Christian Faith will burn
> all the brighter because many who were once rich are
> stripped of their wealth.... Every Christian who takes the
> New Testament seriously must acknowledge that riches
> are throughout it viewed as a peril and that they never can
> be rightly held save in a spirit of detachment ... Never was
> there a greater need of the work and leaven of the Christian
> Church than there is today.

Finally in 'The Church at School' he exhorted for the church to embrace the 'day and the hour':

> They [Christians] have had no clear and direct message for
> this crisis. [A period of many strikes] They have no theory
> of society firmly and justly held. If they have a dogmatic
> theory, they are probably in the wrong.... The truth we
> need for all ages is stored up in the Bible ... The Church
> has a deep motive for social reform, the mighty gospel of
> transformation, the effectual appeal to the Eternal.[89]

WRN was continuing to allay fears for the future, whilst at the same time
seeking to advocate the need for structures and constitutional policies,
rather than just allowing the destructive force of feelings to sweep away
all the positive achievements of Britain's Christian democracy.

WRN developed a good working relationship with Lloyd George,
and they shared many views. "Like his new mentor [Lloyd George],
he did not regard traditional party lines as inviolable.... He went so far
as to endorse the idea of a coalition of Liberal and Labour members on
the ground that joint action in some form would be natural enough",[90]
but this would be regarding WRN's view in too positive a light. Lloyd
George used WRN and his papers to represent and propagate his views.
George Riddell wrote to him "Our friend the Chancellor would be very
much obliged if you could insert it [the paragraph intended for the
British Weekly] in your next issue. He holds a very high opinion of the
Rev. Williams as a preacher and is anxious that you should make some
reference to his powers".[91] In turn, WRN gained an excellent source
inside the Government, so that he could give his readers the most reliably
informed news about what was happening in high places. Indeed, this
close acquaintance with Lloyd George would prove an absolute boon
by the War, all the inside information stemming from it maintaining the
circulation success of the *British Weekly* and WRN's personal sense of
residence in the engine room of power.

As 1914 approached, the cooling support of many Nonconformists
for the Liberal Government was further shown in the new generation of
leaders. To WRN they seemed to compare badly with the leaders of the
past. Although John Clifford was the veteran campaigner, other leaders,
such as R.J. Campbell and Silvester Horne, proved to be disappointments;
the former took up heterodoxy, although Campbell did seek to engage
with politic ideas,[92] and the latter failed to command the impact in the
House of Commons that he had shown on the election platform and in
the pulpit. In May 1914, Silvester Horne[93] died suddenly while on a visit
to America. Horne had embodied the Nonconformist hope for the future,
but had worn himself out as a minister and as an MP. As WRN reflected

"He did not draw a line between his religious and his political activities. He included his politics in his religion, and it was in the Name of the Lord Jesus Christ that he spoke the deepest convictions of his soul".[94] Horne reflected the optimism of Nonconformity at the end of the nineteenth century. However, the Nonconformists had "belatedly ... crossed the threshold into the world of twentieth-century politics; some of them (leaders) mistook it for the Promised Land".[95] Silvester Horne was one such influential leader: "He won from all who knew him both admiration and affection. When he went out to America he was not decided as to his future sphere of work, but he did not doubt that great tasks were before him".[96] WRN appreciated but noted the deficiencies in the dynamic impact the newer leaders failed to have on the society at large.

The First World War

It is generally agreed that the First World War had a devastating effect on Western civilisation and in particular on the Church. "However much a commonplace, it is no exaggeration to say that war, when it came unexpectedly in August 1914, dealt a shattering blow to organised religion. The Churches never recovered from the ordeal, either in terms of communicants or self-possession. Thereafter, men looked elsewhere, if anywhere, for their moral certainties".[97] This is fairly well-explored terrain, particularly in terms of the decline of Nonconformity as a national force and as an element in the decline of the Liberal Party and emergence of the Labour Party. Leaders like WRN were aware of a decline in the standing and general perception of the Church, but they thought it only *temporary*, and that circumstances would change and bring about a revival of interest. WRN genuinely believed that greater political involvement by the Nonconformists would aid this revival of interest.[98] It is also worth noting that studies of the period often tend to fall into one of two camps; those that make too much of the part played by the Nonconformists and those that would ignore them altogether. There were major environmental, demographic, social, educational and spiritual changes taking place in those early years of the twentieth century, but the First World War quickened the pace. It dealt a devastating blow to those in Nonconformity who were pursuing the cause of displaying to the nation their distinctive contribution to the life of the country. Of course, this is all from the benefit of the later historian's hindsight, but at the time, WRN, though a principled believer was also an editor and he took a much more pragmatic view, eager to exploit the immediate opportunities. His concern was to help maintain unity in the Liberal Party by sustaining the support of the Nonconformists, and in displaying the Liberals as *the* party to be entrusted with the responsibility of Government, in peace and war.

WRN, like so many others, hoped against hope for war to be avoided, but when it became a fact, it intensified and galvanised his political commitment into using his resources for the successful resolution of the conflict, something he viewed as his civic and his Christian duty. He was never a warmonger, though his zeal to get the job done was misinterpreted by those who failed to appreciate the seriousness of the hour. WRN's leading article for 31 July 1914 was not only neutral in tone; it also commended the Kaiser's efforts for peace. On 4 August WRN wrote to his son, "It looked as if Germany was hesitating. The cabinet are at one in believing that Germany has been perfidious throughout, and say that she has secretly mobilised a month before the formal order… I never had such difficult job before me as the writing of my leader tonight, but I suppose I shall get through it somehow".[99] However, as with many wavering Nonconformists, the invasion or 'rape' of Belgium drew him to the conviction that Britain had to enter the war. The *British Weekly* for 6 August carried the headline 'United We Stand'. WRN wrote,

> Till Sunday we were working hard for a policy of strict neutrality in the European war. We had hoped to publish today messages from Free Church leaders advocating this policy. Surely it was natural to take this line.... The Free Churches have worked for disarmament, and who can blame them? ... but after Sir Edward Grey's speech on Monday [giving the details of the German invasion of Belgium], our hopes have vanished, as we think, and many of our friends are of the same mind.… Only very grave reasons could justify the breaking of national unity when the nation is fighting for its life.… We must pray as we have never prayed before … let us pray also for peace, and pursue it even when the heart faints. The answer will come.[100]

WRN understood the seriousness of the War, and during the so-called Phoney War period he wrote, "This war has altered everything. One feels sure of nothing now. All the old foundations are shaken, and we do not know what we can keep".[101] WRN's friend and colleague Hodder-Williams remembered a meeting with him at the end of August 1914:

> He looked tired and I wondered if he had strength enough reserved against the days of trouble. We sat in silence

for a time, those pale mystic eyes of his, now clear, now
cloudy, first questioning me almost fiercely across the
table, then looking through me, past me, out beyond into
the frowning future. I know he saw terrible things, for he
had fewer illusions about war than most of us and far more
understanding.... We stood up, and then he told me of his
faith, of his determination to see it through – 'you and I
together', as we had seen through many fights in the past.
'Never fear we shall win – in the end. But we shall pass
through deep waters ... I have no fear' ... Then, with one of
those sudden changes that never cease to startle those who
knew him best – in a voice like naked steel: 'I have no fear.
The blood of my forbears watered the fields of Culloden.'
It was true. He had no fear and he knew the meaning of
sacrifice ... in a few moments we had settled down to the
urgent business of carrying on and defining the policy of
a paper during the Great War.... He was always intolerant
of vagueness.[102]

He stayed at his post and sought to guide his readers through the
uncharted waters of a world war.

WRN was agreeably surprised and heartened by the Nonconformist
support for the war shown at the National Council of Free Churchmen
meeting on 10 November. WRN as chairman stated that, "If we had
not been Christians we should not have been in this war. It is Christ
who has taught us to fight for liberty, righteousness and peace."[103] Then
with R.J. Campbell and John Clifford seconding the motion that was
given by Lloyd George in his best form, the Nonconformists showed
resolve to fight.[104] Lloyd George later paid a warm tribute to WRN's
wartime commitment: "Once he had decided in his mind that there was
no alternative to the dread arbitrament of war – except the abandonment
of liberty and the surrender of national honour – he never hesitated and
he never wavered".[105] A.J.P. Taylor has commented, appreciatively but
ominously: "So in 1914, the Free Churches ... held the key position.
When Lloyd George, sustained by Robertson Nicoll, came down on the
side of war, he determined that there would be national unity, though,
in a longer perspective, the two men sealed the death warrant of the
Free Churches as a great moral force".[106] Would the Nonconformists
have been so united behind the war effort without WRN? Probably
not, although the degree of hyped appreciation for WRN's work here,
both at the time and immediately after the war, was, understandable,

attitudes and became loud supporters of the War, consequently becoming identified with the establishment. Others found the change difficult to take or appreciate, having been in the forefront of movements seeking world peace, they turned their "churches... into adjuncts to recruiting offices and pulpits had become platforms for announcing the latest war news".[111] The Nonconformists campaigned using the ideas and imagery of their faith, willingly sacrificed their ablest young men, and paid further after the war. WRN was one of the main exhorters who used the language of faith to press for the full commitment needed for victory. In an article on September 3 1914, he called for the crushing of the Prussian military system: "There is not a more flagrant iniquity on earth".[112] For WRN the pursuit of victory became a crusade, as Darlow reflected: "To read over again leader after leader which he wrote in hours of national peril, is to feel how 'in his hand the thing became a trumpet, whence he blew soul-animating strains'. Not the least part of his patriotic service was thus to fortify his fellow-countrymen during the darkest months of the dreadful conflict".[113] He used all his powers of argument – practical and religious – to further the cause:

> Free Church [Nonconformist] faith concentrated upon the atoning power of the cross, as did the faith and eucharistic language of other traditions. So there was a potent (and dangerous) source of sacrificial imagery available for Christians to use to idealise the soldiers' deaths and justify the ways of God to men. We should remember the all-pervasive influence of such popular hymns as 'Onward Christian Soldiers', 'Fight the good fight' or 'There is a fountain filled with blood'.[114]

Such were the perceptions of WRN's rallying skills and influence that he was asked to make his contribution to the recruitment drive. He sought to justify the war to the young members of Nonconformity[115] and the War Office published his article, 'Set Down My Name, Sir', in several daily papers. In his article, he states the reasons for supporting the war effort: "Till this evil spirit is cast out there will be no peace or safety. We must have an end of the Prussian military system".[116] WRN also began to publish his 'War Notes' column, which increasingly owed a great deal to his special inside information, obtained mainly from Lloyd George. They were read with great interest and much appreciation[117] – the sales of the *British Weekly* actually increased during the War. WRN was aware that many Nonconformists went contrary to some of their firmly held principles, but it is difficult to imagine that he really appreciated the sacrifice Nonconformity made in the course of the change. At heart he was a Scottish Presbyterian, and held a different outlook to English Nonconformists, and however his English brethren may have felt, to WRN the present emergency was the all-consuming need.

As the war proceeded, he came to see that the voluntary principle of recruitment was insufficient for the emergency and reluctantly became an advocate of the need for conscription, even before it became a political reality in 1916. As the War dragged on, taking its toll of men and principles, WRN continued to urge for greater commitment for victory in articles such as 'The Churches and the War',[118] 'First Righteousness- Then Peace',[119] 'More Men and Still More Men'[120] and 'The Acceptance of Sacrifice'.[121] This approach identified WRN and other Nonconformist leaders with the National Establishment, and was indicative of a growing movement amongst many Nonconformists from radical politics to more conservative ideals. Alan Wilkinson was later to point out,

> The close identification of Nonconformists with the war effort was contrary to some of its deepest instincts, however much there was a continuum between its stance and earlier aggressive crusades. This identification led to a destructive confusion in its own mind and that of others as to what it really stood for now. The hyper-emotional language adopted by some of its leaders during the war was, no doubt, a way of suppressing deep doubts and moral confusions beneath the surface of their own minds. Certainly the war convinced many of the general public that all the churches were impotent, mere pawns of nationalism, and had nothing distinctive to say, or were too cowardly and subservient to say it. And much of the theology received in theological college, church pew or Sunday school, seemed totally inadequate to cope with the experience of war.[122]

WRN was too closely committed to perceive anything like this; for him there was a great task to be done.

Despite this almost fanatical devotion to the war effort, WRN was not blind to the suffering it caused – another facet of his endless work was an ongoing effort to encourage, counsel and comfort his readers. He often wrote personally to those individuals he knew the War had bereaved. He wrote a series of leading articles, seeking to comfort those who were going through times of anguish and distress, and the collection became *Prayer at the Time of War*.[123]

Never were there so many of our people bereaved or about
to be bereaved. What anguished hearts need is the Easter
assurance of life. For we cannot, try as we may, love the
dead as dead. We may, and we do love their memories ...
we may hope much, and very much from the peril and
awfulness and solemnity of their end. Their lives were in
hazard from the first day of fighting. Did they not know it?
Did they not breathe a prayer to the Saviour?[124]

WRN subscribed to the thought, held by a number of contemporary
preachers, that soldiers often made their peace with God as they met
their deaths. Further, his humanitarian feelings were seen when he
found time to join a host of radical writers in an attempt to save Roger
Casement from execution in 1916.[125]

WRN kept the Temperance problem on the boil as a specific necessity
for the duration of the War. He had advocated a policy of prohibition
from the earliest days of the *British Weekly*, and even argued against
compensation for publicans whose businesses might be suppressed. In
truth, WRN never pretended to be an abstainer, he could not stand those
who denounced all alcohol as poison, and felt that extremism hindered
the cause of temperance. He felt that no Christian could condemn all
alcohol – after all, what about the Communion, which was derived
from Christ Himself. Lady Nicoll, in her memoirs, recalled an incident
that underlined WRN's approach to the difficult topic: "Shortly after
a vigorous article by my husband had appeared the Secretary and
Chairman of the Shipbuilders asked to call and see him on the subject.
They told him that nothing less than total prohibition would be of any
value to them if they were to get through the necessary building in their
yards".[126] As to WRN "it appeared not as a gospel, but as a necessary
expedient".[127] In the spring of 1915, the King banned wine, spirits
and beer from being consumed in the royal palaces as long as the war
lasted, but the stricture did not apply to Bay Tree Lodge! This evident
contradiction was an ongoing source of puzzlement to his friends, as
much as his enemies. To WRN's mind, however, it was simple – he
believed he was exercising his Christian freedom and at the same time
being responsible for the national good.

In February 1916 WRN published an article[128] in the *British Weekly* in
which he advocated, quite seriously, that the Government should make
Lord Northcliffe 'Air Minister' and responsible for this new aspect of
modern warfare. Northcliffe[129] was keen but the Government was not so
impressed.[130] WRN was remembered as snapping at a correspondent, "if

Lord Northcliffe had been appointed to the Air Ministry we should have had no fear of Zeppelins".[131] In the same month, he seriously backed a call for Lord Fisher to return to the charge of the Admiralty,[132] but eventually thought better of it, so that Riddell could note in his Diary "Nicoll now thinks that Fisher is in a dangerous state of mind and that his return to the Admiralty would be perilous".[133] WRN wrote in a frank and open way about the terrible losses on the Western front. After the Battle of the Somme (July 1916), he stated

> Day by day we keep looking with dim eyes at the bleeding list of casualties. It seems that if anything could put faith to confusion, if anything could cancel prayer, if anything could quench hope, it would be this welter of war and wounds and death. How can we rise out of our darkness and look behind us and before us with quiet and assured hearts? ... There is a supplication appropriate for the need ... 'Let the beauty of the Lord our God be upon us; and establish thou the work of our hands upon us; yea, the work of our hands establish thou it' [Psalm 90, v17].[134]

WRN shared the growing discontent with lack of decision and determination in the War effort being shown by key members of the Government. He regarded Lloyd George as the leader for the hour, a champion who could get things done in the completely new demands of a total war. Other leaders, such as Asquith, were too attached to the methods of the past, but Lloyd George had the capacity to think of new and fresh ways of doing things. To what extent was WRN aware of Lloyd George's human faults and traits? He was no fool, and though flattered by Lloyd George, he was also in a position to observe the man's methods for himself. The overriding concern was the national emergency, and to WRN's mind there was no one more able to rise to so dire an occasion than Lloyd George. Increasingly WRN's articles in the *British Weekly* became an almost blatant adulation of his friend. A prominent Nonconformist leader, J.D. Jones of Bournemouth, saw this emphasis and the possibility of factional infighting, which would bring about national disunity at such a time. He wrote to WRN a warning letter, only to receive a stinging reply:

> You say that I should warn Mr. George that the Nonconformists will not tolerate division. What does this mean? Does it mean that the Nonconformists will not tolerate his leaving the Government? What does he care whether they tolerate him or not! ... Mr. Lloyd

George is the very last man to whom I would address
a warning ... there are plenty of warnings that might be
addressed to Cabinet ministers, but none that I know to
him. And as for the Nonconformists, you know perfectly
well that I have always been independent of them in the
sense that I have always given my own opinion whether
it accorded with their opinion or not.... Nonconformity
needs to be told very plainly that its place in English life
will be lost if it fails to play its part in this War. Many
have done nobly, but others have done very ill. Scotland,
however, I am glad to say, is as one man.[135]

Jones replied saying that he felt that WRN was being less than just
to Nonconformists. Jones felt that the so-called 'Pacifist' group was
negligible and that Nonconformists had given their sons quite freely.
Jones then sweetened his reply, by saying that in spite of Nicoll's
disclaimer he did speak for the Nonconformists as 'our most potent
voice in the public press'[136]. This episode has much of interest, not
least the degree of objectivity that WRN could muster in examining the
Nonconformist attitudes to the War.

WRN's articles had a rhetorical style which encouraged and exhorted
at the same time. The continuing desperate situation of the War and the
national needs partly account for the tone, but he was the master of
being able to strike a confident note in times of emergency. His 'support
Lloyd George because he knows what is best for us' approach was what
Lloyd George wanted and the country needed at the time. However, the
tactic did come with a 'sell-by' date. WRN used his leading article to
prime the Scottish people for a visit from Lloyd George: "The Prime
Minister will receive this week an enthusiastic and richly merited
welcome to Scotland. When all is said and done, it is he who saved the
country".[137] Predictably, WRN reported the following week of Lloyd
George's fulsome reception in Scotland.

Early in 1917, WRN surveyed the conflict in 'The War after Thirty
Months' (January 25) and simply stated the fact that there was still much
to do. However, his article 'Hail Columbia' (February 8) greeted the
American announcement that they had broken off diplomatic relations
with Germany because Germany had recommenced 'unrestricted'
submarine attacks on all shipping aiding Britain. This was sign that
help was coming soon, and that whole wretched business would end.
Then, in the Christmas special WRN announced 'Jerusalem Delivered'
(December 13) in which the news of General Allenby's victory over

the Turks was celebrated. Yet 1918 saw the German 'last-ditch' offensive to break through on the Western Front and win the War outright, before the arrival of large quantities of American soldiers. His leading articles sought to steady the resolve of his readers: "The war has clutched the heart of the nation as it never has done before. There may have been more critical hours in its history than the hour we are living and dying through, but … the boldest holds his breath … hold on; cease from mere argument in words; pray, look heavenward, hope steadfastly in the loving One".[138] So WRN stuck to his post, continuing to write his articles[139] and his weekly 'War Notes', seeking to keep his readers both encouraged and as informed as he could manage, given his valuable sources of information. The German assault was not only held, but the Allies mounted a successful counter-attack. So by mid-October, he could write "We must not over-estimate the magnitude of the German surrender, and most certainly we must not underrate it … it is not a surrender prompted by repentance in any form. It is simply the enemy's testimony to the solidity of the rock against which he is dashing his already decaying power to pieces".[140]

As the War ended in November 1918, Lloyd George decided to go for a snap election for December. The 'Coupon' Election, as Asquith called it, was where the coalition candidates carried an official letter of Government endorsement, signed by both Lloyd George and Bonar Law. In the jingoistic atmosphere with the ending of the war, it seemed appropriate that Lloyd George continue his coalition as a 'marriage of convenience' with the Conservatives, rather than seek to rejoin with the other 'embittered' Liberals. In this way, he could use his enormous abilities and acclaimed prestige to seek to reconstruct the post-war world. WRN was committed to securing the return of the Coalition Government of Lloyd George and in private memoranda he states how he was persuaded to be involved.

> The Election is to go on. LG wants me to write a brief account, four pages, of the things he has done since the War began, to be published first in the B/W with my signature and to be scattered over the country for electioneering. I said to George [Riddell], 'Of course you and I would have to do it.' Unless the PM revised it and corrected it, I would have nothing to do with it ... but this is to be kept quite private and none to know that he sanctioned it. I said I was exceedingly anxious to have it anonymous but they wanted the name.[141]

In his first article, WRN wrote, "He has stimulated his countrymen to sterner efforts when they failed to realise the magnitude of the task before them, and encouraged them in the dark hours when the cause seemed almost a lost one.... Our own belief is that the British people, who are just, know in their heart of hearts that a great leader is a very special gift of God, and that they have found one in the Prime Minister".[142] Then he followed this with

> Cromwell, Chatham, Lloyd George, are three statesmen who have made Britain great...everywhere we have to note the decisive, practical eye of this man; how he drives towards the practical and practicable; has a genuine insight into what *is* fact...calm, clear-headed and impartial, he won the confidence of masters and men. He can listen as well as talk ... our leader gave all he had, not only of physical and mental force, but also of moral inspiration... the dumb millions found an interpreter.[143]

The result of the election was a massive vote and a victory for the Coalition, with nearly all the leading Liberals, including Asquith being defeated. WRN crowed "We never had a doubt as to the result of the Election, but perhaps no one expected such an overwhelming victory".[144] Lloyd George was head of a predominantly Conservative Government[145] and he became increasingly tainted and shackled by post-War problems. The Election exasperated the division of the Liberal Party, but it also demonstrated that there was division amongst the Nonconformists.

After the War?

After the War, attention was centred on Paris and negotiating the Peace Treaties. WRN wrote, "Does anyone believe that the Germans will be allowed with impunity to sink millions and millions of tons and kill hundreds of thousands of unoffending women and children? Does anyone believe that they will be allowed to burn and destroy the places from which they are driven and to take civilians with them as captives? No, there must be very heavy indemnities".[146] In a post-War leader announcing the abdication of the Kaiser, he wrote "There is an end of the mighty and evil system which Germany has built up with blood and tears. Arrogance has again been evidently rebuked and confounded by the Most High. The chief minister of evil, the worst criminal, has been humiliated to the very dust.... It is best to say, 'This is the Lord's doing, and it is wondrous in our eyes'".[147] Such language reflected a popular mood in the country, which felt the need for Germany to pay for the War, but was also the language of the Coalition Government seeking a mandate from the people to negotiate the Peace Treaty at Versailles. WRN reflected this 'hard line' and even before the hostilities ended, he wrote

> We need to be recalled as Christians [to] the duty of moral indignation. The more we seek to banish from our minds and from the minds of those whom we can influence any temper of vindictiveness, the more we are bound to avoid the danger of condoning crime in the name of Christ.... We who are supremely concerned about a Christian settlement that should leave no rancour behind ... ought to be reminding ourselves that we dare not expect to forgive Germany until we see that our forgiveness carries in its heart an intense condemnation of her crimes.[148]

WRN also wrote, "Plain justice demands that Germany shall pay to the uttermost of her power for the ruin she has wrought in France and Belgium. Civilisation could not endure unless the sternest penalties were inflicted on the kindlers of a world war".[149] This sort of language linked WRN with other 'proprietors of certain popular journals', who called for 'vengeance' on German 'War crimes' and that endorsed the notorious 'war guilt clause'.[150] In these and other ways, WRN appeared to continue to link Nonconformity with the Establishment, which meant that those readers who agreed with him found their Nonconformist distinctiveness was being lost; they were merging with the general national consensus.

Following the War, Lloyd George needed a backing or support constituency in order to retain power, and he thought he could still count on the Nonconformists. Certainly many Nonconformists, like WRN, continued to see him as one of them and gave him their support. However, an increasing number had moved to the right politically, even as Lloyd George himself appeared to do. Others were attracted by the radicalism of the new Labour Party, which had broken away from the Coalition. For many the Government of 'Hard faced Men' was led by their one-time radical hero, seemingly basking in the glow of his own achievements, but too big and remote to care about ordinary problems. This led to a cooling of enthusiasm for Lloyd George and a change to scepticism, disbelief and rejection.

> To an extraordinary extent, the political history of post-Victorian Nonconformity was linked, inexorably and

avowedly, to the fortunes of this single and singular individual. The relationship, progressively less advantageous to either side, was never without its incongruities. Flattered by Lloyd George's attentions, Free Church leaders tended to overlook the disappointments they suffered at his hand. Justly proud of his rapid advancement, which they took as a credit to themselves, they tried their best to ignore the naked opportunism with which he pursued his goals. Occasionally, he went too far; but he was always able to restore himself in their good graces by a fervent appeal to their common inheritance, or, better still, by a rousing attack on privilege, ecclesiastical or otherwise.[151]

The leaders might be taken along, but many of the 'rank and file' in the Churches were growing increasingly disillusioned with Lloyd George and his remote cavalier attitude sounded ever more insincere. WRN remained loyal to Lloyd George, and though occasionally critical of Government policies, he appreciated the dilemma of Lloyd George's position. In February 1920, he wrote to the Prime Minister,

> As I venture to think, your course is to form a Democratic Party, which will be a constitutional party. The foe to fight is direct action, which means strikes of a murderous kind. In fighting these and insisting on all matters being settled in Parliament you would have behind you, not only the Conservatives and Liberals, but also a large portion of the Labour Party. This would allow understandings with the Labour Party on various points. With you at the head of such a party things would go well.[152]

These thoughts remain as portraits of what might have been, but such a possibility would be much debated. In July 1921 WRN had an audience with the King and received the Companion of Honour. Fully deserved for his successful services to his country and his political masters, it was not part of the infamous 'sale of honours' that Lloyd George succumbed to the following year. Lloyd George gave his resignation to the King on October 19 1922. He then fought a "curiously spiritless campaign. Not wishing to accept as final the Conservatives' declaration of independence from him … the *British Weekly* continued to stand by Lloyd George to the extent that WRN refused to publish a pair of highly critical articles, which he had rashly commissioned from A.G. Gardiner over a glass of wine at the Reformed Club".[153] Had Lloyd George come to think of himself as the natural leader of the nation, and, rather like his predecessor, believed that he simply had to wait for his recall? A.J.P. Taylor reflected on WRN and Lloyd George, and thought he saw a measure of distance between the two men. Taylor viewed the criticism of some Government policies that came from WRN's papers as the editor 'putting the boot in'. "It is hardly too much to say that Robertson Nicoll was the man who first, by supporting Lloyd George, raised him up, and then, by withdrawing his support, cast him down".[154] This, however, is far too melodramatic and overblown, with little evidence to support it – WRN always remained loyal to his friends, and, disagreements aside, Lloyd George was no exception.

Conclusion: The *British Weekly* in the New Century

From 1900, there was a discernible change in the political orientation of the *British Weekly*, which led to a more pronounced active political engagement. Twenty years before, the emphasis had been the latest views about books and the church scene, which was pastoral concerns, scholarship and the Bible, but now WRN's paper reflected a change to a more active political engagement with the questions of the day. The papers still contained their religious articles, but the editor and readership were changing to a different view of the world and its priorities. In spite of his avowed intention of keeping the religious emphasis to the fore in his leading articles, there were changes that may be discerned. "The most impressive legislation in the Liberal programme of 1912 concerned land reform and rural housing. Nicoll's leader in the *British Weekly* foreshadowed this – a 'scoop', which created a political sensation and showed Fleet Street how close Nicoll was to the control room".[155] More importantly, and in keeping with the change in orientation of the paper, was WRN's signed column, 'Things in General'. This was always next to the leading article and was almost entirely concerned with the political matters of the day.

   This progressive shift towards greater involvement in politics was reflected in both WRN's interests and those of his readers. The War was not the sole reason for apparent decline in institutional religion, in the influence of Nonconformity in particular. There was a slow ebbing of influence discernible in the Edwardian period, some would say earlier, although it was well disguised to most contemporaries by the many activities and the vigour with which the various personalities, such as WRN, sought to maintain interest. However, the shallow slope of the decline became more precipitate through the events of the War and beyond:

> The War did powerfully accelerate and intensify
> pluralism, secularisation, and the belief in modernity,
> which had proved to be most potent solvents of allegiance
> to institutional religion. It is not so much that faith and
> religious experience have declined in our country, but that
> fewer and fewer people have found it possible to express
> their faith and experience through the means which the
> Churches provide. The War created particular difficulties
> for Nonconformity … they were not new difficulties, but
> the old dilemmas rammed home with apocalyptic force.[156]

WRN's contribution successfully helped Britain to win the War, there he had demonstrated a safe pair of hands on the tiller, but the cost was the weakening of many traditional values[157] that he had championed in his younger days – and, more ominously, there was a perceived weakness of the Christian faith in the minds of the general public.

WRN's Final Years and Legacy

As Britain entered the third decade of the twentieth century there were rapid changes both in the Church and in society, but WRN and his fellow leaders did not succeed in halting the decline of church adherents.[1] What he and his generation handed on was, in spite of their best intentions, a flawed and weakened church, which seemed to have lost its way. Time and circumstances had altered and the situation that was once positive and rewarding had become hard, barren and alien. The devastating effect of the war and the firm measures needed to bring about a successful conclusion deprived the country and the Nonconformists of the cream of their young men, the 'lost generation'. Unsurprisingly, WRN shared the triumphs and the flaws characteristic of the period. There was certainly a perceptible decline: the number of adherents, converts, and ordinands fell, as did the quantity and quality of religious books and other outward indicators. There was also, however, a dilution, a loss of influence of the Church in society. Later generations were to refer to this as 'secularisation' or the marginalisation of Christianity. To what extent WRN and his contemporaries were aware of this is conjectural, but they were at the least conscious of an 'ebbing tide' of support. They cherished the hope that any decline would be temporary and that numbers would resurge. During this time their hope was in a great coming 'revival' or turn-around, bringing the masses back to the Church, as had happened in some parts of Britain in the years 1858-9, 1874-5 and 1904-6.

In terms of demographics, WRN belonged to a unique period in the development of the British electoral system. Gladstone's government in 1884 had passed the Third Reform Act. This continued the advantage given to the Nonconformists by the Reform Act of 1867, but in 1918 the Representation of the People Act was passed, which not only gave the vote to women over thirty, but also brought in universal male suffrage for men over twenty-one. This effectively took away the electoral advantage that the Nonconformists had enjoyed, for the bulk of the working class proved resistant to organised religion.[2] At the turn of the century, there was a unique period of opportunity for the Nonconformists, for they "were particularly well placed to make their mark in politics. Party leaders listened carefully to their views and Nonconformists themselves were eager to exert the maximum leverage on the fulcrum of power. With their growing numbers, they confidently believed that this entitled them to a share in deciding how the nation should be run".[3] Things became very different by the time of WRN's death. The Nonconformist population was beginning to fall off at the end of the nineteenth century. There had been a partial recovery peaking around 1906, but "Thereafter the fall has been almost continuous, and even before 1914 it was provoking serious heart-searching. But up to 1906 people were seldom aware of the ominous decline relative to population. What they knew about was only the absolute growth shown in the annual denominational returns".[4] Circumstances would never be the same again and WRN engaged with those changing attitudes and conditions in social, cultural and theological thought.

In 1917, with a general disenchantment with religion still growing, WRN gave vent to his feeling about a lack of vitality within the churches: "Without being pessimistic, one must confess that the great pulpit thrones of London are not occupied so much by dominant preachers as they used to be. I am referring to preachers who stand out, preachers who draw crowds of Londoners and strangers, preachers who speak to the nation".[5] Was this merely the nostalgic disappointment of an old man? Possibly, but it was also a subject that had always been a passion for WRN, and the decay of something he thrilled to hear – dynamic and vital preaching – was understandably painful. Moreover, he was well positioned to note the great drop in the popularity of the sale of religious books.[6] Ironically, for WRN, people preferred to spend time and money on fiction, culture – anything but religion. Had his 'culture mission' been too successful? Having invested so much in his effort to widen the cultural horizon of his Nonconformist readers, WRN was concerned, but basically 'sanguine' about its lasting effect.[7] Panic, however, was never WRN's style or disposition – the dominant attitude that he strove for in the *British Weekly*, even when reporting crises, was always solidly optimistic. He noted the fears and alarm of those who wrote suggesting some decline in the churches.[8] Though he would voice concerns amidst friends, as when James Denney wrote to him that "There were more students – a great many more – in our Glasgow College when I entered in 1879 than there are now [April 1907]"[9], WRN knew that pessimistic panic was not what his readers wanted. Even in his review of J.H. Shakespeare's book, *The Churches at the*

Cross Roads, he accepted Shakespeare's "statistics to prove that the Free Church communicants in this country are dwindling in numbers"[10]. Such an acceptance, however, was not accompanied by fear or anger. Instead of presenting the argument as a discouraging sign, a sure way to lose readers, he characterised it as a topic of interest, ever trumpeting the belief that 'things' would pick up.

That he read societal changes from a perspective of long-term waxing and waning is quite characteristic – WRN had always watched trends and tendencies in society, particularly amongst the young. He had written, years before, to his friend John Watson of Liverpool,

> I am deeply concerned every day about the love of pleasure and want of seriousness among the young people of our richer classes. They are reading nothing except the worst fiction. They are spending their whole spare time in pleasure, which is growing more doubtful every day. Sunday evening is given to dinners and suppers, and the moral tone is getting very low.... It appears to me that if society is to be saved, and if the Church in especial is to do her proper work; there must be a return to the great Puritan idea of separation from the world. So far as I know, except with a few extreme people – very few now – there is no difference between the Church and the world; they all dance, they all go to music halls... they are all eating and drinking on Sunday, and the younger people are growing up without the fear of God.[11]

He was particularly aware of the problem Nonconformity faced in holding on to its young people and attracting others. He was also particularly aware of where so many of them were fleeing – though he always deprecated any person who left the Church into which they were born, a special vitriol was reserved for those apostates who turned from Nonconformity to the Church of England. Petty sectarianism aside, however, the fundamental root of WRN's concern was, in truth, the declining numbers of young people in all Churches. This was a long-standing worry about life in the churches dating back to his days as a minister, when he would often take the young people's classes himself. From the earliest issues of the *British Weekly* he had a weekly column 'International Sunday School Lesson', written by Alexander Maclaren. In 1889, he began a column, 'Our Page for Young Men' and noted that other initiatives had taken place.[12] At the same time, he warned,

> While we confidently believe that the result will be good, it is not to be denied that difficulties have risen, and

have not always been wisely overcome. These have been mainly connected with amusements. The great danger of the Church becoming a purveyor of amusement is that she should simply stir up the passion for more, and then hand on her youth to more expert and less scrupulous caterers.[13]

He later set up a 'League of Young Worshippers' in 1911, in order to encourage the young to participate in Church life, and then in 1913, he published *The Children for the Church*,[14] maintaining the same concern.

In discussing the positive attitude and resilience WRN displayed in the face of such adversity, it must be remembered that he was able to take the dips and partial declines in Church life because he believed in the doctrine of Revival. He knew enough Church history from both sides of the border (as well as on the other side of the 'pond') to have read about times of dullness and decline often being quickly followed by vital and vigorous growth. His own early experience of the impact of the Moody and Sankey Mission, not to mention WRN's own experience of reporting on the Welsh Revival meant that he saw declining Church numbers as an almost necessary decay for the ensuing rebirth to occur. He was, then, more than a little disappointed by the lack of response after the Great War, to a mind such as his this was an ideal time for such a religious rediscovery. Times had changed, however, from those nineteenth century revivals, and it was with a distinctly Victorian mindset that WRN awaited a mass return to the comforts of the past just as the intoxication of modern life began to truly tighten its grasp upon the British public. He was aware of some of the secularising forces at work, and even partook of a few, but in general these new fads struck him as singularly uninteresting, or at best hardly a distraction from the joys of the Church. Sport, particularly football, left him unmoved, and although very occasionally he did attend the theatre and enjoyed the cinema, his most sincere advice was always to read a good book. It was a lasting source of puzzlement to him that more people did not occupy their time with the sheer joy of reading. Towards other signs of secularisation, WRN displayed a certain ambivalence; he welcomed the rising standard of living and the expectations of life that saw not only the owners and managers moving out to leafy suburbia, but also their clerks and 'lower' staff following suit. He enjoyed holidays and his 'Claudius Clear' celebration of travels encouraged others to explore the places he had described. He used modern advertising, which helped keep the costs down but it made the *British Weekly* look more like a successful secular paper, though it did not read like one. Even in his embrace of an increasingly outspoken political stance, WRN was moving, if unintentionally, with the times. The support of the Liberal Party had been part of his brief from the outset, but the last twenty-five years of his life saw politics dominate his time almost entirely. In this, he reflected what was happening to others in the church. He thought his policy of active involvement was helping the position of the church, but viewed in its entirety, it functioned as part of the greater secularising effect, encouraging his wide body of readers – almost exclusively Nonconformist as late as the turn of the century – to see new attitudes, styles and values as replacements of the Church.

Though increasingly encroached upon by secular society, Nonconformity was simultaneously achieving unheard of parity with the Church of England to the degree that they were, in most ways, equal to the Anglicans and now readily identifiable as part of the Establishment. This new status was not, however, a universally welcomed development – it meant to a number of Nonconformists that their distinct identity as Nonconformists or English Free Churchmen had been eroded. The reasons for 'dissent' or 'nonconforming' had largely been dealt within the legislation of the nineteenth century, and many of the younger generation could see no reason to remain a distinct entity; for they interpreted the achievement gained in status as a reason for merging with the rejuvenated State Church. However, WRN maintained there was a distinct sense of Nonconformist culture and identity and this attitude was seen in 1918 in his discussion over J.H. Shakespeare's book, *The Churches at the Cross Roads*. His view of denominationalism was a traditional 'status quo'; WRN often spoke about Christ having 'sheep of another fold' and he had a distinct love of listening to sermons in the ethos of many small, strict and particular English groups.[15] He applauded when strands of Scottish Presbyterians sought to reunite,[16] as in 1900, for they were from the same stock, as was the proposed reunion of all Methodists. However, he became totally condemnatory and opposed to Shakespeare's suggestions for unity and reconciliation with the Anglicans. "Mr. Shakespeare does not pretend to think Episcopacy is essential to the true church, but he would have us unite with the Anglicans on their own conditions, because [he says] they will resolutely refuse to accept us on any other terms." Then WRN challenged,

> Mr. Shakespeare's fundamental error lies deeper ... it has been said that 'the enemy of true unity is false unity'.... Mr. Shakespeare would accept prelacy because the spirit of the

age demands reunion. But he misreads the temper of the
new time ... for Free Church [Nonconformist] ministers to
accept Episcopal ordination would be to admit solemnly
and publicly that they were receiving some spiritual gift
which they did not possess before.[17]

WRN continued to demonstrate that he was very much aware of the
situation when he wrote a detailed letter to J.D. Jones of Bournemouth.

I think there is a great and just dislike of private conclaves
and conferences ... these people have no mandate from
us, the common peoples of the Churches, We never
authorised them to surrender our principles or betray our
rights. To sum up, I think that Shakespeare has been the
worst enemy of Church Unity I have known ... I think
therefore that whatever good there was in the federation
movement ... has been effectively destroyed by the
Shakespeare plan.[18]

WRN firmly believed that he spoke for the majority of his readers,
many of whom had written in to him, criticising Shakespeare's
proposals. However, his attitude seems to owe as much to his Scottish
Presbyterian roots as to his concern about his Nonconformist readers.
This, also, could open up an intriguing speculation as to whether he
was seeking to bolster a distinct Nonconformist grouping in society
just as it appeared to be reaching the apex of its influence at that
time. When King George V attended a Nonconformist Thanksgiving
Service[19] in the Albert Hall on 16 November 1918, many believed that
the Nonconformists had achieved their aim and were now part of the
Establishment. Trevor Wilson has argued that Nonconformity paid a
staggering price for its right to exult in the Allied victory. "It had become
too closely connected with a regime Conservative in complexion and
nationalist in outlook. Whereas the Church of England might survive,
and even prosper from, identification with the nation in arms, such
identification did violence to the genius of Nonconformity".[20] To
which Stephen Koss added, "The loss was revealed most immediately
in the political sphere, where Free Churchmanship no longer operated
as a tactical unit. Its disintegration mirrored that of the Liberal Party,
to which it contributed in no small measure, and helped to foster a
Labour alternative ... political Nonconformity proved unable to define
its raison d'etre, and consequently was denied one".[21] Even before
the article attacking Shakespeare's proposals, it might be asked, had
WRN been party to perpetuating a 'Nonconformist Ideal' of unity and

significance – an 'Ideal', which he, with others, had doggedly sought to maintain as a sense of identity? Regardless of his role in forcing the question, he did not live to see the answer manifest its full consequences for Nonconformity, aware though he was that the Nonconformist distinctiveness was already fraying round the edges.

WRN's Later Years (1920-1923)

As WRN entered the 1920s he tried, as much as his health would allow, to maintain his usual daily routines. These had been well established after his attack of typhoid in 1885 and though he remained for the rest of his life a semi-invalid, it was a fact that he both accepted and cultivated for its usefulness. He developed the habit of doing a very considerable amount of his work from his bed, surrounded by newspapers and books. Yet, "wherever he was, in whatever state of body, his mind seemed able to function unceasingly".[22] WRN husbanded his energy and was always particularly careful about his health. Dr. Burnett Smith was WRN's doctor and his wife recalls, "They had great tussles during the years, for Nicoll was a difficult patient. His constitution was frail, and he openly defied almost every known law of health, yet managed to turn out work in measure which would have shamed many in perfect health, and to live to pass the allotted span."[23] It is remarkable that in spite of his flawed or enfeebled constitution, he managed to achieve as much as he did. He turned working from bed into an art form: "Nicoll himself dictated many hundreds of articles from his bed. It was weird to watch him as he lay there, amid a medley of newspapers and books and pipes and cigarette ashes and to know his brain was busy absorbing knowledge and incubating ideas all the time".[24] In this observation by Darlow, no mention was made of the usual presence of a cat, for which WRN had a deep affection;[25] he had learned to enjoy his quiet solitude.[26]

Part of his arrangement with Hodder & Stoughton was that he was allowed to have a winter break in a warm environment. Lady Nicoll noted that from 1902 they always wintered in the Riviera every January and February.[27] There was an arrangement that WRN's mail would be forwarded to him, but on one occasion, "the Italian postman, unwilling to be burdened with the load of papers ... had to my husband's agony decided to leave them behind. ... I made for the post office. The placid official allowed me to invade his inner circle; I retrieved the delinquent bundles and triumphantly bore them off – and all was well."[28] WRN was always indebted to his wife and family, receiving and appreciating a maximum of co-operation from both them and their staff, who facilitated his lifestyle around his reading and writing. Indeed, WRN used his disability as an added spur to his concentration on his work, along with the necessity of supporting his family, though he always felt real concern about the length of his own life. Such concerns were certainly not without their legitimate foundations; in spite of the problems with his lungs, WRN was a habitual smoker. He combined this with an aversion to open windows, which made for some most unhealthy atmospheres in his library and his bed sitting room. One visitor who had the temerity to think of opening a window received a full assault from WRN: "'Fresh air! Fresh Air!' he shouted. 'No Sir – It's an invention of the devil. More people have been killed by fresh air than any other disease. If I ever live to have any leisure, I shall certainly employ it in writing an exhaustive treatise on the evils of fresh air'".[29] It would be safe to observe that WRN was essentially an indoor man, and the fire in his study seemed to be always lit, almost throughout the year.

Despite decades of such unseemly habits, WRN remained a force through the first two decades of the new century. However, by 1921 it was

WRN in 1920

clear that the ageing WRN was frail and waning, but he was still regarded as a force in the land, retaining his editorial chair. The frequency of new work of note was, however, much decreased. An appreciative tribute was later made of these latter years; "Behind his frail exterior there lay indomitable energy and an amazing capacity for work. In his heyday he must have been almost the busiest writer and editor in London".[30]

In WRN's final years, quite a number wrote appreciatively to him about his contribution to the welfare of British Christianity. A letter

from the President of the Hartford Seminary Foundation written in 1921 is a characteristic example:

> I resolved to put off no longer sending you this word of personal greeting. It has often been my impulse to tell you of my great gratitude and admiration of your service of the Evangelical cause in England and of the Church of Christ in general. ... You appeared in the world of journalism at the very time when Nonconformity was lowest down in its history. It had lost power, and was being seriously misled by some of those who had most influence.... The *British Weekly* changed the situation. It stimulated scholarly ideals. It made known to the world in a wider way the power of the real scholars who were already in the Nonconformist and Scottish Churches. It gave them courage to take their place where they had a right to be, in the front ranks of the Churches of Great Britain. From these early days until now, your work has been a continuous contribution to the faith, the devotion and the intellectual life of thousands of ministers of Christ. May your strength continue yet for many years.[31]

The letter contains a mixture of flattery, exaggeration with some indisputable facts of genuine appreciation of WRN's success.

Certainly by the 1920s, WRN had become more of a 'figurehead' than the driving-force of his journals. He was increasingly feeling the strain of his responsibilities as Jane Stoddart remembered,

> "Sir Ernest Hodder-Williams took an active share in the editorial work of the paper during Sir William's long illness. Each Monday morning, in the summer of 1922, I called at his house in Sloane Street and spent an hour in consolation with him ... his counsel and guidance was invaluable during the last months of Sir William's life. ... 'the arrangement' – suggested by Nicoll himself – whereby he remained nominal editor of the *British Weekly* to the end, the Rev. J.M.E. Ross was associated with him as co-editor from the beginning of April'.[32]

His able staff led by J.M.E. Ross, who subsequently became the new editor, did the running of the paper. WRN had established a good team who were able to run the periodicals, but despite a drop off in the frequency of his contributions, he remained, right to his death, not only in the editor's chair, but a valuable contributor of ideas for possible copy, if not an active writer.

By early 1923, the onset of the end was evident. Lady Nicoll wrote, "In January [1923] my husband had a very bad attack of influenza, and though he picked up in the early spring days he never recovered. On March 13 he dictated his last paragraph".[33] Again, Jane Stoddart recalls, "Our last interview was in the middle of April, 1923, when I took flowers to his room. He knew me, but that was all. Half-unconsciously, he murmured, 'I may send you something later.' To one of his family he said, 'Have they plenty of copy?' His thoughts were with the paper, which was his own creative life-work".[34] On Easter Day, April 1, WRN's condition became critical. The news of his serious illness brought him many messages from old friends. On 4 April, Lloyd George sent a telegram: "So sorry to hear you are not well. Sincerely trust this improving weather will bring you improved health. We need the inspiration and the wise guidance of your powerful pen more than ever".[35] Darlow concluded, "Through April the sick man lingered on, 'waiting for God's leave to die.' The end came on May 4, when all the buds were breaking into flower. A few days earlier he had whispered to one of his nurses: 'I believe everything that I have written about immortality'".[36] So Sir William Robertson Nicoll died, after a debilitating illness that had begun in January. He had remained nominal editor of the *British Weekly* right to the end.

++++

WRN had firm views about most things and yet many people noticed that there were extraordinary inconsistencies in his personality that often defied explanation. As an individual, he refined his understanding and, occasionally, even changed his mind. His work meant that he dealt with many individuals and functioned on several different planes at the same time, which could produce its own crop of inconsistencies. However, such inconsistencies were apparent in many areas of his life. Although he was a man with an indomitable work capacity and drive, able to be an influence in the corridors of power at the highest levels in the country, "he would seem languid and absent-minded in regard to many outward happenings, he was always keen about things literary, always full of hidden energy about his work," [37] Indeed, WRN's absent-mindedness was 'proverbial' and a contradiction to the usual methodical running of his papers. Darlow writes of him coming home from an engagement in Norwich with Dr. John Clifford's hat, returning in Sir. Robert Hudson's overcoat, or, bringing home Lord George Riddell's shoes in his bag.

Even at his Reform Club, he managed to exchange his own hat with that of the Lord Chief Justice. At work and at home he would continually mislay his pencil, which led him jokingly to consider the nationalisation of pencils.[38] His forgetfulness with cigarette-ends could have proved dangerous, for this included carelessness about fire.

J.D. Jones of Bournemouth also remembered WRN's absentmind-edness and his smoking:

> "He liked to smoke as he talked. He would take a puff and then talk and by the time, he thought again of his pipe, it had gone out and had to be relit.… On one occasion, I saw him off at the station. Just before starting, he felt his pockets and said, 'I've got no matches.' 'Oh,' I said, 'we'll soon remedy that' and I got him a box from the automatic machine. I said, 'You're sure you have got your pipe.' 'Oh yes', he said, 'I've got my pipe.' When I got back to the Manse, however, I found his pipe on the study mantle piece"![39]

Was this a sign that his mind was preoccupied with higher things, or the fact that he became used to his simple personal needs being attended to by others?

It is well to remember that, "With all his love for books, Nicoll [had] never lost touch with common human beings … Aberdeen University had at least this cardinal virtue, that it did not breed snobs".[40] He combined his 'genius' for friendship with an ability to empathise with his friends and readers alike. He had a genuine fellow feeling for people from whatever class. "This power of detached sympathy gives a clue to his many-sided nature, and explains how often he became all things to all men".[41] Darlow explained that his friend was able to move on several different planes in his dealings with people[42] and situations. "On one plane he could be intensely shrewd and practical, alive to the ideas as well as the sales which make a big popular appeal, mixing freely and hopefully among men of the world with whom he had ultimately no real affinity."[43] He was always methodical in preparing and maintaining himself for his work and this included his friendships, for they were a vital part of his life. Those who appreciated WRN understood him and enjoyed the relationship, but his style was capable of other interpretation; some could think him calculating, 'canny' and reserved. All in all he had his likes and dislikes and was prepared to show it. Yet WRN also could be apart and aloof, he withdrew to a different region where he was at home with himself and with the things he prized most and loved best. "He found strength to endure the strain of incessant labour because he possessed a refuge beyond outside worries and weariness. He exemplified his own favourite doctrine of the Inner Room."[44] Beyond the openness and accessibility of his personality, there was the private individual.

He expressed himself in his papers with a kindly, measured tone and appreciation, yet, in private and with friends, reviewing a book or person with devastating and at times highly personalised in his bias and prejudice. Although not one to 'suffer fools gladly'[45], WRN had infinite patience for any youngster who showed a real determination to acquire a skill. Further, his abhorrence of Spiritualism was very much at odds with the fact he at one time became 'strangely intrigued' by palmistry. [46] The evidence seems to be that he was probably totally unaware of the perplexing nature of the mingled yarn, which displayed the web of his life. His family friend, Annie Swan, wrote that WRN "was an extraordinary man. Meredith is reported to have described himself as the possessor of at least six personalities. I am sure Robertson Nicoll had as many. I knew him intimately over a period of years, while we were neighbours in Hampstead ... but I could not attempt a portrait of him. He was a staunch and wonderful friend, but he had a host of enemies, being ruthless in criticism and less than any man I have ever met 'able to suffer fools gladly'".[47]

Despite this tendency to criticise, WRN had an easy, humorous side. His wife tells of WRN attending a conference at Lambeth Palace and all he could tell her about the proceedings was, "I looked at the Archbishop and his apron and I thought – What a nice lap for cats! I have no lap for cats".[48] Such remembered anecdotes show clearly something of the light and shade, which made up WRN's character and approach to living. He remained his own man all his life and in the words of Albert Dawson, "Nicoll's life was a full, opulent, tirelessly industrious, and eminently successful career. He played the game of life bravely and on the whole finely. He enjoyed domestic happiness; he was rich in friendships; he was blessed with children and grandchildren; he attained considerable material prosperity".[49] A man of many, diverse facets of personality and he still seems to resemble the iceberg with a great part unseen.

After his Death

However deeply he understood the future of the Church, WRN had clearly been an embodiment of its present. Following his death, the tributes were fast in coming. The *Punch* said of WRN that he was "The most successful Christian of Modern times".[50] His wily friend and confidant, the Methodist scholar Arthur Peake commented, "He was himself a remarkably successful man.... And as Nicoll grew older he tended to make success more and more a test of merit".[51] Peake goes on to mitigate potential critiques of his friend,

> In justice to Nicoll it should be added that this attitude was not rooted in snobbishness, but in the conviction that if a person did not succeed, the fault lay as a rule, with his laziness. WRN was rarely ready to admit that a man's failure might be to his credit. This rather unattractive feature in his character is the more surprising since he often wrote tenderly about the broken and the disappointed.[52]

Annie Swan was asked to write about WRN as 'a great Christian'. She wrote,

> When I happened to mention to a casual but very able friend that I had asked to write of Robertson Nicoll as a great Christian, he smiled, but made no verbal comment. None was necessary. I did not miss the significance of that smile. Nevertheless, I accepted the task with alacrity, believing that Robertson Nicoll has every right to be numbered among the great Christians of his time. It is certain that he enabled many to hold on to the faith, and confirmed many feeble knees by the richness and beauty of his religious writings, which were inspired by his own unassailable belief in immortality.[53]

She gave a valid testimony as one who knew Nicoll very well as a friend, but others, who only saw him at a distance, might have had more concerns and questions.

The testimonials are effusive, but far from unduly so – WRN always maintained a full, warm, devotional commitment to an Evangelical view of the Christian Faith, and it is only fair to remember him as such. It is worthwhile, however, to approach the man from a more analytical stance as well, employing David Bebbington's familiar quadrilateral[54] 'template' to assess WRN's views and the emphases in his writings. This formulation was a result of Bebbington's assessment of many attempts to grasp 'What was an Evangelical?' and he reduced his findings to four areas that were the special marks and priorities of Evangelicalism. First, WRN's 'Biblicism' was strong, an area that he valued and urged on his reader's as necessary for maintaining a vital personal relationship with a living Christ, both as Lord and Savour, as well as being closer to Christ through sustained reading of the Scriptures. WRN took a liberal Evangelical stance over the Bible and he helped to popularise some of the newer views. His preferred policy was for a slow and gradual progress and change with new teaching, rather than the 'revolutionary' methods and style of those like his tutor, Robertson Smith. As he wrote to Arthur Peake, "The new truths should dawn on the church as gently as the sunlight, and I am not at all sure but that heretics ought to be burnt. I mean the fellows who make a big row and split their Churches".[55] Second, 'Crucicentrism' or the doctrine of the Cross, which WRN considered as central, though Peake considered it as a mark of his essential conservatism: "At this point Nicoll stood resolutely by a strictly substitutionary doctrine of the Atonement. He was also a Calvinist".[56] He stood for and continually wrote about the importance and necessity for the fullest view of the Cross as essential to appreciating the believer's dependence on the Work of Christ and this was, for WRN, what gave Christianity its power and influence.[57]

The third area of Bebbington's template, 'Conversionism' was also of great importance in WRN's view of the Christian life and the point at which the Work of Christ was made personal to the individual. He became concerned over reports coming to him of an absence in preaching with a desire of seeing conversions. He exhorted, "remember also that the ministry which ceases to be evangelistic will soon cease to be Evangelical. If you preach CHRIST and His Cross you will preach for conversions, and you will have them".[58] He was particularly concerned about the reluctance he detected in young preachers to preach evangelistically, he continually sought to counteract against this tendency.[59]

The fourth element of 'activism' was essentially, what WRN was seeking to exhort his readers to be doing; to live a life of faith that would demonstrate that it was alive. This was not just, for him, his explicitly Christian activities, but it was linked to his holistic view of the Christian life.[60] For WRN this embraced culture in the form of literature and a full commitment to politics in his support to the Liberal Party. However, there was more in WRN's understanding of the Evangelical view of the Christian Faith, indeed areas that can easily get excluded or at least played down if the Quadrilateral Template of Bebbington's is too rigidly applied. He regarded the Christian life as dependent on the Work of The Holy Spirit and the reality of the 'New Birth'. He wrote, "The world is increased by every being born into it, but the Church has no natural increase, only a supernatural. The Church lives by capture, by booty, by winning over from the world the citizens that make her number … her life is a perpetual resurrection, and she is forever issuing from the tomb".[61] Sadly, this emphasis seemed to be toned down as WRN got into the twentieth century and he enjoyed the power, influence and rewards of the political world. Perhaps this is reflected by his attitude to the 'Revivals' of 1904-5 in Wales and 1921 in Lowestoft; he carried reports of 'Revivals' that were written by 'reporters on the spot', but made no editorial comment on them himself.

Lasting Legacy

Has WRN left any enduring legacy? Of all his enterprises, his contribution to Hodder & Stoughton has certainly flourished even more than in his day. None of his journals still exist, although the *British Weekly* did survive under different editors, who tried to revive the successful years,[62] until its disappearance in the late 1980s under the banner of the *Christian Week*. The *Expositor*, by contrast, folded not long after WRN's death. The journals, however, were mouthpieces for WRN more than they were independent concerns, and it is not to them that one should look in seeking his contributions to later generations. Through those tools he helped the careers of many others, broadly enough and in so great a variety of ways that the full story can never be known. In literary terms, one must look to WRN as the champion and caretaker of the Kailyard Craze, which he largely 'hyped up' (and there were many other notable writers he helped with strategic reviews, such as William Hale White and Arnold Bennett). Theologically, there were his Scottish friends and companions in his literary achievements.

His political contributions are however, those which stand most clearly forth, with his support of the Liberal Party and Lloyd George in particular. At the same time as he bolstered these powerhouses, he made use of them, admiring and glorying in their prowess– a success he made certain reflected upon him as well.

Despite all these achievements, in the life of the Christian faith in the years after WRN's death his greatest hopes met with failure. There has been no dramatic Revival of the Christian faith in Britain, at least in the way the young WRN expected (following his experiences during the Moody and Sankey meetings of the mid 1870s), and the older WRN exhorted in the early days of the *British Weekly*. The latest phase of his life saw him as a political string-puller in public life and at this time his emphasis on the Work of the Holy Spirit and the expectation of a Revival were noticeably muted. Since that time his writings have suffered a distinct failure to wear well for the new generation of readers. His style was dated, although much of what he wrote about has perennial usefulness, particularly many of his biographical studies.[63] His pattern for society has been left marooned on the beach of changing culture; many of his views strike us now as quaint and bygone – even at the end of his life he felt like a Victorian in a changed landscape.

He seems to have represented a passing generation that rode a high tide of Evangelical dominance – but the tide gradually receded, even beyond the point WRN could have imagined. He sought to help the Church come to terms with the new age, always attempting to employ the changing forces of society to his own ends. The legacy of his efforts, however, leaves the open question of whether WRN just used or unwittingly encouraged the forces of secularisation, critical destruction of the Scriptures, and the downward trending of social morality – all of which have quickened their pace since his day. It remains to say that each generation has to make choices – and WRN chose his way deliberately, succeeding to an extraordinary degree, whilst staying true in intention to his higher calling as a Christian leader. There was always a preacher in him and when he was forced into a change of career, he found a profession that enabled him to maintain his interests in preaching and at the same time make a successful contribution to the culture and life of both the Scottish Free Church and the English Nonconformists. He tried to bring the Church and his old constituency of the Evangelicals into the new age. He felt the message of the times was simple – change or become culturally and politically stranded. There is, however, something of an irony here – though he may have succeeded in his short-term goal of being a modernising influence on Church life, it was ultimately at the cost of undermining or at least weakening his faith's basic defence and foundation – the Bible. The unintentional nature of WRN's contribution to a religious decline is one that our present generation needs to reflect on with care. WRN, for all his sound and solid achievements, was, in the end, a key player in this sad and unhelpful state of affairs. As a prominent editor of a major religious paper he tried conscientiously, with great commitment, and employing all his great abilities to navigate safely through the troubled waters of the Church's problems. He gained much real success, but in the end, the areas he thought he was strengthening only really succeeded in becoming weakened. Of course, some will hold that he did succeed in plotting a reliable course through the strong currents and turbulent seas of transition and change, but in doing so they take a short and simplified view that commits that gravest of historical sins – failing to understand what has come before, and so ensuring it will happen again. The final assessment of WRN's contribution will continue to be debated, but at the time, he did what he believed to be right and most helpful.

Remember me when I am far away,
And still enshrine me in your faithful heart.
Then 'twill not seem such bitterness to part,
For we shall meet in heaven another day.
But not as I am now, dying and weak;
The wafted winds that cool the starry shore
Bring healing to the dwellers evermore,
The rose of life is splendid on their cheek!
Remember me as I was long ago
What time we trode the woodland paths together;
When trees clustered, and the sun was low,
And the proud hills were sweet with scented heather
And the hushed earth lay dreaming, and the skies
Smiled as of old on happy Paradise.[64]

W. Robertson Nicoll

Notes

Preface

1. *Daily Chronicle*: cited by Darlow, T.H.: William Roberson Nicoll: Life and Letters (Hodder & Stoughton, London 1925) p.3
2. Lloyd Jones, D.M: personal letter to the present writer, Sept 21 1974, London

Chapter One

1. Nicoll: *My Father: An Aberdeenshire Minister* (London: Hodder & Stoughton, 1908) p.17
2. The name given to the period of ten years in which the Evangelical majority in the Church of Scotland sought to break away from the principle of patronage, which saw unsuitable men forced on protesting churches. It was hoped by leaders, such as Chalmers, that the Government in London would side with them and bring in legislation to end this perceived abuse.
3. D.F. Wright & G.D. Badcock (eds.): *Disruption to Diversity: Edinburgh Divinity 1846-1996* (Edinburgh: T. & T. Clark) p. 33
4. Nicoll: *My Father, op. cit.*, p.14
5. Drummond, A.L. & Bulloch, J.: *The Church in Late Victorian Scotland,* 1874-1900 (Edinburgh: The Saint Andrew Press, 1978) p.44-5 "The Vale of Alford, good farming country, was stony soil for the Free Church; no minister from it left the National Church and only a small proportion of laity. Before the close of 1843 the microscopic Free Church Presbytery of Alford was founded with two ministers, Harry Nicoll of Auchindoir and William Pirie Smith of Keig and Tough". Ewing, W.: *Annals of the Free Church of Scotland* pp.283, 322
6. Nicoll: My Father, *op. cit,* p.14-15
7. Darlow, T.H., William Robertson Nicoll, Life and Letters (Hodder & Stoughton, London 1925), p.3
8. Nicoll: *My Father, op. cit.,* p.16-17
9. William Robertson (10 Nov 1851-4 May 1923); Maria Rose Thomasina (8 Apr 1853-27 Apr 1894); Elisabeth Williamina (27 Nov 1855-1873); George Smeaton (1856-27 Apr 1858); Henry James (18 Apr 1858-Jan 1885), details obtained from the 'family' historian, Colin Stewart.
10. Nicoll: *My Father, op. cit.,* p.18-19
11. "Her death made a great difference to him, but he seldom spoke of her directly, only whenever anything fortunate happened he was sure to say, even to the very last, 'I wish your mother had been here.'" *ibid.,* p.19-20

12. Nicoll, Catherine Robertson: *Under the Bay Tree* (Private circulation: Nov. 1934), p.154. "My husband would sometimes compare his early home with that of the Brontës – the far away lonely parsonage, the bookish atmosphere, the motherlessness, the Spartan economy." p.55

13. Nicol, cited in Stoddart, Jane T.: *W. Robertson Nicoll LL.D: Editor and Preacher* (London: S.W. Partridge & Co. 1903) p.15

14. Swan, Annie S.: Biographic article in *Great Christians,* edited by R.S. Forman (London: Ivor Nicholson & Watson, 1933) p.385

15. Nicoll: cited in Nicoll, *op. cit*, p.152

16. Nicoll: *James Macdonell, Journalist* (London: Hodder & Stoughton 1890) p.8

17. Nicoll: 'My First Schoolmaster' [Claudius Clear], *British Weekly*, 8 Apr 1915. In the winter, a number of farm servants would come to the school and received a basic education.

18. Nicoll: 'Children's sayings' [Claudius Clear], *British Weekly,* 29 Nov 1900

19. Stoddart: *Nicoll, op. cit.,* p.20 "He loved Horace and Virgil, and read with delight 'Christopher North's' Essays on the translations of Homer – one of the best books, he says for awaking in boys a living interest in the classics."

20. "In the homes from which came the rural students there was a great reverence for learning apart from its rewards ... the scholar was a hero and respected as such. This gave the teachers a very high rank in the parish. They were looked up to for their knowledge." Nicoll: 'The Homes of the Rural Students, 1866-1870', *The Aberdeen University Review*, Nov 1913, p.37.

21. Nicoll: *My Father, op. cit.,* p.29

22. *Ibid.,* p.91

23. *Ibid.,* p.88-9

24. This is 'believing criticism' and will be examined further below.

25. Drummond & Bulloch: *Victorian Scotland, op. cit.,* p.6

26. "In private Mr. Nicoll [Senior] was most genial and pleasant. The extent of his information on every conceivable subject, his rich and sparkling conversation, made his company very agreeable. He possessed a strong vein of humour; and the happy, racy and humorous, while at the same time instructive manner in which he could address or conduct a social meeting was a rare treat." Laing, Rev. T.: 'Rev. H. Nicoll MA, Auchindoir', *Free Church of Scotland Monthly*, 1 Jun 1892: Nicoll Papers, MS 3518, Box 1

27. "He was greatly impressed by the revival hymns and the addresses ... Harry Nicoll had soon after held open-air meetings on the village green at Lumsden". Nicoll, C.R.: *op. cit.,* p.146-7

28. "The boy could go to Aberdeen in October, and compete with some two hundred and fifty of his fellows for perhaps thirty bursaries or scholarships, ranging in value from £30 to £10, or even less, and tenable for four years. As the college season in Aberdeen lasted only five months, and the fees were not exorbitant, a strictly frugal bursar, aided by supplies of oatmeal and butter from home, was able to pay his way." Nicoll: *James Macdonell, op. cit.,* p.18

29. Stoddart: *Nicoll, op. cit.,* p.24

30. Nicoll: Letter to W. McRobbie, 5 Dec 1908, cited Darlow: *op. cit.,* p.14

31. Nicoll: 'The Country Student of Forty Years Ago', *Alma Mater [The Aberdeen University Review]* Sep 1906.

32. Stoddart: *Nicoll, op. cit.,* p.40
33. *Ibid.,* p.26
34. Darlow: *op. cit.,* p.25: Papers included the *Aberdeen Journal* and the *Aberdeen Free Press*. WRN's early interest in periodicals was no doubt fuelled by his accumulation of innumerable back issues of various journals. As he later noted, his father "had a Chinese reverence for the printed matter, and could not bear to destroy anything. In consequence, he accumulated an immense number of journals and magazines. By his careful indexing, he had all [his] collection at his command. His knowledge would have been invaluable to a journalist or an author, though he made no specific use of it himself". Nicoll: *My Father, op. cit.,* p.73-4
35. Nicoll: *Professor W.G. Elmslie, op. cit.,* p.11; Nicoll identified greatly with Elmslie, including their shared delicacy of health
36. Smout T.C.: *A History of the Scottish People* 1530-1830 (London: Collins, 1969) p.480
37. Nicoll: *My Father, op. cit.,* p 92-3
38. Indeed, Donald Carswell quipped, that "Where [WRN] differed from his father ... was that at an early age he made up his mind that the first object in reading a good book and the only object in reading a bad one is to convert them both into hard cash". Carswell, Donald: *Brother Scots,* (London: Constable & Co Ltd, 1927) p.218
39. Swan, Annie S.: 'Robertson Nicoll' in *Great Christians*, edited R.S. Forman (London: Ivor Nicholson & Watson, 1933) p.386-7
40. "He judged his lot ideal, and all he asked from Providence was that things should not grow worse. Though he had few possessions, everything was prized to the full. When he compared his allotment with that of others, he compassionated the others. ." Nicoll: *Seen and Unseen, op. cit.,* p.9
41. Darlow: *op. cit.,* p.25

Chapter Two

1. Darlow: *op. cit.,* p.35
2. One of the motivational forces pursuing this outlook on the Scriptures was Frederick Schleiermacher. He taught that the facts of faith were to be held as of less importance than an individual's sense of 'absolute dependence', a universal, subjective awareness of God rooted in man's inner aesthetic and religious response to reality as a whole.
3. Pattison, Mark: cited Vidler, A.R.: *The Church in an Age of Revolution* (Penguin Books, London 1971) p.22
4. Chadwick, O.: *The Victorian Church*, vol. 2, (Adam & Charles Black, London 1970) p.68
5. Julius Wellhausen (1844-1918) was a biblical scholar and professor of Old Testament at Greifswald, then professor in Semitics at Halle, Marburg and Gottingen. He devoted much of his time to investigating and propagating the Higher Criticism of the Old Testament and later the New Testament. Abraham Kuenan (1828-1891), a dutch biblical scholar, began the 'literary-historial' view of the O.T. Frederick Delitzsch (1813-1890) was a German biblical scholar of more moderate views on the new learning of the Bible.

6. Amongst the papers which accepted his articles were the *Dundee Advertiser,* the *Scotsman,* the *Banffshire Journal,* the *People's Friend,* the *Literary World,* the *British and Foreign Review,* etc.
7. Stoddart: *Nicoll, op. cit.* p.35: "He gained a prize for a poem in the *Peoples Journal* which was afterwards reprinted in *Poems for the People* and praised in the *Spectator*".
8. *Ibid.,* p.35
9. *Ibid.*
10. Both Nicoll's friends entered Free Church ministry and were content simply to do the work of rural pastors.
11. Stoddart: *Nicoll, op. cit.* p.35
12. *Ibid.,* p.37
13. Darlow: *op. cit.,* p.26
14. Nicoll: cited in *ibid.,* p.21
15. William Pirie Smith, the minister of Keig and Tough, and Harry Nicoll of Lumsden were fellow ministers of the same presbytery
16. Nicoll: *British Weekly*, 23 May 1912
17. Nicoll, cited Stoddart: *Nicoll, op. cit.*, 34
18. Nicoll, cited Darlow: *op. cit.*, 24
19. Dabney, R.L.: *Discussions Evangelical and Theological* (Edinburgh, Banner of Truth, 1890, reprinted 1967) p.438-9
20. Norman MacDonald Lockhart Walker (1826-1905) was a Free Church minister and writer and a proponent of the union with the United Presbyterian Church
21. Walker, N.L.: *Chapters from the History of the Free Church of Scotland,* (Anderson & Ferrier, Edinburgh 1895) p.272-3
22. Black, & Chrystal,: *op. cit.,* p.137, cited Cheyne, A.C.: 'Bible and Confession in Scotland: the background to the Robertson Smith case', in *William Robertson Smith, Essays in Reassessment* (Sheffield: Sheffield Academic Press, 1995) p.38
23. Simpson P.C.: *The Life of Principal Rainy* [two volumes] (London: Hodder & Stoughton, 1909) vol. 1, p.334-5
24. Nicoll: 'Professor Robertson Smith,' *British Weekly,* 23 May 1912. Reviewing the Black & Chrystal biography of Smith, Nicoll stated, "It is very much to Dr Black's credit that he has brought out with the utmost distinctness the fact that Smith did, all through and to the last, maintain the [Divine] inspiration. Dr Black, we gather, does not agree with Smith, but there are now not a few critics of authority who do."
25. Walker: *op. cit.,* p.291
26. Black & Chrystal: *op. cit.* p.360
27. Darlow: *op. cit.,* p.38
28. Nicoll: cited *ibid.,* p.356
29. Peake A.S.: *Recollections and Appreciations* (London: Epworth Press, 1938) p.18
30. Nicoll: cited complete by Darlow: *op. cit.,* p.40-3
31. Roughly translated 'wonderful' or 'incredible'
32. *Ibid.,* p.41
33. Rudolf Smend: 'William Robertson Smith and Julius Wellhausen', *William Robertson Smith, Essays in reassessment*, Johnstone, William, ed., (Sheffield: Sheffield Academic Press, 1995) p.235-7

34. Undated letter (D746) cited Smend, Rudolf: 'William Robertson Smith and Julius Wellhausen', Johnstone, William, ed.,: *William Robertson Smith – Essays in Reassessment* (Sheffield: Sheffield Academic Press, 1995) p.236

35. Nicoll: 'Dr. Robertson Smith', *British Weekly,* 5 Apr 1894; also *Princes of the Church, op. cit.,* p.63

36. Peake: *op. cit.,* p.18

37. Darlow: *op. cit.,* p.27

38. Darlow: *ibid.,* p.29

39. Stoddart: *Nicoll, op. cit.,* p.55

40. *Ibid.,* p.43

41. William Cunningham (1805-1861), Principal of New College and controversial defender of orthodox doctrine. Robert Candlish (1806-1873), minister of Free St. George's Edinburgh and Principal of New College. James Bannerman (1807-1868), Professor of Apologetics at New College.

42. Riesen, Richard Allan: '"Higher Criticism" in the Free Church Fathers', *The Scottish Church History Society,* vol. 20, (Edinburgh: 1980) p.139

43. Reisen, R.A: *Criticism and faith in late Victorian Scotland* (University Press of America, Lanham, Maryland, 1985) p.378. "The Free Church themselves ... provided the hard doctrine for their successors to react to, [and] because in their defence of the traditional theories they sometimes asked 'critical' questions and gave 'critical' answers or, what often has the same effect, gave inadequate answers or none at all, thus perhaps accelerating the very process they intended to arrest."

44. Drummond & Bulloch: *Late Victorian Society, op. cit.,* p.220

45. Reisen R.A.: 'Higher Criticism in the Free Church Fathers', *op. cit.,* p.142. "The Traditionalists took both options. Their spirituality required that they take the first; their rationality required that they take the second. But insofar as they took the second they admitted that criticism was with them, if only as an evil to be checked. In other words, they joined battle. Perhaps neither their faith nor their theology would allow them to do otherwise. But the defence of the doctrine of inspiration itself proved to be a double-edged sword. Believing may have fostered believing criticism."

46. There were a few exceptional individuals, who managed to hold these two posts, men such as Thomas Chalmers, but the generality of ministers did not have this ability

47. Finlayson R.A.: *Reformed Theological Writings* (Mentor, Christian Focus Publications, Ross-shire, 1996) p.194

48. Roderick Alexander Finlayson (1895-1989) was a Free Church theologian and writer. He became Professor of Systematic Theology in the Free Church College, Edinburgh (1946-1966)

49. Nicoll: *My Father: op. cit.,* p.26

50. Dwight Lyman Moody (1837-1899) and Ira David Sankey (1840-1908): In 1873, they came from the United Sates as evangelists. Though this was their third visit, this visit saw their amazing impact on the Churches. This was particularly in Edinburgh and Glasgow where their success became a sensation.

51. P. Carnegie Simpson: *The Life of Robert Rainy* (London: Hodder & Stoughton, 1909) vol.1, p.408-9

52. Darlow: *op. cit.,* p.28

53. *Ibid.,*

54. Nicoll: *Calls to Christ,* (London: Morgan & Scott, 1877), Preface iv

55. Darlow: *op. cit.,* p.28

56. Nicoll: Preparatory Note, *Calls to Christ* (London: Morgan & Scott, 1877)

57. Speaking of *Calls to Christ* his biographer noted that this book was given high praise from preachers such as Spurgeon (*Sword and the Trowel*), Parker (*The Fountain*) and Henry Drummond (*Daily Review*), with Parker describing it as, "a model of Christian expostulation and pleading". Darlow: *op. cit.,* p.34

58. "Accordingly I set out on this path. My beginning was with the *Ethics* of Spinoza ... then came Calvin's *Institutes* ... the commentaries of Bishop Lightfoot ... are a few of the books that occupied me during those winters." Nicoll: 'My First House: the Absolution of Snow', *British Weekly*, 20 May 1915

59. "I am fully persuaded that my self-education in Dufftown Manse, amidst the absolving snow had an immense influence over me, which continues to this day." *ibid.*

60. Stoddart: *Nicoll, op. cit.,* p.51

61. Horatius Bonar (1808-1889) was a hymn-writer and preacher, one of the Disruption Fathers of 1843. He was also known for many books, *God's way of peace* (1862) and *God's way of Holiness* (1864) among them

62. Stoddart: *op. cit.,* p.50

63. Maria Nicoll: 'Letter to Harry Nicoll' (10 Apr 1877), cited Lawrence G.W.: "William Robertson Nicoll and religious journalism in the Twentieth Century", (Unpublished Ph.D. Thesis: New College, Edinburgh, 1954) p.68

64. "Nicoll had the homely wit of a Bunyan and the piety of a McCheyne." Cairns, David: *An Autobiography* (London: SCM Press, 1950) p.79.

65. *Ibid.* p.80 "His talk told us about a world of which as yet we knew very little, of letters and journalism. W.T. Stead, of the *Pall Mall Gazette* was then in full flow, with his Maiden Tribute agitation, and Gladstone's ministry of 1880 was in full swing, and the clouds were banking up in Free Church for its great heresy trials. There was plenty to hear about."

66. *Ibid.,*

67. Stoddart J.T.: *My Harvest of the Years* (London: Hodder & Stoughton, 1938) p.23

68. Nicoll: 'The Yale Lectures on Preaching', Reprinted from the *British and Foreign Evangelical Review* for July 1878. This is examined below

69. Stoddart: *Nicoll, op. cit.,* p.57

70. Nicoll: 'The Yale Lectures on Preaching', *op. cit.,* p.21

71. Nicoll: *The Incarnate Saviour: A Life of Jesus Christ* (Edinburgh: T. & T. Clark, 1881 – revised 1897, with a new preface, reprinted 1911) p.110

72. Nicoll: *The Incarnate Saviour,* (Edinburgh: T. & T. Clark, 1881) p.115

73. Nicoll also added to a series begun by his predecessor, Horatius Bonar called 'Kelso Tracts'.

74. Nicoll: 'Life with Christ', A Sermon, Preached in Kelso Free Church, 22 Oct 1882 (Edinburgh: Macniven & Wallace)

75. *Ibid.,* p.26-7

76. Enright, W.G.: "Preaching and Theological in Scotland in the Nineteenth Century: A study of the context and the content of the Evangelical Sermon" (Unpublished PhD. thesis, New College, Edinburgh, 1968) p.212

77. Nicoll displayed his theme from a number of texts in the writings of John and showed, clearly, his maintenance of the traditional approach to the problem of the authorship. Again, this would make him appear to an adherent of orthodox evangelical doctrines. Note there is nothing directly on the Old Testament, such references or antecedents were handled in a traditional way.
78. Nicoll: *The Lamb of God* (Edinburgh: Macniven & Wallace, 1883) p.133
79. *Ibid.,*, Preface in the 1897 edition vi
80. *Ibid.,*, Preface ix
81. Enright, W.G.: 'Preaching and Theology in Scotland in the Nineteenth Century,' *op. cit.*, p.327
82. Ratcliffe S.K.: Review of Darlow's biography, *Observer,* 20 Sept 1925. (Nicoll Papers: MS 3518 Box 41)
83. Stoddart: *My Harvest of the Years, op. cit.,* p.24-5
84. *Ibid.,* p.27-8
85. Henry J. Nicoll (1858-1885) had been to Aberdeen University and after showing some interest in medical studies had developed an interest in journalism and literature. He had shown great promise, not only working on the staff of the *Aberdeen Free Press,* but also becoming the editor of Aberdeen's *Evening Gazette.* Books: *The Life of Carlyle* and *Landmarks in English Literature,* the latter stimulating his elder brother to planning with a study on English Literature in the Victorian Age. This became an unrealised dream for WRN, although he was often setting materials aside for it. His brother died of consumption in the manse at Kelso, where he had been nursed for some time.
86. Darlow: *op. cit.,* p.48
87. Nicoll: 'Resignation of Rev. W.R. Nicoll, MA, Kelso Free Church': Pamphlet (reprint from the *Kelso Mail,* 20 January 1886) p3-4. (Nicoll Papers, MS 3518/46)
88. D. Iverach: *ibid.,* p16-17: "These qualifications ... were also evident in his pulpit ministrations. Conjoined with them were the marks of an orator, that sympathetic realisation of the feelings, opinions, and information of his hearers and the glow of feeling that thrilled them through as he proceeded from point to point, marshalling his facts and arguments till he reached a triumphant conclusion. He was full, too, of practical suggestions which were exactly suited to the situation".
89. Nicoll: 'Letter to Rev. W. M'Robbie,' 27 Feb 1886, cited in Darlow: *op. cit.,* p.50-1
90. *Ibid.,* p.50
91. Unknown letter, cited *ibid.,* p.49
92. *Ibid.,* p.55-6

Chapter Three

1. Matthew Henry Hodder (1830?-1911) saw publishing as an aspect of evangelising. He himself had been converted at the King's Weigh House Chapel, where he also met his future wife Frances Biddulph. In his early career, there was considerable interest in sermons, as Hodder was a connoisseur of sermons, this resulted in many titles. Hodder travelled widely in America, representing the firm and he was Chairman of the General Committee of the YMCA.

2. Attenborough: *A Living Memory* (London: Hodder & Stoughton, 1975*),* p.16

3. Thomas Wilberforce Stoughton (1840-1917)

4. Attenborough*: op. cit.,* p.21

5. *Ibid.,* p.30

6. *Ibid.,* p.30

7. The *Expositor* was a monthly journal, sold for a shilling and numbered clergy and leaders from a variety of churches among its readers.

8. Cox, Samuel: Editor, *The Expositor*, vol. 8, second series, (London: Chas Higham, 1885) Preface v-vi

9. Cox, Samuel to Henry Allon, *Letters to a Victorian Editor,* edited Albert Peel (London: Independent Press, 1929) p.292 This was probably a reference to the fact that Nicoll had voted against Smith in the Assembly debates in 1880 and 1881

10. In his last year as editor, Cox contributed 105 items in 12 issues

11. Darlow: *op. cit.,* p.46

12. "I could only assure you that I entertain no grudge against you, my successor but not my supplanter ... I should be sorry to carry even the semblance of a grudge with me to the grave. And so I send you these papers ... provided you care to have them, in order that, if you wish to use them ... you may insert them in the *Expositor*." *ibid.,* p.46

13. "Competent and impartial criticism of new books will be given. But the great aim of the Magazine will be, as before, to furnish expositions of the Word of God from the most scholarly and reverent writers of the time." Nicoll: 'Preface', *Expositor* [Nicoll's first Preface] (Hodder & Stoughton, May 1885)

14. Glover, Willis B.: *Evangelical Nonconformists and Higher Criticism in the 19th Century* (London: Independent Press, 1954) p.147-8

15. *Ibid.,* p.147

16. Writers such as Henry Drummond; W.G. Elmslie; George Adam Smith; and John Watson

17. Again, Glover's assessment is that: "One Nonconformist had, even by 1890 rendered signal service to the cause of Old Testament criticism though he was not himself a critic. William Robertson Nicoll must be accorded a high place in the history of Biblical criticism in England because of his achievement as the editor of the *Expositor.* Nicoll was himself cautious, sometimes even fearful in the face of the changes criticism was making in English religious life, but he never questioned the principle that free scholarship was the only satisfactory way to settle critical problems, and he practised this principle in editing the *Expositor*, which was the primary vehicle in England for the expression of critical opinion." Glover, W.B.: *op. cit.,* p.258

18. Cox: *Expositor* [Final Preface] 1885, *op. cit.,* p.vi "It has been a leading aim with me – as I announced it would be in the Prospectus of ten years ago – to throw open the Magazine, so far as possible, to all schools of Christian thought. And were I to exclude any of those to whom I have opened the door, I should be untrue to an aim I have steadfastly kept before me."

19. Nicoll: 'The Late Rev. Dr. Driver', *British Weekly*, 5 Mar 1914

20. *Ibid.,* "Dr. Driver has on various occasions contributed to the *British Weekly,* and we recall in particular the noble tribute which he paid in these columns to his venerated friend, Professor A.B. Davidson."

21. *Ibid.,*
22. Wilkinson, John T.: *1662 – And After* (London: Epworth Press, 1962): "Probably the absence of any important theological issue from the controversy over criticism mainly accounted for the fact that there was no splitting of the Nonconformist groups along fundamentalist-modernist lines. Yet the wise presentation of the new viewpoint by many biblical scholars was also responsible for this, and perhaps to Arthur Samuel Peake (1865-1929) more than any other is the credit due, for in his constant aim to transmit the new approach in terms intelligible to the average reader he was unique."
23. James Hastings (1852-1922), held three pastoral charges, but most of his energies were taken up with his editing many significant theological works for T. & T. Clark of Edinburgh. His ambition was to demonstrate that Christians had nothing to fear from the world of academic scholarly research.
24. Ferguson, William: 'Christian Faith and Unbelief in Modern Scotland, in *Scottish Christianity in the Modern World*, Brown, S.J. & Newlands G. (eds.) (Edinburgh: T. & T. Clark, 2000) p.84-5
25. Darlow: *op. cit.,* p.28
26. Dempster J.A.H.: 'Incomparable Encyclopaedist' [The life and work of Dr. James Hastings], article in the *Expository Times,* vol. 100, (Edinburgh: T. & T. Clark, Oct 1988) p.5
27. Nicoll, Catherine R.: *Under the Bay Tree, op. cit.,* "Dr. James Hastings would also visit us on the occasions when he came to London to look up contributors to his great Bible Dictionary.... Being a theologian and a bookman he shared many interests with my husband, and he the virtue in my husband's eyes of being an Aberdonian, born at Huntly in the same strath as Lumsden – 'the only birthplace which at once creates a presumption in favour of a man.'"
28. Dempster: *op. cit.,* p.5
29. *Ibid.,* p.6
30. Nicoll: 'The Age of Encyclopaedias,' *British Weekly*, 15 Oct 1908
31. Nicoll: 'The Rev. Dr James Hastings', *British Weekly*, 19 Oct 1922
32. Warfield, B.B.: letter to Nicoll, 31 Jan 1921, Nicoll Papers: MS 3518/3, Aberdeen University Special Library and Archives. A resolute defender of orthodoxy that Nicoll appreciated and is credited with the comment about Warfield, that it was a thousand pities that Warfield had not continued to make the New Testament his chief field of study in the belief that such were his qualifications as an exegete that had he done so, he might have ranked with Meyer and others as a New Testament commentator. Craig, Samuel G.: 'Biographical preface' to Warfield's *Biblical and Theological Studies,* xiv: (Philadelphia: Presbyterian & Reformed Publishing Company, 1952)
33. Some of the articles became substantial volumes; A.B. Bruce, *St Paul's Conception of Religion*; A.M. Fairbairn, *Studies in the Life of Christ*; Alexander Maclaren, *Expositors Commentary on Colossians*; B.F. Westcott, *Christus Consummator*; A.E. Garvie *Studies in the Inner Life of Jesus*; George Adam Smith, *Historical Geography of the Holy Land*
34. Nicoll: letter to Marcus Dods, 28 Sep 1891, Nicoll Papers, (MS 3518 Box 32)
35. Barbour G.F.: *Alexander Whyte* (London: Hodder & Stoughton, 1923) p.265

36. See Chapter 5, 'Relationships'
37. Moffatt, James: 'In Memoriam,' *Expositor*, June 1923 [Volume 25]
38. When WRN "took over the *Expositor*, he soon began to broaden its outlook ... the original idea of the *Expositor* was to pursue this method [exposition] for the Bible as a whole, to furnish readers and preachers with honest, living interpretations of Scripture, to make them understand what they read and then proceed to make others understand ." Moffatt, James: 'In Memoriam: W. Robertson Nicoll', *Expositor*, Vol. 25, Jun 1923, 401-4
39. Altick, R.D.: *The English Common Reader 1800 - 1900*, (Chicago, 1957) p.361: cited Patrick Scott, *op. cit.*, p.327
40. Darlow: *op. cit.*, p.57
41. Altick, R.D.: *op. cit.*, p.327
42. *Ibid.*, p.336
43. Wolff, Michael: *Victorian Periodicals Newsletter*, (Bloomington, 1970) p.5: cited Patrick Scott: 'Victorian Religious Periodicals: Fragments that remain', Derek Baker, ed., *Studies in Church History*, volume 11, (Oxford: Blackwell, 1975). A contemporary writer estimated in 1862 that, of 516 magazines then in the course of publication, no less than 213 'are of a decidedly religious character.'" p.326
44. Altick: *op. cit.*, p.326
45. *Ibid.*, p.327
46. First published in 1857
47. Nicoll: "the greatest and most influential of Nonconformist journalists." quoted Darlow: *op. cit.*, p.58-9
48. Munson, James: *The Nonconformists* (London: SPCK, 1991) p.73. Clarke saw that Nonconformity could develop a share in the 'newspaper' culture of the Nineteenth Century. He "began to popularise the 'new learning' in Biblical scholarship; he included literary criticism ... serialised novels and encouraged women writers", such as Emma Jane Worboise.
49. Darlow: *op. cit.*,p.59
50. Munson: *op. cit.*, p.74
51. Attenborough: *Living Memory, op. cit.*, p.32
52. Lawrence G.W.: 'Nicoll', citing *Greenock Telegraph*, 9 May 1923: *op. cit.*, p.98-99
53. Darlow: *op. cit.*, p.45
54. Lawrence: *op. cit.*, p.99, citing *Kilmarnock Standard*, 19 May 1923
55. The *Pall Mall Gazette*, when edited by W.T. Stead, was one of Nicoll's examples of good practice
56. Nicoll: Letter to Henry Drummond, Darlow: *op. cit.*, p.69
57. Attenborough: *op. cit.*, p.32
58. Williamson, David: 'Dr. Robertson Nicoll of the *British Weekly*', *Leisure Hour* (c1902), The Nicoll Papers: MS 3518/9
59. Nicoll quoted in Darlow: *op. cit.*, p.79
60. Williamson, David: cited, *op. cit.*
61. Darlow: *op. cit.* p.80
62. *Ibid.*, p.80, "No journal can become powerful which is edited in the temper of a tame rabbit. But this editor had in his blood some drops of the mysterious daemonic quality which creates captains and prophets and raises them above the ruck of common men."

63. *Ibid.,* p.80
64. Nicoll: interview article, *East Anglian Daily Times*, for 1 Apr 1895: cited by Lawrence, G.W.: *op. cit.,* p.81
65. Nicoll: Letter to Marcus Dods, 7 Aug 1886, Darlow: *op. cit.,* p.70
66. Nicoll: *The Day Book of Claudius Clear,* (London: Hodder & Stoughton, 1905) p.288. This was a familiar theme for Nicoll in talking about his success: "A paper is like a meal. Unless well cooked and well laid out it does not tempt, however excellent may be the materials used." Also *People and Books* (London: Hodder & Stoughton, c1926) p.112
67. Darlow: *op. cit.,* p.81. Darlow cites Principal Cairns admitting that it was the one religious paper "Which he could ever read right through; he meant, of course, like thousands of other readers he found it entirely interesting."
68. *Ibid.,* p.325
69. Nicoll: 'How I became a Journalist' (London: *Home Messenger*, Nov 1909), The Nicoll Papers: MS 3518/37
70. Nicoll: 'The Creed and the Hope of Progress', *British Weekly*, 5 Nov 1886.
71. *Ibid.*
72. Stoddart: *Nicoll, op. cit.,* p.70
73. Darlow: *op. cit.,* p.57
74. William Thomas Stead (1849-1912) was a controversial journalist. He introduced new methods into journalism and was the first credited for creating news events rather than just reporting what has happened. His attempt to expose child prostitution backfired on him and he served a term in prison. He also campaigned against leaders over their personal morality, such as Parnell and Charles Dilke and their implications in divorce cases.
75. Nicoll: 'W.T. Stead', *British Weekly*, 25 Apr 1912
76. Darlow: *op. cit.,* p.81
77. Some examples from the early issues of the *British Weekly*: 'The Nonconformist invasion of Oxford', trumpeting the opening of Mansfield College (Issue 2); 'The Influence of Scepticism on character', looking at some of the effects of scepticism in the lives of George Eliot and Thomas Carlyle (Issue 13); 'Is our literature declining?', discussing the older generation of geniuses of literary imagination having no younger successors (Issue 15); 'What can books do for us?', on the need of reading books in order to help inform the consciences of modern society (Issue 25)
78. Darlow: *op. cit.,* p.82
79. 'Prosperous Churches and the causes of their success' – 1) Lyndhurst Road Congregational Church and R.F. Horton [Dec31 1886]; 2) Westbourne Park Chapel and John Clifford [Jan 14 1887]; 3) Broughton Place, Edinburgh and its ministers [Jan 28 1887], 4) Nottingham Tabernacle [Feb 4 1887], 5) Trinity Church, Poplar [Feb 11 1887], 6) Tottenham-Court Road Chapel (Whitefield's Tabernacle) [Feb 18 1887]
80. *British Weekly*, 10 June 1887
81. Contributors included Canon Fausset [Affirmative], Joseph Agar Beet [Negative], H. Grattan Guinness [Affirmative], Principal T.C. Edwards [Negative], Professor Godet [Affirmative] and Principal David Brown [Negative]
82. Nicoll: *British Weekly,* 23 Sep 1887
83. Stoddart: *Nicoll, op. cit.,* p.78

84. K. S. Inglis: *Churches and the Working Classes in Victorian England* (London: Routledge & Kegan, 1963) p.288

85. Brown, C.G.: *The Death of Christian Britain* (London :Routledge, 2001) p.89

86. Chadwick: *op. cit.,* p.233. This census was entrusted to Major Colquhoun, who used several thousand enumerators to count everyone who attended a church or chapel in London on 24 October 1886 (this meant approximately some 1,500 places of worship). To make sure they counted the missions and halls, a further census was taken on the last Sunday in November 1887

87. The poll returns were carefully scrutinised by Nicoll then serialised in the *British Weekly* and afterwards reissued as a book.

88. 'Our Religious Census of London', *British Weekly*, 5 Nov 1886. The final total of attendances in London Churches was 976,292, stated in the *British Weekly*, 17 Dec 1886

89. Gladstone, W.E.: Letter to the Editor (18 Dec 1886), *British Weekly*, 24 Dec 1886. Other notables joined in the follow up correspondence, including General Booth, "I think that you have performed a most valuable public service in compiling your religious census of London, and it would be most discreditable were the tremendous facts you have set before us to pass unnoticed …. The effect of your revelations upon me is that I purpose … to redouble our efforts for poor London." *British Weekly*, 7 Jan 1887

90. Nicoll: 'Our Religious Census of London and its Critics', *British Weekly*, 4 Feb 1887

91. "He was, I suppose, the beginner of the interview, and he held to it when almost everyone else had abandoned it." Nicoll: 'W.T. Stead', *British Weekly*, 25 Apr 1912

92. Nicoll's assistant editor; see later

93. *British Weekly*, 6 Jan 1888 – Canon Liddon; 17 Feb 1888 – C. H. Spurgeon; 8 Jun 1888 – R.W. Dale

94. *British Weekly*, 15 Dec 1898 issued a calendar of Nicoll surrounded by even more of his contributors. [13 Scots and 9 English & Welsh]

95. See below 'Biography & Claudius Clear' in Chapter 7

96. Darlow: *op. cit.,* p.81

97. Attenborough: *op. cit.,* p.32

98. See Chapter 6

99. Attenborough: *op. cit.,* p.34

100. Not to mention the National Liberal Club, the Savage Club, the Reform Club, the Omar Khayyam Club, the Johnson Club, and the Whitefriars Club.

101. Darlow: *op. cit.,* p.416-7

102. *Ibid.,* p.327

103. Attenborough: *op. cit.,* p.60

104. Sir John Ernest Hodder-Williams (1876-1927) was the eldest son of Matthew Hodder's only child Mary. She married John T. Williams, whose uncle George Williams was the founder of the Y.M.C.A. Mary's dynastic ambitions centred on Ernest, for from a child he seemed to be a natural leader. The same year he married Ethel Oddy, but they had no children. He led the firm after the death of his grandfather in 1911, and became senior partner on the death of Thomas Stoughton in 1917. He received a knighthood in 1919.

105. Attenborough, John: *op. cit.,* p.40

106. *Ibid.,* p.41-2

107. *Ibid.,* p.48

108. Nicoll: Letter to E. Hodder-Williams, 19 Dec 1901 (or 02): Hodder & Stoughton Papers, MS 16370

109. The Hodder & Stoughton Papers Collection (MS 16370) has some 87 items of letters written by Nicoll to Hodder-Williams.

110. Stoughton remained as senior partner, but a painful illness severely restricted his involvement.

111. Attenborough: *op. cit.,* p.67-8

112. *Ibid.,* p.74

113. *Ibid.,* p.58

114. Hodder-Williams, J.E.: 'To my friend – from his publisher', *British Weekly,* Memorial Number, 10 May 1923

115. Attenborough: *op. cit.,* p.79

116. Hodder-Williams: 'The Day of glory: The Mall – Peace Day 1919', *British Weekly,* 24 Jul 1919.

117. Hodder-Williams: 'To my friend – from his publisher', *British Weekly,* Memorial Number, 10 May 1923

118. Ernest Hodder-Williams did not long survive his friend and mentor. It was overwork and worry, particularly about things that were "beyond the book publishers' immediate anxieties. It was the old complaint against which Sir William Robertson Nicoll had so often warned him in vain". The General Strike of 1926, and the sudden death of J.M.E. Ross at the *British Weekly,* proved too much, and he died of a heart attack. He was nearly 51.

119. Stoddart: *Harvest* p.20-1

120. *Ibid.,* p.22-3

121. Nicoll was aware of tasks that would 'educate' and thereby increase people's usefulness: "The work on these sermon books was part of my training for it brought me into contact with the best thought of British and American preachers:" *ibid.,* p.57-8

122. *Ibid.,* p.57

123. *British Weekly,* 9 Sep 1887

124. Stoddart: *Harvest, op. cit.,* p.54-5

125. *Ibid.,* p.50

126. Stoddart [Lorna]: 'An interview with Dr. Paton', *British Weekly,* 9 Nov 1893

127. Reid, Charlotte: 'In Memoriam: Jane T. Stoddart', *British Weekly,* 4 Jan 1945

128. Gammie, Alexander: 'Jane T. Stoddart', *British Weekly,* 21 Dec 1944

129. Jane Stoddart's biographical studies included *W Robertson Nicoll, LL D, Editor and Preacher* (1903)

130. Such groups as 'The Brethren', 'The Christadelphians', 'The Spiritualists'

131. Amongst these were both, *The Expositor's Dictionary of Texts* [Vol. 1: 1910; Vol. 2 1911], which contained outlines, expositions, and illustrations of Bible texts, and full reference to the best homiletic literature, and *The Expositor's Treasury of Children's Sermons* [1912], which was a companion volume to the *Expositor's Dictionary of Texts.*

132. Nicoll: Letter to T.W. Stoughton, cited Darlow: *op. cit.,* p.328

133. Attenborough: *op. cit.,* p.34

134. Glover, W.G.: *op. cit.,* p.254

135. Peake, A.S.: *Recollections, op. cit.,* p.24

136. Many of the titles were reprints of short series from the *British Weekly* and indicate that there was a market for more permanent reminders of the original articles.

137. Darlow, *op. cit.,* p.327

138. Nicoll: 'Of log-rolling: some remarks by a person of no consequence' [Claudius Clear], *British Weekly,* 22 Nov 1894

139. Nicoll, C.R.: *op. cit.,* p.112

140. Conan Doyle, A.: 'The Ethics of Criticism', *Daily Chronicle,* 16 May 1899. Cited in Letter to the press [The Unknown Conan Doyle], compiled by Gibson, J.M. & Green, R.L. (London: Secker & Warburg, 1986) p.55

141. Nicoll: 'Conan Doyle and William Robertson Nicoll', *British Weekly,* 25 May 1899: also Stoddart: *Nicoll, op. cit.,* p.129-130

142. Nicoll always tried to mend fences and was publicly complimentary to Doyle's work, particularly his descriptive studies on the First World War

143. Nicoll CR: *op. cit.,* p.114-5

144. *Punch,* cited *ibid.,* p.113

145. Attenborough: *op. cit.,* p.33-4. "The business of book publishing continued – but with a difference. And the difference was William Robertson Nicoll."

146. 'Panjandrum' is a term given to a person who has or claims to have a great deal of authority or influence.

147. Doran, George H.: *Chronicles of Barabbas, op. cit.,* p.73. Doran was a contact and relationship that Ernest Hodder-Williams had gained in his American travels

148. Ratcliffe, S.K.: [review article of Darlow's biography] *Observer,* 20 Sep 1925: Nicoll Papers, MS 3518/1

149. Correspondent: 'Robertson Nicoll – and Claudius Clear', *The Times,* 8 May 1963: Nicoll Papers, MS 3518/46

150. Peake, A.S.: *Reflections, op. cit.,* p.26

Chapter Four

1. Nicoll: Letter to Rev. W. M'Robbie,' 21 Mar 1886, cited Darlow: *op. cit.,* p.53

2. Swann, Annie: 'Robertson Nicoll', Great Christians; R.S. Forman – editor (Ivor Nicholson & Watson, London 1933) p.387-8

3. Darlow: *op. cit.,* p.83

4. *Ibid.,* p.83

5. Nicoll: 'How I became a Journalist', *Home Messenger,* Nov 1909 (Nicoll Papers MS 3518, Folder 37/11)

6. Nicoll, C.R.: *op. cit.,* p.19

7. Stoddart: *Nicoll, op. cit.,* p.88, JTS still tried to maintain the 'myth', for the sake of her boss in 1902!

8. James Macdonell was an Aberdonian who had come south to London and made a successful journalist. He became the leader writer of the *Daily Telegraph* and then the *Times.*

9. Nicoll: *James Macdonell, op. cit.,*p.403
10. Nicoll, Isa: Diary for 22 Nov, cited Darlow: *op. cit.,* p.91
11. William G. Elmslie (1848-1889) was Professor of Hebrew at the English Presbyterian College, London
12. Nicoll, W.R. & Macnicoll A.N.: *Professor W.G. Elmslie DD* (London: Hodder & Stoughton, 1890): Revised and enlarged edition, as *Professor Elmslie: A Memoir* by W.R. Nicoll, 1911
13. See Chapter 6 'Culture'
14. Garden W.G.: *After Fifty Years* (London: Thomas Nelson & Sons, 1893). This was the substance of Blaikie's lectures, particularly the last chapter, 'A Last Word', which caused Nicoll's reaction
15. Nicoll: 'Should Churches cry for the Moon?' *British Weekly*, 13 Apr 1893
16. This was Gladstone, whom Nicoll had come to distrust after initially being an enthusiastic supporter (see Chapter 9 'Politics')
17. Nicoll: 'Should Churches cry for the Moon?' *op. cit.*
18. Nicoll, Isa: Personal diary cited Darlow: *op. cit.,* p.92
19. See chapter 6 'Biography'
20. Darlow: *op. cit.,* p.118
21. Nicoll to A. T. Quiller-Couch: *ibid.,* p.119
22. Stoddart: *Harvest, op. cit.,* p.102
23. Nicoll: 'At the ever green thorn-bush in the wilderness,' *British Weekly,* 28 Mar 1890, the first article
24. Other deaths in Nicoll's family: Mother [34] died 1860; Eliza [18] died 1873; George [2] died 1858; Henry [26] died 1885
25. Nicoll: *The Key Of the Grave* (London: Hodder & Stoughton, 1894) p. vii-viii:
26. Swan, Annie S.: 'Robertson Nicoll': *op. cit.,* p.391
27. Nicoll: 'Letter to Rev. W. M'Robbie, Darlow: *op. cit.,* p.121
28. *Ibid.,* p.124
29. Nicoll: *Ten-Minute Sermons* (London: Isbister & Company Ltd., 1894)
30. Thomas James Wise (1859-1937) was an English bibliographer and book collector. His Ashley Collection was acquired by the British Museum in 1937. He was accused of piracies and forgeries, which he denied, but after his death, there were successive exposures, which destroyed his reputation and showed the extent of his fraudulent activities. Wise had privately printed nearly 300 works of English authors, some of which were exposed by John Carter and Graham Pollard as forgeries in *An Enquiry into the Nature of Certain Nineteenth Century Pamphlets* (1934).
31. Attenborough: *op. cit.,* p.44
32. *Between the lines,* Letters & Memoranda interchanged by H. Buxton Forman and Thomas J. Wise, with introduction, essay and notes by Fannie E. Ratchford (Austin, Texas: University of Texas Press, 1945): also Partington, W.: *Forging Ahead* (New York: G.P. Putnam's Sons, 1939) 'Why did Wise perpetrate these forgeries and piracies?' p.278-81
33. Partington, W.: *Forging Ahead, op. cit.,* p.103
34. *Ibid.,* p.103-4
35. Carter, John and Pollard, Graham: *op. cit.*
36. Attenborough : *op. cit.,* p.44-5
37. Darlow: *op. cit.,* p.124; Darlow had no knowledge of T J Wise whose exposure came after 1937.

38. *Ibid.*
39. *Ibid.,* p.127
40. Attenborough: *op. cit.,* p.45
41. *Ibid.,* p.37
42. *Ibid.*
43. *Ibid.,* p.37 "A year later, it was sold to Horace Marshall, lock stock and barrel, and by 1900 it was well and truly dead."
44. *Ibid.,* p.38; "Never again did they risk their money in the field of the big-circulation magazines."
45. These are noted by Attenborough: *ibid.,* p.43, and include; the Kailyard novels, George Adam Smith's Expositor's Bible Commentary on *Isaiah*; Henry Drummond's *Ascent of Man*; George Adam Smith's *Historical Geography of the Holy Land:* "one of the most famous and long-lived works of scholarship ever published by the firm" [1893]; William Ramsay's *St Paul the Traveller* [1895], and George Adam Smith's *Life of Henry Drummond*
46. Dale R.W.: *Christ and the Future Life* (London: H & S, N/D)
47. Dods, Marcus: *The Visions of a Prophet* (London: H & S, N/D)
48. Forsyth P.T.: *Christian Perfection, The Holy Father, and the Living Christ* (H. & S., N/D)
49. Smith, George Adam: *Four Psalms* (H. & S., N/D)
50. Denney James: *The Church and the Kingdom; Gospel Questions and Answers;* and *The Literal Interpretation of the Sermon on the Mount* [the latter shared with Marcus Dods and James Moffatt] (H. & S., N/D)
51. Whyte Alexander: *The Four Temperaments* (H. & S., N/D)
52. Nicoll: *The Seven Words from the Cross* (H. & S., N/D) also *British Weekly,* 5, 12, 19, 26, Sep; 3, 10, 17, Oct 1895
53. *Ibid.,* p.66-77
54. *Dundee Advertiser:* review, N/D (Nicoll Papers Collection, MS 3518, Box 1)
55. Nicoll: *When the Worst comes to the Worst,* (London: Isbister & Co, 1896)
56. Nicoll: The chapters are, 'The Crowning Sorrow'; 'Haydon, Sir Walter Scott, and Silvio Pellico'; 'Hope Thou in God'
57. *Ibid.,* pp.61-2
58. The company included John Watson (Ian Maclaren) and set sail in the 'Campania' on 26 Sep 1896
59. Stoddart: *Nicoll, op. cit.,* p.104
60. Apparently, his friend Dr. William Wright, of the Bible Society, had introduced him to the lady. Darlow: *op. cit.,,* p.129
61. Nicoll had visited many of the old-world towns of New England and satisfied his curiosity seeing the homes and birthplaces of key individuals, such as Jonathan Edwards, Henry Ward Beecher, Ralph Waldo Emerson, Oliver Wendell Holmes, Henry James, G.W. Cable, as well as others.
62. "On Sunday we heard Dr. [T. De Witt] Talmage preach. I did not like him. His voice is harsh, his language high-flown, and he conveyed no impression of sincerity." Nicoll: Letter to Catherine Pollard, 3 Nov 1896: Darlow: *op. cit.,* p.143
63. Nicoll: Letter to Marcus Dods, Christmas 1896: *ibid.,* p.146
64. "If an idea was turned down by the proprietors, Nicoll was liable to offer his resignation. But Mr. Hodder and Mr. Stoughton seem to have known when to be firm and when to give way. " Attenborough: p.36

65. "The fact that the total correspondence was carefully preserved is a proof of the importance that Mr. Hodder and Mr. Stoughton attached to it." *ibid.*, p.42, and correspondence in Hodder & Stoughton Papers, MS 16355/6

66. *Ibid.*

67. *Ibid.*, p.42-3

68. *Ibid.*, p.43

69. Stoddart: *Nicoll, op. cit.,* p.114. This pattern has also been partly replicated in the Gladstone memorial of St Deiniol's Library, Hawarden.

70. Stoddart: *Harvest, op. cit.,* p.134 -5

71. *Times*, Obituary Article, 10 May 1923, cited Darlow: *op. cit.,* p.148

72. Nicoll: "Weeding a Library," *British Weekly*, 29 Apr 1915. 'This forecast was fulfilled after his death, when 20,000 of his books were sold by auction for little over £1000. It must be owned that most of these volumes were in bad condition, dog-eared and interleaved with tobacco ash. Nicoll treated his books simply as tools, to be caught up when he wanted them and then tossed aside.' *ibid.,* p.149

73. Nicoll: Letter to Catherine Pollard, 14 Dec 1896: *ibid.,* p.145

74. Swan, Annie S.: *My Life: An Autobiography, op. cit.,* p.86

75. *British Weekly,* 6 May 1897

76. His wife retells the story of a friend of hers who told an old Presbyterian minister that she was going to stay with the Nicolls in London. He seemed to disapprove and asked 'Has he not married an English Episcopalian?' To which her friend responded, 'Quite True and he was married by a Bishop.' "This was too much and the poor old minister collapsed at the thought of the backsliding of WRN". Nicoll, C.R.: *op. cit.,* p.83

77. Darlow: *op. cit.,* p.158

78. Stoddart: *Harvest, op. cit.,* p.128-9

79. Nicoll, C.R.: *Under the Bay Tree, op. cit.,* p.23-4

80. Nicoll: *The Lamp of Sacrifice,* (London: Hodder & Stoughton,) title page

81. This is examined in Chapter 8

82. Nicoll: 'Seven-Day Journalism', *British Weekly*, 20 Apr 1899

83. *Ibid.,* "In the first place, this battle must be fought by the Churches." [Various leaders had identified with the cause, such as Monro Gibson, R.F. Horton, John Clifford] "The practical step … is to refuse to buy and read these newspapers." [A boycott]

84. Nicoll: 'More about Seven-Day Journalism', *British Weekly*, 27 Apr 1899

85. Nicoll: 'Notes of the Week', *British Weekly*, 18 May 1899

86. Nicoll: 'Notes of the Week', *British Weekly*, 25 May 1899

87. Nicoll: 'It doth not yet appear', *British Weekly*, 8 Nov 1900

88. MacLeod, James Lachlan: *The Second Disruption* (East Linton: Tuckwell Press, 2000)

89. MacMillan, J.D.: 'Free Church of Scotland, post – 1900' in *Dictionary of Scottish Church History & Theology,* Nigel M. de S. Cameron, ed., (Edinburgh: T. & T. Clark, 1993) p.338

90. Chadwick O.: *The Victorian Church,* op. cit., p.232

91. Koss: *op. cit.,* p.44

92. Simpson, Patrick Carnegie: *Principal Rainy, op. cit.*, p.354

93. Nicoll: 'The Scottish Free Church Trust and its Donors', reprinted from *The Contemporary Review* Oct 1904 (London: Hodder & Stoughton, 1905) p.3

94. *Ibid.,* p.4
95. *Ibid.*
96. *Ibid.,* p.16
97. Nicoll: 'The Scottish Church Case', *British Weekly,* 4 Aug 1904
98. Nicoll: Letter, cited C.R. Nicoll's *Under the Bay Tree, op. cit.,* p.175
99. Nicoll: 'The Living Church or the Dead Hand?' *British Weekly,* 11 Aug 1904
100. Nicoll: *The Lamp of Sacrifice* (London: Hodder & Stoughton, 1906)
101. Of course, of the sixteen sermons that carried text, only three came from the Old Testament, two from the prophet Isaiah and one from Psalms: no historical or critical questions were referred to or examined.
102. Robert Rainy (1826-1906) Principal of New College, Edinburgh and 'leader' of the Free Church Assembly: tried to maintain the evangelical heritage of the Free Church and at the same time help the Church adjust with the rapidity and magnitude of contemporary changes and developments.
103. "The extraordinary series of attacks on him published in the Scotsman for many years have probably no parallel in journalism. We doubt whether Dr Rainy gave them any attention." Nicoll: 'Principal Rainy', *British Weekly,* 3 Jan 1907.
104. Nicoll: 'Principal Rainy', *op. cit.*
105. Simpson, P. Carnegie: *The Life of Principal Rainy,* (London: Hodder & Stoughton, 1909)
106. Nicoll: 'Principal Rainy', *op. cit.* Did Nicoll have a wry smile when writing this, for Rainy could speak his mind freely and incisively? A.S. Peake recorded, "Nicoll had been expressing himself with some freedom to Alex Whyte about Rainy. At last, Whyte was provoked into saying ... 'and shall I tell you what Rainy says about you? He says that what you are chiefly distinguished for is a kind of sloppy Evangelicalism.'" Peake, A.S.: *Reflections op. cit.,* p.17. The reminiscence ended, "It was a remark which it took its victim several years to get over."
107. Nicoll: 'The Life of Principal Rainy', *British Weekly,* 7 Oct 1909
108. *Ibid.*
109. Ross, K.R.: 'Robert Rainy', *Dictionary of Scottish Church History & Theology* (Edinburgh: T. & T. Clark, 1993) p.690
110. See Chapter 5
111. See Chapter 6 on 'Culture', The 'Kailyard School' were a group of Scottish novelists who specialised in domestic whimsical tales and were classified in association with the Scottish cabbage (kale) patch or back garden, where the humble vegetables would be grown.
112. Nicoll: 'Letter to his daughter Constance Miles', Sep 1910: cited in Darlow op. cit 215. "I have been extraordinarily busy, and have ready: *The Round of the Clock* [Claudius Clear Letters], *Sunday Evening*: 52 Sermons, *Poems of Emily Bronte, The Expositor's Greek Testament,* Vols. IV and V, completing the work, *The Expositor's Dictionary of Texts,* Vol. I, (with Miss Stoddart). I am struggling with the proofs."
113. Nicoll: cited Darlow *ibid* 217
114. Nicoll: 'Dr Chalmers: a Reconsideration' *British Weekly,* 27 Oct & 3 Nov 1910, also 'Who shall go over the sea for us?' *British Weekly* 26 Jan 1911

Chapter Five

1. At times WRN could be no more than a literary 'hack', but always with style and polish.
2. Andrew Bruce Davidson (1831-1902) – Hebraist and theologian. Early life in Aberdeenshire graduated from Marischal College, Aberdeen in 1849 and after some teaching experience, entered New College, Edinburgh in 1852. He was asked to assist John Duncan and was appointed professor of Hebrew in 1863. He remained at this post until his death in 1902.
3. Riesen, R.A.: *Criticism and Faith in Late Victorian Scotland, op. cit.,* p.252
4. "Davidson was renowned as a stimulating teacher, one who drew students from overseas to Edinburgh... yet despite his renown, his position was debated within the free Church Presbytery of Edinburgh, though not in the General Assembly, after the William Robertson Smith case; and pamphlets were written against him and his New Testament colleague, Marcus Dods. He always voted for Smith, but – to the puzzlement of many – never spoke for him in public." Wright, D.F. & Badcock, G.D. (Editors): *Disruption to Diversity: Edinburgh Divinity 1846-1996,* (Edinburgh: T. & T. Clark, 1996) p.58-9
5. Such articles included: 'A.B. Davidson in the pulpit' (19 Aug 1887), 'Professor Davidson on the Second Advent' (22 Feb 1889), 'Great sinners making great saints' (4 Oct 1889), Review of John Skinner's *Ezekiel* by A.B. Davidson (11 Apr 1895), 'Dr. A.B. Davidson, Moderator-Elect of the free Church of Scotland' By the late Professor Elmslie (26 Nov 1996)
6. 'Notes of the Week – Professor A.B. Davidson on the Higher Criticism', *British Weekly*, 19 Jan 1893
7. Strachan, James: *Andrew Bruce Davidson* (Hodder & Stoughton, London 1917)
8. C. H. Spurgeon (1834-1892) was a leading Baptist Preacher, speaking regularly to a congregation of 6,000 at his church at the Elephant and Castle in London, The Metropolitan Tabernacle. Conservative in theology and Liberal in politics, he became involved in the Downgrade Controversy due to concern about the spread of radical teaching amongst the Baptists. In October 1887, he withdrew from the Baptist Union, who censured him, but he refused to form a new denomination.
9. The articles were unsigned, but the author was Robert Shindler.
10. Nicoll: 'Mr Spurgeon on the Down-Grade', *British Weekly* No. 40, 5 Aug 1887
11. Nicoll saw Spurgeon in the same light as he saw the Evangelical heroes of the Free Church of Scotland; in that he was deferential but mindful that they represented the past and that, a new day had to be met with different views and methods
12. Porritt, A.: *The Best I Remember* (1922) 1-2: "My instructions were explicit. 'If Spurgeon preaches just a gospel sermon, there is no copy in it. If he says anything about himself, that may make a good paragraph; if he says anything about current questions, give it us in full.'"
13. Nicoll: 'The Coming Battle', *British Weekly*, 12 Aug 1887
14. *Ibid.,* "In the judgement of the vast majority of scholars, Hebrew literature did not begin before the ninth century B.C.; only one half of the Old Testament was written before the exile, and our Pentateuch as we have it

was introduced by Ezra in the year 444 B.C. The Levitical legislation is the work of the exilic period, although the authors used every endeavour to make their work appear to have been written in the wilderness. David wrote no Psalms, all being much later than this period. Solomon had nothing to do with any of the works that bear his name."

15. *Ibid.,* Here Nicoll may well be alluding to a main problem that he had himself in preaching on the Old Testament and could account for his great reluctance in preaching .
16. *Ibid.*
17. Spurgeon: Letter to Nicoll, 31 Aug 1887, Nicoll Papers, MS 3518: Box 46
18. Nicoll: 'What are we to believe about the Old Testament?' *British Weekly*, 9 Sep 1887
19. Nicoll: 'The Week', *British Weekly,* 9 Sep 1887
20. Hopkins, Mark: *Nonconformity's Romantic Generation* (2004): p.397"*The Christian World* was the main newspaper he had in mind." p.200. Further, 'The later Downgrade articles were shaped by the developing debate – Spurgeon made much of the liberal manifesto that appeared in *The Christian World'* , never in the *British Weekly* p.201
21. 'The Case Proved', *British Weekly*, 7 Oct 1887
22. Hopkins: *op. cit.,* p.195-8
23. *Ibid.,* p.200
24. Nicoll: 'The Week', *British Weekly*, 14 Oct 1887
25. Hopkins, *op. cit.,* p.203
26. Nicoll: 'The Week', *British Weekly*, 4 Nov 1887
27. *Ibid.*
28. Nicoll: 'The Week', *British Weekly*, 11 Nov 1887
29. Nicoll: 'The Baptist Union and Mr Spurgeon', *British Weekly*, 27 Jan 1888
30. Nicoll: 'A Word to our Readers', *British Weekly*, 23 Dec 1887
31. Louis Gaussen (1790-1863) was a native of Geneva, Switzerland, known for his love for Reformed theology. *Theopneustia* was his defence of a high view (plenary) of the inspiration of Scripture. Stewart, Kenneth J. 'A Bombshell of a book: Gaussen's *Theopneustia* and its Influence on Subsequent Evangelical Theology', *Evangelical Quarterly* (2003) p.215-37
32. Nicoll: 'Knowledge shall vanish away', *British Weekly*, 11 May 1888
33. *Ibid.*
34. Nicoll: 'The Apology of "The Narrow Minded"', *British Weekly*, 8 Jun 1888
35. Glover: *op. cit.,* p.167-8
36. Nicoll: cited Darlow: *op. cit.,* p.103
37. *Ibid.,* p.103-4
38. *Ibid.,* p.403
39. Nicoll: cited Darlow, op. cit 367; Yet WRN could also write, "His marvellous voice, clear as a silver bell's and winning as a woman's, rose up against the surging multitude, and without effort entered every ear." Nicoll: 'Charles Haddon Spurgeon' *British Weekly* 4 Feb 1892
40. Darlow: op. cit. p.403
41. Carlile, J.C.: cited E.J. Poole-Connor, *Evangelicals in England,* (London: Walter, 1951, revised 1966) p.237
42. Alexander Whyte (1836-1921) minister at Free St George's, Edinburgh from 1873 to 1916 and also Principal of New College, Edinburgh from

1909 to 1918. "A traditionalist himself, Whyte championed the cause of liberty in biblical criticism; a Calvinist in theology, he was catholic in his sympathies with exponents of the devotional life;" Macaulay, A.B. & Matthew H.C.G.: *Dictionary of National Biography* (Oxford: 2004-7)

43. Nicoll: cited Barbour, G.F.: *The Life of Alexander Whyte DD* (London: Hodder & Stoughton, 1923) p.185

44. *Ibid* p.392-5

45. This included such figures as Thomas Goodwin, John Henry Newman, Samuel Rutherford, Santa Teresa, etc.

46. *Ibid.,* p.394

47. Nicoll: 'Dr Alexander Whyte', *British Weekly*, 13 Jan 1921: also *Princes, op. cit.,* p.314

48. Whyte lectured and wrote about his enthusiasms. Newman figured in his lectures, as did St Teresa, Sir Thomas Browne, and Bishop Lancelot Andrewes, which caused raised eyebrows in his Free Church, Protestant circles. "The author of the *Apologia*, in particular, cast a lifelong spell upon him: he paid a visit of homage to the Oratory in 1876, and the two men engaged in desultory correspondence thereafter … Whyte also praised the writings of Lord Acton, paid a friendly visit to the agnostic John Morley, and corresponded amicably with the sceptical Leslie Stephen." Cheyne, A.C.: *Transforming the Kirk, op. cit.,* p.173

49. Marcus Dods (1834-1909) had been the minister of Renfield Free Church, Glasgow (1864), elected to be Professor of New Testament Exegesis at New College, Edinburgh (1889), and briefly Principal of New College (1907)

50. Dods appointment as Professor of New Testament Criticism and Exegesis at New College, 1889, provoked trouble from conservatives in the Free Church, who challenged his published views before the Assembly. He was known for his liberal views on inspiration and his triumph was seen as a sanctioning of such views in the Free Church. Dods' 'new methods' took him a long way from the Free Church Orthodoxy of the Founding Fathers, yet as a 'believing critic' he was conservative on the essentials of his faith. He was certainly most influential in moving the Free Church to a more liberal understanding of the faith.

51. He wrote popular orthodox evangelical books, for example, *The Lord's Prayer* (1866) and was joint-editor of a series of fifty volumes of *Handbooks for Bible Classes* with Alexander Whyte.

52. O'Neill, J.: 'Edinburgh Divinity, New Testament', Wright & Badcock, ed., *Disruption to Diversity, op. cit.,* p.82

53. MacLeod, James Lachlan: *The Second Disruption* (East Lothian: Tuckwell Press, 2000) p.66

54. *Ibid.*

55. "Dods is still spoken about in terms of the utmost obloquy in Free Presbyterian New Year's Day Lectures, and the idea that he might have been a sincere Christian trying in his own way to respond to the desperate challenges being thrown at the faith is quite simply not entertained." MacLeod, J.L.: *Second Disruption, ibid.,* p.124

56. MacLeod, J.L.: *ibid.,* p.66-7 "To men who held to the view of the direct, dictated, verbal inspiration of every word of Scripture, admitting errors of any kind meant admitting errors at source, from the mouth of God

himself. While this meant either denying the existence of the errors or else admitting that their original faith was fundamentally flawed, to men like Dods there was no such problem. This was, in fact, a major reason why Dods was such a controversial figure in the nineteenth-century Free Church. He was perfectly at ease with the idea that there were errors in the Canon of Scripture." *ibid.,* p.67-8

57. MacLeod, J.L.: *Second Disruption, op. cit.,* p.118
58. "Believe me that I am grateful, and that though I can write no more for you my connexion with you has been a very large part of my life." Dods: Letter to WRN, 7 Mar 1909, cited Darlow: *op. cit.,* p.205
59. Edwards, Sterling J.: 'Marcus Dods: with special reference to his Teaching Ministry' (Unpublished PhD Thesis at the University of Edinburgh, University of Edinburgh, 1960) p.354-5
60. 'M' [Nicoll?]: 'Our Young Men's Page: Teachers of Young Men –Professor Marcus Dods DD', *British Weekly,* 25 Feb 1892
61. Dods, Marcus: *Christ and Man – Sermons by the Late Marcus Dods* (London: Hodder & Stoughton, 1909) p.262-3, 265
62. Dods: *Later Letters of Marcus Dods,* (London: Hodder & Stoughton, 1911) p.6
63. *Ibid.,* p.29
64. *Ibid.,* p.212
65. Nicoll: 'Principal Marcus Dods', *British Weekly,* 29 Apr 1909
66. *Ibid.*
67. Many of the young students, whom he trained, found it impossible, on his principles of believing criticism, to make concessions to modern thinking and then to stop where he had – many went much further.
68. Henry Drummond (1851-1897) came to prominence with his assistance of the Moody and Sankey Mission in Scotland (1882); he developed as an evangelist and leader of youth meetings. He sought to combine Evolutionary ideas with his Evangelicalism and his *Natural Law in the Spiritual World* (1883) became a sensational best seller. Drummond followed with other books; *The Greatest Thing in the World* (1890); *The Ascent of Man* (1894); *The Ideal Life* (1897); *The New Evangelism and Other Papers* (1899)
69. Nicoll: 'Professor Henry Drummond', *British Weekly*, 18 Mar 1897
70. Drummond was already an author published by Hodder & Stoughton.
71. "Without a very strictly defined theology, he preached Christ as a potent influence whereby we can become what we are not through intimate communion with perfect love and perfect holiness." Nicoll: 'Drummond', *op. cit.*
72. Bebbington, D.W.: 'Henry Drummond, evangelism and science', *Henry Drummond: A Perpetual Benediction*, edited T.E. Corts (Edinburgh: T. & T. Clark, 1999) p.20-1
73. WRN was not without his criticisms of Drummond's views: "Many – and we count ourselves of the number – believed that he never had a complete intelligence of the religion of redemption, simply because he had no adequate conception of sin, and no sufficient place for it in his teaching." Nicoll: 'Drummond' *op. cit.*
74. Nicoll: 'Friend against friend the polished missile Flinging', *British Weekly*, 7 Oct 1887

75. "He won his immense success with the most difficult classes – especially with students. They saw in him the likeness of Christ, and they gave him earnest heed." Nicoll: 'Drummond' *op. cit.,* Also Smith, G. Adam: *The Life of Henry Drummond,* (London: Hodder & Stoughton, 1902) Chapter 12, p.295-340
76. *Ibid.,* p.71
77. Fountain D.G.: *E.J. Poole-Connor, 1872-1962, Contender for the Faith* (Worthing: Henry G. Walter Ltd, 1966) p.40 Fountain contends that Drummond's influence was given expression in his posthumously published *The New Evangelism* (1899); in it, Drummond's belief in progress signalled his rejection of much of the Old Testament. "He stands out as both a representative and a leader of those who had all the rich ... heritage of the mid-19th century, and exchanged it for a Christianity which was gradually being despiritualised" (p.43)
78. Bebbington, D.W.: 'Henry Drummond' *op. cit.,* p.32
79. Nicoll: *Drummond, op. cit.* "We think he would have said that no reason can be given for that which lies at the basis of all reasoning, and that Christ was a living power before gospels were written, and would be a living power although they perish."
80. Parker had begun his London ministry at the oldest Nonconformist Church, which was in Poultry Chapel, Cheapside, but such was his impact that it became necessary to build the new church to seat a congregation of some 3,000.
81. Tudur Jones, R.: 'Joseph Parker,' *The New National Dictionary of Biography* (Oxford: Oxford Press, 2003) volume x, p.701
82. Parker, J.: *A Preachers Life:* (London: Hodder & Stoughton; 1899) dedication
83. Particularly successful ones, such as, in Scotland: 'Dr Parker in Edinburgh', *British Weekly,* 11 Feb 1887, and America
84. Darlow: *op. cit.,* p.179
85. Nicoll: *British Weekly,* Dec 4 1902; also *British Weekly Extracts No. 4; Joseph Parker: Reminiscences and Appreciations* (London: Hodder & Stoughton); *Princes of the Church: op. cit.,* p.169-182.
86. *Ibid.*
87. *Ibid.*
88. *Ibid.* Nicoll was able to write about Parker's preaching: "As you listened, you saw deeper meanings. The horizon lifted, widened, broadened – the preacher had thrust his hand among your heartstrings. You heard the cry of life, and the Christ preached as the answer to that cry. The preacher had every gift. He was mystical, poetical, ironical, consoling, rebuking by turns."
89. John Clifford (1836-1923) Baptist Pastor, writer and campaigner for religious freedom, who exercised a liberalising influence on his fellow Baptists. He was a liberal evangelical, who ministered at only one Church, Praed Street, Paddington (subsequently Westbourne Park) London.
90. Clifford, John: cited Briggs, J.H.Y.: 'John Clifford', *Biographical Dictionary of Evangelicals,* Timothy Larsen, ed, (Leicester: Inter-Varsity Press, 2003) p.148
91. 'A Layman': 'Westbourne Park Chapel and the Rev. John Clifford, DD,' *British Weekly,* 14 Jan 1887

92. Jeffs, E.H.: *Princes of the Modern Pulpit, op. cit.,* p187

93. *Ibid.,* p.192-3

94. 'M': 'Teachers of Young Men – Dr. Clifford', *British Weekly,* 24 Mar 1892.

95. 'Our Own Correspondents': 'Dr Clifford's Address' *British Weekly,* 27 Apr 1888; Nicoll's leading article for the previous issue [20 Apr] was 'What Justifies Secession?'

96. Clifford, J.: 'Are there errors in the Bible?' *British Weekly,* 28 Sep 1893. The debate lasted from 21 Sep and concluded with Clifford's summing up 28 Dec 1893

97. Marchant, Sir James: *Dr. John Clifford CH,* (London: Cassell & Co. Ltd, 1924) surprisingly makes no mention of Nicoll or Clifford's many articles for the *British Weekly.* "Dr Clifford did not change his opinion with regard to the Education question and the Passive Resistance movement" [In 1922 Clifford received his 57th summons to the Magistrates for his rates non-payment protest] p.144

98. Clifford, J.: 'Personal Tributes', *British Weekly,* 10 May 1923

99. James Denney (1856-1917) began his career as a minister of a church in Dundee, but in 1897, he became Professor of Systematic Theology at the Free Church College in Glasgow. In 1900, he changed to the chair of New Testament Language, Literature and Theology. This he maintained until his death in 1917, though he also served as Principal of the Glasgow College from 1915 to 1917.

100. Denney, J.: *On 'Natural Law in the Spiritual World' by a Brother of the Natural Man* (Paisley: Alex Gardiner, 1885). Later Denney wrote to Nicoll, "I daresay … I allowed this kind of irritation too free expression. I am sorry now when I think of it, for Drummond was the most gentle and gracious of men, and it must have been to him inexplicably and gratuitously rude." cited Darlow: *op. cit.,* p.155

101. Denney wrote in the *Expositor's Commentary Series,* 1&2 Thessalonians (1892), 2 Corinthians (1894), and Romans (1900) in the *Expositor's Greek New Testament*

102. These were mainly theological, but also cultural interests, of which Denney had many; also on issues such as 'Women's Suffrage', various Government policies, and the Great War. Denney wrote many leading articles even when the earlier ones were unsigned. "The contributions Denney made represent a sizeable corpus of his most accessible work, the lucid writing of a journalist theologian. The *British Weekly* was by no means a lightweight publication; it was a newspaper, with an editor instinctively aware of the kind of writing that attracted and retained a loyal readership." Gordon, J.M.: *James Denney (1956-1917) An Intellectual and Contextual Biography* (Bletchley, Milton Keynes: Paternoster, 2006) p.5

103. Nicoll: *Letters of …Denney to …Nicoll, op. cit.,* Appreciation xix

104. *Ibid.,* p.73-4

105. Denney, James: *Letters of Principal James Denney to W. Robertson Nicoll* (London: Hodder & Stoughton, 1920) p.23-4

106. It is regrettable that James Gordon in his admirable book on Denney's lectures spends considerable space on this particular lecture, yet completely overlooked the contribution made by WRN to its published form. Gordon, J

M: *James Denney (1956-1917) An Intellectual and Contextual Biography*, *op. cit.,* p.140-43

107. *Ibid.,* p.204

108. Taylor, J. R.: *God loves like that! op. cit.,* p.133-54

109. *Ibid.,* p.134

110. Denney: *Studies in Theology, op. cit.,* p.204

111. Nicoll: Letter to Denney, cited Darlow: *op. cit.,* p.349

112. WRN suggested, "You should take account of the arguments and thoughts about the Bible that are moving in average minds. In any case, I feel sure you cannot simply ignore the attitude of Christ to the Old Testament. If we could put people just there all would be right – at that standpoint of freedom and fearlessness and yet reverence and love and trust, the difficulty would be over. Is it hopeless?" *ibid.,* p.341-3

113. J.M. Gordon's study of Denney's lecture notes, in New College Library, Edinburgh makes a good case for identifying the original form amongst Denney's papers. He gives a Transcript of DEN09-17, 'Holy Scripture' as his Appendix 2. Gordon, J.M.: *Denney, op. cit.,* p.237-53

114. Denney: *Studies in Theology, op. cit.,* Preface

115. *Ibid.,* p.227

116. Taylor, J.R.: *op. cit.,* p.141-2; also Darlow: *op. cit.,* p.348-50

117. Nicoll, ed., 1920, Some of Denney's letters to WRN are preserved in the Nicoll Papers at Aberdeen University: MS 3518/27/8 (The collection includes a few unpublished letters).

118. Denney, James: The *Atonement and the Modern Mind* (London: Hodder & Stoughton, 1903) p.1-2. "It is the most profound of all truths ... It determines more than anything else our conceptions of God, of man, of history, and even of nature; it determines them, for we must bring them all in some way into accord with it. It is the inspiration of all thought, the impulse and law of all action, the key, in the last resort, to all suffering."

119. For a complete inventory of James Denney's works, see John Randolph Taylor: *God Loves Like That! The Theology of James Denney* (London: SCM Press, 1962) p.191-6

120. Nicoll: *Letters of ...Denney, ibid.,* xxiv-v

121. George Adam Smith (1856-1942) Old Testament scholar, trained at New College, Edinburgh, under A.B. Davidson; ministered at Queen's Cross Church, Aberdeen (1882-92); Professor of Old Testament at Free Church College. Glasgow (1892-1909); Principal and Vice-Chancellor, Aberdeen University (1909-1935). As well as his commentaries on Isaiah and the Minor Prophets, he wrote commentaries on Deuteronomy and Jeremiah. "Smith opposed what he called 'dogmas of verbal inspiration' and was influenced by evolutionary views of the progress of biblical religion." Reisen, R.A.: 'George Adam Smith', *Dictionary of Scottish Church History and Theology, op. cit.,* p.780

122. WRN could and did register some hesitation about Smith's views. In a letter to Marcus Dods, he laments, "I am wrestling with George Adam Smith's 'Isaiah': he has chopped up the prophet terribly." cited Darlow: *op. cit.,* p.87

123. Smith, G. Adam: *Isaiah* [2 Volumes]: *The Books of the Twelve Prophets* [2 Volumes] (London: Hodder & Stoughton)

124. Campbell, Iain D.: *Fixing the Indemnity* (Carlisle: Paternoster Theological Monographs, 2004) p.69

125. Nicoll: 'Modern Criticism and the Preaching of the Old Testament', *British Weekly*, 14 Feb 1901

126. Carnegie Simpson, P: *The Life of Principal Rainy, op. cit.,* Vol. 2, p.270

127. Riesen, R.A.: *Criticism and faith in Late Victorian Scotland, op. cit.,* p.42

128. Riesen: *ibid.,* p.45

129. Johnson, *Destructive Results of the Higher Critics,* p.12-13: cited Riesen, *ibid.,* p.14

130. Reginald J. Campbell (1867-1956) was born an Ulster Presbyterian, before coming to England and entering the United Methodist ministry. Became an Anglican and in 1892 entered Christ Church, Oxford, but subsequently left them in 1895, and entered the Congregational ministry and called to Union Street Chapel, Brighton. [Robbins, Keith: 'The Spiritual Pilgrimage of the Rev. R.J. Campbell', *History, Religion and Identity in Modern Britain* (London: The Hambledon Press, 1993) p.133-47]

131. Nicoll: 'A New Preacher: Mr R.J. Campbell, of Brighton [Claudius Clear], *British Weekly*, 4 Nov 1897

132. *Ibid.*

133. Deane, A.C.: *Time Remembered* (London: Faber & Faber Ltd, N/D c1945) p.116;"I liked him greatly at that first meeting, and … thought him an amazing blend of genuine modesty and egoism. Most humble-minded he seemed, without a trace of pose, yet quietly convinced, thanks to the tributes showered on him, that he was the world's greatest preacher."

134. Campbell, R.J.: 'Recollections of Sir William Robertson Nicoll', *British Weekly*, 7 Nov, 1946.

135. Porritt: *Best I Remember, op. cit.,* p.119

136. *Ibid.,* p.120

137. These sermons caused readers to claim, "That his teaching of the immanence of God was in reality a form of Pantheism, that he denied the miraculous, and that in reality he was forsaking the essentials of the Christian Faith." Lawrence, G.W.: 'Nicoll' *op. cit.,* p.145-6

138. Nicoll: 'City Temple Theology' (24 Jan 1907); 'More about City Temple Theology' (31 Jan 1907); 'The New Theology and Sin' (21 Feb 1907); 'Christianity and the Immanence of God' (28 Feb 1907), all were leading articles in the *British Weekly*

139. Darlow: *op. cit.,* p.194-5

140. Mozley, J.K.: *Some Tendencies in British Theology* (London: SPCK, 1951) p.34

141. Denney, James: 'The New Theology' (21 Mar 1907); 'God, Sin and Atonement' (28 Mar 1907); 'Pantheism and the Churches' (4 Apr 1907) all in the *British Weekly*

142. Forsyth, P. T.: 'The Newest Theology', *British Weekly*, 7 Mar 1907

143. Porritt: *Best I Remember, op. cit.,* p.122

144. Clements, Keith W.: *Lovers of Discord* (London: SPCK, 1988) p.39

145. Nicoll: cited E.J. Poole-Connor, *op. cit.,* p.257

146. Campbell, R. J.: *A Spiritual Pilgrimage* (London: Hodder & Stoughton, 1916)

147. Nicoll: "It is difficult to believe that Mr. Campbell meant what he has allowed himself to say" 'A Foregone Conclusion', *British Weekly,* 12 Oct 1916

148. James Moffatt (1870-1944) was born and educated in Glasgow, trained at

the Free Church College and served as a minister at a number of Churches before lecturing at Mansfield College, Oxford (1911-15), Glasgow (1915-27) and then Union Theological Seminary, New York (1927-39). In America, he tried to lecture and pursue Church History, but his reputation was fixed as a New Testament theologian. He served as the executive secretary of the translation committee for the Revised Standard Version of the Bible.

149. Denney, James: 'The Historical New Testament', *British Weekly*, 21 Feb 1901

150. "A student like Moffatt goes on quietly yielding this and that, and does not see what his admissions mean for the working Church. But he needs, and others need, to be told it. Men ought to know what is at stake in these controversies. You cannot but see that you have a very special responsibility, partly arising from your official position, and partly from your personal qualities." Nicoll: Letter to James Denney, cited Darlow: *op. cit.,* p.348-50

151. *Ibid.,* p.348-50

152. Denney: Letters pf Principal J. Denney, *op. cit.,* p.72

153. *Ibid.,* p.162

154. Reviewed by James Denney: *British Weekly*, 18 May 1911

155. Denney: Letter to Nicoll, *Letters, op. cit.,* p.183

156. Porritt, Arthur: *More and More of Memories, op. cit.,* p.147; "The original idea of a new translation of the Bible into modern English, which Dr Moffatt carried into effect with such conspicuous success, came out of the fertile brain of Robertson Nicoll, who suggested to the theological students of Glasgow Free Church College that each student should make himself responsible for translating a single book of the Bible. When all the other students one by one gave up the task, Moffatt went on to do the work single-handed."

157. Attenborough: *A Living Memory, op. cit.,* p.70-1

158. Porritt, Arthur: *More and More of Memories, op. cit.,* p.147

Chapter Six

1. Nicoll: *My Father, op. cit.,* p.38-9

2. Nicoll: *Songs of Rest,* (Edinburgh: Macniven & Wallace, 1879) 'Prefatory Note – Introduction'

3. He included one of his own and also found a particularly poignant poem from his deceased sister Eliza, who had died in 1873 [aged 18], it is an elegy about a mother's grief and consolation on the death of her child ['For of such is the Kingdom of Heaven']

4. A Correspondent: 'Robertson Nicoll – and Claudius Clear', the *Times*, 8 May 1963: The Nicoll Papers MS 3518/46

5. Willey, B.: *Nineteenth-Century Studies* (London: Chatto & Windus, 1949) "And to them he devotes most of his attention, for he knew them well. Lay school inspectors [Arnold's occupation for thirty years] at that time visited only the Nonconformist schools." p.267-8

6. *Ibid.,* p.268

7. Nicoll: Letter to his friend Rev. W. Robbie cited Darlow, *op. cit.,* p.50

8. Nicoll: 'Faith, Politics and Culture', *British Weekly*, 7 Jan 1887

9. Darlow: *op. cit.,* p.323-4
10. Nicoll: cited V. Cunningham, *Everywhere spoken against,* (Oxford: University Press, 1975) p.210
11. From 1854, Nonconformists were allowed to matriculate at Oxford and Cambridge and take their BA examination, however, it was not until 1871 that Oxford allowed them to take an MA.
12. The President of the United Methodist Free Churches [1902] cited Munson: *op. cit.,* p.84
13. *Ibid.,* p.84, citing Col. J.T. Griffin, the President of the Baptist Union in 1891
14. Andrew Martin Fairbairn (1838-1912) had ministered in the Evangelical Union Church in Aberdeen (1872), but he joined the English Congregationalist, became the Principal of Airedale College (1877-1886) and then Principal of Mansfield College, Oxford (1886-1909)
15. Nicoll: 'The Nonconformist Invasion of Oxford', *British Weekly,* 12 Nov 1886
16. Nicoll: 'Is our Literature declining?' *British Weekly,* 11 Feb 1887
17 Nicoll: 'What can books do for us?' *British Weekly,* 22 Apr 1887
18. Annie Shepherd Swan (1859-1943) . [See below n. 52.]
19. Nicoll: 'Miss Annie S. Swan', *British Weekly,* 29 Apr 1887
20. It should be noted that the series of articles 'Tempted London' was starting at the time and the first part of the series was about young men.
21. Nicoll: 'Can English Literature be taught? *British Weekly,* 11 Nov 1887
22. The name was generic but also derived from a slogan attributed to James Russell Lowell, 'I am a Bookman', cited Lawrence, G.W.: *op. cit.,* p.107
23. Nicoll: Letter to Marcus Dods, Darlow *op. cit.,* p.98; Further, "My experience is that there is a great class of literary aspirants whose wants are met in no way. Then a great many like to know about books and to be guided, but they don't wish it more than once a month."
24. Stoddart: *Nicoll, op. cit.,* p.93
25. Nicoll: letter to Marcus Dods Aug 1881, Darlow: *op. cit.,* p.99
26. Nicoll: letter to Marcus Dods Sep 1891, *ibid.,* p.99
27. It included a front-page portrait of Tennyson, review poetry by William Watson, articles on Thomas Carlyle, Rudyard Kipling, Thomas Hardy's Wessex, Paternoster Row Forty Years Ago, as well as nearly eight pages of news and gossip – a Nicoll speciality!
28. Nicoll: letter to Marcus Dods 28 Sep 1891: Darlow: *op. cit.,* p.100
29. Stoddart: *Nicoll, op. cit.,* p.93
30. George Meredith (1828-1909) – novelist, poet and critic. Meredith never became a popular novelist; at his worst, his style was exhausting and boring, but at best brilliant in his capacity to exhibit subtlety of language and insight. His writing retained an essentially Victorian view and therefore seemed to be dated.
31. Nicoll: 'Memories of Meredith' (1), *A Bookman's Letters, op. cit.,* p.1-8
32. Nicoll: 'What should we read?' *Home Chat,* 14 Dec 1901: Nicoll Papers, MS 3518/9
33. Darlow: *op. cit.,* p.22; Lady Nicoll recalled, "My husband was all his life a Dickens lover, and in his very first printed article, which appeared in a Dundee paper, *The People's Friend* [Published in Aug 1870], when he was only seventeen.

34. Nicoll: *The Problem of Edwin Drood* (London: Hodder & Stoughton, 1912) Preface

35. Nicoll: *Dickens's Own Story: Sidelights on his Life and Personality* (London: Chapman & Hall Ltd, 1923)

36. Darlow: *op. cit.,* p.420

37. Stevenson, R.L.: 'Books which have influenced me', *British Weekly*, 13 May 1887

38. Nicoll: 'Robert Louis Stevenson', *Robert Louis Stevenson: His Work and His Personality*, St John Adcock, ed., (London: Hodder & Stoughton, 1929) p.128-9. [Reprint of a 1901 article]

39. Nicoll: Letter to Marcus Dods, May 1887: Darlow: *op. cit.,* 76; Nicoll maintained that the issue containing Stevenson's article was 200 less than the previous week.

40. William Hale White [Mark Rutherford] (1831-1913) was a friend of Marian Evans (George Eliot) and at a relatively late age began to write and publish novels; *Autobiography of Mark Rutherford* (1881) and *Mark Rutherford's Deliverance* (1885) related to White's own loss of many of the certainties of faith.

41. Stoddart: *Harvest, op. cit.,* p.23-4

42 White had been educated for the Nonconformist ministry, but he .found that he was at odds with the teaching at Cheshunt College and rejected the calling, because of the requirement to give an assent to the inspiration of the Scriptures.

43. Nicoll: 'Memories of Mark Rutherford: The Man and his Books', *A Bookman's Letters* (London: Hodder & Stoughton, 1913) p.365

44. *Ibid.,* p.373

45. *Ibid.,* p.366

46. Munson: *op. cit.,* p.79

47. *Ibid.*

48. Nicoll: 'Memories of Mark Rutherford', *A Bookman's Letters, op. cit.,* p.374

49. Nicoll cited Stoddart: *Nicoll, op. cit.,* p.166

50. Annie Shepherd Swan (1859-1943) was a prolific writer of romantic stories that had a Christian moral to them. Nicoll described her as 'the Scheherazade of modern storytellers'. She later developed her considerable ability as a public speaker and spoke in mission halls and, later in life, at political meetings.

51. Stoddart: *Harvest, op. cit.,* p.76

52. "In the early days, Sir William Robertson Nicoll enrolled a most impressive army of contributors and some of the early volumes included work by Sir James Barrie, Barry Pain, Pett Ridge, Marie Corelli, H.G. Wells, Gertrude Atherton, Sir Walter Besant, W.T. Stead, Mrs. Joseph Parker, Mrs. Belloc Lownes, Sarah Grand, Ellen Thorneycroft Fowler, and one might continue the list almost indefinitely." Head, Alice M.: *The Letters of Annie Swan,* Mildred Nicoll, ed., (London: Hodder & Stoughton, 1945) p.21

53. "The secret was well kept for a great many years, and until now [1934] I have never openly acknowledged my part in the harmless plot. There was much speculation regarding the new author. Sir William himself even accused of being the culprit." Swan, Annie S.: *My Life: An Autobiography, op. cit.,* p.96

54. Swan, Annie S.: 'Personal Tribute,' *British Weekly,* 10 May 1923

55. Nicoll, Mildred R.: *The Letters of Annie S Swan* (London: Hodder & Stoughton, 1945)
56. 'Ian Maclaren': *Beside the Bonnie Brier Bush* (London: Hodder & Stoughton, 1894) Two lines of a rural song were used on the title page, and this gave the critics their ammunition: "There grows a bonnie bush in our kailyard, / And white are the blossoms on't in our kailyard."
57. Blake, George: *Barrie and the Kailyard School,* (London: Arthur Barker Ltd., 1951) p.16
58. Smout, T.C.: cited McLuckie, Craig: 'Kailyard School (1886-1896)', The Literary Dictionary Company Ltd (Internet, Okanagan University College, 23 Jun 2003)
59. Nicoll's capacity to 'puff' an author is looked at with some alarm in A.L. Struthers: *Life and Letters of John Paterson Struthers,* (London: Hodder & Stoughton, N/D) p.289
60. Barrie, J.M.: (1860-1937): Playwright and novelist. From poverty and hardship in Kirriemuir ('Thrums'), Forfarshire, he established a successful career in literature. From 1900 he became successful as a playwright; *Quality Street* (1902); *The Admirable Crichton* (1902), but his most enduring stage presentation was *Peter Pan* (1904).
61. Barrie, J.M.: cited Darlow: *op. cit.,* p.329-330 [From the introduction to *Auld Licht Idylls*]
62. Dunbar, Janet: *J.M. Barrie: The Man Behind the Image* (London: Collins, 1970) p.72
63. Mackail, Denis: *The Story of J.M.B.* (London: Peter Davies, 1941) p.142: "With Nicoll, and Hodder and Stoughton behind it, there would of course be strong and skilful pushing, and in those days all was by no means lost if you couldn't announce a third impression in the first week."
64. *Ibid.,* p.180
65. *Ibid.* also in retrospect: "The time when Barrie had resented his old friend's possessive pride in him had long passed. What they had shared…had made literary history together" p.583
66. Nicoll: cited Darlow: *op. cit.,* p.330
67. Barrie: Letter to Nicoll, 5 Apr 1923: cited *ibid.,* p.445-6
68. John Watson ['Ian Maclaren'] (1850-1907) was educated at Edinburgh University and New College. Called to Sefton Park, Liverpool in 1880, where he stayed for 25 years. He was active in civic affairs and took a prominent role in the creation of Liverpool University. He wrote theological books under his own name, as well as the novels under Ian Maclaren.
69. Nicoll: letter to Marcus Dods, Darlow: *op. cit.,* p.114; Later Nicoll expressed Watson's style differently: "He was the master of a deadly irony, and a withering sarcasm. Generally speaking, it was only in private conversation that he made use of these gifts. *Princes, op. cit.,* p.212
70. Nicoll: *Ian Maclaren: John Watson,* (London: Hodder & Stoughton, 1908) p.165-6
71. No one recognised the name, and some thought that it was Barrie, but Watson's friend George Adam Smith wrote to him in no doubt: "'Bravo, Ian Maclaren!' and was answered by another postcard containing the words, 'Bravo, Higher Criticism!'" *Ibid.,* 166
72. *Ibid.,* p.185
73. Nicoll: cited Darlow: *op. cit.,* p.115

74. Nicoll: 'The Cure of Souls', [review] *British Weekly*, 24 Dec 1896

75. Nicoll: *British Weekly*, 9 May 1907

76. Nicoll: *Princes, op. cit.,* p.214

77. Nicoll: *Ian Maclaren, op. cit.,* p.180

78. *Ibid.,* p.178; "The position of Ian Maclaren seems to be the same as that of Rousseau…At the close of his life Rousseau rejoiced that he had remained faithful to the prejudices of his childhood, and that he had continued a Christian up to the point of membership of the Universal Church. The words precisely describe the religion this is glorified in Ian Maclaren's books."

79. Samuel R. Crockett (1859-1914) was educated at Edinburgh University and New College, and then ministered at the Free Church in Penicuik, Midlothian in 1886. He had also practiced journalism and when he found literary fame in1893/4, he left the church and became a writer. Continued to write, mainly novels up to his death, but he never saw the original popularity for his work again.

80. Nicoll: 'S.R. Crockett' [Claudius Clear], *British Weekly*, 30 Apr 1914

81. *Ibid.*

82. "A 'stickit' minister is one who, having taken his classes and been duly licensed to preach, [but] fails to find a charge [appointment]" Blake George: *Kailyard School, op. cit.,* p.45

83. Nicoll: 'S.R. Crockett' *op. cit.*

84. There was an inconsistency here, for Nicoll objected to his friend James Stalker leaving the pastoral ministry for the theological college, because the pulpit ministry was of 'paramount' importance, but here was acquiescing in Crockett's resignation for secular reasons.

85. Nicoll: Letter to Marcus Dods, cited Darlow: *op. cit.,* p.123

86. Nicoll, Catherine R.: *Bay Tree, op. cit.,* p.30-1; 75-8

87. Nicoll: 'S.R. Crockett', *op. cit.*

88. Hill, C.W.: *Edwardian Scotland,* (Edinburgh: Scottish Academic Press, 1976) p.62

89. Blake, G.: *Kailyard School, op. cit.,* p.27

90. *Ibid.,* p.29

91. *Ibid.,* p.30

92. Buchan, John: 'Nonconformity in Literature', *Glasgow Herald,* 2 Nov 1895: "We are told that the 'deep, serious heart of the country' is to be found in them; that the clatter of hen-wives and clash of a country street are things of paramount importance…these men in a hatred of morbidity fly to what seems to us the opposite extreme and enter the land of vapidity and promises." cited Janet A. Smith, *John Buchan,* (London: Hart-Davies, 1965) p.86

93. *Ibid.,* p.87: Buchan is cited from a letter, "I got a letter from the editor in which he practically apologies and offers as recompense to print anything I like to send him in the *B.W.* and pay me well for it. I have also received a letter from the *Bookman* asking for personal details to furnish up a New Writer article."

94. Kent, John: 'A late 19th Century Nonconformist Renaissance,' *Studies in Church History,* Vol. 14, (Oxford: Blackwell, 1975) p.357

95. *Ibid.,* p.357-8

96. Nicoll: 'A Bennett's *Clayhanger*' [Claudius Clear], *British Weekly*, 29 Sep 1910

97. Nicoll: 'Weeding a library', *British Weekly*, 29 Apr 1915

98. Enright, W.G.: "Preaching and Theology in Scotland in the Nineteenth Century": *op. cit.,* p.341

99. Enright, W.G.: *ibid.,* p.342 "The appropriation of the Bible as a human book was most evident in the many sermons based on the personalities of the Bible. Indeed, the vibrance of the character sermon was the most significant contribution of the liberal evangelical pulpit to nineteenth century homiletics."

100. Blake, George: *Kailyard School, op. cit.,* p.27-9. "The letters were ultimately sold at Sotheby's for a tidy sum: to whom I do not know."

101. Nicoll alias Wace Walter E.: *Alfred Tennyson* (Edinburgh: Macniven & Wallace, 1881)

102. Darlow: *op. cit.,* p.44; "Nicoll records that the book 'had the high compliment of being referred to by Francis Turner Palgrave in [his article on Tennyson] *Chamber's Encyclopaedia* [1892]. That is enough to show that Tennyson was pleased with it."

103. Nicoll: 'John Bunyan' *The Evangelical Succession* [Third Series] (Edinburgh: Macniven & Wallace, 1884)

104. *Ibid.,* p.41

105. *Ibid.,* p.65-7

106. Nicoll: *James Macdonell,* (London: Hodder & Stoughton, 1890)

107. *Ibid.,* and Darlow: *op. cit.,* p.91-2

108. *Ibid.,* p.401

109. *Ibid.* 401/2/3/4

110. *Punch* review: N/D; c.1890, Nicoll Papers MS 3518/27/3

111. William G. Elmslie (1848-1889) was an able teacher and preacher and Nicoll had entertained high hopes of his future usefulness to the Church. Nicoll & Macnicol A.N.: *Professor W G Elmslie DD: Memoir and Sermons* (London: Hodder & Stoughton, 1890). Sermons and addresses were added from Nicoll's papers.

112. Nicoll: 'Professor Elmslie' *British Weekly,* 22 Nov 1889. "In Biblical criticism he was a master, and he was very well abreast of scientific thought. But the problems thus suggested never threw one shadow on the clearness of his assurance. He held his faith with a certain large simplicity, but with absolute conviction. He dwelt in the positive."

113. Darlow: *op. cit.,* p.84

114. Review, *Church Family Newspaper:* (no date – Nicoll Papers, MS 3518)

115. Republished in 1911, with just the memoir filling out the recollections and appreciation with testimony from friends and in particular Andrew Harper of Sydney, but not including any of Elmslie's own work.

116. *British Weekly,* 4 Feb 1892

117. Nicoll: *Robert Louis Stevenson* [*Bookman booklets series*] (London: Hodder & Stoughton, 1902)

118. Nicoll: 'Henry Drummond: A Memorial Sketch' in *The Ideal Life* (London: Hodder & Stoughton, 1897)

119. Nicoll: *Hugh Price Hughes as We Knew Him* (London: H. Marshall & Sons, 1902) p.14

120. Nicoll: 'Introduction' to *John Clifford* by C.T. Bateman (London: National Free Church Council, 1904)

121. Nicoll: 'Introduction' to *Memoirs of the Late Dr Barnardo,* by Mrs Barnardo & J. Marchant (London; Hodder & Stoughton, 1907)

122. Mrs Gaskell's *Cranford and the Moorland Cottage* (1898), Charlotte Bronte's *Jane Eyre* (1902), Robert Southey's *Journal of a tour in the Netherlands* (1903), George Fox's *Journal* (1903), Oliver Wendell Holmes' *The Professor at the Breakfast Table* (1906), Mrs Oliphant's *Salem Chapel* (1907), etc

123. Nicoll & Seccombe T.: *A History of English Literature* [In three volumes] (London: Hodder & Stoughton 1906) Preface (This was originally issued as *The Bookman Illustrated History of English Literature* [in 12 monthly parts])

124. Darlow: *op. cit.,* p.308

125. Nicoll C.R.: *Under the Bay Tree, op. cit.,* p.192

126. Annie Thwaite's biography of both Gosses has established that Edmund Gosse's recollections of his childhood were often inaccurate. Thwaite cites a dozen occasions on which either Edmund's memory betrayed him, or he "changed things deliberately to make a better story." Thwaite, Annie: *Glimpses of the Wonderful: The Life of Philip Henry Gosse, 1810-1888* (London: Faber & Faber, 2002)

127. Nicoll: *My Father op. cit.,* preface ix

128. Munson James: *op. cit.,* p.77

129. Swan, Annie S.: 'Robertson Nicoll', *op. cit.,* p.387

130. Nicoll: *Ian Maclaren: op. cit.,* preface [vii]

131. Lucy, Sir H.W.: Nicoll Papers, MS 3518 Box 37 also publicity for Nicoll's books – Hodder & Stoughton

132. See Chapter 5.

133. Denney, Robert[brother to James]: letter to Nicoll, 9 Nov 1920: Nicoll Papers, MS 3518/19

134. Smith, G Adam to Nicoll: Nicoll Papers MS, 3518/19

135. Whyte, Alexander: Note to Nicoll: Nicoll Papers, MS 3518/19

136. Nicoll: *Princes of the Church, op. cit.,* 'Prefatory Note'

137. Stoddart: *Nicoll, op. cit.,* p.78

138. Oliver Wendell Holmes (1809-1894) was an American man of letters. He became an essayist and conversationalist, modelling himself on Addison and Steele, but in the tradition of Dr Johnson. Holmes was fiercely anti-Calvinist, here WRN would have dissented.

139. Williamson, David: 'Claudius Clear of the *British Weekly*', *op. cit*: Nicoll Papers, MS 3518/27/3

140. Darlow: *op. cit.,* p.320-1

141. *Ibid.,* p.321

142. Nicoll: Letter to Rev. W. M'Robbie, 10 Mar 1888, cited in Darlow: *ibid.,* p.85

143. Darlow: *ibid.,* p.321

144. *Ibid.,* p.322 [*The Day Book of Claudius Clear* published in USA as *The Key of the Blue Closet*]

145. *Ibid.,* p.322

146. Nicoll: cited *ibid.,* p.322

147. Nicoll: *A Bookman's Letters* (London: Hodder & Stoughton, 1913) preface

148. Darlow: *op. cit.,* p.322-3

149. Review of *Letters on Life*: 30 Aug 1901: *Daily Free Press* [American], Nicoll Papers MS 3518/9

150. Review: *The Chicago Record,* Apr 1902: Nicoll Papers MS 3518/9
151. Review: 'The Art of Life: A pedigree of counsellors', *Academy* [American] 1902? Nicoll Papers: MS 3518/9
152. Nicoll: 'A Library for £5' [Claudius Clear], *British Weekly*, 5, 12, 19, 26, Jul; 2, 9, Aug 1917
153. Cairns D.: *An Autobiography,* (London: SCM, 1950) p.80-1
154. Darlow: *ibid.,* p.324 "To raise the general level of intelligence and culture among churchgoing folk was no light task; but Nicoll probably did more towards its accomplishment than any other man of his generation",
155. Clifford, John: 'Personal Tributes' *British Weekly,* 10 May 1923
156. Hocking, S.: My Book of Memory, (1923) cited V. Cunningham, op. cit., p.45

Chapter Seven

1. In fairness Darlow knew the later Nicoll and at a time when politics had captured his interest.
2. Evan Herber Evans (1836-1896) was a Welsh Nonconformist minister. He trained in Swansea and Brecon and entered the ministry in 1862. His preaching was characterised by his earnestness, his eloquence, and he achieved a position of great influence in Wales.
3. Thomas Charles Edwards (1837-1900) became the first Principal of the University College of Wales and later became Principal of the Calvinistic Methodist ministerial training College at Aberystwyth. Edwards was a great help to Nicoll and they shared a great passion in preaching: "Principal Edwards was thoroughly convinced that preaching came before everything else". He once said that 'A great preacher is Christ's last resource'. He meant that when faith was decaying, when the Church was cooling, the hope was in the sudden appearance of the great preacher. Nicoll: *Princes, op. cit.,* p.128-9
4. See below
5. Darlow: *op. cit.,* p.377-8
6. Nicoll: *My Father, op. cit.,* p.88-9
7. The Nicoll Papers were kept at the family residence, the old Manse in Lumsden, but in 1995, following the death of Nicoll's daughter Mildred; the family donated them to Aberdeen University Special Library and Archives. This is MS 3518 and contains family items from Nicoll's second wife, Catherine and from his daughter Mildred, besides material from Nicoll himself.
8. One typical example survives in the Nicoll Collection (Nicoll: MS 3518, Box 30, Folder 1): Sermon (based on Colossians 2 vs 5-7) [dated] 2 Sep 1877:
   1 Faith then order – in churchyard the order of death
   2 The order of flowers – the beauty of the garden
   Rooted – planted
   Established – growing
   Thanksgiving – blossoming
9. Some of Nicoll's sermons have survived in pamphlet form: *The Father's House* (John 14 v2) – 'A sermon preached in Free Church of Rayne (1874) Printed by request – Memorial of 6 months ministry' (Nicoll: MS 3518, Box 29, file 4)

10. Henry Ward Beecher (1813-1887) was a prominent, American Congregationalist minister, social reformer and abolitionist and Minister of the Plymouth Church of Brooklyn from 1847 to1887.
11. Nicoll: 'The Yale Lectures on Preaching', Reprinted from the *British and Foreign Evangelical Review* for Jul 1878, p.4
12. Phillips Brooks (1835-1893) was a minister and eventually bishop in the Protestant Episcopal Church and he served at Trinity Church, Boston 1862-1891.
13. Nicoll: 'Yale Lectures', *op. cit.,* p.6
14. *Ibid.*, p.7: For R.W. Dale, see below.
15. *Ibid.,* p.10
16. *Ibid.,* p.11-12
17. Nicoll edited *Household Library of Exposition* (1879-80); *The Contemporary Pulpit* (1884-1893): *The Foreign Biblical Library* (from 1886) and *The Theological Educator* (begun 1887)
18. Nicoll: 'Is Preaching Doomed?' *British Weekly*, 13 May 1887
19. *Ibid.*
20. Nicoll: 'Present-day preaching', *British Weekly*, 21 or 28 Sept., 1888
21. Nicoll: 'A Rare Volume of Sermons', *British Weekly,* 15 Jan 1891
22. Nicoll: cited Darlow, *op. cit.,* p.54
23. Nicoll: 'Correspondence of Claudius Clear - Rev. Eli Julius, Minister of Blossoming Lane Chapel, Surrey,' *British Weekly,* 3 Feb 1888
24. Nicoll: cited Stoddart, *Nicoll, op. cit.,* p.82
25. Nicoll then gave a few extracts and appraised them. Nicoll: 'A Rare Volume of Sermons'*, British Weekly,* 15 Jan 1891
26. Nicoll: 'The Next Revival of Religion', *British Weekly,* 12 Oct 1899
27. Stoddart: *Nicoll, op. cit.,*, p.123-4
28. Nicoll: 'The Next Revival' *op. cit.*
29. *Ibid.*
30. In brief Nicoll's concerns were: "The next revival will make CHRIST and Him crucified to shine before the souls of men … is this theology? Yes, but it is theology that may be sung."; "The next revival will, I think, concern itself much more than some others with the perfecting of the saints"; "The next revival will certainly be an ethical revival, the revival in every sphere of righteousness towards GOD and man. I am assured that in the next revival more deference will be paid to the claims of the intellect ... "The next great revival will be a revival of justice … when we read the Bible with open eyes we shall see that the deepest word in it is not grace but righteousness … when CHRIST truly rules the world, the offices of mercy, which have been the glory of Christianity, will take quite a secondary place, and justice will bear sway." *Ibid.*
31. Nicoll: *Ten-Minute Sermons* (Isbister & Co Ltd, 1894 – reprinted 1908 & 1910)
32. Interestingly the actual texts, which are conspicuous in the book, were not given in the original *British Weekly* articles.
33. The Cambridge Trio were F.J.A. Hort (1828-1892), J.B. Lightfoot (1828-1889), and B.F. Westcott (1825-1901). They "had been making plans, at the instance of Macmillan the publisher, for the production of a series of commentaries on the whole of the New Testament with a view to meeting the critics on their own ground.]" Vidler, A.R.: *The Church in the Age of*

Revolution (London: Penguin Books, 1961) p.130-1
34. Darlow: *op. cit.*, p.355
35. Robert William Dale (1829-1895) was a leading Nonconformist Congregational preacher, who from 1853 ministered at Carr's Lane, Birmingham. He was Liberal in politics and seeking to be progressive in his theology. Dale sought to bring the Churches to engage with social and educational issues, as well as challenging the accepted orthodoxy in some areas; he was anti-Calvinist, upheld conditional immortality, rejected verbal inspiration of the Scriptures, but he maintained a high orthodox view of the atonement.
36. *British Weekly*, 29 Oct 1891
37. *British Weekly*, 24 Mar 1892
38. 'Our Young Men's Page – Dr. Dale', *British Weekly*, 7 Apr 1892 Possibly Nicoll but the article was anonymous, the custom in the early issues of *British Weekly*.
39. Nicoll, *Princes, op. cit.*, p.83
40. Nicoll did not accept Dale's view on conditional immortality
41. Dale, A.W.W.: *The Life of R.W. Dale*, (London: Hodder & Stoughton, 1898) p.593
42. Dale, R.W.: 'Letter': *ibid.*, p.679. "Dr Nicoll in his notice of my new book [*Christian Doctrine*] in the *British Weekly* has stated with great precision what, to use a pretentious word, is the 'method' which I have endeavoured to apply to theological truth."
43. *Ibid.*, p.598
44. Mark Hopkins, *Romantic Generation, op. cit.*, p.81-2, 83-4
45. Dale "was so affectionate, so generous, so magnanimous, so truehearted, so entirely forgetful of self, that he won the hearts of all associated with him.." Nicoll: 'Dr. R.W. Dale', *British Weekly*, 21 Mar 1895
46. Nicoll: *The Return to the Cross* (Isbister & Co Ltd, London 1897: Reprinted Hodder & Stoughton, London 1910)
47. *Ibid.*, 'A Listener unto Death' (89[1897]) given at Smith College, Northampton, Mass. 11 Oct 1896
48. Nicoll: *Return to the Cross*, op. cit. p.80: here Nicoll was reviewing .Alexander Whyte's book on Jacob Behmen – the mystic.
49. *Ibid.*, 'The Secret of Christian Experience', p.20-1; "The fact is no less than this, that the springs of our life and power lie outside of ourselves in Christ, are independent of the changes in our personal condition, and furnish us with joy and a strength which it is out of our power to understand or account for save as we know that His infinitude is under our finitude, that we are rooted in the Eternal Son".
50. *The Dundee Advertiser*: 28 Oct 1897 (Nicoll Papers, MS 3518, Box 1)
51. Various: *The Clerical Life – A Series of Letters to Ministers* (London: Hodder & Stoughton, 1898)
52. Other contributors included, John Watson, Marcus Dods, T.C. Edwards, James Denney, T.H. Darlow, T.G. Selby, and J.T. Stoddart, although they all signed themselves in code; 'omicron', 'Lorna', 'oo' [another of Nicoll's own marks], etc.
53. *The Clerical Life*: op. cit., p.67
54. Nicoll: cited Darlow, op. cit., p.349
55. *Ibid.*, p.343-4, Peake: *Recollection, op. cit.*, p.20

56. Peake: *Recollections, op. cit.,* p.20
57. Darlow: *op. cit.,* p.356
58. *Ibid.,* p.358
59. Nicoll: *The Church's One Foundation* (Hodder & Stoughton, London, 1901) title page
60. *Ibid.,* p.22
61. *Ibid.,* p.10-11
62. Thomas Kelly Cheyne (1841-1915) was an Oxford Old Testament scholar and critic. He contributed to the Revised Version, but became reckless and unconventional in his last biblical criticism and ideas.
63. Alexander Balmain Bruce (1831-1899) was a Free Church of Scotland New Testament scholar. From a conservative alignment in his early work, he became progressively more liberal and increasingly sceptical.
64. "The Free Church [of Scotland] had to face the long and hard battle of Old Testament criticism. Now at last in Dr. George Adam Smith's *Modern Criticism and the Preaching of the Old Testament,* has received an honest attempt at construction, at making the new views of the Old Testament not only compatible with preaching, but contributory to the power of preaching." Nicoll: *One Foundation, op. cit.,* p.41
65. *Ibid.,* 53, 55-56; 57-58
66. *Ibid.,* p.71: citing Robertson Smith's *The Old Testament in the Jewish Church,* 27f
67. *Ibid.,* p.73-4
68. *Ibid.,* p.81-2
69. *Ibid.,* p.88-9
70. "Let it be observed that the evangelists have taken this wonderful character into the business of life. They have shown us how He demeaned himself under all circumstances, whether blasphemed or adored, whether triumphant or suffering ... they have given us the picture of a living personality." Nicoll maintained that idealised characters as described in literature are so often very vague. *ibid.,* p.94-6
71 *Ibid.,* p.115
72. *Ibid.,* p.119
73. *Ibid.,* p.151-2
74. "The Christian Church which finds room for such teaching will soon discover that her lights and fires are low. But after all, the faith is in the hands of the saints. To them it was delivered and they will keep it. They have entered into the eternal and divine order, they have obtained redemption, they are justified by faith, and they have peace with God through our Lord Jesus Christ." *ibid.,* p.208-9
75. *Ibid.,* 'Keep' p. 226
76. *Ibid.,* p. 227
77. Nicoll: 'Twenty-one years in the *Expositor*'s chair', *Expositor,* Jan 1906
78. Nicoll: 'We have an Altar', *British Weekly,* 4 May 1899; "You must preach your very best. The sermon must be the result and efflux of your best thoughts and feelings during the week. You must live ... for your sermon and in your sermon."
79. "Read above all things your Bible, and whatever books you add to your Bible, add some of the volumes of your great apostle Charles Spurgeon." *Ibid.*

80. Clifford John: 'Personal Tributes' *British Weekly*, 10 May 1923
81. Nicoll C.R.: *Under the Bay Tree* (*op. cit.*) p,138
82. Nicoll: *My Father*, *op. cit.*, p.32
83. "Christian mysticism emphasizes if possible the Christian doctrine that the chief business of life is to find God, and that in the finding of God all is included." Nicoll: cited Darlow: *op. cit.*, p.396
84. Nicoll: 'The Wisdom of God in a Mystery', *British Weekly* 6 Dec 1894
85. Nicoll: cited Darlow, *op. cit.*, p.396
86. *Ibid.*, p.400
87. *Ibid.*, p.398
88. *Ibid.*, p.403
89. Nicoll: *The Garden of Nuts*, (Hodder & Stoughton, London 1905) 22
90. Dorothy [Dora] Greenwell (1821-1882) wrote poetry and essays, which were well received: *Stories that might be True, with Other poems* (1850), *The Patience of Hope* (1860), *Carmina crucis* (1869), *Essays on Spiritual and Social Life* (1875), and *Selected Poems* (1889). She was active in the fields of philanthropy and women's rights and always wrote with passionate religious fervour.
91. Nicoll often drew his reader's attention to Dora Greenwell: "As all readers of her books – and it is to be desired that they were much more numerous – are aware, she possessed the true mystic note of passionate religious feeling. " Darlow: *op. cit.*, 402
92. Nicoll: cited Darlow *op. cit.*, p.405
93. G.F. Barbour: *Alexander Whyte*, *op. cit.*, p.533
94. Nicoll had consulted Arthur Waite, who was, according to Nicoll, "the exponent in poetical and prose writings of sacramental religion and the higher mysticism, understood in its absolute separation from psychic and occult phenomena". Nicoll: *Garden*, *op. cit.*, Preface
95. *ibid.*, p.33-4
96. *Ibid.*, p.39
97. *Ibid.*, p.40
98. *Ibid,.* p.40
99. *Ibid.*, p.42-3
100. *Ibid.*, p.52
101. "It was wrought in darkness because the full, far-reaching meaning and result cannot be beheld of finite mind. Tell me the death of the Lord Jesus was a grand example of self-sacrifice – I can see that and much more. Tell me it was the bearing of what ought to have been borne by myriads of sinners of the human race, as chastisement of their sin – I can see that and found my best hope upon it. But do not tell me that this is all that is in the Cross." Spurgeon, C.H.: cited *ibid.*, p.54-5
102. *Ibid.*, p.55
103. *Ibid.*, p.58
104. *Ibid.*, p.69
105. *Ibid.*, p.70
106. 1 Corinthians 7, v20
107. Song of Songs 6, v11
108. Nicoll: *Garden*, *op. cit.*, p.81
109. *Ibid.* p.82
110. "The references to the Bible in sermons, so far as we hear and read them,

are surprisingly small. Yet nothing is more sure than that the Church can, as a whole, have no commentary on Scripture but Scripture itself... in this respect the preaching of the present day has fallen far below the level of the past." *Ibid.,* p.82

111. *Ibid.,* p.83-5; Darlow cited a remark of Nicoll to a friend, just before he died: "I believe in the Old Testament, interpreted by common sense and taken back as far as may be to its parabolic and allegoric use. Christ Himself preached the truth by parable, and 'without parable spake he not unto them.' Why should not God speak in parables to His poor people?" Darlow: *op. cit.,* p.405

112. *Ibid.,* p.86-7

113. *Ibid.,* p.230-1

114. In his Prefatory Note, Nicoll said, "In this I hope to supply a bibliography as full as I can make it of English works on Mysticism." Nothing more was heard of this project.

115. Elliott-Binns L.E.: *English Thought 1860-1900* (London: Longmans 1956) p.323

116. *Ibid.,* p.323

117. "When we have done our best, and when we have used the Bible to the full, there still remains much mystery and we can only wait till the mystery of God shall be finished." Nicoll: cited unknown letter 'during the war', Darlow: *op. cit.,* p.405

118. Nicoll: *Garden, op. cit.,* p.129-30

119. Peake, A.S.: *Recollections, op. cit.,* p.26-7

120. Ratcliffe, S.K.: Review of Darlow: *Observer,* 20 Sept 1925 (Nicoll Paper MS 3518/41)

121. *Ibid.*

122. Hermann, E.: 'The Work of the Preacher: The Preacher's Equipment and the Church's Task: An Interview with Rev. William Robertson Nicoll, LL. D. (N/D: Nicoll Papers: MS 3518/37/12))

123. *Ibid.*

124. "With great felicity of speech, with frequent apt quotations from many a writer, with lucid illustration and with tender appeal, Dr Nicoll delivers his message." 'Review article' from the *Hebden Bridge District News,* 13 Jun 1913 (Nicoll Papers, MS 3518/1)

125. Nicoll: cited Darlow, *op. cit.,* p.217

Chapter Eight

1. Higgins, Roisin: 'William R. Nicoll and the Liberal Nonconformist Press (1886-1923)', unpublished PhD thesis, (University of St Andrews, 1995) p. xi

2. Silvester Horne, a leading Congregational preacher epitomised this mood: "It is too early to chronicle the results of this great national movement, but at least proof has been given that the Free Churches realise their opportunity, and are determined to discharge the responsibility resting on them as the legitimate heirs of Protestant Christendom." Horne, C.S.: *Nonconformity in the Nineteenth Century* (London: Thomas Law, 1907) p.160. see also Horne's *A Popular History of the Free Churches* (London: James Clarke & Co., 1903) p.426

3. See below
4. Lawrence: 'Nicoll', *op. cit.,* p.126-7
5. Dale A.W.W.: *op. cit.,* p.649-50
6. Govett, R.: 'The Christian and Politics', a tract from Surrey Chapel, Norwich (Norwich: Fletcher, J., N/D [c1880])
7. Baldwin, Stanley: cited Munson, *op. cit.,* p. 301
8. Mark 12, v17
9. Nicoll: 'Faith, Politics, and Culture', *British Weekly,* 7 Jan 1887
10. Lawrence: *op. cit.,* p.129
11. Dunckley, H.: 'Should women have the vote?' *British Weekly,* 29 Nov 1889; on this occasion WRN did venture a reply
12. There were such figures as Sir Edward T. Cook (1857-1919) of the *Daily News*; Alfred Harmsworth [Lord Northcliffe] (1865-1922) of the *Daily Mail*, L.T. Hobhouse (1864-1929) of the *Manchester Guardian*; H.W. Massingham (1860-1924) of the *Daily Chronicle*; C.P. Scott (1846-1932) of the *Manchester Guardian*; J.A. Spender (1862-1922) of the *Westminster Gazette*; George Riddell (1865-1934) of the *News of the World* – these with others supported the Liberal Party
13. Bebbington, D.W.: *The Nonconformist Conscience, op. cit.,* p.45 "In the following year, when Dilke re-entered Parliament, Nicoll threatened official Liberalism with the loss of Nonconformist votes if Dilke were offered a place in government. 'There is no political object, however much desired, he declared, 'that can compare with the maintenance of family life and New Testament morality." [citing the *British Weekly,* 21 Jul 1892]
14. William Ewart Gladstone (1809-1898) was an outstanding Victorian Parliamentarian. He began his career as a Conservative, under Sir Robert Peel, serving in a number of posts, such as Chancellor of Exchequer. Adhering to his principles, such as free trade, saw him become the leader of the Liberal Party. He was Prime Minister from 1868-1874, 1880-1885, 1886, and 1892-1894. Gladstone dominated the politics of his day and left a remarkable legacy of achievement.
15. Nicoll: cited in Darlow: *op. cit.,* p.38
16. Nicoll: 'The Death of Mr Gladstone', *British Weekly,* 26 May 1898
17. *Ibid.* "He knew that Christian morality, especially on its higher side, is not to be defended by the light of nature. But while he was keenly interested in these subjects and entered into discussions with zest, he was never for a moment shaken, never for a moment dismayed
18 A reference to Nicoll's life as a minister at Kelso indicates that, even then his hero worship of Gladstone was tempered. "Nicoll had no uncritical admiration of Gladstone, which was the prevailing key in our manse. Indeed, he once, I think, in my hearing, said that the two outstanding statesmen in our days, Gladstone and Disraeli had fundamentally Jesuitical minds". Cairns, David: *Autobiography, op. cit.,* p.80
19. Nicoll: 'Joseph Chamberlain', *British Weekly,* [*Claudius Clear*] 9 Jul 1914
20. Joseph Chamberlain (1836-1914) was a Nonconformist (Unitarian), radical member of the Liberal Party in his early days. He entered Parliament and the cabinet at the Board of Trade, but later split with Gladstone and in 1885 became a Liberal Unionist. Though never Prime Minister, he held important posts in the Conservative Government (Colonial Secretary),

his oratory and style marked him out as one of the most important and colourful politicians of his era.

21. Nicoll: 'Joseph Chamberlain', *op. cit.*
22. *Ibid.*
23. *Ibid.*
24. *Ibid.*
25. Nicoll: 'Catechism of the Education Bill, as it affects Nonconformity', *British Weekly*, 2 Oct 1902. Nicoll cites previous Chamberlain speeches on education and passive resistance
26. Archibald Philip Primrose, Earl of Rosebery (1847-1929): Queen Victoria had sent for Rosebery when Gladstone retired. He was popular in the country, but was distrusted by the Liberal rank and file, and, after losing office, he seemed to espouse more right wing views, in particular his horse racing, Imperialism and opposition to the People's Budget (1909) offended many of the Nonconformist supporters of the Liberals.
27. In December 1904, Nicoll confided to a friend, "Rosebery is the only possible man", cited McKinstry, Leo: *Rosebery, Statesman in Turmoil* (London: John Murray, 2005) p.464.
28. Denney, James: Letter to Nicoll, 29 Jul 1895, *Letters Nicoll, op. cit.*, p.7
29. Darlow: *op. cit.,* p.126
30. The Nicoll Papers: MS 3518/26/5, 6 & 7
31. Darlow: *op. cit.,* p.188, also Nicoll Papers: MS 3518/26/9
32. "In politics Stoddart was a strong Liberal Imperialist and quite influential on Nonconformity in that respect." Matthew, H.C.G.: *New National Biography, op. cit.,* p.844
33. The Jameson Raid was an attempt to help a planned internal 'coup d' etat' in the Boer State of the Transvaal [29 Dec 1895]. The internal coup did not happen, the raid was contained, and the Jameson force captured. This was part of an expansionist plan by Cecil Rhodes. It is balanced by the fact that the Boers under their leader Kruger also had plans in the region at Britain's expense, and this success possibly gave an exaggerated confidence in their ability to cope with the British.
34. Nicoll: 'Notes of the Week', *British Weekly*, 5 Oct 1899
35. British settlers in the Boer States were treated as 'Uitlanders' [outsiders] and heavily discriminated against. The British government had proposed a franchise scheme and to settle matters by arbitration.
36. Nicoll: 'Notes of the Week', *British Weekly*, 12 Oct 1899
37. Nicoll's friend and editor of the *Daily Chronicle*, H.W. Massingham had resigned because of disagreement with the proprietors. Nicoll honoured him but disagreed with his standpoint.
38. *British Weekly* articles included, 'Is might right?' (28 Dec 1899), 'Shall we win?' (By a South African – 11 Jan 1900), 'Will there be peace after the War?' (By a South African – 18 Jan 1900), 'Are the Cape Dutch disloyal?' (By a South African – 25 Jan 1900), 'What is the Task before us?' (By a South African – 1 Feb 1900); 'The Dutch Reformed Church and the War' (By a South African – 15 Mar 1900)
39. Nicoll: 'Notes of the Week', *British Weekly*, 2 Nov 1899
40. Nicoll: 'Notes of the Week', *British Weekly*, 14 Dec 1899
41. In truth, this was a skill he had acquired in seeking to keep the divergent groups within Nonconformity continuing to read his paper. Nicoll could

appear to spread his sympathy very wide – even when he clearly spoke his mind over many of the disputed issues.

42. Stoddart: *Nicoll, op. cit.,* p.136
43. Nicoll: 'The True Issue of the Battle', *British Weekly,* 27 Sep 1900
44. Nicoll: 'The Tasks before us', *British Weekly,* 4 Oct 1900
45. Perks, R.W.: 'After the Election', *British Weekly,* 18 Oct 1900
46. Intriguingly Nicoll could privately voice his limited pleasure with politics, as in a letter to his wife, "At the Ritz to meet Lloyd George ... Lloyd George very pleasant. But I do hate talking politics." Nicoll, C.R.: *Under the Bay Tree, op. cit.,* p.190
47. Only in 1901 Nicoll had written, "It is the duty of Christian men to take part in politics and administration ... but Christian men, each following his best lights, will come to different conclusions ... No Christian minister has the right to pledge the Church to the service of any of these [political] parties. 'Twenty-Five Years, 1876-1901', *British Weekly,* 24 Dec 1901
48. Koss, Stephen: *Nonconformity in Modern British Politics* (London: B.T. Batsford, 1975) p.38
49. Ensor R.C.K.: *England 1870-1914* (Oxford: Clarendon Press, 1936) p.355
50. Chadwick O.: *Victorian Church, op. cit.,* p.232 Also Koss: *op. cit.,* p.170, Koss pointed out that there was an upsurge of numbers and morale, which continued amongst Nonconformists with the impact of the Welsh Revival of 1904 and the successful rallies of R.A. Torrey and C.M. Alexander (1903-1905).
51. Stoddart: *Nicoll, op. cit.,* p.170
52. Nicoll: 'The New Duty of Nonconformists', *British Weekly,* 3 Apr 1902
53. Stoddart: *Nicoll, op. cit.,* p.161
54. Nicoll: 'Nonconformity on its Trial', *British Weekly,* 24 Jul 1902. In the same article, he quotes extensively from the old speeches of Joseph Chamberlain who, back in 1872, had advocated passive resistance, but was now in the Balfour camp!
55. Nicoll: 'Set Down My Name, Sir', *British Weekly,* 31 Jul 1902
56. Porritt A.: *More and More Memories* (Allen & Unwin, London 1947) p.77
57. Stoddart: *Nicoll, op. cit.,* p.156
58. David Lloyd George (1863-1945) began, as a solicitor in North Wales and in 1890 became the Liberal MP for Caernarfon, which his represented for fifty-five years. He was seen as a radical; he took a pro-Boer stand [1899-1902] and identified with particular causes that were the concern of his Welsh Constituents. He was brought into the Liberal Government as President of the Board of Trade and eventually he was made chancellor in 1908. He was identified with social reforms such as The Old Age Pension Act (1908), National Health Insurance Act (1911). He produced his 'People's Budget' (1909), which brought about the constitutional crisis with the House of Lords. During the First World War, he became Minister of Munitions in 1915 and Prime Minister in December 1916. At the time a dynamic leader who seemed to be full of ideas, he would nevertheless, after his resignation in 1922, never hold any office of state again.
59. Koss: *op. cit.,* p.47-8
60. Nicoll: 'Mr Balfour and an injured innocent' (*British Weekly,* 19 Jun); 'The Next Step' (*British Weekly,* 14 Aug); 'The Priesthood and Education'

(*British Weekly*, 18 Sep); 'For Conscience Sake' (*British Weekly*, 25 Sep); 'The Liberal League and the education Bill' (*British Weekly*, 2 Oct); 'On courage and faith' (*British Weekly*, 16 Oct); 'The Church of Scotland and the Education Bill' (*British Weekly*, 23 Oct); as well as signed articles in several papers, including the *Daily Mail* and the *Contemporary Review*

61. "Some leaders of the movement, including Nicoll, found complications in their own individual cases because they were exempt from paying the rate ...Nicoll, living in London, would not have the opportunity of refusing the rate, which did not affect the metropolis. To overcome this, he planned to take a cottage in the country." Lawrence, G.W.: 'Nicoll', *op. cit.,* p.179-80

62. See Chapter 5, 'Personalities'

63. Cocks H.F.: *The Nonconformist Conscience* (London: Allen & Unwin, 1982) p. ix

64. Porritt A.: *More and More Memories, op. cit.,* p.77

65. Nicoll: *British Weekly,* 8 Jan 1906

66. Koss: *op. cit.,* p.70

67. Bebbington D.W.: *Nonconformist,* op. cit., ix

68. *Ibid.,* p.157

69. Koss: *op. cit.,* p.88

70. Taylor A.J.P.: *From the Boer War to the Cold War: Essays on Twentieth-Century Europe* (London: Penguin Books, 1996) p.202

71. "Nicoll was prepared to sacrifice some of his independence in order to move into Lloyd George's inner circle because he felt it was important that Free Church Leaders should have the ear of a senior minister. It had been a source of anger that Gladstone never had a Nonconformist close friend. The Free Churches finally had someone in a position of power that was truly responsive to their particular demands." Higgins, Roisin: 'William R. Nicoll and the Liberal Nonconformist Press', *op. cit.,* p.378

72. Lloyd George: Private letter to Nicoll, 6 Jun 1909; Nicoll Collection: MS 15941, *ibid.*

73. Nicoll: 'Letter to James Denney', cited by Darlow: *op. cit.,* p.208

74. Sir George Allardice Riddell (1865-1934). He was chairman of George Newnes Ltd., C. Arthur Pearson Ltd. and News of the World Ltd and became a liaison officer between the Government and the Press between 1914 and 1918. ()

75. Riddell, Lord [George]: *More Pages from my Diary – 1908-1914* (London: Country Life Ltd, 1934) p.1

76. Riddell, Lord: *More Pages, ibid.,* p.17

77. "In everything and in every place he brings the same enthusiasm for sound literature and sound religion. So far as in him lay, he has made popular journalism literary and he has made religious journalism interesting." Daily Chronicle, 12 Nov 1909: Nicoll Papers MS 3518/3

78. Nicoll Papers MS 3518/3: also Darlow: op. cit., p.210-11

79. Lathbury, D.C.: 'Letter to Nicoll': Darlow: *op. cit.,* p.211

80. Darlow: footnote, *op. cit.,* p.213

81. Nicoll: letter to James Denney, 31 Jan 1910, cited Darlow: *ibid.,* p.213

82. N. Blewett, *The Peers, the Parties and the people: the British General Elections of 1910* (London: 1972) quoted by Koss, *op. cit.,* p.108

83. It should be remembered that the clergy were the main readers of the *British Weekly*

84. Wilkinson, Alan: *Dissent or Conform?* (London: SCM, 1986) p.75

85. Stoddart: *The New Socialism: An impartial inquiry* (London: Hodder & Stoughton, 1909)

86. Nicoll: 'What is Socialism?' *British* Weekly, 30 Sep 1909 and then with an election pending 'New Socialism', *British Weekly*, 7 Oct 1909

87. Porritt A.: *The Best I Remember, op. cit.,* p.24

88. Such as, Arthur Henderson, John Clynes, William Abraham, James H. Thomas, George Barnes, etc. From A. Porritt: *ibid.,* p.25-6

89. Nicoll: et al *British Weekly*, 21 Sep 1911, 7, 21, Mar 11 Apr 1912, later published as *The Christian Attitude towards Democracy,* (London: Hodder & Stoughton, 1912)

90. Koss, *op. cit.,* p.113-4

91. Riddell, George: Letter to Nicoll, 20 Mar 1913: The Nicoll Papers, MS 3518/26/1

92. Campbell did recant, but left Nonconformity for the Anglican Church (See chapter 5, 'Personalities')

93. Charles Silvester Horne (1865-1914) was one of the new generation of Nonconformists from Mansfield College, Oxford. Horne became an activist in Nonconformist/Political circles – opposed the Boer War, and resisted the Education act of 1902; was seen as "an advanced radical"' He was also minister of Whitfield's Memorial Church in Tottenham Court Road and an MP for Ipswich (1910-1914). He had outstanding gifts of oratory, so much so that R.W. Dale had wanted him as his successor at Birmingham.

94. Nicoll: 'Silvester Horne', *British Weekly*, 7 May 1914

95. Koss: *op. cit.,* p.37

96. Nicoll: 'Silvester Horne' *op. cit.*

97. Koss: *op. cit.,* p.125

98. He may have begun the twentieth Century with the same high hopes as other Nonconformists, but during the second decade, he began to seem less and less confident about the role of the Churches in inspiring such a revival.

99. Nicoll, Letter to 'Dearest Sonny', 4 August 1914, Nicoll Papers, MS 3518 Box 27

100. Nicoll: *British Weekly,* 6 Aug 1914

101. Nicoll: Letter to Miss Maud Coe [secretary] cited Darlow: *op. cit.,* p.235

102. Hodder-Williams J.E.: 'To my friend – from his publisher', *British Weekly Memorial Number,* 10 May 1923

103. Nicoll: cited Koss, *op. cit.,* p.130; "It is He who taught us to care for small nations and to protect the rights of the weak, over whom He has flung His shield. The devil would have counselled neutrality, but Christ has put His Sword into our hands"

104. Nicoll: 'Letter to Strachey', 11 Nov 1914, cited *ibid.,* p.131 "The vast Nonconformist meetings held last night surprised everybody. They showed a far more militant spirit in English Nonconformity than I had dared to hope for ... Dr Clifford, our Grand Old Man, who was a keen pro-Boer, appeared as a Cromwell Ironsides, taunting the shirkers and urging that the War should be pursued ... and brought to an end as soon as possible".

105. Lloyd George: appreciation after Nicoll's death: *British Weekly,* 10 May 1923
106. A.J.P. Taylor: *Essays on Twentieth Century Europe* (London: Penguin, 1995) p.239
107. 'Obituary', *Daily Telegraph*, 5 May 1923
108. Riddell Lord: *Intimate Diary of the Peace Conference* (London: Victor Gollancz, 1933) p.406
109. Darlow: *op. cit.,* p.236-7
110. *Ibid.,* p.237
111. Wilkinson: *op. cit.,* p.35
112. Nicoll: cited Bebbington, D.W.: *The Nonconformist Conscience, op. cit.,* p.126
113. Darlow: *op. cit.,* p.237
114. Wilkinson: *op. cit.,* p.42-3
115. "At the request of the Publicity Department of the War Office we wrote a short paper giving reasons why young men, and in particular young Nonconformists, should enrol themselves". He then stated that Britain had not sought the War but was being true to its 'sacred and solemn obligations'. Germany had to be opposed and Britain had to defend itself and defend 'the common people', indeed he believed Britain was fighting for its children. Nicoll: 'Set Down My Name, Sir', *British Weekly* 3 Sep 1914
116. *Ibid.*
117. Editorial in *John Bull*, 12 Sep 1914; "my purpose in writing is to thank you for your Appeal to Nonconformists to join the Army – which is one of the most sane and manly pronouncements issued since the war began."
118. Nicoll: *British Weekly*, 22 Oct 1914
119. Nicoll: *British Weekly*, 5 Nov 1914
120. Nicoll: *British Weekly*, 12 Nov 1914
121. Nicoll: *British Weekly*, 13 Apr 1916
122. Wilkinson: *op. cit.,* p.54-5
123. Nicoll: *Prayer at the Time of War* (London: Hodder & Stoughton, 1916)
124. Nicoll: 'When the Wounded go home', *British Weekly*, 1 Apr 1915
125. Koss, S.: *Fleet Street Radical: A.G. Gardiner and the Daily News* (London: 1973) p.196
126. Nicoll, C.R.: *Bay Tree, op. cit.,* p.255
127. Darlow: *op. cit.,* p.243
128. Nicoll: 'Work for Lord Northcliffe', *British Weekly*, 10 Feb 1916
129. Alfred Charles William Harmsworth (1865-1922) was a newspaper magnate and propagandist. Beginning in 1888 when he founded a weekly paper, he built up a successful business in periodicals. He bought the *Evening News* (1894), founded the *Daily Mail* (1896), founded the *Daily Mirror* (1903), bought the *Observer* (1905 until 1911), then the *Times* (1908). He was one who pressed for a more vigorous direction of the war-effort and was made Director of Propaganda to Enemy Countries in 1917.
130. The *Glasgow Weekly Herald* and *The Bailie* published a cartoon of Nicoll as Daedalus (a practical dreamer) handing a pair of wings to Northcliffe, as Icarus – adding, "when the young man soared into the Empyrean the Gods grew jealous, and Jupiter (Asquith) shot forth his hot rays and melted the wax with which the Wings were fastened, and Icarus came kerflop to the ground".

131. Nicoll: Letter to a 'Correspondent', Darlow, *op. cit.,* p.257
132. Douglas, James: 'Lord Fisher', *British Weekly*, 24 Feb 1916
133. Riddell, Lord: *War Diaries, op. cit.,* p.185
134. Nicoll: 'The Casualty Lists', *British Weekly*, 14 Sep 1916
135. Nicoll letter to Jones, (Oct 1915), cited Jones, J.D.: *Three Score Years and Ten* (London: Hodder & Stoughton, 1940) p.232-4
136. Jones letter to Nicoll, (25 Oct 1915), *ibid.,* p.235. Jones went on to note, "this difference did not disturb the friendship between Sir William and myself. He was several times our guest at the manse." p.236
137. Nicoll: 'The Premier in Scotland', *British Weekly,* 5 Jul 1917
138. Nicoll: 'A Time for Faith', *British Weekly,* 28 Mar 1918
139. So in the following weeks, 'A Time for Hope' (4 Apr 1918); 'The Great Promise of God' (11 Apr 1918); 'Peace in Believing' (25 Apr 1918); 'Bearing up' (16 May 1918), etc
140. Nicoll: 'Is it Peace?' *British Weekly*, 17 Oct 1918
141. Nicoll: Private memoranda, dictated 8 Nov 1918, Nicoll Papers MS3518, Box 26, Folder 7
142. Nicoll: 'The Premier's War Record', *British Weekly*, 21 Nov 1918
143. Nicoll: 'The Hero as Statesman', *British Weekly,* 28 Nov 1918
144. Nicoll: 'The Election Result', *British Weekly*, 2 Jan 1919
145. Arthur Henderson and the Labour Party had withdrawn from the Coalition and fought the election under their own colours.
146. Nicoll: 'Is it Peace?' *British Weekly, op. cit.*
147. Nicoll: 'Beholding the fallen Satan', *British Weekly*, 14 Nov 1918
148. Nicoll: 'Three Duties of the Day', *British Weekly*, 21 Feb 1918
149. Nicoll: 'The Terms of Peace', *British Weekly*, 15 May 1919
150. Lawrence: *op. cit.,* p.215
151. Koss: *op. cit.,* p.101
152. Nicoll: Letter to Lloyd George, 4 Feb 1920: Nicoll Papers, MS 3518/27/ Folder 10
153. Koss: *op. cit.,* p.163-4
154. Taylor, A.J.P.: *op. cit.,* p.233; Nicoll's lack of enthusiasm for Lloyd George in 1922, compared to 1918, seemed tuned in to Lloyd George's own subdued campaign, hoping, perhaps, to be re-invited to front a National Coalition government.
155. Attenborough: *op. cit.,* p.75
156. Wilkinson: *op. cit.,* p.55
157. "The militarism of the *British Weekly* left it implicated in the destructiveness of the war effort and left much of its Christian stoicism sounding hollow … the *British Weekly* supported fully an interventionist approach on behalf of the Government and became dislocated from the debate over the true nature of liberalism. When it did attempt to recreate its Liberal persona in the post-war world, much of the language sounded more convenient than passionate. Lloyd George had lost credibility as a Liberal and the *British Weekly* was heavily defined by its association with him." Higgins, Roisin: 'William R. Nicoll and the Liberal Nonconformist Press', *op. cit.,* p.293-4

Chapter Nine

1. It would perhaps be fairer to say that Nicoll's generation helped slow the rate of decline, which became more rapid and dramatic later.
2. McLeod, H.: *Religion and Society in England, 1850-1914* (London: Macmillan Press, 1996) p.92; "Only in 1918 did class supplant religion as the key variable – a major reason for this probably being the extension of the franchise in that year, which considerably increased the proportion of working-class voters in the electorate."
3. Bebbington D.W.: *Nonconformist Conscience*, op. cit., p.ix
4. *Ibid* p.2
5. Nicoll: 'Wanted – Great Preachers in London', *British Weekly*, 18 Jan 1917
6. Attenborough: *op. cit.*, p.49. "The *Publishers' Circulars* of the 1900s record a reduction of religious books published each year."
7. True WRN had sought to encourage moral and specifically religious fiction, seen in his weekly serials in the *British Weekly*, but the picture often presented, and particularly in his dated hero of fiction, 'Mark Rutherford' and his own 'Kailyard School' of novelists, an atmosphere that was increasingly out of touch with the perceptions of modern life.
8. 'The growing Difficulties of the Ministry', *British Weekly*, 31 May 1894: 'The Alleged Decline of Churchgoing' [a 3 week series], *British Weekly*, 27 Aug– 10 Sep 1896: 'Is Nonconformity worth preserving?' *British Weekly,* 1 Oct 1903, etc
9. Denney J.: *Letters of Robertson Nicoll, op. cit.*, p.89-90
10. Nicoll: 'Mr. Shakespeare at the Cross Roads' [Review], *British Weekly*, 5 Dec 1918
11. Nicoll: letter to John Watson, 10 Jan 1900, Darlow: *op. cit.,* p.165-6
12. Such as competitions and encouragement to send the editor their literary efforts
13. Nicoll: 'Our Page for Young Men', *British Weekly,* 20 Sep 1889
14. Nicoll and Butcher, J. Williams: *The Children for the Church: The League of Young Worshippers* (London: Hodder & Stoughton, 1913) [reprinted articles from the *British Weekly*]
15. Darlow: *ibid.,* p.403; "…he set store by periodicals such as the *Gospel Standard* and the *Earthen Vessel,* belonging to the same school, and containing memoirs of godly old men and women who worshipped in humble village chapels".
16. Nicoll: 'Letter to Carnegie Simpson', Dec 1921: "It will be heart-breaking if the Scottish Churches refuse to unite. They are infinitely more hopeful than anything connected with Lambeth", cited Darlow *ibid.,* p.394
17. Nicoll: 'Mr. Shakespeare at the Cross Roads', *op.cit.*, "For a Free Church minister to submit to re-ordination by a bishop, because the minister considers the act to be a harmless form, whereas the bishop himself holds it to be a most solemn and vital necessity, must appear to plain men as shockingly insincere."
18. Nicoll letter to J.D. Jones (11 Jan 1919) cited *Jones, J.D.: op. cit.,* p.209-11; WRN wrote, "I shall put down my propositions as they occur to me. [1] I have not been able to hear of any true concessions made by any representative man in the Church of England. [2] We shall not agree on this

point, but for my part, I am thoroughly opposed to Episcopacy as a form of Church Government. [3] The question [of] Re-ordination … is quite out of the question. [4] I highly approve of the increased friendliness between the Church and Nonconformity. [5] I should most highly approve of reunion between the Methodist bodies. [6] I do not see why we should not have Federal Committees … to prevent the duplication of Chapels and arrange for union in places when it seems to be desirable. [7] I most strongly object to the minatory talk … they ['Shakespeare and his friends'] say, submit to Episcopacy or go under. I do not believe this in the slightest degree. I think there may be better times before Nonconformity than Nonconformity has ever seen.

19. "This service … marked an epoch in English religious life. For the first time in history the King and Queen, accompanied by … other members of the Royal Family joined in public worship with the Free Church [Nonconformity] subjects of the throne." Porritt, A.: *J.H. Jowett, op. cit.,* p.197

20. Wilson, Trevor: cited Koss, *op. cit.,* p.144

21. *Ibid.*

22. Swan, Annie: 'Robertson Nicoll', *op. cit.,* p.387

23. Swan, Annie: *Autobiography, op. cit.,* p.258-9

24. Darlow: *op. cit.,* p.409

25. In her memoirs, Nicoll's wife quoted her husband, "In my opinion the great charm of cats has never been properly noticed. It is their purring. What can be more restful than to listen to the loud purring of a cat?" Nicoll, C.R.: *Under the Bay Tree, op.* cit., p.236-7; also 'Claudius Clear on Cats', *British Weekly*, 13 & 20 May 1914

26. "I seem to see him now, lying in bed among his papers and books and saying when I entered the room, 'I hope to have a perfectly quiet day today – a good day. *Nobody* is coming.'" Miles, Constance: cited Darlow: *op. cit.,* p.412

27. Nicoll, C. R.: *op. cit.*, p.129

28. Nicoll, C. R.: *ibid.,* p.132

29. Swan, Annie: *Autobiography, op. cit.,* p.259

30. 'Tribute' (unnamed), *Christian World* cited *British Weekly*, 17 May 1923

31. Mackenzie, William Douglas: Personal letter to Nicoll, 30 Nov 1921. Nicoll Papers Collection: MS 3518, Box 27/1/7

32. Stoddart: *Harvest, op. cit.,* p.244

33. Nicoll, C.R.: *Under the Bay Tree, op. cit.,* p.297

34. Stoddart: *Harvest, op. cit.,* p.244-5

35. Lloyd George: 'Telegram to Nicoll', 4 Apr 1923, cited Darlow: *op. cit.,* p.445

36. *Ibid.,* p.446

37. *Ibid.,* p.411-2

38. *Ibid.,* p.411

39. Jones, J.D.: op. cit 237. Jones also recorded seeing Nicoll at a conference, having refused coffee, "absentmindedly taking the half-emptied cup of the Baptist minister sitting next to him, and finishing it for himself".

40. "In rural Scotland, moreover, a young minister mixes on equal terms with all sorts and conditions of men." Darlow: *op. cit.,* p.427

41. *Ibid.,* p.427-8

42. "I think my husband was exceptionally sympathetic with any who were suffering from illness or physical handicap, but he felt a special compassion for the blind – for those who could not read!" Nicoll, C.R.: *op. cit.,* p.234
43. Darlow: *op. cit.,* p.428
44. *Ibid.*
45. Swan, Annie: *Autobiography, op. cit.,* p.79
46. Darlow: *op. cit.,* p.409
47. Swan, Annie: *Autobiography, op. cit.,* p.79
48. Nicoll, C.R., *op. cit.,* p.237
49. Dawson, Albert: 'Review of Darlow's biography of Nicoll', *Great Thoughts,* U/K [c1925] p.81: Nicoll Papers, MS 3518/1 & 41
50. *Punch Magazine:* cited Peake, A.S.: *Recollections and Appreciations* (London: Epworth Press, 1938) p.28
51. *Ibid.,* p.28
52. *Ibid.*
53. Swan, Annie: *op. cit.,* p.385
54. Bebbington, D.W.: *Evangelicalism in Modern Britain, op. cit.,* p.2-3
55. Nicoll: Letter to Peake, 22 Oct 1897, cited in Darlow: *op. cit.,* p.160
56. Peake, A.S.: *Reflections, op. cit.,* p.16
57. Nicoll: 'Aspects of the Cross: The Consecration of Jesus' [2], *British Weekly,* 13 Nov 1890; "Still the Cross remains the pattern and the inspiration of love. In meditation and prayer beneath its shadow, and nowhere else, the lost enthusiasm will revive. There men's burden falls from them, there they waken from the dull stupefaction of things temporal."
58. Nicoll: 'We have an Altar', *British Weekly,* May 4 1899. Also, 'Twnety-Five Years, 1876-1901' *British Weekly,* Dec 24 1901: "The Church exists for the conversion and the sanctification of souls, for the promotion of inward peace and purity."
59. Nicoll: Letter to Arthur Peake, 4 Feb 1898, cited in Darlow: *op. cit.,* p.344; "I feel very deeply that if Primitive Methodists lose their evangelistic power they will lose their savour."
60. *Ibid.,* p.325; "In editing a religious newspaper it is more than ever necessary that the whole range of subjects in which men and women are interested should be dealt with from a frankly and distinctly Christian standpoint, especially now that the secular press inclines less and less to make definite Christian assumptions."
61. Nicoll: 'Revival Christianity: Principal Brown', *British Weekly,* 2 Jun 1898
62. Scott, Patrick: 'Victorian Religious Periodicals,' *op. cit.,* p.336. WRN, in his day, managed to challenge the secular press, "But the number of years in which such ambitions were possible was limited, because of the further developments in the secular press. The growth of the weekly newspaper was followed by the growth of the daily newspaper. The daily-newspaper-buying public doubled in the period 1896-1906, and doubled again by the First World War. By 1920, five million national newspapers were sold each day, and thirteen million Sunday newspapers each weekend. Just as the Victorian, news-medium of the weekly survey was overtaken by the daily newspaper, so the Victorian entertainment-medium of serial fiction was in time overtaken by the cinema and television. The imitative innovations which had so much increased the circulation of the religious press were

precisely what made it vulnerable to subsequent changes in the secular media."

63. See *Princes of the Church*, op. cit.
64. Nicoll: 'An Early Sonnet', cited Darlow: *op. cit.,* p.447, Prudence Kennard told the author that this poem was used by the family at funerals and memorial services (For the memorial service for WRN's daughter Mildred in 1995, and for the funeral of his granddaughter, Rosemary in 2005)

Bibliography

Archive (Manuscript) Sources and Places of Research

Aberdeen University Special Library and Archives: The Nicoll Papers Collection: (MS 3518)

Edinburgh, National Library of Scotland: The Nicoll Letters Collection

Edinburgh, New College Library & Archives: The Papers of Marcus Dods, James Denney, and William Robertson Nicoll

Edinburgh: University Library

Edinburgh: Library of Rutherford House, Leith

London (St Pancras) British Library & General Printed Books Collection

London (Colindale) British Newspaper Library

London: The Evangelical Library, Chiltern Street

London: Guildhall Manuscripts Library: The Hodder & Stoughton Collection of Papers

St Andrews: The University Library

Primary Sources (including the Writings of WRN)

Nicoll, W.R. (1877) *Calls to Christ,* Morgan & Scott, London

Nicoll, W.R. (1878) *Yale Lectures on Preaching:* Reprinted from the *British and Foreign Evangelical Review*

Nicoll, W.R. (1879) *Songs of Rest* [First Series], Macniven & Wallace, Edinburgh: combined with Second Series (1893), Hodder & Stoughton, London

Nicoll, W.R. (1881) *Incarnate Saviour*, T & T Clark, Edinburgh

Nicoll, W.R. (1883) *Lamb of God*, Macniven & Wallace, Edinburgh

Nicoll, W.R. (1884) 'John Bunyan' in *Evangelical Succession,* Macniven & Wallace, Edinburgh

Nicoll, W.R. (1890) *James Macdonell, Journalist,* Hodder & Stoughton, London

Nicoll, W.R. & Macnicoll, A.N. (1890) *Professor W.G. Elmslie DD*, Hodder & Stoughton, London:

Nicoll, W.R. (1894) *Key of the Grave*, Hodder & Stoughton, London

Nicoll, W.R. (1894) *Ten Minute Sermons*, Isbister & Co: reprinted 1910, Hodder & Stoughton, London

Nicoll, W.R. (1895) *Seven Words from the Cross*, Hodder & Stoughton, London

Nicoll, W.R. (1896) *When the Worst comes to the Worst*, Isbister & Co

Nicoll, W.R. (1897) *Return to the Cross*, reprint 1910, Hodder & Stoughton, London

Nicoll, W.R. & others (1898) *Letters to Ministers on the Clerical Life*, Hodder & Stoughton, London

Nicoll, W.R. (1899) *Ascent of the Soul*, Isbister & Co

Nicoll, W.R. (1901) *Letters on Life: by Claudius Clear*, Hodder & Stoughton, London

Nicoll, W.R. (1901) *Church's One Foundation*, Hodder & Stoughton, London

Nicoll, W.R. (1905) *Garden of Nuts*, Hodder & Stoughton, London

Nicoll, W.R. (1905) *Day Book of Claudius Clear*, Hodder & Stoughton, London

Nicoll, W.R. (1906) *Lamp of Sacrifice,* Hodder & Stoughton, London

Nicoll, W.R. (1908) *My Father: An Aberdeenshire Minister*, Hodder & Stoughton, London

Nicoll, W.R. (1908) *Ian Maclaren, Life of the Rev. John Watson D.D.* Hodder & Stoughton, London

Nicoll, W.R. (1910) 'Introduction' to Jane Stoddart's *Against the Referendum*, Hodder & Stoughton, London

Nicoll, W.R. (1910) *Round of the Clock: Story of Our Lives from Year to Year* [Claudius Clear], Hodder & Stoughton, London

Nicoll, W.R. (N/D: but after 1910) Sermons *of C.H. Spurgeon,* Nelson & Sons, London

Nicoll, W.R. (1912) *Christian Attitude towards Democracy* [reprinted from the *British Weekly*], Hodder & Stoughton, London

Nicoll, W.R. (1912) *Problem of 'Edwin Drood'* (A study in the Methods of Dickens), Hodder & Stoughton, London

Nicoll, W.R. (1913) *Bookman's Letters*, Hodder & Stoughton, London

Nicoll, W.R. (1914) *Difference Christ is Making* [reprinted from the *British Weekly*], Hodder & Stoughton, London

Nicoll, W.R. (1916) *Prayer in War Time,* Hodder & Stoughton, London

Nicoll, W.R. (1918) *Reunion in Eternity,* Hodder & Stoughton, London

Nicoll, W.R. (1920) *Letters of Principal James Denney to W. Robertson Nicoll*, Hodder & Stoughton, London

Nicoll, W.R. (1921) *Princes of the Church*, Hodder & Stoughton, London

Nicoll, W.R. (1924) *Memories of Mark Rutherford (William Hale White)* [reprints from 'Claudius Clear' in the *British Weekly*], T Fisher Unwin, London

Nicoll, W.R. (N/D c.1926) *Seen and the Unseen,* An Anthology of religious extracts made by Lady Nicoll [C.R. Nicoll] & Mrs C. Miles [daughter], Hodder & Stoughton, London

Nicoll, W.R. (N/D c.1926) *People and Books*, An Anthology of literary observations by C. R. Nicoll & Mrs C. Miles, Hodder & Stoughton, London

Stoddart, Jane T. (1904) *William Robertson Nicoll: Editor and Preacher*, S.W. Partridge & Co, London

Stoddart, Jane T. (1938) *My Harvest of the Years*, Hodder & Stoughton, London

Darlow, T.H. (1925) *William Robertson Nicoll: Life and Letters*, Hodder & Stoughton, London

Nicoll, C.R. (1934) *Under the Bay Tree*, Private edition (copy in New College Library, Edinburgh)

Swan, Annie S. (1945) *Letters of Annie S Swan*, edited Nicoll, Mildred Robertson, Hodder & Stoughton, London

Secondary Sources

Attenborough, J. (1975) *A Living Memory*, Hodder & Stoughton, London

Barbour, G.F. (1923) *Life of Alexander Whyte*, Hodder & Stoughton, London.

Bebbington, D.W. (1982) *Nonconformist Conscience,* Allen & Unwin, London.

Bebbington, D.W. (1989) *Evangelicalism in Modern Britain: 1730s-1980s*, reprint by Routledge, London.

Bebbington, D.W. (1992) *Victorian Nonconformity*, Headstart History, Bangor.

Bebbington, D.W. (2005) *Dominance of Evangelicalism,* Inter-Varsity Press, Leicester

Binfield, C (1984) *Pastors and People:* Alan Sutton Pub. Ltd, Coventry

Black, J.S. & Chrystal, G. (1912) *Life of William Robertson Smith*, A & C Black, London

Blaikie, William Garden (1893) *After Fifty Years or Letters of a Grandfather*, Thomas Nelson & Sons, Edinburgh

Blaikie, W.G. (1898) *David Brown: A Memoir*, Hodder & Stoughton, London

Blake, George (1951) *Barrie and the Kailyard School*, Arthur Barker Ltd, London

Blakey, Ronald S. (1978) *Man in the Manse*, Handsel Press, Edinburgh

Briggs, J. & Sellers, I. (1973) *Victorian Nonconformity*, Edward Arnold, London

Brown, Callum G. (1997) *Religion and Society in Scotland since 1707*, Edinburgh University Press, Edinburgh.

Brown, C.G. (2001) *Death of Christian Britain: Understanding secularisation 1800-2000*, Routledge, London.

Bruce, Steve (ed.) (1992) *Religion and Modernization: Sociologists and Historians debate the Secularisation Thesis,* Clarendon Press, Oxford

Cairns, D. (1950) *David Cairns: An Autobiography*, S.C.M. Press, London.

Cameron, N.M. de S. (1987) *Biblical Higher Criticism and the Defence of Infallibilism in Nineteenth Century Britain*, Edwin Mellen Press, New York

Cameron, N.M. de S. (1993) *Dictionary of Scottish Church History & Theology*, T. & T. Clark, Edinburgh

Campbell, Iain D. (2004) *Fixing the Indemnity: The Life and Work of Sir George Adam Smith (1856-1942)*, Paternoster Theological Monographs, Paternoster, London.

Campbell, R.J. (1916) A *Spiritual Pilgrimage*, Hodder & Stoughton, London

Chadwick, O. (1966) *Victorian Church* [two volumes], A. & C. Black, London

Cheyne, A.C. (1983) *Transforming of the Kirk*, Saint Andrew Press, Edinburgh

Cheyne, A.C. (1999) *Studies in Scottish Church History,* T & T Clark, Edinburgh

Clements, K.W. (1988) *Lovers of Discord*, SPCK, London

Collins, G.N.M. (1976) *Heritage of our Fathers*, Knox Press, Edinburgh.

Corts, T.E. (ed.) (1999) *Henry Drummond: Perpetual Benediction*, T. & T. Clark, Edinburgh

Cox, J. (1982) *Churches in a Secular Society*, Oxford University Press, Oxford

Crosland, T.W.H. (1902) *Unspeakable Scot*, Grant Richard, London

Cunningham, V. (1975) *Everywhere Spoken Against*, Oxford University Press, Oxford

Dabney, R.L. (1890, Republished 1967) *Discussions: Evangelical and Theological*, Banner of Truth, Edinburgh

Dale, A.W.W. (1898) *Life of R.W. Dale of Birmingham*, Hodder & Stoughton, London

Dale, R.W. (1890) *Living Christ and the Four Gospels*, C.H. Kelly, London

Davies, Horton (1952) *English Free Churches*, Oxford University, Oxford Press, London

Davies, Horton (1953) *Varieties of English Preaching 1900-1960,* SCM Press Ltd, London.

Deane, A.C. (1945) *Time Remembered*: Faber & Faber, London.

Denney, James (1895) *Studies in Theology*, Hodder & Stoughton, London: also reprint in 1976, with Introduction by David Wells, Baker Book Company, Grand Rapids, Michigan

Denney, James (N/D: c1920) *Letters of Principal James Denney to W. Robertson Nicoll*, Hodder & Stoughton, London

Dickson, Beth (1987) 'Foundations of the Scottish Novel', *The History of Scottish Literature,* edited Cairns Craig, Volume 4: Twentieth Century, Aberdeen University Press, Aberdeen

Dods, M. (1909) *Christ and Man - Sermons by the late Marcus Dods*, Hodder & Stoughton, London

Dods, M. [son] (1910) *Early Letters of Marcus Dods*, Hodder & Stoughton, London

Dods, M. [son] (1911) *Later Letters of Marcus Dods*, Hodder & Stoughton, London

Donaldson, William (1989) *The Language of the People: Scots Prose from the Victorian Revival,* Aberdeen University Press, Aberdeen

Doran, George H. (1935) *Chronicles of Barabbas: 1884–1934,* Methuen Ltd, London.

Doyle, A. Conan (1986) *Letters to the Press: the unknown Conan Doyle* compiled by J.M. Gibson & R.L. Green: Secker & Warburg, London

Drummond, A.L. & Bulloch, J. (1978) *Church in Late Victorian Scotland: 1874-1900*, Saint Andrew Press, Edinburgh

Dunbar, Janet (1970) *J.M. Barrie: The Man Behind the Image*, Collins, London

Elliott-Binns, L.E. (1936) *Religion in the Victorian Era,* Lutterworth Press, London

Finlayson, R.A. (1996) *Reformed Theological Writings*, Christian Focus Pub, Ross-shire

Forman, R.S. (1933) *Great Christians*, Ivor Nicholson & Watson, London

Fountain, David G. (1966) *E.J. Poole-Connor – Contender for the Faith,* Worthing, H.E. Walter Ltd

Gammie, A. (N/D-individual articles dated, c.1945) *Preachers I Have Heard*: Pickering & Inglis, London.

Gill, Robin (1993) *Myth of the Empty Church* SPCK: London, also *The Empty Church revisited* (2003) Ashgate for the University of Kent

Glover, W.B. (1954) *Evangelical Nonconformity and Higher Criticism in the Nineteenth Century*, Independent Press, London

Gordon, J.M. (2006) *James Denney (1856-1917): An Intellectual and Contextual Biography*, Paternoster Press, Bletchley, Milton Keynes

Green, S.J.D. (1996) *Religion in the Age of Decline 1870 – 1920* Cambridge University Press, Cambridge

Hill, C.W. (1976) *Edwardian Scotland*: Scottish Academic Press, Edinburgh

Hopkins, Mark (2004) *Nonconformity's Romantic Generation,* Paternoster Press, London

Horne, C.S. (1907) *Nonconformity in the XIXth Century,* Thomas Law for the National Council of Evangelical Free Churches, London

Jeffs, Ernest H. (N/D: c1931) *Princes of the Modern Pulpit in England*, Cokesbury Press, Nashville

Johnson, D.A. (1999) *Changing Shape of English Nonconformity, 1825-1925,* Oxford University Press, Oxford

Johnson, Mark D. (1987) *Dissolution of Dissent: 1850-1918*, Garland Publishing, New York & London

Johnson, W. (ed.) (1995): *W.R. Smith: Essays in Reassessment*, Sheffield Academic Press

Jones, J.D. (1940) *Three Score Years and Ten*, Hodder & Stoughton, London

Jones, R. Tudur (1962) *Congregationalism in England 1662-1962*: Independent Press, London

Kent, John (1977) 'A late Nineteenth-Century Nonconformist Renaissance' in *Studies in Church History: Renaissance and Renewal in Christian History*, edited Baker, B. Basil Blackwell, Oxford

Koss, S. (1975) *Nonconformity in Modern British Politics*, Batsford, London

Larsen, Timothy (ed.) (2003) *Biographical Dictionary of Evangelicals*, Inter-Varsity Press, Leicester

Machin, G.I.T. (1987) *Politics and the Churches in Great Britain 1869-1921*, Clarendon Press, Oxford

Mackail, D. (1941) *Story of J. M. B.* [Barrie], Peter Davies, London

MacLeod, James L. (2000) *The Second Disruption*: Tuckwell Press, East Linton

Marchant, J. (1924) *Dr. John Clifford, C.H.*, Cassell & Co, London

Martin, David (1967) *A Sociology of English Religion*, Heinemann, London

McLeod, H. (1996) *Religion and Society in England, 1850-1914,* Macmillan Press, London

Munson, J. (1991) *Nonconformists*, SPCK, London.

Murray, I.H. (1966, second edition 1973) *The Forgotten Spurgeon,* The Banner of Truth, Edinburgh

Nash, Andrew (2004) 'William Robertson Nicoll, The Kailyard Novel and the Question of Popular Culture', *Scottish Studies Review,* Volume 5, Spring 2004, Association for Scottish Literary Studies

Partington, W. (1939) *Forging Ahead,* G P Putnam's Sons, New York

Payne, E.A. (1944) *Free Church Tradition in the Life of England*, S.C.M. Press Ltd, London

Peake, A.S. (1938) *Recollections and Appreciations*, Epworth, London.

Peel, A. (ed.) (1929) *Letters to a Victorian Editor* (Henry Allon), Independent Press, London

Porritt, A. (1922) *Best I Can Remember*, Cassell & Co, London

Porritt, A. (1947) *More and More Memories,* Allen & Unwin, London

Read, D. (1972) *Edwardian England 1901-1915*, Harrap & Co, London

Riesen, R.A. (1985) *Criticism and Faith in Late Victorian Scotland*, University Press of America, New York.

Riddell, Lord (1933) *War Diary*, Ivor Nicholson & Watson, London

Riddell, Lord (1934) *More pages from my Diary*, Country Life Ltd, London

Scott, P. (1975) 'Victorian Religious Periodicals: fragments that remain,' in *Studies in Church History: Materials Sources and Methods of Ecclesiastical History*, edited Baker, D, Basil Blackwell, Oxford

Sell, A.P.F. (1987) *Defending and Declaring the Faith: Some Scottish Examples, 1860-1920*, Paternoster Press, Exeter

Sellers, I. (1977) *Nineteenth-Century Nonconformity*, Edward Arnold, London

Simpson, P. Carnegie (1909) *Life of Principal Rainy*: Hodder & Stoughton, London.

Simpson, P. Carnegie (1943) *Recollections*, Nisbet & Co Ltd, London

Smith, G.A. (1902) *Life of Henry Drummond*, Hodder & Stoughton, London

Smith, J.A. (1965) *John Buchan*, Rupert Hart-Davis, London

Smith, L.A. (1943) *George Adam Smith*, Hodder & Stoughton, London

Smout, T.C. (1986) *Century of the Scottish People 1830-1950*, Collins/Fontana, London

Stiles, A. (1995) *Religion, Society and Reform 1800-1914,* Hodder & Stoughton, London

Strahan, James (1917) *Andrew Bruce Davidson*, Hodder & Stoughton, London

Swan, Annie S. (1934) *My Life: An Autobiography*, Ivor Nicholson & Watson Ltd, London

Taylor, John R. (1962) *God Loves Like That! The Theology of James Denney*, SCM Press Ltd, London

Thompson, D. M. (ed.) (1972) *Nonconformity in the Nineteenth Century*, Routledge & Kegan Paul, London

Thompson, F.M.L. (1988) *The Rise of Respectable Society*, Fontana Press, London.

Todd, W.B. (1959) *Thomas J. Wise: Centenary Studies,* University of Texas Press/ Thomas Nelson & Sons, Edinburgh

Walker, N.L. (1895) *Chapters from the History of the Free Church of Scotland*, Oliphant Anderson & Ferrier, Edinburgh

Watt, Michael R. (1995) *Dissenters: Volume 2 Expansion of Evangelical Nonconformity*, Clarendon Press, Oxford

Watts, M.R. (1995) *Why did the English stop going to Church?* Dr. Williams' Trust, London

Wilkinson, A. (1986) *Dissent or Conform? War, Peace and the English Churches 1900 – 1945*, SCM Press, London

Willey, B. (1949) *Nineteenth-Century Studies*, Chatto & Windus, London

Willey, B. (1956) More *Nineteenth - Century Studies*, Chatto & Windus, London

Wright, D.F. & Badcock, G.D. (1996) *Disruption to Diversity; Edinburgh Divinity 1846-1996'*, T. & T. Clark, Edinburgh

Unpublished Sources

Lawrence, G.L. (1954) 'William Robertson Nicoll (1851-1923) and religious journalism in the Twentieth Century', (unpublished Ph.D. thesis, University of Edinburgh, New College Library)

Edwards, S.J. (1960) 'Marcus Dods: with special reference to his teaching ministry', (unpublished Ph.D. thesis, University of Edinburgh, New College Library)

Enright, W.G. (1968) 'Preaching and Theology in Scotland in the Nineteenth Century: A study of the context and the content of the Evangelical Sermon', (unpublished Ph.D. thesis for the University of Edinburgh, New College Library)

Gardiner, Edmond Forbes (1977) 'Literary Phenomenon and Woman of Compassion' [Annie S Swan], thesis submitted for the Fellowship of the Library Association, The British Library, St Pancras, London

Higgins, Roisin (1995) 'William Robertson Nicoll and the Liberal Nonconformist Press (1886-1923)', (unpublished Ph.D. thesis, St Andrew's University)

Ives, Keith A. (2000) 'William Robertson Nicoll and the Great Decline', (unpublished MTh. thesis, Brunel University, London School of Theology)

Index